PRAISE FOR
STEPHEN SONDHEIM: A LIFE

"A must-read for anyone interested in the musical theater. . . . In *Stephen Sondheim: A Life,* Meryle Secrest sheds some light on the complex sensibility that grew out of a golden yet emotionally ragged childhood."

—*New York*

"Definitive . . . Secrest has connected Sondheim the human being with Sondheim the genius. Secrest's is the first to combine discussion of Sondheim's public career with an in-depth look at his private life, heretofore largely unexplored. Secrest's capably written and painstakingly researched volume boasts inherent interest."

—*Houston Chronicle*

"Impressively researched, eminently readable . . . Secrest, who offers revealing glimpses of Sondheim's working methods as well as perceptive analyses of his music and lyrics, seems to have spoken with nearly everyone who ever knew or worked with him. [She] does a remarkable job of integrating the life and the work. The result is a portrait of a brilliant, deeply sensitive man."

—*The Philadelphia Inquirer*

"Secrest's book on Sondheim is so fascinating that anyone can enjoy it. [She] does an excellent job of reconciling the two sides of Sondheim. She spent hours talking with him and clearly gained his confidence. In her hands, Sondheim emerges as a brilliant man. The book is also loaded with backstage tidbits that will have special appeal to musical buffs."

—*Minneapolis Star Tribune*

Please turn the page for more extraordinary acclaim. . . .

"What distinguishes Secrest's work is her access to the very private, vulnerable and sometimes quite prickly composer himself, and through that, the first detailed study of his complex personal life."
—*Chicago Tribune*

"[A] meticulously researched book . . . Secrest's ability to link Sondheim's formative influences with his later creative output is the smoothly written biography's main strength . . . the well-illustrated book is a bonanza."
—*The Denver Post*

"A portrait of a complicated, contradictory and compelling artist. . . . Secrest does much to illuminate some of the darker corners of Sondheim's life, as well as to describe his long years in the spotlight."
—*The Miami Herald*

"Meryle Secrest has not only revealed the inner life of this complex man but has also given us new and fascinating material about his extraordinary shows and their productions."
—Paul Salsini, *The Sondheim Review*

"*Stephen Sondheim: A Life* is a must-read for anyone in the unique genre of American musical theater."
—*Rocky Mountain News*

"The first full biography of the most important creative force in American musical theater . . . Secrest and Sondheim seem to have discussed pretty much everything, and have produced a fascinating book. [Secrest] is a hard worker, obviously a good listener, a thorough interviewer and a clear, even graceful writer."
—*San Jose Mercury News*

"A surprisingly close look at the personal and professional development of a figure who has a reputation for being private and reticent. Secrest has done a consummate job of research . . . the vast amount of material from the author's conversations with the composer—reflective, fresh, and filled with juicy revelations—gives the book its depth and vigor."
—*Biography*

"Admirable. . . . In a most unostentatious, unpretentious way, [Secrest] often puts Sondheim on the psychoanalyst's couch. [She] is clearly a tireless researcher and marathon interviewer . . . those with and those without a specialist interest in the musical theater are kept happy."
—*The New York Times Book Review*

"Superb . . . *Stephen Sondheim: A Life* garners our trust, seducing us into a delicious and uncommonly erudite show-biz read."
—*Newsday*

"It's a superb book—informative, impeccably written, and an extraordinary portrait of one of the major American artists of our time."
—Schuyler G. Chapin

"Remarkable . . . One of the most satisfying show-business biographies in recent memory. . . . This book makes it possible to appreciate the work of Stephen Sondheim through his life in a new, more complete way. The chronology and detail of Sondheim's professional life is impeccable . . . the final portrait is of a man as complex, fascinating, deep and rewarding as the songs he has been creating for his entire life."
—*Toronto Globe and Mail*

"Secrest has written a wonderful biography of an uncompromising musical dramatist who uses irony, wit and disillusion to probe painful emotions. Decked out with memorable photographs, her moving and perceptive portrait, full of Broadway lore, provides an incomparable peek into the genesis of such musicals as *West Side Story, Gypsy, A Little Night Music* and *Passion.*"
—*Publishers Weekly*

"Memorable . . . Secrest's biography of Sondheim brilliantly captures the uncertainties of a life in the theater."
—*People*

"This excellent, absorbing biography of an extraordinarily talented, true American original should be of interest to a very large audience . . . insightful and readable. Drawing on extensive interviews with Sondheim, his friends, and colleagues, she has brought vividly to life a person who says he is difficult to describe."
—*BookPage*

STEPHEN SONDHEIM

A LIFE

MERYLE SECREST

Delta
Trade Paperbacks

A Delta Book
Published by
Dell Publishing
a division of
Random House, Inc.
1540 Broadway
New York, New York 10036

ISBN: 0-385-33412-5

Reprinted by arrangement with Alfred A. Knopf, Inc.

Manufactured in the United States of America

Published simultaneously in Canada

June 1999

10 9 8 7 6 5 4 3 2 1

MN

For Cary

. . . My heart has built a precious shrine for the ashes of dead hopes.

—BERTRAND RUSSELL
The Perplexities of John Forstice

Contents

CONTENTS

STEPHEN SONDHEIM

CHAPTER I

An Institutionalized Child

T HE S A N R E M O apartment building on Central Park West, to which Stephen Joshua Sondheim was taken in 1930 when he was six months old, has been a landmark in New York City almost since the day it first opened that same year. Like the familiar view of the domes, spires, and towers of Whitehall as seen from the bridge of St. James's Park, London, the twin towers of the San Remo are distinctive for the silhouette they present when viewed from the Lake in Central Park. They rise serenely from the broken line of trees at their base, their genteel reflections trailing at the water's edge. The juxtaposition of such a sophisticated architectural style with a pastoral setting, of man living in harmony with nature, one as old as Arcadia, brings thoughts of Andrea Palladio and Inigo Jones. By no accident Emery Roth, architect of the San Remo, was as dedicated as were his famous precursors to the study of Greek and Roman architecture; he was also a fervent adherent of the Italian Renaissance revival that swept the country at the turn of the century. Like other architects of the period, Roth saw his role less as the builder of gilded drawing rooms than as a calling: that of a high priest designing temporal cathedrals in the manner of those European counterparts who were expressing, they felt, the human links between art and habitation.

However, one cannot take the analogy between these views of the London scene and the San Remo too far. The dreaming vistas of Whitehall have the same air of ancient splendor, but they are farther away and their outlines tend toward the horizontal. The emphasis is all on the foreground, the silhouettes of boats, a fountain in full flood: the bewitching promise of an oasis in the middle of a metropolis. As seen from Central Park, the San Remo commands as much awe as admiration. It is as if a citadel had soared into the air beside that urban refuge, one designed to defend and exclude: the emblem of prohibitive chic.

That the parents of Stephen Sondheim, Herbert and Janet Sondheim, should have chosen such a background was perhaps no accident, since, like their architect, the Sondheims had dedicated themselves to "les arts de vivre" and were newly rich. Although Herbert Sondheim was only thirty-five when he moved into the San Remo, he had made a rapid advance from lowly beginnings in the garment trade to found his own dress house before he was thirty. Both husband and wife were involved in the firm, he as president—he had just become sole owner of the house he co-founded seven years before—and she as chief designer. Sondheim had begun at the very bottom of the ladder, but that he was destined to prosper seems unsurprising, given his paternal ancestors. He was the grandson of German Jewish immigrants. His grandfather, Isaac, born in Bessen-Darmstadt, emigrated to the United States in 1848 and settled with his wife, Rosa, on the Lower East Side. Family legend gives no clue to his occupation, but in the city directory of 1866 there is an Isaac Sondheim listed as a peddler; no doubt Rosa took in lodgers. Isaac died at the age of sixty-five in a freak accident. He was hit by a streetcar in his own neighborhood in 1883 and succumbed as the result of his injuries about two months later. His wife lived on in quiet obscurity until 1914, but by then she had moved to a much better address.

Isaac and Rosa Sondheim had four sons. Three of them, Meyer, Joseph, and Abraham, died young, mute testimony perhaps to the conditions to which they had been exposed as children in the New York slums. The first-born, Simon (who became Samuel), survived and prospered. Before long he was in business for himself, making shirtwaists, or "waists," as they were called, the tailored blouses with starched collars and cuffs that were all the rage for working girls at the turn of the century. He had two locations, on Broadway and on East Thirty-eighth Street, and was soon well enough off to move his widowed mother to a better address just off Fifth Avenue, on East Eighty-eighth Street. His marriage to Bertha Guttenstein in the summer of 1894 in the fashionable Temple Emanu-El must have been a splendid affair. Quite soon thereafter they were living two blocks away from Rosa Sondheim, at 23 East Ninetieth Street. In due course three children arrived: Herbert, born on July 2, 1895; Walter, born a year later; and Edna, born in 1900.

Grandfather Simon Sondheim
with his sons Herbert (Sondheim's father) at left and Walter:
a photograph taken at the turn of
the century

Grandmother Bertha Sondheim
with Walter at left, Herbert, and
Edna

Family photographs of about 1905 show the two boys in starched collars, ties, belted jackets, and knickerbockers; Edna has a big bow in her hair; and their mother stands in the background, wearing a severe summer dress and a pale expression. If it was a privileged upbringing, it was an unbending one. Stephen Sondheim recalls his father saying that his grandparents were "strict German disciplinarians, you know, keep your hands folded and don't put your elbows on the table." There was also the fact that Samuel, who was almost forty by the time he married, soon took on a portly look and had, perhaps, the reactions of any middle-aged man, with pressing problems at the office and a heavy dinner inside him, when confronted with a roomful of boisterous children. All one can tell from his photograph is that he cut his hair very short, in the German style, wore a military mustache, and that if his views matched his eyebrows, they were most emphatic. His sons bore him no resemblance. As children they had heads as delicately modeled as Botticelli angels and faces as grave and unfathomable.

Then, when Herbert was in his early teens, disaster struck. There was a run on the Knickerbocker Trust Company in Wall Street which led to a general bank panic. Some respectable companies collapsed in 1908; Samuel Sondheim's was one of them. The family was forced to move to a house on Elm Street in New Rochelle, a location they chose because, as everyone knew, one could live there comfortably on much less than one could in Manhattan. By 1910 he had a business in men's hats. Or perhaps he was just a salesman; no one was quite sure. There could be no thought of further education for Herbert; he was fifteen and went to work. He began by pushing carts in the garment district and graduated to carrying the packing trunks of salesmen.

That Herbert Sondheim advanced at such a rapid pace in the rough and tumble of the garment district must have had something to do with his appearance. In adulthood he had acquired his father's strongly marked brows, which punctuated his otherwise unremarkable features and gave his face a certain distinction. An air of natural gentility was perhaps emphasized by the sleek head, hair flattened in the fashionable twenties style, a fondness for well-tailored suits, beautiful manners, and a way of standing with a quizzical smile, developed a decade before Clark Gable discovered its virtues—it is said that ladies found Herbert very attractive. He had a "wonderful, sly sense of humor," his son Stephen said, an aptitude for business and an elusive something else that must have aided his ascent. Perhaps it was the virtue of resourcefulness; at any rate, he demonstrated this at an early stage when he decided to start a dance studio in the evenings. As luck would have it, one night his pupil was a dress manufacturer, who naturally saw all sorts of promise in Herbert and gave him a job. All that pushing and carrying was over; from now on, Herbert was a dress salesman and young man about town.

By 1923, when he was twenty-eight, Herbert Sondheim had become president of the Sondheim-Levy Company, with offices on West Thirty-ninth Street; and by 1930, at the height of the Depression, he had bought out his partner. He was established as a manufacturer of beautifully made clothes of marked style and taste, selling to select stores. Still, nothing quite explains the rapid transformation of this poorly educated, penniless young man into a position on Seventh Avenue, if not quite that of haute-couturier, certainly far above his peers, who were turning out cheap dresses in the thousands, a man who knew what his particular client wanted almost before she did herself. The mystery about his rise is equaled by an enigmatic aspect to his personality. Behind the energy and persuasive charm was someone whose gentle manner concealed a melancholic view of life, and whose emotions were as elusive as his smile; when he was faced with an unpleasant confrontation, his solution was to slide away.

If the picture of Herbert Sondheim's personality is blurred—people who met him later in life often dismissed him as a "good, gray businessman"—the same cannot be said of his wife. Here was someone with whom you immediately came to grips, for good or ill, a sprawling personality who escaped ordinary definitions, the kind of person who came crashing into your life and left some kind of mark—usually a scar—before she crashed out again. Janet Fox had the same penurious upbringing as her husband; she shared his ambitious dreams and, like him, had a special gift that had catapulted her up the fashion ladder.

There, however, the resemblance ends. Whilst the Sondheims had long since made the transition from working poor to genteel middle class, and from immigrant status to that of native born, the Foxes were new arrivals with rough manners, still fighting for a foothold in the New World, unsure of themselves and struggling to acquire, sometimes with comical results, the veneer of savoir faire that would mark their transition into the bourgeoisie. Janet Fox, always called "Foxy," was the fifth child of Joseph M. and Bessie Fox. They were Lithuanian Jews from Vilna who had arrived in the United States by a circuitous route. The family's history is sketchy, and no one knows what Joseph Fox's name was originally—it certainly was not Fox. But it is believed that he and his wife, Bessie, had their first two children, Anna Leah (1883) and Rose Sarah (1890), in Vilna, before emigrating to England, where they had relatives in Nottingham. They stayed there for a decade, and two more children were born, Frances (1892) and Victor (1894). In 1895 they emigrated again, to Fall River, Massachusetts, where one of Bessie's brothers was already established. There the last two children arrived. Etta Janet was born on March 13, 1897, followed by Marienne Gladys in 1900. Six children, the financial demands of two major migrations, the need for shoes, coats, plates, pans, mattresses, blankets, and piano lessons—one wonders how any man, even one who is being helped by his relatives, could have survived. The one photograph that exists of Joseph Fox gives a certain clue. He stands, hat on the back of his head, as if momentarily arrested from the grinding daily round, like a man who has discovered how tired he is. In one hand a traveling bag, in the other a steel box: these were the tools of his trade, since he dealt in precious stones. His granddaughter Joan Barnet recalled that he traveled constantly. She thought he had fled from Vilna to evade conscription in the Russian army. He and his wife were members of the Hasidim and, when they were living on Sherwood Rise, a hilly section near Sherwood Forest in Nottingham, they had sent their children to Hebrew school. When a father is hardly ever at home, perhaps it does not matter so much that he is mean-tempered and unpleasant; even so, that is the only thing that is said about Joseph. Their grandchildren have kinder things to say about Bessie. Like all the Fox women, she was tiny and slim-hipped, with a generous bosom. She kept a kosher household and wore a wig like other Hasidic women, speaking in Yiddish or heavily accented English, and the grandchildren all remember how tender she was, how generous with her gestures, and forgiving.

Several of the girls turned out to be artistic. Rose painted on china; Frances (Frankie) played the piano beautifully; and Foxy showed a precocious interest in fashion design. Anna was the Latinist and family scholar, who completed a four-year college course in three at Brown and went on to get a master's degree in education. Victor was the one to whom no one paid much attention. But there were certain disconnections, certain fault lines running through the family that must have shown themselves before they all became adults and drifted away. Anna and Rose had grown up in the Pale of Settlement and had to learn a new language and new, foreign ways in Nottingham; Frances and Victor had grown up in Nottingham and then had to make their own adjustments to an industrial American city. Etta Janet and Marienne would not have understood any of these psychic shocks. As adults they were concerned about each other in a businesslike kind of way, but if they felt warmth they did not show it.

Anna, as oldest, was perhaps the most involved with the fates of her brother and sisters. "She cared about everybody," her daughter Joan Barnet recalled. "She was the regretter in the family." Frankie was the pretty one; her daughter, Myra Berzoff, recalled, "Anna was the smart one, Foxy was artistic, but my mother was absolutely beautiful." She was also unreliable. "She told elaborate *Little Women* stories about skating on the pond and hot chocolate, but she lied so much that I never knew what to believe. It was self-fulfilling, self-gratifying; a way to make herself look better." Mrs. Berzoff's brother, Arthur Persky, said his mother was like all the Fox women. "All of them considered themselves superior. My mother was a New England Scarlett O'Hara who never raised a finger and was quite above doing anything considered work, and the world's worst cook. She couldn't boil water." A clue to the evolving aspirations of Stephen Sondheim's mother can be gleaned from a photograph taken in 1913, when Etta Janet, who soon dropped her first name, no doubt for aesthetic reasons, was about sixteen and her sister Marienne in her early teens. Their fond mother looks benevolently at the camera, signaling her approval while Foxy, with some kind of flower garland in her hair, and wearing a dress in the "artistic" style that could have been her own design, takes center stage. These were girls whose father dealt in small objects of great beauty and value, and who had given Anna a present of a diamond surrounded by sapphires, even if the diamond was flawed and one he therefore could not sell. Joan Barnet said, "Look at Herman Wouk's portrait of Marjorie Morningstar. The values are what you wear and how you look."

At some point the Fox family moved to New York and were living in Harlem in the days when it was a Jewish neighborhood. Foxy went to Parsons, the famous design school. While there, she made friends with a young woman destined to become even more successful than she was: Jo Copeland. Her daughter, the novelist Lois Gould, recalled that Jo Copeland had achieved such success by the age of seventeen that she was able to put her brother through Harvard Law School. They were "young women traveling together," Gould said. Stephen Sondheim said, "Jo Copeland was very commanding. When she came into the room, you knew she was a dress designer. When my mother came in, it was this woman who had good taste in clothes."

Foxy might have looked demure—her son suspected that in certain situations she could even be quite shy—but no one who knew her was misled. Myra Berzoff said, "Stephen's mother was a doozie. The most pretentious, self-centered, narcissistic woman I have ever known in my life. My father [Robert Persky] adored Herbert and couldn't bear her. She was a snob who didn't like the fact that she came from a working-class background. She was a very brilliant designer, very successful, one who falsified her background and assumed a false accent. She was pretentious beyond belief."

Joan Barnet thought Foxy was capable of generous gestures, even affectionate, although "one never got a real feeling of warmth. She was vain. I remember seeing twenty little hats in her wardrobe and twenty little bottles

Janet Fox, Sondheim's mother, center, with her youngest sister, Marienne, at left and her mother, Bessie Fox, at right, circa 1913

Joseph Fox, Sondheim's maternal grandfather, and the tools of his trade

of perfume, everything in order and very elegant. She could be so generous. She would bring me lots of presents, things like exquisite little doll's carriages from Paris. And she was very good to her mother; I think that Bessie's apartment on West Eighty-first Street was underwritten by Foxy after my grandfather died." She particularly recalls a photograph of herself as a little girl being hugged by Foxy, who was wearing a flapper hat, and the memory made her feel sad. "That is my warmest memory of her. I think she must have been very hurt to become so tough." That was before Foxy had her prominent nose reconfigured. Being the plain one in a family so concerned with personal appearance must have been a trial, which could have partly explained her meticulous interest in such matters, although it was one more reason for others to find her wanting. The novelist Jill Robinson, who met her on the West Coast in the early 1950s, took a charitable view. She said, "I remember her as very stylish and aloof in that 1940s way, wearing cocked hats with veils. Someone who could walk well in high heels and handle a cigarette with style. She was probably an Anna Wintour sort of person, full of guts and gumption," which was her misfortune. "In those days a lot of women who were ambitious, comic, raunchy, and sexy were considered bitchy, because they weren't sexy-cute. A woman could be self-destructive sexy, like Marilyn, or reserved sexy, like Gloria Swanson, or icy sexy, like Grace Kelly, but she could not be aggressive, bawdy sexy. She could not be comic sexy. That was dangerous."

STEPHEN SONDHEIM THOUGHT his father had married his mother for practical reasons. "I *think*—this is my opinion—that it was a bargain. I think my mother was in love with my father, and he was not in love with her, but needed a designer. That's a guess." Nevertheless, there were other reasons why Foxy might have seemed an ideal wife. For someone as emotionally distant and evasive as Herbert, Foxy's ability to blurt out every thought that came into her head, good or bad, to express her views forthrightly (as he might have thought), might have seemed an attractive quality, at least at first. She might even have been giving voice to some of the things he longed to say himself but had been thoroughly inhibited from expressing. To him she might have looked like a rough, gutsy character, full of life and high spirits. She had a knack for gathering people around her, and a staggering amount of chutzpah; Susan Blanchard, Oscar Hammerstein's stepdaughter, said she was the kind of person who could talk a jeweler like Van Cleef and Arpels into lending her a priceless necklace and matching earrings to wear for the evening; perhaps that was something else her husband admired. "She invented herself," another friend commented. The writer Dominick Dunne liked her gift of the riposte most of all: it was true she could be cutting, but she was also very funny, he said. She could be charming. She loved parties, and any fashion designer has to become a relentless social climber. In the days when even the Sears catalogue was using the names of Loretta Young, Joan Marsh, and Fay Wray to promote its evening gowns, hats, and handbags, every fashion house needed a retinue of actresses and film stars. Foxy had already befriended Florence Desmond, Glenda Farrell, Colleen Moore, Helen Kane (the baby-faced "boop-boop-a-doop" girl), and many others. She was always seeking to add to her collection and was an indefatigable first-nighter at Broadway shows. All this made her very useful if one were selling a line of expensive clothes.

One can easily see why Foxy Sondheim had decided that the San Remo was the perfect background for the kind of sophisticated life she wanted to have. The new apartment building, which was to occupy a whole block between West Seventy-fourth and Seventy-fifth Streets, had been in the news since 1928, when a building syndicate had announced plans to buy the hotel of the same name that was on the site and erect a splendid edifice of twenty-seven floors, placing it among the city's tallest apartment buildings at the time.

Roth's ingenious interior plan dispensed with the usual long, echoing corridors, making use of semiprivate elevators to carry tenants to within a few feet of their own front doors, which was considered a great improvement. The San Remo's lobbies were richly detailed with large terrazzo-square floors, marble walls in various subtle shades, and dark beige marble panels. In terms of design, the San Remo was a transitional building, and Art Moderne details were making their appearance beside the Beaux-Arts bas reliefs and ceiling vaultings. The average rent was two hundred dollars a month, in days when a sales clerk at Woolworth's made seven dollars a week and scores of the homeless were living in Central Park in a shanty-town "Hooverville" erected on the Great Lawn between Seventy-ninth and Eighty-sixth Streets, just five blocks away.

Herbert and Foxy could not afford the grandest apartments of all, the duplexes in the south tower, which consisted of fourteen rooms, including seven bedrooms, seven bathrooms, and a library—those were among the finest apartments in the city. Nor could they afford to live on the park, which did not prevent them from entering their apartment from either of the two splendid lobbies on Central Park West as well as from a relatively obscure one on Seventy-fifth Street. Nevertheless, they had the comfort of knowing that their neighbors were all well-heeled and influential.

Herbert and Foxy's first and only child was born on March 22, 1930, while

Herbert Sondheim

they were waiting to take possession of their new quarters. In the interim, they lived in a hotel.

As a mother, Foxy took the kind of progressive position one would expect of someone whose livelihood depended on being absolutely up to the minute, if not in front of it. If fashion decreed that a baby's skin should have lavish doses of sunlight, the infant Stephen must be divested of his clothes and paraded about in his carriage. "I was strolled naked!" he said, his tone conveying the helplessness of someone whose life was being organized by a determined woman, an image reinforced by an early photograph in which the two-year-old is standing between his mother's knees, each tiny hand imprisoned at arm's length, looking like a puzzled puppet. He had a nurse, a Miss Daly, whom he does not remember at all, and at the age of four he was enrolled in a prekindergarten class. The school chosen for him was twelve blocks to the south on Central Park West. It had been founded by Felix Adler, a nineteenth-century social reformer who had begun life as a rabbinical student but who had decided that religion was inadequate to deal with the problems of the modern world. Being born into an observant household seemed to have left no mark on Etta Janet, or rather, seemed to have convinced her that she wanted nothing more to do with it. She declared on numerous occasions that she had been educated in a convent, a claim her son considered too preposterous to be believed, adding to his suspicion that she was ashamed of being Jewish. If this were the case, the Ethical Culture School was the ideal solution for parents uneasily poised between a strict adherence to old dogmas and atheism: although it was considered a radical school, it might have looked to both Sondheims as the only alternative. As for religious instruction, Stephen Joshua Sondheim received none at all. He never had a bar mitzvah ceremony, he knew nothing about the observances of the Jewish calendar, and he did not enter a synagogue until he was nineteen years old.

While Mommy and Daddy were at their office at 530 Seventh Avenue, Stephen, often called Stevie or Sonny, had to be kept occupied. He remembers going to Miss Mabel Walker's prekindergarten class, then skipping kindergarten and entering first grade in 1935, at the age of five, taught by Mrs. Esther Burnham. He took second grade with Miss Marian Stevens and third grade with Miss Louise Welles. After school every day he would go looking for his friends Henry ("Skippy") and Felicia Steiner, who lived a few floors below him at 146 Central Park West. Their parents, Ethel and Howard Steiner, were friendly with the Sondheims. They would all play games in the Steiner apartment or various forms of skip ball on the street. Six o'clock was suppertime, and Stephen would listen to the radio until his father got home from work. He has no memory at all of his mother in those days. "My father would come into my bedroom every night, and often he would hold out his hand and I could touch his hand and I might get a quarter out of it, or something like that," he said. "Little bribes."

On Saturdays he went to "something called Group, which was a way of parents getting rid of their kids. And Group would either be in Central Park or Van Cortlandt Park [in the Bronx]. Mostly Jewish kids, and mostly from the West Side. It started at nine in the morning and went until six in the evening, and we'd do games like Hare and Hounds and stuff like that. So those were my Saturdays." Sunday mornings would be spent breakfasting with his parents; in the afternoons his father might take him to a football or baseball game on the Polo Grounds or at Yankee Stadium.

He enjoyed school. "One of the reasons I love teachers, obviously, is that where I felt *great* was in school, because . . . whether there was competition with my peers or not, I didn't feel any backlash from it. The teachers obviously thought I was terrific because I was smart. And then I had Skippy and Felicia for fun after school, and so, who should complain? And I loved Group. It wasn't that I thought, Oh, I wish I could be with Mommy and

The young Stephen Sondheim (the nurse is not identified); and below, in a formal portrait

Daddy. I *loved* running around the park, you know, looking for clues and doing chasing games. I thought it was swell!"

Those long summer holidays were another problem Foxy tackled with her usual determination and panache. She chose Camp Androscoggin, a famous all-boys' camp in Wayne, Maine, where campers lived in simple cabins in the pine woods beside a large lake. It was, said Robert W. Bloch, who also went there, patronized by prominent German-Jewish families from the New York area and emphasized athletics from dawn to dusk: archery, tennis, boating, swimming, basketball, soccer, gymnastics. Each hour of the day was closely supervised. Bloch remembers that Stephen was a member of the Milk Squad, comprised of children who were considered to need extra nutrition, and early photographs do show him as one of the smaller boys, in the front row, looking forlorn. Bloch disliked Camp Androscoggin, but Sondheim has only warm memories of the five summers he spent there which, to him, were an extension of Saturdays with the Group, deliciously and endlessly prolonged. Bloch remembers that once they all went to be fitted for gray wool tops bearing large letter A's, and how swamped Stephen looked in his new top, standing out there by himself on the soccer field.

Although at home he was almost entirely cared for by servants, Sondheim remembers them as benevolent presences. There was an Irish cook named Mary, whose husband, Paddy, was a doorman at the Beresford six blocks north, the other luxury apartment building on Central Park West designed by Emery Roth during the same period. Paddy was on duty at the side entrance on Eighty-first Street, and once school was out Stephen would be allowed to open the door for people as a special treat. Paddy also taught him to play chess, and Stephen promptly gave lessons to Skippy. A great deal of his young life was spent listening to the radio (Fred Allen and Charlie McCarthy—"I was brought up on those") and sending away for such things as Little Orphan Annie rings. "So my parents would have to put up with a box of . . . whatever cereal it was, because it came with a decoder ring. I think I was a very ordinary kid."

When he was sick in bed, his mother's cousin Peggy Schlesinger would leave her job to sit with him and play games, something his mother never did. He was healthy as a youngster, but he did have asthma, which later would disqualify him for military service. There was a great emphasis on manners. "You are polite, you look people in the eye, you get up when a woman comes into the room. . . . I was brought up in a genteel, upper-middle-class way," he said. As a toddler he was dressed in knitted two-piece outfits, a fashion that survives to this day for small French boys, usually accompanied by nautical stripes. Or he might be photographed with the family dog, whose name

A birthday party at the San Remo: Sondheim is seated fifth from left in a pirate's outfit. "Skippy" Steiner is the soldier standing at far right, Felicia Steiner is seated on the floor, second from right, and Sondheim's cousin Janet Schwab is fourth from left in the back row.

was Scotty, in front of the family fireplace, graced with Oriental urns, wearing suits with short pants and Little Lord Fauntleroy collars. At this age he bore a strong resemblance to his father, with the same delicate features and finely modeled head.

Sondheim learned to read at an early age. He remembers that, in those days, children at the Ethical Culture School were taught to sound out words by syllables, a method he mastered so well that, at the age of five, he used to stand in front of his first-grade class reading the *New York Times*. Thanks to this method, he could even pronounce the hard words he could not possibly be expected to know with some success. But even before he could read he had mastered the ability to identify record albums simply by recognizing the pattern that the words made on the spine, and his parents would trot him out in the evenings to demonstrate this parlor trick before the guests. It is significant that words and music should have been closely allied so soon, although he says he became interested in the music because he was fascinated by a phonograph player they had at the time, a Capehart.

"A Capehart was a wonderful invention with a console record player, and what it did was play both sides of a record. The gimmick was, if you're looking at it, and it was glass-fronted, there is a sort of rim around the turntable, and then there is what looked like a music stand, so you pile your records onto that, you press the button, and the record slides down, and when that side is over, this rim thing picks up the record and does it . . . like that," he said, almost tying his arms in knots in an effort to demonstrate how the ingenious mechanism performed this feat. "Now the record slides down on the second side! And when that's done it spits it out someplace and the next record comes in." He remembers an old 78 of Fats Waller singing "Ain't Misbehavin' " and a collection of show albums on ten-inch records that had been put out by Liberty Records. He would lie on the floor, listening to the music and watching the Capehart turning the records over and over.

There were always show tunes in the house, because Herbert Sondheim's favorite form of recreation was playing the piano. He was entirely self-taught and had mastered, his son said, seven or eight basic chords, which worked perfectly well for most popular tunes; less well for composers who used more inventive harmonies. Perhaps it was his willingness to sit down and play, combined with his charm of manner, but Sondheim the couturier who also performed became a familiar figure on Seventh Avenue. Alice Crouthers, who was formerly the buyer for the exclusive Wedgwood Room of F. & R. Lazarus & Co. in Columbus, Ohio, said that one of the highlights of a fashion show by Sondheim was his willingness to play Broadway numbers at the end of the program. An advertisement for some of his summer dresses, which was printed in the 1940s and widely reproduced, was decorated with drawings of musicians playing violins, drums, and double bass, along with an impressionistic sketch of the great man himself in the lower right-hand corner. The headline was "The Sondheim Straw Hat Chorus," which seems prescient.

Sondheim had a group of cronies who saw each other on Thursday nights and went to sports events on weekends, but one of his closest friends was Lloyd Weill, also in the dress business and living in the San Remo. Weill, who was a natural tenor, was a clever lyricist who would write parody lyrics to a popular song for a specific occasion; Sondheim would learn the accompaniment, and they would perform the song for charity. They made numerous appearances for the New York and Brooklyn Federation of Jewish Philanthropies and other organizations such as the young Museum of Costume Art, one of Sondheim's special interests. They became so well known that they were called "the Rodgers and Hart of Seventh Avenue." Curiously enough, another friend of Sondheim's was Dorothy Fields, the famous lyricist. Her father, Lew Fields, once part of the famous vaudeville comedy team of Weber and Fields, later became a producer and launched the careers of Rodgers and

Hart, among others. Dorothy Fields worked with a wide range of composers, from Fritz Kreisler to Jerome Kern, and she and Kern won an Academy Award in 1936 for "The Way You Look Tonight." Sondheim said that his father introduced another of his close friends, Eli Lahm, to Dorothy Fields and "made a *shiddach*," i.e., a match. After they married and had children, Aunt Dorothy was at their apartment constantly, but Sondheim had no idea what she did until he became an adolescent.

Musical evenings were a large part of the Sondheim entertaining at home. Felicia Steiner Lemonick remembers grown-up parties when Lloyd Weill sang—"he was outgoing and fun and crazy"—and hearing Herbert Sondheim play the piano, and her father as well, since he was also a part-time musician and composer. A group of parents went to dinner parties at each other's apartments, and sometimes Skippy would be trotted out to play a duet with his father, while his nurse waited in the background. And so would Stephen.

He started to take piano lessons from the age of about seven, studying with a Mrs. Moss, who had a small studio on West Eighty-fourth Street just off Central Park West. "My father would sit me at the piano bench and have

Herbert Sondheim's favorite pastime

me put my hand on his little finger, which played the melody over the top," and that led to weekly piano lessons. "At the end of each year we would have to give recitals for all the little kids. I had a very fleet right hand, so one of the first pieces I would play was 'The Flight of the Bumblebee' by Rimsky-Korsakov. My father and mother used to take me out of bed at cocktail time if they had clients, they'd drag me out in my pajamas to play 'The Flight of the Bumblebee.' I took lessons for about two years. I don't remember why I stopped, but I am very right-handed and at the piano my left hand is really a lump, very difficult to make work except for *oompah, oompah*."

He did not recall having any marked interest in music. He did concede, "I can't remember when I didn't go around humming things," but dismissed the idea that this was in any way indicative of special talent. All children had similar gifts, he believed, but their interests were not allowed to develop, or were even discouraged by misguided parents and teachers. He could just have easily been a mathematician, and was "very strongly attracted" by the idea. He had no interest in art and poetry, and his inability to conjure up a visual image remains striking. When asked to describe his mother, he said helplessly, "You'll have to see pictures of her." As the description of the Capehart phonograph would indicate, he was intensely interested in how things worked, and once took a slot machine apart—it took him three days—because it had jammed and he wanted to solve the puzzle. He was taken to the movies—he vividly remembers seeing Disney's *Snow White*—and to the theatre on rare occasions. He saw his first live theatre at age six, Benatzky's operetta *White Horse Inn.* He remembers seeing Rodgers and Hart's *The Boys from Syracuse,* which opened on Broadway in the late fall of 1938, and Oscar Hammerstein II's *Very Warm for May* the following year. He also met the great man himself that year but remembers nothing about it.

He moved to the Ethical Culture's Fieldston campus in Riverdale, a bus ride away, when he was in fourth grade, although he does not remember why. "What I remember most is that they were teaching you how to take care of yourself financially. You were issued a checkbook and you'd go to the canteen and make a check out for five cents for a pack of gum, or something. You had a bank account of, say, a dollar fifty, and you had to balance your account. I loved that. That was great. That's what I mostly remember about Fieldston."

His lack of any memory of his mother at that period, even though she was seldom at home, seems unusual. When he came to undertake analysis in adulthood, the paucity of these early memories caused his therapist to wonder whether some painful memories were being repressed. It was finally concluded that this was not the case.

"I don't remember my mother at all during those years . . . I don't think

Sondheim at Camp Androscoggin in 1937; he is sixth from left in the first row.

she was around. I don't think she cared. I think my father wanted to share things with me; I think my mother did not. I have no memory of my mother doing anything with me. And my father, it was only on occasional Sundays that we would go to ball games. Otherwise I was what they call an institutionalized child, meaning one who has no contact with any kind of family. You're in, though it's luxurious, you're in an environment that supplies you with everything but human contact. No brothers and sisters, no parents, and yet plenty to eat, and friends to play with, and a warm bed, you know? And a radio."

Felicia Lemonick had a sad memory of visiting him. "Because he just didn't have the affection, attention, and love that other children had. I thought of him as a child pressing his nose against the glass." Myra Berzoff thought he was "a truly neglected child emotionally, left with governesses and servants and badly abused." Joan Barnet went to visit the Sondheims when she was about fourteen and Stephen around eight years old. "He was a very beautiful boy dressed in English clothes. I remember him in their large living room with this piano and servants and a dog, and how lonely he seemed."

Sondheim said, "You will find people who will say, 'Gee, he was an unhappy kid.' Because I've heard that. And so obviously people could look at me from the outside . . . but I don't remember it. I really don't. I didn't cry myself to sleep . . . And I was very popular in school, and I remember being happy there; and since most of my life was spent in school and camp, where, again, I was popular and accomplished, eighty percent of my waking hours I was being supported. I didn't know that I was missing my parents."

Then one night when he was ten years old, his whole world came apart.

He was awakened by the sound of sobbing coming from his mother's room. "A rainy night, a sudden awakening," he wrote later, "a voice sobbing loudly, incessantly, a frightened voice, a lonely voice." His mother took him into her bedroom and "wept all over me and clung to me and held me all night and that's how I found out. I don't remember how I felt. I guess I was just upset for her. I didn't make any judgments or recriminations."

Herbert Sondheim had written a note, packed up his clothes, and walked out.

CHAPTER 2

Children Will Listen

I N T H O S E Y E A R S before World War II, Herbert and Foxy Sondheim traveled to Paris regularly for the haute couture collections. To copy the latest Paris fashions for mass reproduction in New York was the unvarying practice of the Seventh Avenue rag trade. On rare occasions a manufacturer might buy the rights to a particular design, but as a rule sketchers were employed to attend the showings, memorize the most popular designs, rush back to their hotel rooms, and reproduce them. A matter of weeks later a cheap copy would be in the stores, usually with some kind of brazen label identifying the garment as a "Parisian Mode." When Jo Copeland and Janet Fox began their careers, all American fashion followed the dictates from Paris. There was no American look until Copeland, one in a wave of young innovators, began to launch her own version of the clothes Americans should wear: fresh, inventive, casual, and smart. Copeland was particularly well-known for her dress-and-jacket ensembles, a ladylike outfit that Foxy Sondheim also favored, and no doubt Copeland's early success and influential contacts had helped launch her friend. The American look was emerging, but both women still went to Paris for the spring and fall collections. Foxy Sondheim's special usefulness for Herbert Sondheim, Inc., was her ability to spot fashion trends that would appeal to his upper-bracket clientele. They often traveled together. However, on one particular occasion Herbert Sondheim was alone, and fell in love.

Alicia Babé was born in Cuba, arriving in the United States at the age of seven; and could converse in Spanish although her English was without flaw. She was tall, blond, and Catholic and, when Herbert Sondheim met her, married to a publishing executive named Bill Walling. "One of his coups was the Crime File series," Stephen Sondheim said. "The idea was that they got well-known crime writers to help them put together a dossier of clues: letters, documents, bullets, and the like, and then you recreated the investigation . . . And they had something of a vogue." The Wallings had no children, and Alicia, then in her late thirties, was in charge of fashion promotion at Macy's. Marjorie Pleshette, who was working in those days as a buyer in costume jewelry, remembered her as having an exquisite sense of chic in the style of Givenchy. She had "sort of a receding chin. I can still see her. She wasn't pretty by conventional standards, but good looking. And she had an aura, an air. We were all in awe of her. Even the way she spoke. We thought she was English for a while." She was particularly kind to the junior women in other departments: "She was wonderful."

"The real point was that it was exactly like the film *Love Affair*," said Sondheim, whose frames of reference were often cinematic. "They decided they would not do anything but see in six months whether they still wanted each other. So they let six months go by and then decided that they did want to see each other, so she left her husband—even though she was a Catholic—and he left my mother."

The event brought about a complete upheaval in Stephen Sondheim's life. He found his parents sitting on a couch in their apartment one day, discussing his future. He was to go to military school. "And that did not particularly disturb me, not that I remember anyway. I was sort of startled. And the surprise is that I loved military school. Because I knew where I was going to be at 9:03 and 9:58 and 12:50 and I needed structure and it gave me that, and made me feel the world was not in chaos. Because everything fell apart. You accept, even if your parents aren't there (and remember, I was not unhappy), that you have the setup. You go to school, you come home, there's Mommy and Daddy, the school, then on Sunday you see Mommy and Daddy, the whole routine. Then suddenly there's no Daddy there, and there's an upset Mommy, and suddenly you're in boarding school, where you have to establish yourself in a new community, you are living with strangers. You don't get to go home every night and see Skippy and Felicia. And to my surprise now, I just adored it; I thought it was terrific."

Many years later, driving in upstate New York, Sondheim realized he was very near the New York Military Academy at Cornwall on Hudson, where he had spent the two years from 1940 to 1942. He said to Peter Jones, his traveling companion, " 'I don't know exactly where it is, but there are these huge gates and this huge quad,' and we kept driving, and we finally saw a little gate, and it was open, and we parked the car and went in." That of course was the front gate, distorted by the magnifying effect of memory. As they walked into the gates toward the quad, which was equally unimpressive, a platoon of children, aged ten or eleven, were being drilled, dressed in their best uniforms. "It was Sunday, parents' visiting day, and I saw myself, you know. Our guns were wooden guns. They looked like regular rifles but didn't weigh as much and they were not comparable in any way, shape, or form. But we went through all the drill. We did all the present arms and that sort of stuff. And polished our brass and had our Sunday uniforms."

They walked into the main building, "and suddenly I got a memory of it, and I sort of knew where the corridors were, and what I wanted to do was go upstairs to the second floor, where the chapel was, where the organ was, but I didn't have the nerve to ask." The New York Military Academy owned an enormous pipe organ, almost as magnificent as the pipe organ in the Radio City Music Hall, and so Sondheim spent a year learning to play such immortal classics as MacDowell's "To a Wild Rose" on this immense instrument. "At the age of eleven I was there with my feet hardly able to touch the pedals, sitting on the edge of the chair, pulling every green button and every red button, and manual after manual, and having a great time."

Sondheim remembers very little else about his military years in grades six and eight—he skipped seventh. There are a few photographs of him in his dress uniform, a kind of hotel-pageboy outfit with vertical rows of brass buttons, a white cap, and smart white stripes on the pants. Boys led very closely regimented lives, went to bed early, were taught to be obsessively tidy, and were given plenty of athletic training, including football, swimming, tennis, and boxing; in 1941, Sondheim was manager of the baseball team. Certain decorations were awarded for excellence in academic work, neatness, good conduct, and the like, and a photograph of the young cadet, displaying what would become his typically lopsided smile, shows him wearing three medals, although for what is no longer clear. That the military training had its effect was evident a year later, when he spent his usual summer at Camp Androscoggin. He stands "at ease" in his photograph, feet planted well apart, his hands behind his back and his shoulders square. The list of his accomplishments was long: he had a swimming certificate, a junior lifesaving

Sondheim at Camp Androscoggin

With his father at New York Military Academy, 1940

Sondheim showing off his medals

With his father on a military picnic. He is seated center rear, holding a cup and sandwich.

emblem, an archery championship, was in the Glee Club, the Dramatics Club, the Players' Guild, on the Androlog Board and the baseball team. His nickname was still Sonny. That summer he appeared as Reckless Richard, the hero of a melodrama called *Out in the Cold,* played Mary Livingstone in a skit about Jack Benny, and was editor of the weekly newspaper. To all appearances he was making a surprisingly good adjustment to the upheaval in his family life.

In the summer of 1941 Sondheim's address was given as the Hotel Pierre in New York, where he was living with his mother. When his father left his mother, she also lost her job, so she went to work as a designer for Hattie Carnegie. Some time after that, she started her own dress business, which did not put her in direct competition with her husband, since she specialized in made-to-order things. She called her company Foxy, Inc., with offices somewhat north of his on Seventh Avenue. No doubt they still saw each other at the Paris collections.

By the time Herbert Sondheim met Alicia Babé, he was in his middle forties and Foxy would have been about forty-three. To have her husband fall in love with a younger woman who was everything she was not—tall, blond, and a *shiksa*—was hurtful enough, but to lose her job as well threw her life into complete turmoil. She obviously could not go on living at the San Remo. One can sympathize with someone who has been rejected in such a cavalier fashion, and if she saw herself in hackneyed terms as the "wronged" wife, it was the conventional view of her day.

Once she had recovered from the shock, Foxy Sondheim did indeed see herself in those terms. One doubts that she spent ten minutes wondering what she herself might have done to contribute to the failure of her marriage. Her thoughts were entirely focused on the undeniable fact that a younger, prettier woman had stolen her husband. Alicia and Herbert had run off together and were living in sin. This was also true: New York divorces were extremely difficult to obtain, adultery being the only ground, and although Herbert Sondheim immediately obtained a Mexican divorce, it was not recognized in the state of New York. There was also the White Slave Traffic Act (known as the Mann Act), which had been passed at the turn of the century as part of an international effort to suppress the worldwide trade in prostitution, and provided stiff penalties for the interstate transportation of women for "immoral purposes." Anyone who took a woman across a state line, as Herbert Sondheim did every time he and Alicia drove to their Fifth Avenue apartment from their home in Stamford, Connecticut, could be placed in an embarrassing position if charges were brought. Perhaps this was why, once a legal separation was agreed upon in the autumn of 1941 and custody of

Stephen was granted to her, Foxy told her son she could "have his father put in jail" if he ever saw his stepmother, because "she was an immoral woman." After he and his mother moved out of the San Remo, his father would come to visit him on Sundays at the Pierre or, later, the Ritz Towers (they finally moved into an apartment at 25 West Fifty-fourth Street), and Sondheim often went back to his father's apartment at 1010 Fifth Avenue. That was when Sondheim became aware that his mother was having him followed. One day he went for lunch, "and the phone rang and Alicia picked it up and somebody hung up at the other end, and my father, you know, gave her a look," and he knew it was his mother. It seemed to him in retrospect that his mother had lied to him about being able to put his father in jail (although in fact, Miriam Noël, Frank Lloyd Wright's second wife, could and did get her husband arraigned on Mann Act charges in 1926). In any event, in those days, at the age of eleven or twelve, Sondheim believed her. "Of course I did. Sure. What do you do when you're twelve? She was having me trailed. My mother was a very vindictive woman, because she'd been scorned."

Like Miriam Noël, Foxy Sondheim soon had new cause for her outrage. After believing she could not have children, Alicia Babé discovered early in 1943 that she was pregnant. In an attempt to legitimize their coming parenthood, she and Herbert were married in a registry office in Stamford, and their

Alicia and Herbert Sondheim around the time of their marriage

son, Herbert Sondheim Jr., was born in the autumn of that year. Their second son, Walter, was born in February of 1946, the year Herbert finally obtained his divorce from Foxy in the state of New York. Presumably by then Alicia had also obtained hers. "The minute Alicia had the kids, of course she was thrilled beyond belief," Stephen Sondheim said, "and she built a little fortress up in Stamford—with an actual stockade fence, and it was all a metaphor . . ." Sondheim remembers the occasion when his father and Alicia went through a second marriage ceremony in Stamford. He wrote a short story about that from the point of view of the son who was "sort of" the best man at his father's wedding, in the presence of his father's two sons. Two divorce actions, two marriage ceremonies—it all went over the heads of the little boys. Walter Sondheim came upon Sondheim's short story years later and learned for the first time that he and his brother had been conceived out of wedlock. It was quite a surprise, he said. He also said that he had not known of his parents' previous marriages, and did not know his true relationship with Stephen Sondheim until adulthood.

In a family where such secrets are kept, all kinds of crucial misunderstandings can arise. In retrospect Sondheim realized that, as the guilty party in the divorce, his father could not have gained custody of him. "In those days women got custody; men rarely did. Dad would have taken me in a second." At the time, he believed his father had abandoned him. For in fact, Foxy was outraged, vindictive, and frustrated, with no target for those feelings except her ten-year-old son.

After Herbert left, most of his mother's effort, Sondheim said, was focused on poisoning his mind against his father. A college friend also thought Foxy blamed her son for the failure of her marriage and succeeded in making him believe it. She also began to act very strangely. Sondheim said, "She would hold my hand in theatres . . . I remember going to a play with her and she not only held my hand but looked at me during the entire play. It was really upsetting." Then he became aware that she was trying to seduce him. "Well, she would sit across from me with her legs aspread. She would lower her blouse and that sort of stuff." This happened often during his teenage years, and he was "surprised rather than shocked. At the time I was innocent and didn't know. Remember, I grew up in a generation in which sex and such matters were not discussed openly, and we were all moderately naive." As he remembers, this kind of behavior did not take place until he and his mother were alone, but the assumption that Stephen would become the man of the house, in every sense, began soon. Joan Barnet recalls going to baby-sit with Stephen when he was about twelve. "As I came in the door I heard her saying to Steve in her whisky-sour voice, 'Darling, pour me another drink,' " Joan Barnet said. "She was on her way to a party and off she whirled." Stephen Sondheim said, "When my father left her, she substituted me for him. And she used me the way she had used him, to come on to and to berate, beat up on, you see. What she did for five years was treat me like dirt, but come on to me at the same time."

Foxy Sondheim's behavior fits a pattern often found, of women whose husbands have left and who turn to their sons for their emotional and sexual satisfactions. They tend to be domineering, controlling, and overpossessive. Such a mother can have problems with alcohol or drugs and "lacks appropriate sexual controls and boundaries and is overtly seductive or sexual in front of her son." Just as a high proportion of abusing men are found to have been abused themselves as children, it is believed that incestuous mothers have had similar histories. Taking the charitable view, that Foxy Sondheim had no possible way of knowing that she was behaving destructively, the results would be the same. Writers have stressed the psychic damage that is done to an adolescent boy when his mother is using him as a substitute for his father. Evelyn S. Bassoff writes in *Between Mothers and Sons*, "The incesting mother forces [her son] to fuse with her and thereby lose the separateness and individuality—the distinct, bounded selfness—that he has struggled since early childhood to achieve."

Along with the damage done to a boy's sense of emerging sexuality is the even larger damage done to his sense of trust. He has been betrayed, and instead of love he has experienced a distorted substitute. Alice Miller writes, in *Thou Shalt Not Be Aware*, "To have one's helplessness and . . . dependency taken advantage of by the person one loves . . . soon produces *an interlinking of love and hate*. Because anger toward the loved person cannot be expressed for fear of losing that person . . . Ambivalence, the interlinking of love and hate, remains *an important characteristic of later object relationships*. Many people, for instance, cannot even imagine that love is possible at all without suffering and sacrifice, without fear of being abused, without being hurt and humiliated." There is the horrible secret of the abuse itself, there are anger and feelings of guilt that cannot be explained, can hardly be admitted, and certainly cannot be discussed; one is alone in the lion's den. Every stray resentment has to be rigorously suppressed, but the very act of swallowing the hurt brings with it an unconscious compulsion to reenact the drama of childhood, what Miller calls "the repetition compulsion." She writes, "The unremembered plight of *being at someone else's mercy* and being abused by a love object is perpetuated either in a passive or an active role."

In years to come Sondheim would be very much on his guard against overtures, imagined or real, from women, and would strive to maintain a safe psychic distance. The playwright Arthur Laurents recalled that a mutual friend of theirs, a successful figure in her own right, spent an evening with Sondheim. He feigned a headache at her door and she was quite insulted that he would consider such a stratagem necessary. There were other incidents: a woman visitor to his house, finding him seated on a sofa, chose a nearby chair. He leapt up and removed himself to the sofa's far corner with devastating dispatch. Leonard Bernstein's sister Shirley recalled going to dinner at her brother's Park Avenue apartment years ago. The hosts were still getting dressed, so she went into the thickly carpeted library, where Sondheim was already waiting. She said he did not see her enter but hearing a noise as she advanced, he spun around and said, "Don't touch me!"

THAT NIGHT WHEN Joan Barnet went to act as baby-sitter and found Stephen pouring drinks for his mother, there was a friend at the apartment, Jamie Hammerstein, then called Jimmy. The boys wanted to go to a shooting gallery on Broadway, but their baby-sitter did not think that was a very good idea. So Stephen asked her if she would like to see the new hit musical by Richard Rodgers and Oscar Hammerstein, *Oklahoma!* He rang up his friend "Ockie," Jimmy's father, they got standing-room tickets, and off they went to see *Oklahoma!* Foxy had become friendly with the Hammersteins in about 1940 after having lunch with Oscar's wife, Dorothy, who happened to be an interior decorator. The Hammersteins had recently moved to the East Coast from Hollywood; Oscar's illustrious career was in something of a slump, and Dorothy's income as an interior decorator was important to the family. She was looking for clients and contacts and found both in Foxy Sondheim, who engaged her to refurbish their San Remo apartment and introduced her around. Susan Blanchard, Dorothy's daughter by a previous marriage, said, "She got hooked up with Foxy, and I think she got sorry for her. She was very tolerant of her shortcomings, and I was amazed the friendship lasted as long as it did. My mother had been born in Australia and lived in London, so there were aspects of American life she didn't understand, and Foxy's chutzpa opened doors she never would have opened otherwise."

Their sons, just a year apart in age, had discovered a mutual passion for Monopoly and other games and often played together. Jamie Hammerstein recalled that his parents moved to Highland Farm, outside Doylestown in Bucks County, Pennsylvania, and shortly afterwards, in June of 1942, Stephen came for a visit. "He was supposed to go off to camp for the summer, but he had such a good time that he said, 'Do I have to go to camp?' and his mother canceled it and he came to us instead. He was the boy who came to dinner."

Sondheim described it as "infiltrating the house." Jamie Hammerstein said he soon established himself as a relative. "If Susan and I would come into the house, we'd ask, 'Where's Steve?' "

Shortly after that, Herbert Sondheim gave Foxy a financial settlement and she bought a farm of her own in Bucks County, on the opposite side of Doylestown, just four miles away from the Hammersteins. She called it Fox Hill Farm and leased out her land to local farmers for growing alfalfa. Sondheim remembers it as an old frame building (not unlike the one he would eventually buy in Connecticut), tastefully decorated by his mother. In those days Doylestown was little more than a village. Jimmy Hammerstein had taught him to ride a bicycle, and he would bike to Highland Farm. He believes his mother moved to Bucks County because it was chic, and that only a coincidence brought Foxy and himself so near the Hammersteins in Bucks County. But there is at least a possibility that she, ever alert to the value of connections, decided to place Stephen where he could have easy access to these important friends. Since he seemed to have inherited his father's talent for music, it could not do him any harm.

Just like Alicia and Herbert, Oscar and Dorothy Hammerstein had met on a boat going to Europe. They, too, were already married, and they also fell in love "across a crowded room." By the time Stephen came on the scene they had been married for a decade. Their son said, "They were very much in love and you could feel it. They didn't put their kids first; they put each other first. They weren't clutchy in the Mediterranean way. They were Anglo down to their toes. Oscar was the man of the house, and mother set about making it as perfect as possible: an old-fashioned marriage."

In that Highland Farm living room, dark and cool, with uninterrupted vistas of countryside all around, a troop of children came and went. Oscar had a boy and a girl, Billy and Alice, by his first wife, Myra, and Dorothy had Henry and Susan by her first husband, Henry Jacobson; then Jimmy, who was a year younger than Stephen, arrived. Then there were the waifs of the war years. Dorothy's niece Jennifer Watanabe, who had a Japanese father, was living with them (the Hammersteins took her in after her father was arrested and sent for a time to Ellis Island). There were two other girls in residence, both of them, like Stephen, the victims of neglectful and abusive mothers. Shawn Lynch, daughter of an English actress friend of Dorothy's, had survived the London blitz and used to "go into the bathroom and scream," Susan Blanchard said. Margot Devauchier, daughter of an American mother and a French father, was in a similar situation. But somehow there were enough bedrooms for everyone.

Susan Blanchard said, "About those children—the dynamics were very

Oscar and Dorothy Hammerstein
shortly after their marriage in 1929

complicated. We were brought up in a time when there was no awareness of psychology, and our parents plunged in, in a good-hearted way, without altogether being aware of the consequences. Stevie spent a good deal of time with us." Susan worked briefly for Foxy, Inc., and went to Paris with Foxy in 1947 or 1948, making sketches of the collections. "The thing about Foxy was that she was not reliable. She'd promise and then not come through. She'd say, 'I want you to meet me at eight a.m.,' and then she wouldn't be there. What she did to Stephen was unforgivable. When he was still a preadolescent she would have house parties in her farm with everyone drunk out of their minds. You didn't dare walk into a bedroom. It was not a nurturing, loving atmosphere, to say the least. Anything good she might have done she turned around and undid the next day. She looked a lot like Stevie, but not so great on a woman. Stevie in drag, with dark red lipstick and froufrou bows and bustles. She had an incredible ego. She always thought everyone was trying to get her into bed."

Jamie Hammerstein called her "an extraordinarily selfish woman, in her early forties and worried about getting laid. All she wanted to do was get her kid out of her hair. Also don't forget, Stephen could criticize her friends so you wouldn't want to know . . . His relationship with his mother reminded me of Albee's play [*Who's Afraid of*] *Virginia Woolf?* Even at the age of twelve he could be as bitchy as she was. They were incredible, the way they could dish it out. I didn't understand it, then or now."

Susan Blanchard said, "I heard stories about Foxy reducing Stevie to tears. He'd be out of his mind with rage and pain." He would get on his bicycle and rush to the Hammersteins and they would comfort him. "They were extremely loyal," he said. "They never, never, *never* undermined my mother to me. I won't say they defended her, but they tried to make me understand, you know, that it was difficult and she was upset." Her son was making himself so much at home with the Hammersteins that his mother began to get worried. She would say to him, "You're not to go to the Hammersteins any more; I'm suing them for alienation of affection." He said, "That was her phrase; of course, at the age of eleven or twelve, what do you know what that phrase means? But she wanted to cling to the Hammersteins' friendship because Oscar was a celebrity and it was difficult for her to juggle these two things, making me alienated from the Hammersteins at the same time that she wanted to be close to them." Jamie Hammerstein said, "If Foxy showed up at our place my father would disappear upstairs. We none of us wanted to see Foxy ever." Sondheim's solution was to live at Fox Hill Farm during the week and move to the Hammersteins for the weekend, whenever his mother arrived. There would be the regulation Friday-

The Hammersteins in later years, outside Highland Farm

night dinner at home and then he would go. He did not think she really minded.

Sondheim has memories of long bicycle rides through the countryside—occasionally, Jimmy would come to visit him, but mostly he went to Highland Farm—and then going to see movies in Doylestown at one of the two evening showings, seven or nine o'clock. They also played tennis with Oscar, who was a fine player. Jamie Hammerstein said, "I was a good athlete and Steve wasn't quite as good. I betrayed him once: I ditched him as a double in a tennis match after pressure from my coach and still feel guilty about that." There was a nine-hole golf course abutting Oscar's property, and they used to sneak in through the fence and play a few holes. One summer they raised rabbits. Sondheim said, "We took all our allowance money and bought rabbits, built hutches and spent the summer chasing them because they'd always get out and we'd have to get them back."

The Hammerstein family would see Stevie wandering around the farm teaching himself Greek, Susan Blanchard said, "and we were all somewhat wary of him because he had a terrific temper. One time we were playing Monopoly and I accused him of cheating and he hit me. Much later, he told me he had hit me because he *was* cheating." Jamie Hammerstein said their friendship contained elements of sibling rivalry. "I loved him as a brother, but Steve was not warm. Steve was brittle, competitive, and sarcastic. More so than other kids his age and better at it. There was nothing cuddly about him. He spoke and thought very quickly, and perhaps had a genius IQ." In retrospect, Jamie was sure they had "some pretty bitchy fights," because they were competing to be first to do something: "there would be a fight to get to the piano first." That, one assumes, happened when Oscar was in the room.

When Oscar Hammerstein II and Stephen Sondheim met, Hammerstein was not yet launched upon his famous series of musicals with Richard Rodgers, although he was about to begin work on the first of these, *Oklahoma!*. At that point Hammerstein was known for "a romantic, florid kind of theatre, more operetta than musical comedy," Richard Rodgers wrote, since he had worked with Rudolf Friml and Sigmund Romberg. But he was also responsible, along with Jerome Kern, for *Show Boat* in 1927, a work Rodgers very much admired. Hammerstein had not had a major hit on Broadway for almost a decade.

He was tall and as a young man had been handsome, but surviving photographs and films of him in midlife invariably show him sporting an unbecoming crewcut, and his skin was heavily pockmarked. He is usually characterized as a benevolent figure, but that portrait is challenged by those who saw a ruthlessness behind the charm and a marked contrast between what could be the saccharine sweetness of his lyrics and the sophistication of his manner. "He talked a good game," said Mary Rodgers Guettel, Richard Rodgers's daughter, "but he didn't want intimacy."

Hammerstein had lost both parents at an early age. His mother died when he was fifteen and his father when he was nineteen, which may have accounted for his sympathy for those to whom he gave such generous hospitality. Even Sondheim, who loved and defended him, did not think "Ockie" had much sense of how to be a father. "He and my father shared something, I think, which is that they were not good parents until you were at a rational age, and the trouble with that is, by the time you are at a rational age a number of wounds have been inflicted and scars have formed."

All of Hammerstein's children were to some extent subjected to his brand of humor, which usually meant making them the butt of a joke. Mary Rodgers Guettel said, "His idea of fun would be to trip up his kids with a branch just as they were learning to ice-skate." Susan Blanchard said of her stepfather, "He was extremely sweet and kind on the one hand, but because words were his main talent he could cut you down in a very abrupt way. For instance I might be gossiping with a girlfriend on the couch and he'd be eavesdropping behind the couch without our knowing it. Then he might get up and say, 'Very boring,' or wait until dinner and give an imitation of what he had heard. He was worse with the boys. He would tease Jimmy mercilessly at the dinner table and my mother would say, 'Stop it this minute!' "

Sondheim was aware that Hammerstein's cutting humor "would reduce everyone at the dinner table"—except himself. He was the one whose point of view was listened to sympathetically and whose ideas were praised and encouraged. A famous photograph of Sondheim standing with Oscar, Dorothy, Mimi Lynch (Shawn's mother), and Jamie Hammerstein makes the family situation very clear. Jamie is at far left, with a hesitant half-smile, almost a grimace, on his face, and his mother has her arm around him protectively. Oscar is second from right, smiling, both hands in his jacket pockets, and Stephen is beside him, smiling, with both hands in his pants pockets. That he might have displaced one of Oscar's children in the bid for his affection troubled Sondheim for many years. He was talking about this with his analyst one day and suddenly realized that, even though Oscar loved him, he loved his own children more. This was why he was so critical and demanding: he wanted higher standards from them. Sondheim found that thought reassuring.

Hammerstein had many redeeming qualities. Susan Blanchard was tolerant of his attacks, loved him anyway and considered him a stabilizing influence. Her mother "tended to get emotional," and Oscar's gift was to stand in the middle of the storm chuckling, until he had calmed everyone down. Even though he felt the lash of his father's tongue, Jamie Hammerstein said, "he made you laugh despite yourself." What was remarkable was his father's disciplined approach to work. "He worked for five and a half hours every day creatively and for another one and a half on other stuff. Day in and day out, except for Sunday. He began at 8:30 a.m. and we only saw him at lunch. But when he came out of his study at 4:30 p.m. he brought none of the angst with him. He was ready to go for a walk," or play backgammon, or tennis, a game of any kind. Stephen fitted in perfectly.

One of Sondheim's first acts on joining the Hammerstein household was to teach Ockie how to play chess. He said, "The first time we played, I taught him the rules and of course I beat him. The second time I beat him, but not as easily as the first time. The third time I set up something like a two- or three-move trap, which was as far as I could go, and he started to move a piece, and in chess the rule is you haven't completed the move until you have actually taken your finger off the piece. He moved a piece forward, and

From left, Jamie Hammerstein, Dorothy Hammerstein, Mimi Lynch, Oscar Hammerstein, and Sondheim

thought about it, and looked at me, and took it back. And then he moved another piece. I said, 'Gosh, you're getting good. You saw what I was setting up,' and he said, 'No, I heard your heart beating.' "

OSCAR TAUGHT HIM bridge and a "genteel form" of anagrams and backyard croquet. This was a tame version of the croquet they played at the Richard Rodgers house on Black Rock Turnpike in Fairfield, Connecticut, in those days. "The whole idea of serious croquet is that it's team," Sondheim said. "It's two against two, and the strategy is as important as the shots, so what happens is you shoot, and then you confer for five minutes, then you shoot and confer again. A *very* serious game." It sounded more like military maneuvers than an afternoon's diversion, more competitive even than the games Oscar liked. But that they were learning this kind of croquet was an indication of the growing role Rodgers, who also had a wife named Dorothy, and his daughters Mary and Linda, were beginning to play in the Hammerstein household. Mary was just fourteen when she went to stay at the Hammerstein farm with her parents one weekend. She had been enrolled in a work farm, where she was going to harvest vegetables and help the war effort, but her stay was cancelled because of an outbreak of polio. So she went to the Hammersteins instead.

"And then this boy showed up," she said. "I don't remember what we started talking about, but I know that at first he probably didn't know what to do with me, so we started to play chess. And he beat me three games in a row, so fast. And then somehow he made his way to the piano, and I had either never heard *Rhapsody in Blue* or *An American in Paris,* or something. And he sat down and played a great hunk of it. I was just done in by this, not only by what I was listening to, because I'm still a huge Gershwin fan, but by the ability of this guy to do that." It never occurred to her to ask Stephen whether he was going to be a pianist or a composer. (He was then fifteen.) "I just knew that this was an incredibly talented person with an incredible musical sensitivity and was the smartest person I had ever met in my whole life." She "fell in love with him," just like that. One of the Hammerstein orphans, Shawn Lynch, was also there that weekend, "so I got Shawn in a corner and said, 'Can you get him to write me a letter?' It was like a little girl being madly in love. I said, 'Here's my address,' and Shawn said, 'I'll try.' Every day after I got back to Connecticut I walked to the mailbox from the driveway, which was half a mile. There never was any letter. And finally I got back to Shawn and said, 'Can't you get him to write me a letter?' and she said no, she

Herbert and Stephen Sond-
heim in Connecticut

A tense game of chess with
Herbie on the living room
floor, 1950

Herbert Sondheim with Stephen, at right, and sons Walter and Herbert Jr.

Stephen Sondheim at the piano

didn't think she could. I'm not sure she even tried! I trudged down there every single day of that summer."

DORIS CROCKETT, daughter of Rose and Charles Crockett, Sondheim's cousin on his mother's side, married Manny Gorman in the autumn of 1938. They went to live in Alexandria, Virginia, and invited the nine-year-old Stephen to visit them a year later. She met him in New York and they went down on the plane together. It was her first trip, and she was apprehensive, but he was very self-assured. "Don't worry," he said, "if you get sick there's a bag you can use to throw up in." He had visited a novelty shop at Broadway and Forty-ninth on the way to the airport, so when she went into the bathroom to wash her hands perhaps she should not have been surprised to find a different kind of soap. The more she washed her hands, the dirtier they got. That was a great trick, but then there was the spoon that was presented for her coffee. "That's a spoon that falls apart, that goes *nnnnng,* like that, when you try to use it," Sondheim said, demonstrating. "I was very into glasses that dribbled water through hidden holes disguised as floral decorations." And he loved the pack of cards he was sometimes able to substitute for the real ones when his mother and her friends sat down to play canasta-like games, in which all the hearts and diamonds were black and all the spades and clubs were red. "The women didn't notice it, but they would start to get extremely nervous." It was all just good-natured fun, and there was a moment in early adolescence when he thought he might become a magician. "Between the ages of ten and fourteen I spent a lot of my allowance on sending away for magic tricks to a place in Michigan called, I think, Abbott's. I never gave shows, but I used to do card tricks and mechanical illusions, things like producing scarves from a box, and I liked mechanical things where you put a card in a frame and put a pencil through it and it comes out whole, although I was never very good at that. The idea is, I'm so busy with my left hand that you don't notice that my right hand is holding something. It's just misdirection."

For the fact was that the grownups in his life had played a trick on him. While he was not looking they had, with malicious sleight-of-hand, demolished the framework of his life and left him stranded. There is a parallel event in a work for which Sondheim later wrote words and music, *Pacific Overtures,* about the trade treaty Commodore Matthew Perry signed with Japan in the mid–nineteenth century. The signing of the actual treaty takes place in secrecy, but it is witnessed by a young boy hiding in a tree—curiously, he is just ten years old. He can see people, movement and argument, and knows something of immense significance is taking place. Yet his testimony has a dreamlike ambiguity, as if some part of himself were aware that he cannot possibly fathom the meaning of the drama unfolding before his eyes. The boy sings, "I'm a fragment of the day," just as Sondheim would write years later that he was "the remnant" of his parents' divorce, as if the torrent that had blotted out their marriage had swept him away with it. Yet the boy, nevertheless, has his own tenacious story to tell. He sings, "I am there still."

Sondheim said he had only recently realized that his interest in games and conundrums dated from the failure of his parents' marriage, and that moment when "nothing made sense any more." The puzzle was a metaphor, a reassurance he desperately needed that there really was a path through the maze, that magical secrets waited to be revealed, that a world in fragments could be reassembled, however painfully, and that a key existed to every riddle if he searched diligently enough. For that reason he was never interested in games in which the rules were flexible and open to challenge. These did not suit him at all. He wanted games for which the rules were inflexible, where one always knew exactly what was coming next, as in military school, as if to "face out the black terrors of life," as Anthony Shaffer wrote in *Sleuth*.

If the puzzle was the metaphor, art was the solution, because of its equally crucial emphasis upon structure and form. His interest in music had been precipitated by the same crisis. This must be true, he reasoned, because he "hadn't given much of a damn" about his piano lessons when he was six or seven. Music became charged with meaning only when it could make order out of chaos, and this goal became the leitmotif of his life. Years later Keith Warner, who directed a revival of *Pacific Overtures* at the English National Opera in London, recalled sitting in a box with Sondheim at the back of the stalls. "When 'Someone in a Tree' started, all of a sudden he grabbed my arm. He said, 'Just think, this orchestra is playing my music, and this is my favorite song of anything I have ever written.' There were tears in his eyes."

CHAPTER 3

The Brass Goddess

Foxy Sondheim's operation to improve her nose took place when Stephen was about twelve. He said, "She got into a minor car accident at a place called the Jenkintown Circle, which was on the way to the farm, and used that as a pretext to get her nose changed." He thought she fondly believed he would not notice. Instead of the emphatic contours she was born with, she was given a delicate replacement, one that doubtless satisfied her surgeon's notions of beauty but which robbed her face of its undeniable character. With her straight, bobbed nose she looked like anyone. But she was apparently very satisfied, because "one night she got drunk and took out the pictures of her old nose in various frames around the house and tore them up." He secretly retrieved one of the photographs, wanting, he said, to be able to prove that her story about the accident altering her appearance was a fabrication and that he, at least, had not been fooled. He hid the photograph in his desk, where she discovered it a month later and was furious.

He was beginning to fantasize about leaving home. A short story he wrote later, as a college freshman, makes his state of mind at this time clear, since it is plainly autobiographical and the main character is even called Foxy. The fictional Foxy in "The Brass Goddess" is always complaining about how miserly her monthly alimony check is, although her daughter, Ellen, knows they live extravagantly and that their old New England house is full of beautiful things: a Chippendale sideboard, Sheraton tables, and sumptuous objets d'art, including a silver cigarette box given to Foxy by the Prince of Sweden. "She says, 'It's got the Swedish Royal shield engraved on it here, you see? Weighs sixteen ounces: solid silver.' And then that maddening smirk—owning for the sake of owning." Ellen feels she is just one more object to be possessed and ignored: "left with the run-down victrola, the static radio, the torn murder-mysteries, the expensive, polished, lonely house." The fictional Foxy is entertaining executives from her dress company for the weekend, and during dinner she and Ellen start to wrangle. When Ellen accuses her mother of trying to "climb the social ladder," her mother, in tears, complains that Ellen does nothing except "sit around all day . . . only sulking and making yourself unpleasant and trying to hurt me, while I work from morning to night to support you!" Ellen later complains to one of the dinner guests, "She deliberately tries to hurt me all the time. She humiliates me in front of everyone; never alone, only when it's in front of everyone! I hate her! I hate her!"

That Steve and Foxy were at loggerheads was hardly a secret to her friends, including Jo Copeland. For Copeland's daughter Lois Gould, the saga of Foxy and Steve was so much a part of her own childhood that the two of them, somewhat disguised, appear in her novel *Necessary Objects*. The portraits are not flattering. Foxy has become Elly, youngest of four daughters, whose self-made father has left them Lowen's, a great Fifth Avenue department store. All of the "Lowen girls" are caught up in possessions and appearance, but Elly is the most superficial of them all, unhappily married, secretly a lesbian, so terrified of gaining weight that she exists on sliced tomatoes and champagne. Her son, Jason, aged fifteen, is expelled from boarding school for using drugs and is probably a homosexual.

Sondheim dismissed this portrait of his mother as completely inaccurate and that of himself as a not very kind caricature. He thought he had been almost too well behaved as an adolescent, and if he had been angry, he was not aware of it. Doing what was expected of him had been too well ingrained by his father, who obviously believed with Bishop Wykeham that "manners makyth man," or, as Sondheim explained it, "Don't stand out in the crowd. Duck in the corner. Don't raise your voice. Don't make a spectacle of yourself. Don't brag."

There were some aspects of Jason that did, however, resemble Stephen. He, too, tended to stammer when his words could not keep up with his thoughts. He, too, had severe acne as an adolescent: "I used to go for treatments where they squeezed every pimple; it was painful and dreadful." Like Jason, whose nose was "forever running," Stephen suffered from hay fever until he was about thirty. "Lots and lots of coughing, wheezing, and tearing. In my teens I had a series of allergenic tests and it turned out I was allergic to house dust." And, like Jason, he was playing the piano.

In *Necessary Objects* Jason is a musical prodigy who writes brilliant compositions but is under such a compulsion to shock and offend that he keeps destroying his chances. Rather than remove some offensive lyrics that he has written for the annual school production, Jason destroys the score. That is very much at variance with the way Stephen Sondheim was leading his life at the time. After the happy experience of playing the organ at the New York Military Academy, he took a year or two of piano lessons at the George School and even was encouraged to consider a career as a concert pianist. But there were some problems. In the first place, he did not enjoy the teacher, and then he discovered that he did not enjoy performing, either. At one concert he played Rachmaninoff's Concerto No. 2 in C minor (the first movement—his teacher played the second) and then a Chopin polonaise, and to his horror he blanked out in the middle of the latter. That was when he realized he had lost interest in a concert career. Composing was quite another matter.

As Gwen Raverat observed in her delightful book *Period Piece,* the problem for great men is that people often do not know what to make of them, especially when they are young. E. M. Forster, who was a friend of Raverat's family, was judged to have no talent for writing by her aunt Etty, who hoped he would soon turn to a more promising occupation, although she did not know what. The same aunt despaired of Ralph Vaughan Williams, who *would* go on working at music when he was "so hopelessly bad at it." But then, the author wrote, "this is what you have to go through to become great."

So although Sondheim, aged twelve, intended to do well, as usual, at the George School, where he would spend the next four years, to his contemporaries he simply looked lost. He was short and unkempt-looking, usually wearing the same black herringbone jacket, with his shirt wrinkled at the collar and his shoes lacking any polish. He was on the outside of the group, wanting to be included and not sure how to go about it. Then he found Hugh and Roz.

Sixteen-year-old Hugh Cronister was a handsome boy, and one of the stars at the George School: prominent in the student government, the head of several committees, a three-star athlete, and a force behind the junior and senior plays. (He returned to the school as a teacher of English and theatre.) He was a good friend of Rosamond Earle, with whom he ran the dance committee. She was the daughter of a professor who taught at the Institute for Advanced Studies at Princeton, and a figure in her own right: literary editor of *Life,* the George School publication, head of the Girls' Council, archery manager, and much else. Cronister said, "I'd be with some people and you could see Steve thirty feet away edging towards us. Socially we were on different circuits, and here's this little puppy hugging our knees." They took to him in a good-natured way. "I think he felt socially inept unless he were included. I can remember that forelock, that flip of hair, and the way he had of tossing it back." Cronister recalled Sondheim was very moody as an adolescent, excitable and high-keyed and liable to erupt unpredictably. But his peers liked him very much—he could make a joke out of anything—and the twosome gradually became a threesome. "I guessed he would end up as a pianist or a serious composer. I never knew he was going to be famous," Cronister said.

By the time Sondheim arrived at George School he was two grades ahead of his contemporaries, "and throughout my school years I wanted to be accepted." So he was careful not to make a point of his good grades, "because I was precocious and people don't like that." If his mother had taken to using British pronunciation, using a double *s* sound in "tissue" instead of *sh,* for instance, then he would make a point of doing the reverse. "I used to drop *g*'s at the ends of—I'd say 'goin' ' instead of 'going'—so that nobody would think I was hoity-toity," he said. It does not appear that anyone did. Rosamond Earle Matthews said, "He was full of energy and bright as could be." They both had the same favorite teacher: Lucille Pollock, who taught Latin in a stimulating way. They studied Cicero at an early stage and would make up songs in Latin. Sondheim had begun to study Latin in military school, but because he had skipped seventh grade he had missed some basic lessons. "My memory is that the very first day of class Miss Pollock started talking about nouns, verbs, and adverbs and I didn't know what they were. So she told me to come and see her afterwards and proceeded to give me a lesson." He picked it up quickly and got through a four-year course in two years. Miss Pollock was, he said, the first teacher who changed his life, because she allowed him to move ahead and excited him about language. Steve would take Hugh and Rosamond to the Hammersteins' on weekends and they would "horse around" under the piano, Rosamond said. Her mother was going through a phase of calling them all "lambs," "and I remember Steve gave me a stuffed lamb. His entry in the yearbook said, 'I hope you will continue to gambol,' and he signed it 'Ewe.' " She thought he had a crush on her, and on Hugh as well. Sondheim said, "I had no family, and the only time I had a family was in school."

THE GEORGE SCHOOL, a coeducational college-preparatory school, is situated in Bucks County on former Indian settlements in Newtown, about fifteen miles outside Philadelphia. It was founded in 1893 by John M. George, a wealthy Quaker, and its original enrollment was eighty-five percent Quaker. (It is now eighty-five percent non-Quaker.) The school was favored by New York Jewish families, whose children could get a first-class education there with no social bias, although Cronister said that Newtown was very prejudiced and one would hear talk about "these kikes." Alger Hiss's stepson, Tim Hobson, was in the class of 1944; Irene Mayer Selznick's son went there, and so did Mary Martin's daughter. James Michener taught there in the 1930s, and distinguished lecturers made regular visits to the campus, among them Hammerstein and Langston Hughes.

Boys went to class in jackets and ties. Girls had shoulder-length hair, wore skirts and blouses, and socks with their saddle shoes and loafers. In that inno-cent time smoking was forbidden, only seniors drank coffee, and there was, of course, no alcohol. When Roz Earle became head of the Girls' Council she led a "crusade" to get permission for the girls to wear lipstick and earrings on Saturday nights. During the war years observing a blackout was patriotically enforced, food was rationed, and every autumn students were recruited to help harvest root vegetables on the Annual Farm Day. In the main, life con-tinued at its unruffled pace, enlivened by parties, musical events, plays, dances, and arts and crafts of all kinds. The staff chaperone was a constant presence. Group activities were the norm, dating was discouraged, and at the dances they would check, Sondheim said, to make sure the boys did not dance too close to the girls. "No firearms, no drinking / Not even coed wink-ing / All they allow is thinking," Sondheim would observe in his song "What to Do at George School."

Like Roz Earle and Hugh Cronister, Stephen took an active part in the dramatics program, which was at its peak while he was there. "Uncle Jack" Talbot, who had played in summer stock, mounted productions of every-thing from Shakespeare and Sheridan to Wilde, Barrie, and Kaufman and Hart during his thirty-seven years at the school (he retired in 1970), unde-terred by the improvised nature of the facilities. The stage of the old assembly room, where plays were performed, was so shallow that scenery flats had to be laid against the back wall. There was only one entrance, from stage left, so

Sondheim at the George School in about 1945

anyone who left the scene on stage right had to wait in the wings until the curtain came down. Girls were given the only dressing room; boys improvised their own on a nearby staircase. When Sondheim first arrived, he was too small to play leading roles, Cronister said. One of his early parts was as the heroine's brother in the J. M. Barrie comedy *Alice Sit-by-the-Fire*. He got a mention in the school newspaper.

He was given an early example of the importance of learning to improvise when he appeared in a one-act play by Edna St. Vincent Millay called *Aria da Capo*. It was "about two shepherds who are on opposite sides of some kind of invisible barrier, and there's a godlike figure with a prompt book. The shepherds are friends but come to blows at some point," he said. He played one of the shepherds, and during the dress rehearsal the other shepherd came crashing out of his chair to the floor in a fall that had not been rehearsed. Sondheim, not knowing how to respond to this new bit of business, was paralyzed. Then "Uncle Jack" leapt onto the stage and carried the boy out; he had had an epileptic fit.

He remembered another occasion, when he was playing the detective in a melodrama by N. Richard Nash called *Incognito.* Ten minutes into the second act he had to find a gun concealed in a woman's purse. As he made his triumphant discovery the stage manager, mistaking this cue for the one that ended the act, rang down the curtain. "None of us knew what to do," he said. So the curtain went up again, they picked up their lines, and the next act ran for an hour and forty-five minutes.

By the time of the senior class play early in 1946, Sondheim, at almost sixteen, was tall enough to play some leading roles. He was cast as Charles Condomine in Noël Coward's play *Blithe Spirit,* wearing a blatantly artificial mustache. His father loved the image and kept a photograph of him in that role on his office wall. Sondheim said, "I can remember the opening line. I came in shaking a cocktail shaker and saying, 'No sign of the advancing hordes yet?' which was my idea of real sophistication when I was sixteen."

Oklahoma!, Oscar Hammerstein's famous collaboration of 1943 with Richard Rodgers, and particularly the evolution of the opening song, "Oh, What a Beautiful Mornin'!" were described in an essay, *Notes on Lyrics,* that Hammerstein wrote in 1949. The authors had set about turning *Green Grow the Lilacs,* a play by Lynn Riggs, into a musical, but immediately ran into difficulties. The play opened with a quiet rural scene. A woman is churning butter outside a farmhouse in the early morning, but no musical could do that. Tradition dictated that every musical had to begin with a chorus line of pretty girls. What could they substitute? A quilting bee? A strawberry festival? They stared at each other, "unable to think of anything at all," and finally made their decision. They would begin their story where it needed to begin. "We realized that such a course was experimental, amounting almost to the breach of an implied contract with a musical comedy audience," Hammerstein wrote. "I cannot say truthfully that we were worried . . . Once we had made the decision, everything seemed to work . . . and we had that inner confidence people feel when they have adopted the direct and honest approach." There would be the farmhouse, the woman with the butter churn, and a cowboy singing offstage.

Hammerstein had read the playwright's description of the opening scene, and it seemed that some of the images: the blades of young corn, the streams, and a golden emanation over the whole scene, were too good to waste on stage directions. He would incorporate these ideas into his song. He also remembered a moment on his own porch in Pennsylvania when he had watched a herd of motionless cows on a hillside some distance away. That had led to a quatrain about "the cows on the hill / Are as still as the grass," a verse he recalled when writing the cowboy's song. The image had stayed in his mind, "quietly waiting to be used," he wrote, until it was transformed into "All the cattle are standin' like statues." The words and music are now so universally familiar that it is hard to remember that "Oh, What a Beautiful Mornin'!" signaled the beginning of a completely new approach to musical theatre.

At a moment when the famous Rodgers and Hammerstein collaboration was having its first success, it is not surprising that Sondheim should have conceived the ambition to become just like Oscar. Oscar was his surrogate father; he loved Oscar, and if Oscar had pursued any other profession, Sondheim believed, he would have followed him blindly. But he could become like Oscar without risking any disloyalty toward his own father, since that unusual man had a musical gift of his own. The examples of both men pointed in the direction of his own talents and needs. "The Hammersteins were more than a balm," he said. "They were not only comforting. They gave me an outlet; they opened up all the worlds of creative possibilities."

Sondheim's first attempt at writing songs began in the spring of 1945, when he and another classmate launched the idea of a musical about life at the George School. The plan was postponed for almost a year, but then picked up again enthusiastically by Sondheim, working with two new partners and with plenty of help from Uncle Jack Talbot and other faculty members. It eventually developed into *By George,* with three acts, twenty songs, dances, and a cast of about fifty, and was performed in May of 1946. It was the surprise hit of the season, perhaps because the lyrics made knowing references to the triumphs and frustrations of life at school, the faculty received a fair amount of gentle ribbing, and the actors, if inexperienced, were engagingly enthusiastic. One of the most popular songs was about "The Doughnut," a leather-upholstered seat wrapped around a pillar that was the unofficial meeting place for dating couples; other songs celebrated the joys of homework, Monday mornings, and being late for breakfast. It was the biggest success George School had seen for many a year, and since Sondheim had played the piano for the performance, as well as written the music and collaborated on the lyrics, he was justifiably excited. *Babes in Arms,* the successful musical by Richard Rodgers and Lorenz Hart, had advanced the fable that teenagers (in this case the children of vaudeville veterans whose profession had disappeared with the advent of talking pictures) could, with their clever new ideas, succeed where their parents had failed. The musical was subsequently made into a popular film starring Mickey Rooney and Judy Garland. The moment seemed right for yet another hit that would demonstrate the superior talents of the new generation. Sondheim could hardly wait to show the script to Ockie so that he could become the first sixteen-year-old to have a musical on Broadway.

When he came to write *Notes on Lyrics,* Oscar Hammerstein felt he would be doing a disservice to the truth if he pretended that he had never made any early mistakes or written truly bad lyrics. It was not fair to the novice to pretend that the successful man starts life being perfect. Even after he had several shows produced, he was still capable of coming up with something like "My Little Redskin," a song about Indians sung by a female chorus in bathing suits and deep suntans—"and the lyric featured the double meaning of 'redskin' . . . Get it?" he wrote. He did not remember the actual lyrics and was not going to look for them. "There are limits to which I will debase myself, even to encourage the young."

He did not want an amateur to get the idea that writing a song was easy. His impression was that amateurs were "money mad." They seemed to think all they needed to do was pull the right strings, without taking the time to correct their errors and perfect their work, so "instead of writing what they honestly feel, they invent fancy rhymes and foolish jokes and tricky titles and . . . lines that merely 'fill in.' " Thoughts of this kind may have gone through his head after he had perused Sondheim's *By George.* Sondheim recalled him saying, "Now, do you want my opinion as though I didn't know you? Well, it's the worst thing I've ever read." As he saw Sondheim's expression, Hammerstein added, "I didn't say that it was untalented, I said it was terrible. And if you want to know *why* it's terrible, I'll tell you."

Sondheim learned the importance of choosing every word with meticulous care, while at the same time finding the right balance between saying too little and too much. Most poetry, which the eye could absorb at its own pace, was too dense with meaning to be appreciated by the ear alone. Lyrics needed to be more repetitious. "Oh, what a beautiful mornin'! / Oh, what a beautiful day!," which looked merely silly on a page, was absolutely right for that particular melody. Oscar taught that a song had to be singable. One of his songs from *Carousel,* "What's the Use of Wond'rin'," which Sondheim would later cite as being just about perfect, did not quite please Oscar: he thought it should have ended with an open vowel instead of a closed one ("talk"), which made it more difficult to sing. A song should be sincere, representing one's own feelings and experiences; listeners were not fooled and would reject false sentimentality. Hammerstein also discussed the issue that, by general agreement, made his collaboration with Rodgers so valuable in the history of the American musical. He wrote: "It must be understood that the musician is just as much an author as the man who writes the words. He expresses the story in his medium just as the librettist expresses the story in his. Or, more accurately, they weld their two crafts and two kinds of talent into a single expression. This is the great secret of the well-integrated musical play." Songs should not be inserted at arbitrary intervals, but seamlessly intertwined so that everything, dialogue, melody, and lyrics, worked to further the plot and give it dramatic force. It was a lesson Sondheim never forgot.

Despite Hammerstein's unpromising response to this evidence of talent in his protégé, he began to make the occasional overture in Sondheim's direction. Sondheim remembers the day that Ockie and Richard Rodgers, who were writing *Carousel,* were contemplating beginning the second act with a treasure hunt. Since Sondheim was already refining what would become advanced skills in that particular game, his advice was asked. "It was my first major contribution to the American musical theatre," he said; but in the end they used a clambake instead. Then he remembered going to see *Carousel.* "When Jimmy was fourteen and I was fifteen and it was our spring break at George School, Oscar took us to New Haven for the first-night performance." He was so moved at the end of Act One "that I wept copious tears on Dorothy Hammerstein's fur wrap. Apparently certain kinds of fur will stain from tears, and I stained hers irrevocably." For years he was unable to watch *Carousel* again, "because it moved me so much."

WHEN WORK BEGAN on *Allegro* in the summer of 1947 Hammerstein suggested that Sondheim come onto the set as a glorified office boy, for twenty-five dollars a week. Sondheim said, "It was a seminal influence on my life, because it showed me a lot of smart people doing something wrong. Years later, in talking over the show with Oscar—I don't think I recognized it at the time—I realized he was trying to tell the story of his life. It's about a doctor who grows up in a small town and marries an ambitious woman and becomes very successful in New York and ends up giving vitamin injections to rich people and laying cornerstones of hospitals . . . His wife is cheating on him and he's disillusioned, but his loving nurse persuades him to go back to the country and . . . be a doctor with a capital D. Oscar meant it as a metaphor for what had happened to him. He had become so successful with the results of *Oklahoma!* and *Carousel* that he was suddenly in demand all over the place. What he was talking about was the trappings, not so much of success, but of losing sight of what your goal is . . . To the end of his days

Oscar said, 'I want to rewrite the second act of *Allegro* so people will under-stand what I was talking about,' because all the critics pounced on it as being a corny story, the doctor who gets corrupted by money. That's not what he meant . . . It wasn't about money; it was about losing sight of your goal. On the highest level it's about—an artist has to be selfish. That's not what Oscar meant, but that's what I think it's about."

In the manner of Thornton Wilder, who popularized the genre with *Our Town*, Hammerstein had wanted to tell a universal story about the life of a man from birth to death, but was pressured to redeem his hero, Joseph Taylor Jr., in mid-life because to have him die on stage would be too depressing. He was writing the book and lyrics himself and one of the reasons why Act Two remained unpolished was that he, predictably ignoring his own moral, had wasted too many hours making speeches and producing other people's plays. A re-reading of *Allegro* also suggests that Hammerstein as dramatist was not up to the challenge of writing a modern allegory.

As a musical, despite its respectable Broadway run, *Allegro* was a failure. But as an experiment it was audacious and ahead of its time. "It occurred to Oscar to use a Greek chorus as a chorus," Sondheim said. "I don't think any-body had put those two ideas together before. The chorus in *Allegro* is used not only to comment on the action but to explore the inner thoughts of the main characters; something two thousand years old, but I don't think anybody's done it in the commercial theatre." The other innovation was in terms of set design. Hammerstein and the designer, Jo Mielziner, created an S-shaped curtain to slide on a wide floor-length track all along the stage to accommodate several sets at once; the action could then flow from one to the other with almost cinematic effortlessness.

Sondheim continued, "The other thing I remember is that it was Agnes de Mille's first job as a director" (she had worked as the choreographer for *Oklahoma!* and *Carousel*) "and she was a horror. She treated the actors and singers like dirt and treated the dancers like gods, and at one point I remem-ber something dramatic. The stage manager was a man named Jerry [Jerome] Whyte, who was sort of Dick Rodgers's closest friend . . . and Agnes was treating the cast so badly during rehearsal that Jerry Whyte came out and in front of the whole company said, 'Miss de Mille, if you keep this up the com-pany will quit,' or something like that. But Agnes de Mille was . . . I think, an extremely insensitive woman, an excellent writer and a terrible director, in terms of morale anyway. That was my first experience of bad behavior in the theatre." Perhaps it was shortly after that incident that Hammerstein took over as director of *Allegro*.

Sondheim still has vivid memories of the famous opening night in New Haven in September 1947, when everything went wrong. He said, "There were four major catastrophes that night, one funny and the other three not. The first was that during the freshman dance" (the future doctor having reached college) "which was a tap ballet, Ray Harrison, who was the leading dancer, got his tap caught in the curtain track and ripped every ligament in his right leg. He was carried off screaming from the stage.

"The second thing that happened was, there's a song called 'A Fellow Needs a Girl,' and a small platform trundled in from stage left, there was a wall behind it, and Annamary Dickey, [as] Joe's mother, sits down, and William Ching, playing the father, stands behind her, and he sings the song. It's a very tender, very Rodgers-esque song. And as he did so he became aware of a movement behind him": the wall was about to fall on him. "The stage-hands eventually noticed, the wall was yanked back, and it was okay."

During the second act, Lisa Kirk, who would be making her Broadway debut playing Dr. Taylor's faithful nurse, Emily, was singing "The Gentleman Is a Dope." "The costume designer had decided she should wear a nurse's white shoes, but they had high heels. So as she stepped forward and got to the moment in the song, 'He's somebody else's problem,' her foot got caught in the same track and she fell into the orchestra pit.

"Now, at the Shubert in New Haven there *is* no orchestra pit, so luckily she just fell onto the string section. And luckily they all had their bows raised, so they were able to hoist her back on stage. And I know it may be my memory playing tricks, but I swear she didn't miss a beat." He was a good friend of Lisa Kirk's, "her mascot," he said, so he was waiting when she came offstage. She was in tears but grateful to be unhurt. "Need I tell you, the audience was giving her an ovation the Pope has never received. Everybody pushed her back on stage and she had to take two bows. Next day, in the New York *Herald Tribune,* a column . . . written by Billy Rose of all people, said, 'A star is born.' Next night she comes back, gets to the same point in the song, and starts to fall again, and the entire audience gasps, because they'd all read the *Herald Tribune.* She recovers quickly, they all sigh, and she gets another ovation. Oscar came backstage at the end and said, 'You do that a third time and you're fired.'

"The last thing that happened that night was that in the quietest and most uplifting moment of the show there is a song called 'Come Home,' the equivalent of 'You'll Never Walk Alone' in *Carousel.* And as it started there was a vague smell of smoke in the theatre, and it went on, and the smell got stronger. A couple got up in the second or third row and made their way up the aisle, trying not to run, and then four people over in the other aisle, and eight people, and a mass panic started. There probably were between fifty and sixty people going up the aisles when a voice from the back of the house yelled, 'It's just an ashcan fire in the alley!' " Since it was a hot night, doors were open and smoke from the alley was drifting in. The man who calmed the crowd that night was Joshua Logan, who would go on to direct *South Pacific* and would perfect many of *Allegro's* cinematic techniques, incidentally influencing a whole new generation of designers and directors. Next time the crowd rioted, during opening night in Boston, it would be Hammerstein's turn. The musical was all but shut down by a rowdy group of conventioneers. Hammerstein rose and commanded them to be quiet; they obeyed.

Allegro had a formative influence on Sondheim, he decided years later, not just because it was highly innovative: "Right away I accepted the idea of telling stories in space, of skipping time and using gimmicks like the Greek chorus. All the stuff that's in *Allegro*, of somebody playing with the idea of theatre, Pirandello-ish almost." It also influenced him because it had failed. "That's why I'm drawn to experiment . . . I realize that I am trying to recreate *Allegro* all the time."

DURING THE SUMMER MONTHS Jimmy Hammerstein and Stephen Sondheim saw every movie that came to Doylestown—the program changed twice a week—and Stephen would be taken to see a film at Radio City Music Hall whenever he visited his father. He said, "During my formative years movies really molded my entire view of the world." When he came to write "The Brass Goddess," he described Ellen (Foxy's daughter) as thinking of herself "in a perpetual movie, as if there were some unseen cameraman making the story of her life and showing it, scene for scene, in a small theatre somewhere, to a small, interested audience, who would live there and see everything through her eyes."

He remembered films like *Days of Glory,* the first one Gregory Peck ever made, and a film called *Winter Carnival.* That did not particularly interest him, but *Hangover Square,* an American film made in England, did. It starred Linda Darnell, George Sanders, and Laird Cregar, the latter playing George Harvey Bone, a tall and socially prominent composer with a guilty secret. As the film opened Bone was about to make his debut as a pianist and composer. The piano concerto was written for the film by Bernard Herrmann, who would write more than sixty scores, for such films as *Citizen Kane* and *North by Northwest.* Herrmann's bleak and percussive opening bars had the guise of Sergei Rachmaninoff as revisited by Charles Ives; Sondheim was entranced.

He and Jimmy went for the seven o'clock showing. Then Jimmy went home and Sondheim stayed for the nine o'clock so as to memorize the first six or eight bars of the score, the pages of which are seen for a matter of seconds. After playing the theme over and over again, he wrote a fan letter care of Twentieth Century–Fox. About three months later, "I got a reply back from Herrmann. It turned out he lived right around the corner from where I lived with my mother in New York. In tiny handwriting he said how rare it was that composers got fan letters." He would never forget that piano concerto and gave it credit for influencing one of his major works decades later.

The movie was an early example of film noir, and just the sort of melodrama that would fascinate an uncritical adolescent. The plot has to do with a protagonist who feels compelled to go out and strangle somebody whenever he hears the right high-pitched screeching sounds. Bone has no idea what he has done, and apart from this ungentlemanly lapse, he is about as menacing as a Pekinese. He cannot help it, poor chap, says George Sanders consolingly (playing the doctor in his silkiest and smoothest manner). He must be locked up for his own good. All of this happens just before his piano concerto is to receive its first performance. Bone gives the doctor the slip and, in the middle of his performance, has another one of his fits and sets the whole place on fire. As the flames mount higher, he plays on and on, and then . . .

The reason for Bone's guilty secret is never made clear in *Hangover Square,* which, it must be said, does not go in much for profundity of thought or dialogue. Something of the same sort happens in *Bequest,* a novel Sondheim began to write two or three years later while at Williams College. (It was never finished.) Edward Gold, the hero, is also a pianist and composer. As the novel opens he is giving the first performance of his own concerto for piano and orchestra at Carnegie Hall when, in the middle of a crescendo, he has a memory lapse and cannot play for a few crucial seconds. The moment passes and his memory returns, but the incident is deeply frightening. Although at the peak of his career, with a wife and baby son, he is plagued by headaches, nightmares, and erratic mood swings. In dreams he runs in terror from a nameless pursuer. By day he grows increasingly anxious, and when his wife tries to persuade him to get help, he discovers sinister motives in her most innocent remarks. He accuses her of treating him like a child and humiliating him. He vacillates between a rush of tender feelings and moments when he wants to strangle her.

Sondheim dismissed *Bequest* as the result of watching "too many Bette Davis movies." He had intended to have Gold discover that he was suffering from paresis, an idea that, in turn, had been inspired by Ibsen's *Ghosts.* But the novel never reaches that point. It is still describing its character at the end of ninety pages, causing the anonymous professor who had read it to protest mildly that it was time for the plot to develop. But Sondheim did not want to, or could not, go any further, and what remains is a detailed description of a man who suspects he may be going insane. The similarities between the hero of *Hangover Square* and that of *Bequest* are evident, but there are differences. Gold is less likable, experiences his feelings more directly, and also has some idea of the cause of his illness.

His mother has died, and there is a cryptic reference to the fact that she was highly promiscuous. In his dreams he sees hands with long red fingernails. He has a sensation of running and looking back over his shoulder and the fear that he is close to remembering something horrible. There is another dream about the mother, who is presenting a red-ribboned box that contains "a gray-black mass of soft, watery material." Meantime Gold experiences bizarre symptoms. He is, he fears, "falling into the pit."

One can see how a lonely and isolated adolescent might be attracted to themes in which artists take center stage, their every move portrayed on camera the way his heroine Ellen, in "The Brass Goddess," wishes the camera would record her own loveless existence. One can also see why the hackneyed theme that art demands an emotional sacrifice might have its consoling aspects, although the belief that the artist is helplessly bound to act out a kind of destructive rage could lead to the state of diffuse and deep-seated depression that Sondheim said he suffered during those years. What is fascinating about *Bequest* is the obviously sexual metaphor of the box tied with red ribbon. Young as he was, the author of the work seemed to have a precocious awareness of the cause of his anxiety, even if it was one he could never breathe aloud. The references are even more overtly biographical in "The Brass Goddess," a less ambitious but more completely realized work. The conversations between parent and child have the ring of verisimilitude, as do Ellen's confused feelings, which veer between frustration and rage and a longing for reconciliation. For if Sondheim could remember only his anger toward his mother in later years, it is clear from "The Brass Goddess" that as an adolescent he had the normal child's desire for a loving mother. In the opening paragraphs Ellen wants to write a story about a daughter who once "worshiped"—her word—her "nervous, brilliant" mother. And later, after they have quarreled, Ellen allows herself to be persuaded that Foxy really loves her and wants to be reconciled. Her mother, who is feeling ill—her asthma is troubling her—is in the bedroom. As Ellen goes up the stairs she starts to run, "longing to get in her mother's arms, to hug her, to kiss her, to make her happy." But when she arrives in the bedroom her mother's response is hostile.

Foxy uses Ellen's sense of guilt to make her apologize, and Ellen, while despising herself for capitulating, has no choice. Emotionally, she is paralyzed.

In the real-life game of control being played, Foxy's asthma—attacks of which can be triggered, at least partly, by stress—did have its frightening aspects. But while she was genuinely at risk, she was also using her illness as a weapon to elicit the appropriate feelings from Stephen. At the root of her complicated emotional state was the normal human need for reassurance, and proof that she was loved and needed. But if she ever had felt sure of love (and one doubts that she did, because she appeared to think that its withdrawal meant her death), her husband's desertion had destroyed any such belief. Little wonder that she sought to obtain by unscrupulous means what was not being freely given. A revelation of her seductiveness was far too explosive to appear even as fiction; by giving his brass goddess the name of Foxy, Sondheim went as far as he dared. But he felt obliged to disguise the real sex of her child and, incidentally, the deepest roots of his antagonism. Nevertheless, the short story did convey his central dilemma. Foxy had managed to convince him that her asthmatic attacks were his fault.

Finally, in the story, there is a medical crisis. Most nights when Foxy's asthma is particularly bad, Ellen is asked to sleep in the same room and even the same bed, although she very much resents having to go to bed with her mother, and is even terrified of the thought, which may be taken as an indication of the author's state of mind. On this particular evening Foxy decides to sleep downstairs, sitting up. In the middle of the night Ellen is awakened by a spasm of coughing, harsh wheezing sounds, a silence, and then "another spasm, and a strange, new sound, a sort of weeping, tired and painful." Then Ellen hears Foxy's heavy footsteps mounting the stairs. She is in a panic. She wants to say, "You think you can get back at me for tonight, don't you, by scaring me with your asthma, but you can't, you can't. No, not this time. Stop faking." These thoughts are never given voice, because Foxy really is ill and has to be hospitalized.

The story is concluded in a few more paragraphs. Ellen is waiting for her mother to return from the hospital, feeling all the old feelings of terror, loathing and helplessness. But as Foxy comes through the door it is clear she is suffering a relapse. Ellen goes to get a glass of water, but by the time she returns, Foxy is dead. Ellen wants to feel vindictive triumph. She wants to be cold and unfeeling, like brass. But all she can feel is "a sick, empty, lonely feeling in the pit of her stomach."

Speaking of these mixed and painful feelings, Sondheim said, "The business about being ill was not being ill. It's every Jewish mother's thing—the blackmail of 'If you don't take care of me I'll die.' It's not about being ill. It's about, How do you get to a kid who's not paying enough attention to you? You say, 'Well, you don't happen to know it but your mother happens to be terribly sick.' Totally made up. It's all to make the kid feel guilty, and tie the kid to the apron strings by virtue of that: 'If you leave me, I will die.' " Almost as an afterthought, he added that "of course" he believed her, at least then.

He did not remember when he stopped believing her. But by the time he reached Williams he was frantically trying to convince himself that his mother's periodic attacks were imaginary. Andrew Heineman, a future lawyer who would eventually represent Sondheim's uncle Walter Sondheim, was one of his roommates at Williams. Heineman also suffered from severe asthmatic attacks. The first time he was coughing, sneezing, and wheezing he was astounded at Sondheim's reaction. "He was totally unstable when it happened, a madman," he said. He danced around screaming "Stop it right now!" as if, Heineman said, Heineman were inventing the attack and making a cheap bid for Sondheim's sympathy. "It was totally illogical, childish and emotional." Several such attacks brought the same reaction. Finally one day he and Sondheim were on a car trip, "so I had him captive," he said. He demanded an explanation and Sondheim said that it all reminded him too much of his mother. He was, Heineman thought, "perplexed and possessed" by her.

CHAPTER 4

No Sad Songs

S TEPHEN SONDHEIM LEFT his mother and moved in with his father during his freshman year at Williams College, the year his parents' divorce became final and he became sixteen. He does not remember the actual moment of packing up and leaving. "It was not dramatic," and that seemed strange, given the previous trauma. "It may be that I had prepared her for it." He paused. "Incidentally, I'm not sure that she wanted me around."

Herbert Sondheim's apartment at 1010 Fifth Avenue, opposite the Metropolitan Museum of Art, was a spacious, three-bedroom affair, with a couple of servants' rooms behind the kitchen, in the fashion of New York floor plans. Just the same, Herbert could not provide his firstborn with a bedroom of his own. Herbert Jr., then aged three, was sickly and became a diabetic when he was seven years old; Walter, the second child, was an infant when Stephen moved in. Alicia's mother was also living with them so all the bedrooms in New York were taken—in Stamford, Stephen had one of his own—and Stephen slept on a sleeper sofa in the dining room for the next several years. He seems not to have minded, although his friends minded for him. That he had to be accommodated in this fashion is evidence that his father was taken by surprise at his son's decision to move in with them. Nevertheless the transition was smooth. "Steve wasn't on the outside," his half-brother Walter said. "Mother loved Steve and accepted him as part of the family." So did he and his brother. "Herbie and I played a lot of board games with him as little kids. We'd sit around and try to invent them. Sort of like a criminal detective game, a big board with a wheel on it and windows in it. A lot of fun. He was great to have around. He'd help with our homework once we were in grade school and play in the yard with us in Connecticut in the summers. He was old enough and gone often enough for there not to be any rivalry." Sondheim, who thought his father felt uncomfortable around young children, made a special effort to pay attention to Herbie and Walt. Walter Sondheim said of Sondheim Sr., "He was an absentee father. He cared for us but he was not the one to pick you up and give you a hug. He wanted you to entertain yourself." Stephen Sondheim, curiously, confused himself with his father in later years when, speaking of one his brothers, he said, "I had a stepson too."

Walter Sondheim said that he and Herbert were brought up as Catholics. In addition to being kept in ignorance about their parents' previous marriages and their own illegitimacy, the boys did not know their father was Jewish. In a family where secrets were kept assiduously there was the predictable Victorian prudery about sexuality; once when his mother learned that Walter had discovered some of her old love letters, she was horrified. Avoiding confrontations and keeping unpleasant revelations at bay seemed important to both parents. But his father's evasiveness and insistence upon the polite social lie were particularly sore points with Stephen Sondheim. Whenever his father had arrived to take him out, "unfortunately he would always ask, 'How's your mother?' in a solicitous way, because he felt so guilty he wanted me to take care of her," he said. "He never asked, 'Is your mother mistreating you?'" Sondheim continued, "When you really get down to it, the most damaging thing was that my father abandoned me and left me in—in the lion's den, in the cave." He would find himself becoming tense and wanting to back away whenever his father tried to embrace him. It took years before he understood why.

Alicia Sondheim's good looks were the subject of general comment, and one of her young admirers was the writer Dominick Dunne, who went to Williams with Sondheim and often visited the family in Stamford. He said, "You hear that guys marry the same woman—Herbert Sondheim didn't. A whole different type: an outdoors woman. I can imagine her wearing slacks, which was a big deal in those days. She was lovely looking, with long blond hair, and glamorous." The Stamford house was relaxed and family-focused, in contrast to the kind of formality Foxy preferred.

Stephen Sondheim said, "Much as I loved her—she was a terrific lady—she had no sense of humor at all. Dad would make little jokes and Herbie and Walter would get them, young as they were, and Alicia would not. I don't mean she was humorless or stern. She was very relaxed, but she didn't get it. I think it frustrated Dad a bit." Sondheim thought his father might have had some discreet affairs, because he heard rumors to that effect. It was not the kind of subject he could have discussed with his father: "My father wouldn't have wanted to recognize that he wasn't happy," he said. Herbert and Alicia were united in their concern for little Herbie, with his continuing medical problems. Every day he needed an injection of insulin, and since he was so thin as a child it was sometimes difficult to find a vein. The threat of a diabetic coma was constant and real.

Whilst Alicia and her mother fretted over, and pampered, little Herbie, his father was increasingly caught up in the demands of his career. During World War II he served on advisory committees for the War Production Board and the Office of Price Administration and was sought after as an industry spokesman; he continued his heavy schedule of charitable performances. His collection was shown with those of other famous designers such as Vera Maxwell, Sally Victor, Lilly Daché, Jo Copeland, Adèle Simpson, Hattie Carnegie, and Pauline Trigère, and appeared in advertisements for such stores as Neiman-Marcus of Dallas, Harzfeld's of Kansas City, and Henri Bendel of New York, as well as in the editorial pages of *Vogue* and *Harper's Bazaar*. Reporting on the colors and shapes for autumn, the Hartford *Times* of July 1947 reported that Herbert Sondheim, "as usual, was the most popular designer-host of the day. His showing is quick and smartly paced . . . Herbert Sondheim's clothes are praised for their design and cut . . ." The hemlines had dropped that season. " 'They will get longer before they get shorter,' he says, 'and heaven help Seventh Avenue if they get shorter too soon.' " Sondheim liked to say that he tried to manage his business with as much humor as possible because "no drape, no matter how trend-setting, is worth an ulcer." It was his way of keeping at bay the truth of the matter, that every season was a throw of the dice, that he stood to lose his business with as much abruptness as his father had lost his and that, along with luck, the only asset he could count on was his own intuition. For the next twenty years he gambled successfully, with a cavalcade of outfits designed to be worn from luncheon onwards, accompanied by hats, gloves, and high-heeled shoes. His flair for spotting new designers continued—he hired the young Chester Weinberg—and his company continued to prosper.

As for Foxy Sondheim, as she approached the age of fifty her enthusiasm for her profession began to wane. Perhaps, as her son thought, her decision to retire from dress design was motivated mainly by the fact that she was a poor businesswoman. Perhaps, too, the pressure to come up with something fresh and new season after season was bound to take its toll, bringing with it the inevitable creative slump. True to form, Foxy Sondheim was not going to stay defeated. She had a close friend in the actress Vivienne Segal, a favorite of Rodgers and Hart's who had created the role of Vera in *Pal Joey*. Segal was married to Hubbell Robinson, a well-known television executive with CBS-TV, and living on the West Coast. Perhaps it was while visiting her there that Foxy Sondheim met Ed Leshin, one of the lesser lights at CBS-TV, a bachelor some years older than herself. Leshin, always called "Lesh," "was somewhat ineffective but an incredibly nice man," Dunne said. To everyone's surprise he proposed, and Foxy moved to the West Coast. They bought a pretty house in the right part of Beverly Hills, which Foxy decorated—she had taken up a new career as an interior decorator—and they began to move in the best circles. Dunne said, "She needed a husband and was good for him. She maneuvered him, gathering people around him. I would see them at all the CBS parties. She was always hilariously funny in a smart, sophisticated way. There was always something gutsy about her that I liked."

Sondheim remembered the day of the wedding, which took place in his mother's apartment, because it was the day that *All About Eve* opened at the Roxy. His mother's cousin Peggy Schlesinger, who had taken care of him as a child whenever he was sick, had arranged the whole apartment and helped his mother dress, but Foxy Sondheim would not let her attend the actual ceremony on the pretext that it was just for close family members. She had to wait in the bedroom. "I was appalled," Sondheim said, "but I didn't fight hard enough, and I'm sorry I didn't. I should have said to my mother, 'I won't appear.' I do remember arguing. But it was all about poor relatives. It was awful."

Just the same he remembered "the enormous sense of relief that she was out there and not on my back in New York . . . In those days I thought of her as a nagging, demanding mother, rather than a hateful one." If she criticized him harshly to his face, privately she did nothing but sing his praises. Dominick Dunne believed she was genuinely proud of her son, and the writer Stephen Birmingham agreed: "She was full of Jewish-motherly pride." She used to tell people Stephen had ambitions to become the next Noël Coward or George Gershwin, which of course he denied. After they were separated by a continent, his feelings of relief gradually were succeeded by something close to affection, and he remembered writing her some warm letters. "It's hard for me to recapture the emotions, but I know she once said, 'Whatever happened to the fun times and the fun letters we had?' I have every reason to believe she was telling the truth." He also said that he left his mother just in time. If he had not managed to move away, "I might have been institutionalized."

WILLIAMS COLLEGE, to which Stephen Sondheim went in the autumn of 1946, was a small (its 1950 graduating class was three hundred), all-male institution, ranking just below the Ivy League schools of Harvard, Yale, and Princeton, exclusive and sought-after. It was named for Ephraim Williams, who as a reward for his services in the Revolutionary War was given land in the northwest corner of Massachusetts. Williamstown, within which Williams is situated, is a village of unspoiled charm, with pre-Revolutionary houses and ancient trees, whilst the college owns a fine art museum, a library of rare books on English literature and Americana, and the oldest observatory in the United States. When Sondheim arrived there it had just built a new theatre. Sondheim said that his George School advisor had suggested Swarthmore, outside Philadelphia, the college to which many of the school's graduates went. But Sondheim wanted to get out of Pennsylvania, partly, he recalled, to get away from his mother, who still owned the farm in Bucks County. He wanted a small college, was attracted by Williams's theatre, and was undeterred by its lack of a strong music department because, at the time, he said, "I didn't care about music." He enrolled as an English major, taking music as an elective.

John Anderson, who would become an editorial writer for the Washington *Post* and was at the college in that immediate postwar period, thought Williams an unlikely choice for Sondheim. "He is a very urban type, and Williams, like most of the northeast colleges, is very much the possession of the upper-class WASP, Anglophile natives," Anderson said. "It's less the case now, but then it was very much so. Like most of those colleges, all the required courses for an English major were English literature and the electives were American literature. I was a history major, and the big course in the sequence was British constitutional law." Sondheim, with his sophisticated New York manners, "breathed something that was larger than that little town." Ford Wright, in the class of 1950, said, "I view myself and my generation as holdovers from Victorian times. By the time I got to Williams we were being called the 'silent generation,' which simply meant we were doing things quietly. Form was very important, and we were taught to use it. The eastern establishment used a lot of English expressions, and I can remember people saying that certain things 'weren't done.' " Their surroundings were genteel. Dormitory walls were paneled, the ceilings were high, and there were working fireplaces, as befitted young gentlemen who would go on to become bankers, doctors, lawyers, directors of companies, and heirs to discreet fortunes. Anderson said, "There was a smell of money about the place."

The concept of Williams College as a finishing school for elegant young men, however, was changing. The campus was swarming with young veterans from World War II who were strolling around in their Army fatigue jackets rather than the tailored tweeds and chinos that had been the standard attire. The situation was further complicated by the fact that young men might arrive as freshmen, leave after a year to do the required two years of military service, and return to college three years later. Youngsters out of prep school would be consorting with undergraduates who had been in combat or had learned to fly fighter planes; some were even married. These older men were far less impressed by the social rituals that had characterized life at college before the war. Ford Wright said, "When you arrived at Williams you were considered a 'legacy' of the fraternity your father or uncle had attended—that's how important the hierarchy was. Not to make one was almost like being branded with a scarlet letter." But to the men returning from the war, fraternities were irrelevant. "I felt I was past all that nonsense," Anderson said. Stephen Sondheim, however, was only sixteen.

Stephen Birmingham remembered, "Stephen Sondheim was one of the first people I met the first week of fraternity rushing. He fell in step beside me and said, 'We both have the same name,' and we became friends. They called us the two Steves." Anderson was surprised to learn that Sondheim had joined a fraternity. He said, "Fraternity houses did not pledge Jews. God, no! There must have been some obfuscation of the fact that Steve was Jewish. Because I had a roommate who was Jewish who, unlike myself, was a very sociable soul, and had been told by one of the fraternity houses, 'Ben, we love you, you can come over here any time you want, spend as much time here as you like. Regard yourself as a member, but we can't pledge you.' It was very explicit."

Sondheim spent his first year in the freshman quad. Professor Emeritus Irwin Shainman, who was one of his music teachers, recalled that Sondheim lived in West College, the old dormitory just opposite the president's house, where he had a room on the top floor and thought that Sondheim had owned one of the first television sets on campus, but Sondheim said this was not true. Sondheim applied to Beta Theta Pi, the oldest college fraternity west of the Allegheny Mountains (founded in 1839), known as the "singing fraternity," the motto supposedly being "When two Betas gather, they talk; if three, they sing." Sondheim was blackballed twice, but the objections were overridden. "It was the only anti-Semitism I encountered," he said. Ford Wright said that the house was not on the main fraternity row but on a side street. "The glue that held us together was our group of freshmen, who were terribly nice, unsnobbish, and unprejudiced. We never batted an eye over who was Jewish. And remember, in those days Jewish boys tried to blend in with the eastern establishment and emulate it." One of the things Wright liked most about it was the musical atmosphere: "You would come in from classes for lunch and someone was always playing the piano in the living room, and not just college songs, but classics and jazz."

Sondheim had a vivid memory of Hell Week, when, before being initiated, the pledges were subjected to a week-long ordeal. "There was mild hazing, nothing of any corporal danger like—I dunno—running in your underwear through cold weather or who knows what, but mostly having to do with taking orders and standing up straight at the dinner table, sort of like military school.

"But the climactic moment, which I rather liked, was the very last night of Hell Week. The pledges were brought into the house and the atmosphere became very serious and each pledge was led into one of the rooms of someone who lived in the house. You were asked to sit there and think about which meant more to you, the college or the fraternity. Then you were brought down to the living room one by one, and there were the brothers and the president of the fraternity, sitting behind candles, just looking very solemn, all wearing their robes. And you sat in a chair in front of these candles and were asked, 'Which means more to you, the fraternity or the college?,' and you gave your little speech and everybody looked serious, and you were taken back to your room.

"Then they brought you down again. Now the entire pledge class was in this room with candles, very dimly lit, and the president announced, 'The evening has been very interesting. There are, out of the—' let's say there were twelve or fifteen pledges—'two members whose answers we feel are somewhat inadequate. In order to avoid any embarrassment we'll blow out the candles, and'—each person had a pledge master who had taken you through it, so there was somebody standing behind you—'your pledge master will tap the rejected members on the shoulder and they can leave the room and there will be no embarrassment.' Of course every pledge master tapped everybody. Then they turned on the lights and said, 'Surprise!' It was so sadistic. I totally fell for it and was so relieved when I was accepted."

SONDHEIM'S FIRST LOVES, musically speaking, were the Russian romantics: Tchaikovsky, Rachmaninoff, and Prokofiev, as well as Brahms; he was "brought up on them," he said. Perhaps as a result of watching too many Hollywood films, he had formed the impression that "you made music late at night, sitting in your penthouse or your study, looking out over the lights of New York. The muse came and you suddenly started *Rhapsody in Blue*, or whatever it was." He was soon to be disabused of this notion. His teacher at Williams was Robert Barrow, who had served as organist at the National Cathedral in Washington, D.C., and was a former student of Paul Hindemith's at Yale. Professor Shainman called him "a very, very dogmatic and difficult person, and probably the best common-practice harmony teacher in America, the kind of music you sing in front of church, four-part harmony." Sondheim agreed Barrow was "very hard-headed and cold. He taught from a little black book that he had compiled over the years, and most people took the course because they thought it was a gut course, but in fact it wasn't." Instead of waiting for inspiration, Barrow taught "that music is a matter of craft and technique like, as it turns out, all art, and the fact that art is work and not inspiration, that invention comes with craft."

The one other professor in the music department was Joaquín Nin-Culmell, a fastidious pianist and composer better known for being the brother of the diarist Anaïs Nin. Sondheim wrote a couple of papers while in Professor Nin-Culmell's class, on Aaron Copland and Maurice Ravel, two of his favorite composers, and Nin-Culmell commented on Sondheim's conclusions in a flowing hand. Sondheim also took courses with Shainman, who was invited to replace Nin-Culmell for a year after he had finished his Ph.D. thesis at Columbia University in New York. Shainman almost did not take the appointment because, he was told, the music department was so small that he would not have a decent student. As luck would have it, one of his first was Sondheim, who under Barrow's influence would soon change his major to music. Shainman taught a general history course, more or less a survey of nineteenth-century symphonies, concerti, operas, and chamber music. He said, "We hit it off very well, because after high school I became a professional trumpet player and played for two years before going to college. So I knew all the Broadway shows. I remember we talked about *Allegro* a lot, *Me and Juliet*, and shows that didn't appeal to a lot of other people: *Billion Dollar Baby, Beg-*

gar's Holiday, and *A Day Before Spring*." Sondheim always spoke of Barrow as the great influence on his career. But Shainman thought Barrow would have wanted his promising pupil to write a string quartet, or the great American symphony, and not waste his time on musicals. "I would honestly say that I doubt Bob Barrow ever attended a performance of a Sondheim show while he was at Williams, and I don't think he ever went to one in New York, either."

What made Williams unique as a college, Shainman said, was the emphasis its music department placed upon performance. At his alma mater, Columbia, musicology students did not fraternize with those studying composition. But at Williams, "they were required to make music, not just teach it." Sondheim immediately began to compose. He vaguely remembers his earliest work, called the *Oscar Hacker Suite*, which he wrote early in 1947. That was an in-joke, since his roommate Josiah T. S. (Joe) Horton, with whom he would work on a musical, was the campus humorist and had invented a character called Oscar Hacker. But the great thing was that the music department was in the basement of the Adams Memorial Theatre, Sondheim's reason for choosing Williams in the first place. Sondheim said, "It had two features that were quite extraordinary, and I assume they're still there. The lighting board was in the orchestra pit, so that you could light the show and change the lights as you watched the action, as opposed to most theatres, which had lighting boards in the wings, where you could not see what was happening. Then it had an iron curtain off stage right with a sound-proofed shop, so you could actually build new scenery or make repairs while the show was going on."

Compared with the facilities at the George School, this was luxury indeed, a chance to experiment on a fully professional stage. But the college had spent so much money on the theatre's construction that there was none left for the production of plays by the undergraduate theatre group, Cap and Bells, Inc., under the supervision of the English department. Besides, the college's idea of what constituted experimental drama was limited, Sondheim said, to Oscar Wilde or the daringly modern works of Noël Coward and George Bernard Shaw. Nor did he have any very great opinion of David Bryant, who had been hired to supervise the drama program, finding him pompous. However, when Sondheim proposed a college musical and was rebuffed on the grounds that there were no funds, it is entirely likely that Bryant helped smooth the way, because he told Shainman that Sondheim was the most talented student he had ever met. Sondheim said he fought for the musical "all the way up to the head of the university." The authorities finally relented, and *Phinney's Rainbow* (a play on the name of the hit musical *Finian's Rainbow*) was given four performances in the spring of 1948.

Sondheim presumably won his argument because, "We hoped [a musical] would get the students in the theatregoing habit, and that this, in turn, would make some money for the theatre," Sondheim said later. Besides, Cap and Bells had never attempted a "college musical" before, the kind of "harebrained, hopefully satirical book musical with its line of chorus 'girls' recruited from the football team," as John S. Wilson described the genre. The title referred to the president of Williams College, James Phinney Baxter III, a distinguished historian. Sondheim and Joe Horton concocted the frothy plot, which centered around the efforts of Dogma Nu fraternity at Swindlehurst Prep to replace their compulsory PT with more house parties, their motto being Strength Through Sex. That led to a series of songs and dances conducted at mass meetings, in a bedroom, in the prexy's office, at a faculty meeting, at a clandestine house party, and in the Dogma Nu "Goat Room," a scene that opened the second act.

"A 'Goat Room' was where all the rituals of initiation were performed," Sondheim said, and so he took Beta Theta Pi's ceremony "with just a slight smidgen of variation and exaggeration and put it on the stage. All the brothers were horrified, but of course everybody else thought it was screamingly funny; it seemed like a work of the imagination. And I told everybody at the house, 'Don't get into an uproar. If you don't tell anybody it's real, they won't believe it.'"

The chorus line for *Phinney's Rainbow,* May 1948

In retrospect, what most people remember about *Phinney's Rainbow* was "The Q-Ladies Waltz." This was a play on the name of the P-ladies, so-called because, in the days before indoor plumbing, they came every morning to empty the chamber pots under the beds. Maids were called P-ladies ever afterwards. The future producer Charles ("Chuck") Hollerith Jr., who played Petunia, wearing a flowered dress, apron, and knee-length hose and brandishing a broom, was very upset because another of the Q-ladies, Pete Nielson, had a plunger for a prop, "and he got to bang it down and pop it up, and it was a much better prop than I had." The whole production, said Howard Erskine, another close friend of Sondheim's who became a theatrical producer, was at a considerably higher level than that of most college musicals. A subsequent poll showed that it had been seen by over half the student body. More important, it made the handsome profit of $1,500, which, Erskine said, practically financed the rest of the theatrical season. Sondheim wrote over twenty musical numbers for the show, and three of them, "Phinney's Rainbow," "Still Got My Heart," and "How Do I Know?," were subsequently published by Broadcast Music Inc. (BMI) of New York.

"How Do I Know?" (that I love you) is an early parody of Irving Berlin's many songs that pose a question as well as a venture into the kind of musical ambivalence at which Sondheim, as a lyricist, would excel. Its words run, in part:

> You said goodbye
> When I said hello,
> And I asked you why
> And you said I would know,
> But how will I know
> When I know
> That you said 'no'?
> I just don't know.

Another former classmate, Edward T. Gushée Jr., recalled the writing of that song. "We were in dress rehearsal for *Phinney's Rainbow* the night before opening. During a scene change it became apparent that redressing the stage was going to take too long and the auditorium would be black for as long as a minute," Gushée wrote. "That was unacceptable. Something had to be done. Steve suggested he write a song and have it sung solo in front of the curtain. The director agreed and we took a break. Steve returned within the hour with a brand-new parody, entitled 'How Do I Know?,' that became the highlight of the show."

He seemed to have developed his skill for lyric writing almost as an after-thought. It was a dull but necessary craft that one pursued in order to arrive at the sheer delight of writing music, and Sondheim found himself being drawn increasingly to Maurice Ravel. He had admired Ravel ever since, in an effort to educate Hammerstein's ear, he had given him a record of the composer's Piano Trio for his birthday. Sondheim was thirteen at the time. That Ravel would become a large influence was perhaps inevitable because, Sondheim said, Ravel was the one responsible for "most popular music that has been written in the twentieth century. That is to say his harmonic influence, all the secondary sevenths, is what pop music has existed on even into the age of rock." Ravel's *Valses nobles et sentimentales* and *La Valse* were particularly important to him. Sondheim wrote to the English musicologist Stephen Banfield, then writing his book *Sondheim's Broadway Musicals,* "The reason, incidentally, for the preponderance of the two specific colors ('dark' versus 'romantic') of the waltzes that you bring attention to is the pervasive influence in my writing of Ravel." The drama critic David Richards, who would review a number of Sondheim's works for the *New York Times,* thought it would be interesting to look at his work in the context of the three dramatic categories expounded by the French playwright Jean Anouilh: "les pièces roses, noirs et étincelants."

As an apprentice to an exacting craft, he had been given an invaluable piece of advice by Oscar Hammerstein on the famous afternoon when all hope had been dashed of taking *By George* to Broadway. Hammerstein suggested he write four works that would serve as lessons in the art of writing musicals. "First take a play that you like and musicalize it. Then take a play that you like but you feel has flaws and try to improve them, and musicalize it," Sondheim recalled him saying. "Then he said, 'Take something that is *not* a play but that somebody else has written, a novel or a short story, so that you don't have to invent the characters or plot, and musicalize that, make it into a play. Dramatize it. And then finally write an original, your own story, and dramatize that.'"

Sondheim began on Oscar's course during his junior year in college, taking his advice one step at a time. He very much admired a play by George S. Kaufman and Marc Connelly called *Beggar on Horseback.* Kaufman, a quintessential man of the theatre who was a director as well as a playwright during his thirty-year career, was a friend of Hammerstein's and had visited the Bucks County farm. The story goes that one evening as the friends were sitting on the porch, looking out over the fields, Hammerstein remarked on what a luxury it was to sit and not have to think of anything. Kaufman supposedly replied, "Anybody can sit and think of nothing. The trick is to think of *something!*" Kaufman's wit was celebrated. Once he was obliged to accompany his wife on a shopping trip for household furnishings, and when the manager of the department store asked if there was anything he needed, Kaufman replied briskly, "Yes. Do you have any good second-act curtains?" The anguish behind the mock appeal would become familiar to Sondheim once he began the formidable task of translating plays into musical theatre, and *Beggar on Horseback* was not a particularly easy choice. Although Brooks Atkinson thought it a remarkable work, it owed its origins to an expressionistic drama by the German playwright Paul Apel, almost all of which took place in the hero's imagination, calling for advanced dramatic skills. It was the by-now-familiar theme of youthful promise in danger of being corrupted by worldly temptations; and by no coincidence, perhaps, Sondheim began working on the book, music, and lyrics for *All That Glitters,* his title for the musical, not long after witnessing the failure of *Allegro.* Instead of a young doctor, there is a composer, torn between true love in a garret and the prospect of marrying a rich girl for her money, who finally chooses "honest garrets," as the Williams *Record* reviewer noted drily.

That Sondheim should be attracted to a theme that had already caught the imaginations of Hammerstein and Kaufman is perhaps not surprising, but that a writer still in adolescence should want to explore a cautionary tale about the loss of integrity is interesting for the light it throws on his character as well as his attitude toward his future career. Sondheim at his most optimistic bursts with quixotic idealism. It is, as Harold Clurman observed, "the spirit of the romantic Artist raising the standard of his self-appointed mission to redeem humanity." Clurman said this of Clifford Odets, but he might just as well have written it of Sondheim, who at this stage of his life cherished a conviction that it was literally possible to live happily ever after (as in Anouilh's "rose-colored" plays). In the plot as imagined by Kaufman, his young composer has pulled back from the brink, even if he does linger over the temptations of money and fame. The impression left by *All That Glitters* is that only love could have saved the hero from a future the adapter saw only too clearly, with a kind of savage disillusion striking in one so young (Anouilh's "black" plays). As for Anouilh's third category, plays carried by the sheer brilliance of their style, there is not enough evidence in this early work of what would become one of Sondheim's strengths. Predictably, BMI approved of the sweet sentiment and published five songs from *All That Glitters:* "When I See You," "Let's Not Fall in Love," "I Love you, Etc.," "I Need Love," and "I Must Be Dreaming." BMI did not publish what by general agreement was the best number in the show, a sparkling parody of Cole Porter's "Begin the Beguine" called "The Bordelaise."

Shortly after writing *All That Glitters* Sondheim was invited to play his score for Porter. Porter had just had his latest success, *Kiss Me, Kate,* a triumph achieved although he, then aged fifty-eight, had been in constant pain for a decade, both legs having been shattered in a riding accident. The Porters owned an estate in Williamstown but took little part in the life of the town or college. However, Dave Bryant asked them whether he could bring his very talented student to meet them, and they all went up one Sunday afternoon, his widow, Jean Bryant, said. Sondheim's version is that he was taken there by Dr. Albert Sirmay, a Hungarian composer who had emigrated to the United States and became head of the show-music publishing division of Chappell Music. Sondheim recalled that he always wore a smock like a chemist's. He believed he had met Dr. Sirmay through Hammerstein and would go to his office periodically to play his compositions.

Mrs. Bryant recalled, "Steve would play some bits of music and Cole would come to the piano and pick it up right away and say, 'Wouldn't that sound a little better this way?' " Then Sondheim played his "Bordelaise," that included such lines as:

> It beats all your sambas and calypsos—
> Everybody dances it—even the dipsos.
> All you have to do is wiggle your hipsos
> And pucker up those tasty lips, so
> Sing a couple Chiles and a Paraguay
> With Rio de Janeiro baba lu ai ay!

"Poor thing, he knew exactly what I was doing," Sondheim said, but Porter's only comment was "You should extend the ending more." He added, "I extend endings a lot." Sondheim said that he learned from studying Porter, as well as from Hammerstein, the necessity of having some kind of rhythm in one's head when one began to write lyrics even if the music had not yet begun to shape itself. The sooner words and music began to entwine and reinforce each other, the closer to ideal the match was likely to be. He had also taken to heart Hammerstein's dictum that lyrics must not overtax the ear. Achieving the right balance in lyric writing was so difficult and elusive that one's only recourse was to develop a kind of instinct for it. He did not mean to overstate its importance, however. It was a minor talent, like "pewter ashtray making," he said. "How much paint do you put on a canvas, you know."

IN THE CLASS ELECTIONS of 1949–50 Sondheim was voted among the most versatile, the most brilliant, the most original, the most likely to succeed, and those who had done the most for Williams. He was at the center of musical life from the start, Ford Wright said, and anyone who had the slightest connections with music or the theatre soon knew who he was. Howard Erskine was president of Cap and Bells during Sondheim's junior year and almost lived at the theatre. He and Sondheim had both been to see previews of *Kiss Me, Kate* and had enjoyed it, but Sondheim insisted that "Bianca," one of the songs, was unnecessary and should never have been in the show. Erskine liked and defended it: "We had serious arguments about this, as we used to do in those days." Erskine, a fine actor, had been cast as one of the professors in *Phinney's Rainbow*, although he was not much of a singer. The day came when each actor had to step up to the footlights and sing. Erskine said, "Whoever it was would walk down, Steve would hit their note at the piano to get them on key and introduce them, and then they'd get into the song. He made it very easy. So when it came to be my turn to walk down, I heard nothing. And then as I got to the footlights I heard . . . 'Bianca' . . . and I didn't know what show I was in! Steve is very funny, something a lot of people don't realize." According to John Anderson, his humor was appreciated at Williams. "He certainly had the quickest wit. I remember there was a kind of competition to see who could construct phrases that had internal rhymes and riddles. His entries tended to get repeated. Here's the one I remember. Question: What do you call a place where a New York Dutchman keeps his bottled goods? Answer: A Knickerbocker liquor locker."

Campus life centered around the theatre, the fraternities, and the outdoors because with few television sets, few cars (most undergraduates did not drive their own), and no girls, you had to like fishing, hiking, and skiing. Sondheim remarked that it was always snowing in Williamstown. Certainly the winters were long, and "you'd walk down the middle of the street with a wall of white on either side," Wright said. So many people wore raccoon coats it "looked a bit like a bear colony." People wore coats and ties for dinner, and when parents came for homecoming weekends, "we'd dress impeccably above the waist and wear blue jeans below, our small rebellion," Wright said. Two or three fraternities would join forces to give house parties and bring girls from Bennington, the nearest girls' school, fifteen miles away, who stayed at designated guest houses. "It was very much a chaperone situation, and they had to be back by midnight," Wright added. After a big football game there might be a big party centering around Purple Passion, a punch made from a lethal combination of grape juice and gin. Eventually the younger girls would have to be slung over someone's shoulder and returned to their guest houses. They would be invited to recover on Sunday mornings with milk punch, well laced with brandy.

Jamie Hammerstein has a vague memory of a conversation during their college years in which Sondheim described what he was discovering about himself sexually. All through George School Sondheim had a steady girl-friend named Janet Long; they "did a lot of smooching," but never went to bed, which would have been difficult to arrange in any event. His family never discussed sex, and neither did the Hammersteins; "Where would I learn about such things?" Sondheim asked. His father did warn him against masturbation, at a time when he barely knew what the word meant. All this changed during his freshman class at Williams. "Half of my class were as naive as I was, and the other half, being returning veterans, were very experienced, you know," he said. That is when he began to realize that there was "something different" about him. His first homosexual experience was shortly after college, when he attended a Hollywood dinner party at which Irene Dunne was one of the guests. Another guest, a moderately well-known composer, and much older, gave him a ride home, parked the car, and the overture was made. Sondheim was not attracted. The second time was on Cape Cod, with a writer, another older man. Again, the car was parked and the fumbling advance rebuffed. It would be some years before such an overture was successful, and he does not remember exactly when. "I was sexually very late blooming," he said. "I've also got to tell you—I think people tried to make passes at me and I didn't know what they were doing."

SONDHEIM, usually wearing a heavy flannel shirt, with uncombed hair and looking rather scruffy, would hang around the College Restaurant, which Hollerith called "a grubby little greasy spoon with a counter and booths, and Steve would play the pinball machine." Hollerith had a car at college, either a Mercury or a Chevrolet, and taught Steve to drive in the back parking lot of the Adams Memorial Theatre. He also taught him to play bridge, but the pupil rapidly outshone the teacher. And he taught him to drink. Hollerith liked to give black-tie parties when gin, bourbon, Scotch, and rum flowed freely. No one drank anything as banal as rum and Coke. The idea was to mix very sophisticated cocktails, their favorite after-dinner drink being a stinger made with white crème de menthe and brandy. Vodka stingers came in later and would appear in one of Sondheim's best known songs.

They all adored movies. Hollerith recalled driving down to Radio City Music Hall, a trip that took five and a half hours, to see the latest Margaret Sullavan movie. Sondheim would later write a song called "Party of the Stars" for Hollerith, and there was a whole section in it about Margaret Sullavan. "I know every movie of hers," Sondheim said. "In her last movie, *No Sad Songs for Me*, she has a child and husband whom she adores, and Viveca Lindfors plays a woman who is teaching the child the piano, and Margaret Sullavan arranges a romance between her husband and Viveca, so that he won't be alone, without telling them she's dying of cancer, of course . . . So it's self-sacrifice on two levels," he said. "But you see, the way she acted, there was a toughness in her that prevented any of her movies from becoming really silly. I can remember, when she looked in the camera, to the doctor who was telling her, and she said, 'You mean—cancer?' " He gasped this in a hoarse voice. "You know she always spoke like that. Something in her voice. So I wrote a song, because she died of everything. She died of a rifle shot, she died of a machine gun, she died in childbirth, she died of TB," he continued, deadpan. "But she never died of the same thing twice, and I swear it was in her contract." Dominick Dunne said, "We used to worship Margaret Sullavan. Worship. And we could all imitate her speaking voice. We were camp before camp was in style."

Sondheim had his detractors. Ford Wright said, "I looked on Sondheim as being a bit of an intellectual snob. He paid a lot of attention to anyone in Beta who played the piano or had an artistic gift, not someone like me, who did not." Stephen Birmingham, who was another fraternity brother and also a neighbor in the West College dormitory, thought that Sondheim was "very New York and sophisticated. He used words I had never heard of and had to look up. He became such a smarty-pants. The genius at the putdown or send-up. He had professors scared of him. He'd say, 'Excuse me, but that's not right,' and he'd be right." He was acquiring a reputation for not suffering fools at all, which was contradicted by people like Professor Shainman, who saw him as very shy, "rather self-effacing in many ways." Howard Erskine, who worked with him closely, agreed. "Oh, he was very shy. Always very much in the background." They knew that he was "very good at what he did," Erskine said. He was gathering around him a small circle of close and loyal friends: Erskine, Chuck Hollerith, "Nick" Dunne, and Ford Schumann, a wealthy composer and painter. Hollerith said, "We used to call Steve the CO [commanding officer]."

Sondheim and Birmingham served as editors of the college's magazine, *The Purple Cow*, and also collaborated on a radio show for the college radio station. Birmingham said, "It was a parody of a soap opera that ran for a couple of weeks. We thought it was terribly funny. One character was slowly going blind and the other was losing his hearing. So one would say, 'Where are my glasses?' and the other one would say, 'What?' " Sondheim contributed some short stories; one, "The Adventurous Guy," was an encounter between a college boy and a taxi driver, and another, "The Ritual," another vignette of life in the big city, concerned a cocktail-hour conversation between a husband, his wife, and the wife's woman friend, which was published in the autumn of 1947, six months after "The Brass Goddess." The wife, who talks in relentless trivialities and contradicts whatever her husband says, bears perhaps an inevitable resemblance to Foxy of the earlier tale. Her friend, in an almost word-for-word repetition of the complaint leveled against Foxy, protests that she is controlling her husband and treating him like a child. The husband limits himself to silent agreement and an inner dialogue in which he criticizes and ridicules his wife. At the end of the story he manufactures an excuse to slip away to a movie, having perfected Herbert Sondheim's art of passive resistance.

Sondheim also contributed some successful pieces of comic writing. H. Baekeland Roll, who also served as a co-editor, remembered a playlet Sondheim had written set in ancient Rome which had an effervescent sense of humor and must, he thought, have served as the genesis of Sondheim's later musical in a similar setting, *A Funny Thing Happened on the Way to the Forum,* but Sondheim said it was just a coincidence. Then there was "The Wade Caper," by someone named Hashiell Dammit, in which Sondheim parodied the genre, including the moment when the hero felt a sharp thump on the back of his neck, heard a dull thud as something hit the floor, and realized it was himself. There was the inevitable parody of that musical folk play by Rodgers and Hammerstein, *Utah,* which was somewhat less successful but did include some sprightly lyrics and the lines

> Chicks and frogs and pigs better hustle
> When I call for you in your bustle—
> When I take you out in the Howdah with the fringe on top!

Sondheim was still at work on Hammerstein's course. Having satisfied the first category, that he musicalize a play he liked, with *All That Glitters,* he then turned his attention to a play he liked but that he thought had flaws. He chose *High Tor,* a verse play by Maxwell Anderson, set on a mountaintop with some promising characters, including an Indian, Dutch settlers, unscrupulous real-estate agents and a romantic backwoodsman. It was a useful exercise since, he said later, it taught him how to remove extraneous material and build a structure of ideas. He had written to Kaufman and readily obtained permission to give a performance of *All That Glitters*. But when he wrote to Anderson asking for the same courtesy, the playwright refused, giving the excuse that he was planning his own musical version of *High Tor*. That said something for Sondheim's taste as well as his daring—*High Tor* won a Pulitzer Prize—but it was a setback nevertheless, and his musical adaptation was never performed.

It was his first real disappointment, but there would be another. Taking the third Hammerstein category, that he make a musical out of a novel or short story, he chose the stories P. L. Travers had written about her famous character Mary Poppins. Sondheim said, "I did about two-thirds of it and realized I couldn't complete it because I could not solve the problem of taking disparate short stories, even though they are interconnected, and making a larger form. A footnote to that is that about ten years ago, when I was in London for some purpose, I had a call from P. L. Travers, who said, 'Mr. Sondheim, I would like you to adapt *Mary Poppins* for the stage,' and I said, 'Funny you should call, because when I was nineteen years old this is exactly what I did.' She was astonished; I was flattered and astonished." By then Sondheim had convinced himself that he did not have the makings of a playwright. In the case of *Mary Poppins* that is a pity, because his own portrait of the insufferably perfect governess is much more nuanced and believable than the one offered by the famous film starring Julie Andrews. Similarly, the governess's young charges, while entranced by her magical abilities, are not instantly transformed into perfectly behaved little ciphers, but stage at least one rebellion which baffles Mary Poppins. It also confounded Sondheim, and that was the end of that idea.

AS PROFESSOR SHAINMAN OBSERVED, for people like Sondheim the theatre department became a surrogate fraternity. When Sondheim was not writing music—during 1949–50 he wrote a piano sonata as part of his music major—or trying to write a musical, he was involved in some aspect of the major Cap and Bells productions each semester, as either stage manager or actor. The theatre's only musical instruments were two pianos, and so Sondheim, along with classmate Gerald O'Brien, was the orchestra as well. Since the music department was in the basement of the theatre there was hardly ever any reason to leave the building.

Sondheim began acting shortly after he arrived. He had a role in the chorus of *Antigone* by Sophocles early in 1947 and was then cast in a new play, *Trade Name,* about how spies were trained during World War II. It was written by Peggy Lamson, who was married to Roy Lamson, an associate professor in the English department. She was an accomplished playwright and had already won the DuBose Heyward prize. Howard Erskine said, "Steve and I both played potential spies; it all took place in a house somewhere, and you had to take on different identities. It was very well written. The play was under option to Gilbert Miller, bound for Broadway. Miller came to see the Williams production and got very enthusiastic, but nothing ever happened."

Sondheim's first big break as an actor came when he took the role of the son, Henry Antrobus, in Thornton Wilder's *The Skin of Our Teeth*. There is a moment when Henry, who is also Cain, has to part his hair to show a large ocher-and-scarlet scar on his forehead. There is another moment when the same character who, with his family has endured all of history's catastrophes, from prehistoric times to the present day, returns from a war determined to take his revenge for the ill treatment he has received from his father. However, when Sondheim drew a large C on his forehead with the aid of a mirror, he forgot that the letter would be reversed. He recalled that when the moment came ("my Pirandello moment," he said, somewhat derisively) to talk about his murderous impulses, ones that stemmed from traumatic childhood abuse, the audience simply thought it was funny.

Sondheim played Garth in Maxwell Anderson's *Winterset* in May of the same year; and when he returned as a sophomore in the autumn of 1947, he began rehearsals for the role of the blind seer, Tiresias, in *King Oedipus* by Sophocles. In March of 1948 he repeated the role in Jean Cocteau's modern-dress version of the Sophoclean tragedy, and was praised for his performance, although the Williams *Record* reviewer thought he seemed "held back by a fear of over-acting, and of reaching too high a pitch before his climaxes. When he let himself go he was strikingly effective." He kept on performing. He played Cassius in *Julius Caesar* and then took the part of a gangster who threatens to sink a boat belonging to two fishermen in Irwin Shaw's *The Gentle People*. The fishermen are good friends, and one of them, played by Edward Gushée, is delegated to lure the gangster into a rowboat and then murder him, which is why Gushée now jokes that he got to "kill" Sondheim every night for a week. (The play actually had three performances in February of 1950.) Whether playing bit parts or more substantial ones, Sondheim received respectful notices. He was given credit for rescuing a ragged production of *Waiting for Lefty*, Clifford Odets's one-act play about a taxi-driver strike, in the pivotal role of Agate Keller. But the only part he says he ever really wanted was that of Dan, the psychopathic killer in *Night Must Fall* by Emlyn Williams. It was a "spectacular kind of show-off part," which

Sondheim in the role of Henry Antrobus in Thornton Wilder's *The Skin of Our Teeth* at Williams College in March 1947, with Madeline Goodrich as Gladys

Sondheim, far left, in Emlyn Williams's *Night Must Fall* at Williams College, 1948

Williams had written for himself. Sondheim had already discovered Williams the playwright and loved *The Corn Is Green* as well as *Night Must Fall.* He did not know why he was so attracted to the part of Dan but was determined to do anything to get it, including learning to smoke, since the character is a chain smoker. "I became a confirmed and addicted smoker after that, but it was worth it."

The play is set in an English bungalow in the middle of a forest, the home of Mrs. Bramson, a wealthy, spoiled hypochondriac who is in a wheelchair. She is cared for by a nurse, servants, and Olivia Grayne, a young woman who is her niece by marriage. Dan, who works as a bellhop in a nearby hotel, insinuates himself into the household. He claims to have trained as a male nurse and readily admits that he got Mrs. Bramson's unmarried maid-of-all-work pregnant. Mrs. Bramson has summoned him to lecture him but is seduced by his childlike charm, his willingness to cater to her whims, and his half-flirtatious manner, and hires him as her nurse. He cajoles and flatters her, but Olivia Grayne is not so easily deceived and begins to suspect Dan when the decapitated body of a middle-aged woman is discovered buried nearby. Her suspicions become stronger when a sealed hatbox is found in his room, but there seems no way to warn the gullible Mrs. Bramson, who takes up the sentimental notion that, as Dan says, she reminds him of his mother.

Then the discovery is made that he and the murdered woman were having an affair and that he had been blackmailing her. Realizing what must be in the hatbox, Olivia Grayne packs a suitcase and runs from the house. That night Mrs. Bramson is helped into her wheelchair by "the baby son she never had." Duped and trusting, she allows herself to be cajoled and humored to the moment when she is smothered with a pillow. When Olivia Grayne returns unexpectedly, Dan threatens to murder her as well, but is prevented from doing so by the arrival of the police. They have surrounded the house and are spying on him from the windows. "Nobody would dare to watch, I'm the one that watches!" he screams as he is being arrested.

Sondheim said that after *Night Must Fall* he lost all interest in becoming an actor; "the orgasm was over." Curiously, his ambition faded just as an acting career seemed within reach, if the review in the Williams *Record* is to be believed. He was coming into his own at last, the reviewer said, giving rein "to the high talents which have previously been confined." That must have been gratifying, but he remained unaffected and his final contribution to theatrical life at Williams was a single song written for *Where To From Here,* a student revue in May 1950, the year he graduated magna cum laude. The song took its title, "No Sad Songs for Me," from the Margaret Sullavan film about the young wife dying of cancer who nobly sacrifices herself to her husband and child's happiness. That title in turn was based on a poem by the Victorian poet Christina Rossetti: "When I am dead, my dearest, / Sing no sad songs for me." Sondheim's lyrics have an adolescent awkwardness, not to be compared with the exquisite precision of Rossetti's paean to reticence and renunciation, but that they are genuinely felt there can be no doubt. It was evidence of a delicate ability to empathize that would be a marked characteristic of his best work. Behind the raillery was something else: a sense of shared pain.

CHAPTER 5

Climbing High

H E HAD ENJOYED his stay at Williams, but the final year
became tedious: "Suddenly . . . I looked around and I thought,
'What the hell am I doing here?' " he said. He had done everything he
wanted to do, and nothing stood between him and a future career except two
years of compulsory military service. He applied for the Air Force but was
excused because of childhood hay fever and asthma. He had won the Hub-
bard Hutchinson Prize, a two-year fellowship to study music. The stipend
was $3,000 a year, which compared well with the average yearly salary for an
assistant professor of about $3,500, and was adequate if one did not need to
pay rent; and for two more years, he slept in his father's dining room. Professor Shainman said Sondheim "made it very clear that he wasn't planning to
write a symphony and wasn't planning to write an opera. He wanted to be the
best on Broadway."

By an extraordinary piece of luck he had already met, or would soon
meet, a man who would be a pivotal figure in his life for the next thirty years
and the most important single figure in making that career possible: Harold
Prince. The future producer of such Sondheim successes as *West Side Story,*
*A Funny Thing Happened on the Way to the Forum, Company, Follies, A Little
Night Music, Pacific Overtures,* and *Sweeney Todd* believed they were introduced by their mutual friend Mary Rodgers at the opening of Rodgers and

Hammerstein's *South Pacific* in the spring of 1949. The story is that they subsequently met for coffee in Times Square and declared their joint determination to become the next Rodgers and Hammerstein. Prince said, "It wasn't in Times Square but at Walgreen's at the corner of Fifty-seventh and Broadway. And I didn't say we were the logical heirs to Rodgers and Hammerstein, never would have. I did say that with a little luck we would be part of the future of musical theatre. Much more modest than that. But you know, it's kids daydreaming. I think I was about nineteen or twenty, and it could have been six months after I went to work for the producer George Abbott." Prince began working for Abbott in 1948, when he was twenty, so the possibility that he and Sondheim met at Walgreen's just after their introduction at the opening of *South Pacific* is plausible. Sondheim does not remember the encounter in the drugstore at all, or even meeting that soon. He said, "I got to know Hal, as far as I'm concerned, when he got out of the Army." (Prince was in the Army from 1950 to 1952.) "He'd been going around with Mary Rodgers and she gave a homecoming party for him, and that's how I remember starting the friendship, and that's a good deal later. Could have been in our early twenties."

Prince does remember that he was optimistic and that his future collaborator was much more cautious about making rosy predictions. The avantgarde composer Milton Babbitt, with whom Sondheim had been studying, had reservations of another kind. "Steve was extremely sweet and very soft and I was very concerned about his ambition, because I didn't know how much he could take," he said. "I knew something about Broadway and show business, and I don't care what's involved, you can have it. Especially in the twenties and thirties, it was a totally unscrupulous world. The best you can say is that they were uneducated vulgarians." Sondheim's own postscript to that thought came years later. "You know, I had the idealistic notion, when I was twenty, that I was going into the theatre. I wasn't; I was going into show business, and I was a fool to think otherwise."

Sondheim had decided to study with Babbitt after consulting with Professor Nin-Culmell at Williams. Babbitt, who taught at Princeton and took a few private pupils, seemed like a strange choice to those who knew what Sondheim's ambitions were, because Babbitt, a disciple of Arnold Schoenberg, had developed a theory of serialism in which the process of composition was subjugated to a preordained order of notes, rhythms, and intervals. Babbitt was aware that his theories were of interest mainly to specialists; eight years later, he would publish a controversial article with the title of "Who Cares If You Listen?" He now says that the title was deeply misleading and that he very much cared that the public was not listening. To Sondheim, though, the choice of Babbitt was quite logical. He said recently, "I just wanted to study composition, theory, and harmony without the attendant musicology that comes in graduate school. But I knew I wanted to write for the theatre, so I wanted someone who did not disdain theatre music. Milton, who was a frustrated show composer, was a perfect combination." Babbitt had written popular songs, film scores, and a musical, *Fabulous Voyage,* four years before (in 1946) and was then working on another musical, about Helen of Troy, which he hoped would star Mary Martin. Together he and Sondheim would dissect the songs of Jerome Kern, and those of Buddy De Sylva, Lew Brown and Ray Henderson, the writing team, and occasionally Rodgers and Gershwin, as intensely as the music of Beethoven and Mozart. Afterwards, Sondheim and the Babbitts would all go out to dinner. Babbitt said, "Sylvia and I became almost his second parents."

Babbitt was also puzzled at first because Sondheim "wasn't interested in becoming what one would call a serious composer, but he wanted to know a great deal more about serious music because he thought it would be suggestive and useful . . . Steve was always very principled. He wanted to improve himself in every conceivable way. He had grown up in a society of celebrities and he wanted to be a fellow celebrity. He was simply going to make it."

The choice was not as farfetched as it might seem, Professor Shainman said. "If you ever met Milton Babbitt you'd know why they would hit it off very well, because Babbitt was first of all a mathematician, a very, very scientific, analytical musician. He is also a great raconteur who loves Broadway shows, knows how to tell jokes, loves baseball, loves New York, that sort of thing. He and Steve would get together and discuss where they could get the best corned beef sandwich in New York."

Babbitt said that Sondheim wanted a basic study of analysis, counterpoint, and large-scale structural relationships in the standard repertoire. They never looked at a twelve-tone piece, and, Babbitt said, "he seemed very uncomfortable about serious composers and never went to a single concert of mine." Sondheim wanted to study Copland and Ravel, his major interests in college, and made exhaustive analyses of Beethoven symphonies and Mozart sonatas. He later described one of the most valuable lessons he learned from Babbitt, i.e., how to structure a piece of music so that it will make a coherent whole whether it goes on for three minutes or forty, what he called "long-line" compositions. He would discover that most Broadway composers had not studied from this perspective and did not know how to sustain a musical idea. The knowledge "stood me in very good stead for shows that I've written which have extended developments in them because I am pretty good (not quite as good as I'd like, but pretty good) at writing what Lenny [Bernstein] would call *scenas*, something that goes on for twelve or fourteen minutes that's more than a song." He praised Jerome Kern's ability "to develop a single motif through tiny variations into a long and never boring line and his maximum development of the minimum of material." When Sondheim went to Oxford University to become its first Visiting Professor of Contemporary Theatre in 1990, he presented his students with an analysis of Kern's "All the Things You Are" that was a result of his work with Babbitt. He said, "I am his maverick, his one student who went into the popular arts armed with all his serious artillery."

What Babbitt called Sondheim's "sweet," or vulnerable, side, was a reference to the waiflike image he presented in those days. "When he came to me he was about as sad a young man as I have ever seen," he said. The impression of Stevie as someone who was always on the outside, and whose emotional needs were not being met, seemed symbolized, once he reached young manhood, by his general appearance. His hair was uncombed, and if his clothes did not exactly look slept in, they were definitely rumpled. He was forgetful in his personal habits—he "tended to 'nif' a bit," one friend said—as if he were, consciously or not, trying to keep people at a distance. Despite it all he was considered very good looking, with a mobile, amused face, and would astound his friends by the transformation whenever he remembered to wash

A recent photograph
of Milton Babbitt

his hair. Sondheim said that his appearance (he called himself "a slob") was a reaction to his father's exhortations to buy himself some decent suits and smarten up. In any event it became a sore subject between father and son and a career in music was another. Herbert Sondheim naturally saw no future in such a precarious profession. Music was for relaxation, something one did on one's off hours. He wanted Steve to get a "real job," not become a "feckless artist," his son said. To underline the point, Sondheim was made to pay his own bills, including the dentist—even his weekly laundry.

Over at the Babbitt household he was being given a different message. Someone as bright as Sondheim could have written major symphonic works, and Babbitt gave the impression that this is what he would have liked to see. But when his pupil's path became clear, he listened respectfully to the work Sondheim had done so far. Some of the songs he had written in college were wonderful, Babbitt said. Sondheim had a new project, which he began in his senior year and worked on for the next two or three years. He had reached the final item on Oscar's course, an original musical, and had started to write *Climb High,* which takes its title from a motto, dating back to the nineteenth century, on a set of steps leading to one of the dormitories at Williams. It reads:

> Climb high
> Climb far
> Your goal the sky
> Your aim the star.

Sondheim said, "And so I wrote a show about a guy I knew at Williams who was in a class ahead of me who came to New York and wanted to be an actor, and about how he fucked his way to the top, because he was a charmer and a ladies' man." As his capsule summary would indicate, the playwright had no great opinion of his hero, David Alton, and the main impetus behind the work seemed the desire to lampoon those who will do anything to get ahead. It is another version of the moral drawn from *Allegro* and *All That Glitters.* College graduates arrive in the big city every year in waves, bringing innocence, enthusiasm, and talent. David Alton sings, "One good break— / (I'm telling you!) / That's all I need to make my dream true." But they soon discover the harsh realities of an overcrowded and jaundiced profession ("Too much take here; / It's all fake here"), become ruthless and unscrupulous, and either succeed or not, but in any event the theatregoer knows what the playwright thinks of them. No longer is "the spirit of the romantic Artist raising the standard of his . . . mission to redeem humanity," as Clurman wrote. The romantic Artist has already thrown in the towel. His principal character is mean-minded, boastful, and superficial; his leading lady is well on her way to becoming an alcoholic; and the supporting characters are frivolous and venal. Whatever youthful idealism might have once been there has evaporated almost before the play begins. At the final curtain, true love (this time, the girl is rich) rescues the hero, but one suspects that the reprieve is temporary. The repeated theme has become almost a leitmotif. Was it true, as Hal Prince believed, that his friend's pessimism was already a marked trait, and would be the reason why recognition of his talent took longer than it should?

Sondheim gave the two-act play to Hammerstein to read. His mentor returned it with a detailed letter and comments in block capitals at various points in the script. The fact that Sondheim would invent a cast of unlikable characters deeply worried Oscar. He did not expect them to be paragons of virtue, but they should have some redeeming qualities. Then, if the principal character strayed from the right path, one would be concerned for him and want him to succeed. Hammerstein was concerned that Sondheim would go to so much trouble to write at such length about someone he did not like. There were copious annotations throughout, some having to do with possible cuts and some with the choice of words. There were encouraging comments, and the occasional "Good" and exclamation marks in the margins. But Hammerstein was mostly concerned with the hero's shortcomings. Unlike the character flaws of Billy Bigelow in *Carousel,* which did have a certain tragic grandeur, those of David Alton simply seemed petty and mean.

There is a good deal to like about *Climb High.* A group of scenes in which the hero tries to find work and is repeatedly turned away with the same refrain:

> Mr. Rodgers is out.
> Mr. Hammerstein's home.
> Mr. Rodgers is home.
> Mr. Hammerstein's out.
> Leave your name and we'll call you if we need you

strike just the right note of rueful disillusion. And Hammerstein did praise a song by the only sympathetic character, an older woman theatrical agent who falls for David, "I'm in Love with a Boy," which prefigures, in its irony and delicate understatement, the kind of emotional impact that would be characteristic of his best work. She sings:

I'm in love with a boy,
And the boy's just a baby.
He's no bundle of joy—
Well, he may be,
But something's amiss, girl;
Someone's throwing curves.
That bundle of joy leaves this girl
A bundle of nerves.

In *Sondheim's Broadway Musicals,* Stephen Banfield wrote, "Time and again the force of Sondheim's personality is brought home to us by foretastes of phrases, techniques, or preoccupations from the later shows." He might have added that *Climb High* includes some in-jokes that only those familiar with his life at the time could appreciate. David Alton boasts that he wants Margaret Sullavan for a play he is about to produce, and there is a toast at the end of *Climb High* that his group of close friends would have recognized. It was adapted from Robert Burns and taught to them by Ford Schumann: "Here's *to* us. Who's like us? Damn few!"

As if anticipating Sondheim's response, Hammerstein wrote on one of the pages of script, "Don't bristle." Sondheim's reply has been lost, but it is clear that Hammerstein was trying to impress on his gifted pupil that he felt an author was not writing to satisfy himself, or even the actors who would play the parts. His main consideration should be how to relate the work to the audience's experience. Without exactly saying so, he was trying to convey the fact that if the sympathies of the audience were not engaged, it did not matter how brilliant the work was. It was a point that his pupil may have missed. Sondheim's complaint, to judge from Hammerstein's reply, seemed to be that his mentor had found the book irritating. That was not the issue, Hammerstein said. This, however, was not the right way to launch a career. "Granting the uncertainties in the theatre, I feel quite certain that you will not succeed in getting an audience's interest, and certainly not in sustaining this interest throughout an evening for this group of characters."

Hammerstein had advised him not to let anyone produce the play, but it was too late. He had already aroused the interest of a young man-about-town with theatrical ambitions, John Barry Ryan III, who was working at the Westport County Playhouse in the summer of 1950 when Sondheim arrived to do summer stock as an apprentice and learn about the theatre. The famous playhouse was only a half-hour from Stamford up the Merritt Parkway, and Sondheim had just received a second-hand car from his father as a graduation present: a small blue Chevrolet with a stick shift, which his friends named the

Blue Beetle. Most of the apprentices at Westport stayed at the theatre—the jobs were unpaid, but they got their living quarters free—but he commuted in the Blue Beetle.

"As an apprentice you either cleaned buildings and bathrooms, sold Coca-Cola, parked cars, or were assistant stage managers. I was an assistant stage manager on a play called *My Fiddle's Got Three Strings* by Arnold Schulman. It starred Maureen Stapleton, J. Edward Bromberg, Steven Hill, Betsy Blair, and an old-time *Follies* singer named Fritzi Scheff. It was directed by Lee Strasberg, and the first day of the rehearsal at the Theatre Guild headquarters in New York everybody sat around the table reading and I couldn't hear a word. Everybody mumbled. It was like the joke about the Actors Studio. But I didn't know about the Actors Studio at the time; I just thought, Why can't I hear these people? Listening to [Strasberg] talk I thought, He's the most brilliant man I've ever heard in my life.

"Then when it came to the dress rehearsal I . . . realized you couldn't follow anything that was going on. He had so much simultaneous action; it was a two-level-set house and there were three or four rooms, maybe a living room downstairs and two bedrooms upstairs, and while the action was going on downstairs Betsy Blair would be turning the pages of a magazine upstairs. It was so busy it was ghastly, and one of those examples of a completely coherent theatrical direction that is dreadful in practical terms . . . The only other thing I remember about it was there was a voice-over racetrack announcer, and Arnie [Schulman] asked me to do it and I was terrible. They had to get somebody else."

A close friend during his Westport summer was Mary Rodgers, who, at the age of eighteen, was also commuting from her home about five miles away to learn about theatre. They were inseparable, and he was also very friendly with "Johnnie" Ryan, who was heir to two of the nation's great fortunes, since he was descended from both Otto Kahn, American banker and arts patron, and Thomas Fortune Ryan, a multimillionaire industrialist. Ryan went on from Westport to become stage manager for a number of Broadway shows, including *Make a Wish* and the revival of *Pal Joey* in 1952. He was ambitious to become a producer and loved *Climb High,* Sondheim said. He made a record of the composer singing his own music and spent much time and energy looking for an out-of-town production before abandoning the idea. "It never went anywhere," Sondheim said, and perhaps this experience accounted for Sondheim's pronounced dislike, in later years, of plots that had anything to do with show business.

Thanks to Johnnie Ryan, Sondheim had an unforgettable spring of 1953. Ryan had been hired to assist the director John Huston, who was making a

Humphrey Bogart in *Beat the Devil*

film in Italy called *Beat the Devil,* a comedy thriller with a stellar cast: Humphrey Bogart, Peter Lorre, Robert Morley, Gina Lollobrigida, and Jennifer Jones. But the film was floundering, and Truman Capote had been summoned at the eleventh hour to act as script doctor. (He ended up rewriting the film.) Ryan invited Sondheim to go to Europe with him in March. Sondheim said, "I had seven hundred bucks in the bank. I said, 'Why not?,' because his family had an expensive flat in Grosvenor Square and we could stay there, which was my first time in England." From there they planned to go on to Ravello on the Amalfi coast south of Naples, where the filming would take place.

Sondheim already owned a movie camera and, along with pals like Ryan and Ford and Caroline Schumann, had been making short horror movies and thoroughly enjoying the editing process. But it was complicated to operate, so he did not want to take it with him and instead borrowed Ryan's sixteen-millimeter Bolex. He got the idea of making a short film about what happens when a Hollywood production company takes over a small Italian town. He even started keeping a diary for the only time in his life, but got tired of it after about ten days. He and Ryan stayed in one of the two hotels in Ravello along with Huston and most of the cast. He became friendly with Bogart, who was a first-class chess player and excelled in the kind of mental gymnastics required for a game of chess without a board. Sondheim said, "I'd come down to breakfast and Bogart would say, 'All right, pawn to king's four,' and I'd say, 'Pawn to king's four, all right.' Then he'd say, 'Knight to bishop's three . . .' By about the fifth move I'd be thinking, Wait a minute, knight's on the fifth square. No, no! Knight's on the fourth square. No, I moved the bishop . . ." and Bogart would sit there smiling.

Making movies, he told the Schumanns in a letter from Ravello, was largely a matter of waiting: "waiting for an airplane to pass, waiting for the mules to stop braying, the children to stop chattering, Bogie to stop coughing . . . Morley to learn his lines, Jennifer to adjust her wig . . . the generators to start running, the lights to be adjusted, Sondheim to stop tripping over cables." He had been learning about film technique and playing poker with Jennifer Jones's husband, David O. Selznick, a large man in every sense. "We've played poker every other night and the man will bet on anything . . . Money obviously has almost no value . . . for him. He'll bet 30,000 lire (approximately fifty bucks) and call it 30,000 dollars by mistake. John [Huston] told me that he's been completely broke a number of times." The unit was mostly English, and Sondheim had become quite an Anglophile. There was "only one psychotic in the group and she's a bore besides." He had met a wonderful girl, secretary to the producer, whom he was trying to persuade to move to New York. "We have a great time, tearing everybody apart—I might as well have stayed home . . ."

Sondheim visiting the Colosseum in Rome during his first trip to Italy, 1953

Sondheim's money ran out after a few weeks. When he announced his departure Huston suggested that he might want to hang around until the company returned from shooting in Africa. He was sure that some kind of job could be found for him in London in the music department. But Sondheim could not afford to linger on the vague promise of work and returned home. He had, however, become a real fan of Bogart's. One day Ingrid Bergman and George Sanders, who were making a film for Roberto Rossellini, came on the set, followed by a pack of photographers. There was much picture-taking, and at a certain point, Bogart waved Sondheim into the shot and put his arm around him. Next morning, when he came to breakfast, there was a picture of himself with Bogart at his place setting. "He knew how starstruck I was," Sondheim said.

Sondheim's fascination with the puzzle-making aspect of film continued for several years. After *West Side Story* he used to visit Leonard Bernstein and his wife, Felicia Montealegre, every summer on Martha's Vineyard, where they rented a house near Lillian Hellman's. He would arrive on a Friday night with his black-and-white Ciné Kodak sixteen-millimeter camera, and they would plan to spend the next day filming. Their first effort was based on the films *Golden Boy*, about a prize fighter who plays the violin—a role played by Luther Adler on stage—and *Humoresque,* the famous camp movie starring Joan Crawford (she of the "wide-shouldered negligées, wide-hipped tights and wide-bosomed suits," he joked). Crawford played a rich, neurotic woman and John Garfield was the violinist whom she befriends. At the end of the film Crawford, her love unrequited, walks into the sea. Bernstein took the part of the combination concert trombonist and prize fighter ("He used to overact dreadfully," Sondheim said), and his wife took the Crawford role. Ofra Bikel, Theodore Bikel's first wife, was in it, and so was Bernstein's younger brother, Burton, playing a rabbi. The house had a dock leading down to a pond, and at the end Montealegre was shown taking her last walk along the dock to the sea, and Sondheim's camera panned along behind her as she relinquished her jewels one by one: a bracelet, a tiara . . . Sondheim was devastated to discover, once the film had been developed, that the bottom third of every frame had somehow been ruined.

A couple of summers later, in 1961, they made a new film based on the last ten minutes of the second act of Puccini's *Tosca.* Making judicious use of fabrics and props, Montealegre, who harbored a secret ambition to be an opera singer, transformed the house into an opera stage and mimed her arias to a Maria Callas soundtrack. Her husband played the villain, Scarpia, in a false nose and mustache. They had great hopes for this film, but then it transpired that the action and sound were slightly out of alignment, which ruined the

Felicia Montealegre, wife of Leonard Bernstein, performs in Sondheim's home-movie take-off of Puccini's *Tosca*.

effect. Bernstein rented an expensive machine, one of the few then existing, that could alter the speed of a soundtrack without changing the pitch, and the spoof was effectively saved. After Felicia Montealegre died in 1978, the film was shown at her memorial service in Alice Tully Hall. "It was really fun," Sondheim said. "Franco Zeffirelli saw it and said it was the best opera film he ever saw." There were two other films, one that would have cast Mike Nichols as a vampire (Lee Remick contributed a cobweb-making machine), which was never made, and the other a takeoff on *Whatever Happened to Baby Jane?* Montealegre played that one in a wheelchair, and Bernstein was a seductive stranger (in the manner of the hero of *Orpheus Descending* by Tennessee Williams), who arrives with a guitar and causes amorous havoc.

IT WAS CHARACTERISTIC of Sondheim's silver-spooned entrance into life after college that his first experience of London should be from a flat in Grosvenor Square and that his first job should result from an influential dinner party. The deus ex machina was, not surprisingly, Oscar Hammerstein, who had used his influence to launch his sons Billy and Jamie into show business and now, no doubt, thought it was time to do something for Stevie. So one evening Sondheim was invited along with the Hammersteins to have dinner with Donald and Pat Klopfer at their country house in Clinton, New Jersey. Hammerstein was an old friend of Mrs. Klopfer's (her family owned and operated several Broadway theatres), and Donald Klopfer, a prominent publisher, had co-founded Random House with Bennett Cerf. Among the other guests that evening was George Oppenheimer, a well-known playwright and screenwriter, who had just sold a pilot film for a television series and was looking for a co-author. As it happened, Sondheim had been trying his hand at scriptwriting. After *Beat the Devil* he had written a spy script on the Hitchcock model called *The Man with the Squeaky Shoes,* specifically for Jack Lemmon, whom he had seen and admired on the stage in *Room Service.* He thought he might have had one or two other scripts to show. Oppenheimer hired him at $300 a week.

Oppenheimer's series was based on the novel *The Jovial Ghosts* by Thorne Smith, about "an elegant, rich, Martini-swigging couple who die in an accident and come back to haunt a man named Cosmo Topper. And constantly screw up his life," Sondheim said. The book was made into a successful film with Cary Grant and Constance Bennett as the ghostly couple and Roland Young as the constantly bemused Topper: several successful films followed.

Leo G. Carroll in the title role of *Topper,* with Robert Sterling and Anne Jeffreys as his ghostly persecutors. The series appeared on television from 1953 to 1955.

The television series was to star Robert Sterling and Anne Jeffreys in the Grant and Bennett roles, with Leo G. Carroll as Topper. Oppenheimer and Sondheim were under intense pressure, since they had to write twenty-nine episodes in just six months.

By the summer of 1953, Sondheim told Ford and Caroline Schumann, they had written six scripts; shooting was to begin in ten days and he was very excited. "The schedule calls for an entire program to be shot every two and a half days. I don't know how the hell they're going to do it." His co-author was a gentle man who had been very good to him but who suffered from moods of manic elation and depression, so that he often found himself in the role of "general bucker-up." Oppenheimer had two distinct traits, a fondness for chewing on paper (which he did not swallow) and an insistence upon exactly sharpened pencil points. Sondheim was working hard, although not as hard as Oppenheimer, and had decided it was not the kind of work he wanted to spend his life doing.

Once in Hollywood, Sondheim had the advantage of his mother's influential contacts. One of her good friends was Lillian Schary, married to a well-known agent, Paul Small, about whom it was said, Sondheim joked, that whenever he entered a room he cast a small pall. Mrs. Small was the sister of Dore Schary, then head of production at Metro-Goldwyn-Mayer. "He's a bright, sweet, simple man . . . A kind of movie counterpart of Ockie." Sondheim was dating Schary's daughter, now the novelist Jill Robinson, who remembered him as "special and shy, looking like a proper good boy." He told his friends she was "cute and fun," but she thought she had fared badly in his opinion, partly because his East Coast education was so superior to her own, and "he wasn't crazy about girls." Growing up in Los Angeles had given her a precocious awareness of homosexuality. "My godfather, Leonard Spiegalgass, a screenwriter, used to have Sunday lunches to which I was invited, full of beautiful young men. I wanted to be a boy in those days so I could have boys like that in love with me. I sensed that [trait] in Steve, but it was something you never talked about."

Sondheim's one encounter with the swimming-pool life led to another friendship. He was invited to a birthday party around the Small swimming pool, and Lucy Geringer, later Beldock, was there. She remembered, "I'm sitting at a table near the pool playing Scrabble with Walter Goetz, not winning, and waiting for lunch. I have the word 'train' on my rack and an extra *c* and a *u* I don't know what to do with. Somebody gets out of the pool behind me and says, 'You've got the word "curtain."' I get eight hundred points and win the game. Then I get up and say, 'Who was that man?'"

Lucy Geringer was living at home and grateful to have her fifty-dollar-a-week "play" job at a time when there was not much opportunity for women. She invited Sondheim to dinner and the two became good friends. "I knew I was pretty close to someone unique." She also knew he was as movie-struck as she was. Then one day Sondheim came to her with a special request. He wanted to make a musical out of a film called *The Clock,* and was longing to see a copy of the script, which was against all the rules. She smuggled one out to him one evening ("It meant my job if he didn't get it back"), and he spent all night typing a copy. He was at her house by eight the next morning with the script, which she returned with no one any the wiser.

Sondheim went to visit Bogart on the set of *The Caine Mutiny.* Apart from visiting the Scharys and meeting his mother's friends, life was quiet. Speaking of Mom, "The old Fox just came in and tried to read this letter which I hid from her prying orbs," he wrote. "Her ostensible reason for dropping in was to hang a huge picture . . . which is now covering three walls of my one-room Murphy-bed apartment. She thinks it's great because his eyes follow you wherever you go. It isn't bad, as a matter of fact."

There were one or two "glamorous" experiences in Hollywood during the *Topper* series and later, when he was writing what he hoped would become his first musical on Broadway, *Saturday Night.* "Dore would occasionally invite me to previews at the Westwood Theatre, where I'd get to see movies before anybody else. One time they previewed a movie called *Rhapsody,* with Elizabeth Taylor, and I took the audience comment sheet and wrote answers on it, but in the form of a letter, and sent it back to Chuck Hollerith." By then his friend was married, had become a banker, and was living in Jackson, Michigan, but secretly longing to go into the theatre. That letter was partly the inspiration for a new game, as were some maps Sondheim found that gave addresses of all the stars. "So I sent them this road map with a note attached saying, 'Spread this out on the dining room table and see who gets to Joan Crawford's the fastest.' And it suddenly suggested a game to me, so I invented this game, very elaborate and quite good, called Stardom, about how you fuck your way to the top, literally. The board, which my mother painted—that was her contribution—is made of eighty homes of stars in the categories of extra, bit player, starlet, and star to Great Star, who is Norma Desmond. She has her own estate in the corner of the board. And you travel around, you get a bid by picking a card from the pack, who you are going to sleep with, and once you sleep with that person it gets you onto the next category. But other people can play Louella Parsons cards and figure out who you're with, and reveal it to the newspaper, which sends you back. By following your moves they can make accusations."

He "hung around a bit" with Jean Stein, daughter of Jules Stein, a wealthy tycoon who had founded the MCA agency. "She invited me to her parents' house one evening, sort of a castle, and I sat next to Irene Dunne." This was the dinner after which he was almost seduced by a composer. He went to a preview of *Torch Song*, starring Joan Crawford and Michael Wilding, with the Scharys and daughter Jill, and met Crawford afterwards. "Just a hello and a feel," he wrote. "She was great—held court from her limousine. God, how the fans love her! Why don't they love me the same way?" Then Nick Dunne invited him to go on a double date with Grace Kelly and Maureen Connolly, then the United States tennis champion. "Maureen Connolly was unfortunately my date, and I knew about as much about sports as she knew about the theatre." Kelly was not yet famous, staggeringly lovely but unfortunately nearsighted. "When we sat down to look at the menu she literally held it an inch from her nose, which was not my idea of glamour."

Chuck Hollerith and his wife, Catherine, soon became parents of a baby girl, and Sondheim wrote a song for the occasion titled "A Star Is Born," after the version that starred Judy Garland, a gentle, tongue-in-cheek celebration of the baby's arrival. It was also a successful example of Sondheim's effort to apply to an extended form the lessons learned from Babbitt; one senses a new note of mastery and self-assurance.

Of the presents that were deluging the new arrival, Sondheim wrote,

> Ethel Merman sent an ermine bib in mauve and blue,
> Joanie [Bennett] Wanger sent a manger lined with marabou.
> Ann Doran sent a can of Flit,
> Irene Dunne sent a nun to babysit.
> Swanson sent a pale magenta mink upholstered car,
> Rita Gam a silent samovar.
> Olivia de Havilland sent some gravel and half a ton of tile,
>   cement and tar
> To pave the driveway round the home of the star!
> Ona Munson sent a Bunsen burner just for kicks,
> Osa Massen sent a bassinet and swizzle sticks.
> Alan Ladd sent some mad perfume,
> Myrna Loy sent a toy projection room.
> Rossellini sent Martini mix for formula,
> Anthony Quinn sent a sequin bra.
> A maid of Kit Cornell's sent a doll that yells,
> "Really dahling!" instead of "Ma"—
> The perfect present for a budding young stah . . .

In this one song he managed to mention the names of sixty-nine stars, bearing witness to his knowledge of films which, at the time, was encyclopedic. He said he was almost accepted as a contestant on *The $64,000 Question* when he was twenty-five, but then the producers found he was working in a related field and disqualified him. "They wanted nuns who were experts on boxing," he said. "My memory for trivia is failing rapidly now, but if you'd asked me twenty years ago I could probably have told you all the statistics of any movie from about 1942 until the studios broke up in the mid-fifties, which is when I lost interest." He was far more interested in watching films than in reading books, and his interest was close to omnivorous, including foreign films of all kinds. He used to haunt the museum programs and film societies, he said. He was especially fond of film noir. He would even go to westerns and the occasional comedy provided it were sophisticated enough. The only kind of film that did not interest him at all was the movie musical.

SONDHEIM HAD ORIGINALLY planned to stay in Hollywood for six months but left after five, having written eleven *Topper* scripts. He was getting bored, and besides, his principle reason for taking the job had been to save money for an apartment of his own. He had already moved from his father's apartment before he went to California, sharing an apartment around the corner on East Eighty-third Street with Tom Bull, a friend from Williams. Bull was in advertising and kept regular hours. "He was very much a yuppie," Sondheim said. "When he came home from work he used phrases like, 'Can I build you a Martin?' by which he meant a Martini. It was very gray-flannel-suit." When he came back from California he found an apartment in a brownstone in a good neighborhood just three blocks away, at 11 East Eightieth Street, between Fifth and Madison. "It was a back apartment, but it had a twenty-foot living room with a kitchenette, meaning just an area, and a hallway going to a large bathroom, all of which had been the master bedroom suite of the original house. The hallway was just wide enough and long enough to get a bed in there. But it was so narrow that I had to get a special bed from Bloomingdale's, thirty-three inches wide instead of the regular thirty-six, so that I could squeeze past it." Small as it was, he now had a sleeping area he could shut behind a door. The rent was $175 a month, and he would live there for the next seven years.

He was seeing a lot of Nancy Ryan, daughter of one of New York's famous beauties, Mrs. William Rhinelander Stewart. Ryan, who later married the English novelist and journalist Alan Brien, was a friend of Truman Capote's, whose biographer characterized her as "the typical Capote woman, bright,

Decorating with games: an early example

brash and somewhat scatty." She gave Stephen a Victorian "Game of Jew" as a bad-taste joke: "Everything is in bad taste when you're twenty to twenty-five, right?" Sondheim said. "It's also an interesting piece of social history." He was already collecting and displaying games and puzzles. Ford Schumann, his painter friend from Williams, gave him a large color print of a Miró, which he had framed, and Gloria Vanderbilt gave him one of her paintings. Dorothy Hammerstein gave him a couch and wall-to-wall carpeting, and his mother helped him decorate.

He was spending his time with a number of close friends, among them John Barry Ryan, Nick Dunne and his wife, Howard Erskine and his wife, Hal Prince, and the Holleriths. He said, "When you're in your twenties you see people almost every night. There was rarely an evening when I didn't have somewhere to go or somebody to see. Also, you know, people were newly married and they wanted to entertain. I remember giving a cocktail party

Hal and Judy Prince in early married life

after I got my apartment and the only celebrities who accepted were Arlene Francis and Martin Gabel, so she was always on my good list from then on. Believe me, there was nobody there except a lot of us young folk." He "hung around a lot" with Mary Rodgers, who had married a lawyer, Julian Bonar Beaty Jr. Sondheim gave few parties because his apartment was so small, but Mary Rodgers liked to give them and he was always invited. By then he had bought a piano. It was an upright Steinway, called the "GI piano," made with an absolute minimum of frills so that it could be shipped overseas. "After the war they discontinued the model. The piano was still available for $1,100 and was the cheapest they had, so that's what I bought."

He wrote a piano concerto in three movements, not for piano and orchestra but for two pianos, in 1952. The first movement was subtitled "Letters from Aaron Copland to Maurice Ravel," the second used a number of experimental techniques, such as plucking the piano strings. He also wrote a violin sonata that languished for years until one day the lyricist Sheldon Harnick, who also played violin, asked whether he had composed anything for that instrument and took away a copy. "Two years later the doorbell rang in the middle of the afternoon and there was Sheldon. He said 'Here' and thrust a recording of the work into my hand." The first piece of his music performed on a professional stage had been for a play by S. N. Behrman called *I Know My Love.* It was performed at the Walnut Street Theatre in 1950 and starred Alfred Lunt and Lynn Fontanne. Brooks Atkinson called the play "ramshackle," but it did have a Christmas carol, sung at the opening of Act One, that Sondheim arranged. He got the job because the play's stage manager, Charles Bowden, had been head of the apprentices at Westport when he was there the previous summer. His second venture presumably came about because of his collaboration with George Oppenheimer, author of a play called *A Mighty Man Is He.* It starred Claudette Colbert as an ex-showgirl who has to remember a tune and sing it a capella; the tune was Sondheim's song "Rag Me That Mendelssohn March." The play began at the Cape Playhouse in Dennis, Massachusetts, and went on to Broadway in 1955. It was a flop, Sondheim said, but his tune was in it.

Sondheim's influential contact with the Hammersteins had led to his first professional job, writing television scripts; and after the success of the *Topper* series it looked like a promising way of earning some money. Through her influential friends at CBS, his mother did what she could to get work for him. He was often considered, but one promising project after another came to nothing. There was "Teddy and the Magician," an episode for the *Kodak Family Adventure* series that he was commissioned to write by Hubbell Robinson. "I don't think it was ever produced, but I got paid for it," he said. He was hired to write two other television plays, *Mr. Blandings and the Tree Surgeon* and *The Education of Mr. Blandings,* based on *Blanding's Way,* that did not get produced, either. With Larry Gelbart he wrote a treatment, *The King of Diamonds,* that was "an industrial espionage drama, something nobody had ever done before. The hero was an epileptic, so every time he was creeping through some place or cracking a safe he would feel the aura and know he was going to have a fit." It did not sell. There was a radio script, *The Rats,* told in the form of a monologue and adapted from an H. P. Lovecraft short story, that he wrote in college. There was a television musical called *I Believe in You,* which he wrote with Elaine Carrington, a writer of radio soap opera (*Pepper Young's Family*), whom he got to know as a result of meeting her son Robert at Williams. "I wrote the title song," he said. "It was a ghastly script. She was a terrible writer. She wrote like a soap-opera lady: half an hour to do one incident, you know. Nowadays soap operas are different, but in the old radio days nothing happened. The idea was you just got involved in the characters. It never sold."

Then there was *The Last Resorts*, which was to have been based on the title of a book by Cleveland Amory. It was about an author, modeled after Richard Bissell, who had written the hit musical *The Pajama Game*, who goes to Florida to do an article about the visiting Duke and Duchess of Windsor. By then Hal Prince, who had just produced *Pajama Game*, was very interested in adapting the book for a musical and had bought the rights to the title. The play was being written by the humorist Jean Kerr, wife of the New York *Herald Tribune* drama critic Walter Kerr, and Sondheim was hired to write the music. Sondheim said, "So I went to play some songs for Walter and Jean Kerr. All I really remember is I played a few and they didn't like them—as he subsequently proved in all of his reviews of everything I wrote. But my main memory is that Jean Kerr sat in a big wing chair, and at the end of every song (I'm overstating it) she would just say to Walter, 'Butt me.' And he would give her a cigarette." Nothing came of that project, either, not just because the Kerrs did not like Sondheim, but because Hal Prince did not like Jean Kerr's script and wanted it rewritten, which she declined to do. Prince said, "It was just a disagreement among creators, but the thing that is larger about all of that is that until Steve broke through there was great reluctance to appreciate the nature of his talent."

One of the few projects in which Sondheim was involved in those days that did get produced was *In an Early Winter*, a television adaptation, starring Kim Hunter, of a story by Roger Angell about an accident-prone family. It was commissioned by his friend Howard Erskine, who had become a producer at CBS and hired Sondheim to write it for a series called *Rendezvous*. Sometimes Sondheim was being paid and sometimes not. What is striking about this period is the singlemindedness with which he was approaching the problem of how to become established as a writer/composer/lyricist. Nothing seemed to deter him; he was full of ideas and kept coming up with new ones.

One of the projects he tried hard to make work was *The Lady or the Tiger*, a musical based on a short story by Frank R. Stockton that had a huge success when it was published in *The Century* in 1882; it subsequently became an operetta. It is a fable about an ancient king with a novel method of sentencing prisoners. They are brought into an arena and forced to choose whatever is behind one of two doors. If they choose the right door they are pronounced innocent and marry a beautiful girl. If they make the wrong choice they are pronounced guilty and eaten by a tiger. When a young man falls in love with the king's beautiful daughter, he is about to be presented with the same dilemma. But the princess has discovered the secret of the doors and tells him which one to open. The story ends: "And so I leave it with all of you. Which came out of the opened door—the lady or the tiger?" Sondheim was so intrigued with the idea that he first wrote a musical version with Miriam Dubin, one of his collaborators on *By George,* and then reworked the same material with Mary Rodgers. One of the songs, "Another World," has lyrics that curiously prefigure those of "Somewhere," the famous song from *West Side Story:* "There has to be another world / Another place for us to start . . ." The musical was never finished.

Then there was *The Jet-Propelled Couch,* based on a book, *The Fifty-Minute Hour,* published in 1954 by Robert Mitchell Lindner, a psychiatrist. "It was a series of case histories. One of them was about a guy who had invented an entire planetary universe which he had mapped thoroughly and to which he would retreat. In the course of trying to cure him of this the psychiatrist decides to get into the man's fantasy. So the idea is, the psychiatrist gets so involved in the fantasy that, one day when the patient comes in and says he has made it all up, by then the psychiatrist is caught in the fantasy. Stanley Roberts, who was a writer in California whom I knew socially, heard some of my stuff. He wanted to write a musical, so we selected this. I actually wrote a couple of songs, and the music of one of them, called 'Yes,' I eventually used in a film called *Stavisky.* And there was a song called 'Nobody Reads Books,' and there was a third song whose name I cannot remember. I wrote at least three songs for it, but we never did anything with it."

Perhaps the idea that interested him most was to write a musical based on the lives of Addison and Wilson Mizner, two flamboyant figures of the early twentieth century. Anita Loos pointed out that the brothers had handsome pedigrees; they were descended from Sir Joshua Reynolds and were the sons of an ambassador. Addison Mizner was a successful architect who designed houses for the wealthy and prominent in Palm Beach and Boca Raton. His brother, Wilson, was a Gold Rush prospector, gambler, boxing promoter, and bon vivant who became a playwright and screenwriter. Alva Johnston, who wrote about them both, said of Wilson, "He was fundamentally a confidence man whom circumstances occasionally induced to go straight." Although his celebrated humor could be crass, Loos said, the gentlemanly air with which it was delivered not only absolved Wilson of vulgarity but "gave it a unique shock value. To hear that imposing and elegant creature come out with a statement such as the one he made about Hollywood during the Fatty Arbuckle scandal produced a rather special effect. 'Living in Hollywood,' said Wilson, 'is like floating down a sewer in a glass-bottomed boat.' "

Wilson Mizner is also quoted as having said, speaking of prospecting versus the gentler charms of the Klondike's saloons and dance halls, "Flesh beats scenery," a profundity that, to his chagrin, Sondheim misquoted for years. He thought Wilson had said, "People beat scenery." But he loved the idea of writing about those two outsize figures and their sprawling lives, formidable as the prospect seemed, and he was saving his *Topper* money in order to take out an option on Alva Johnston's *The Legendary Mizners,* published in 1953. Oscar Hammerstein also thought this was a wonderful idea, but then Sondheim found out that the rights had been sold to David Merrick. Irving Berlin planned to make a musical with S. N. Behrman. So that, at least for then, was that.

Of all the ideas for a musical or a play in the early fifties, the one that was closest to being realized came through his friendship with John Barry Ryan. Ryan had fallen in love with a young woman of arresting style and artistic gifts who was a protégée of Diana Vreeland's and working at *Harper's Bazaar.* They were married in 1954 in a fashionable wedding that is still remembered with awe by their friends. D. D. Ryan said, "I wanted a country wedding but we decided that it had to be in the city, so I dressed my bridesmaids" (one was Gloria Vanderbilt and another Mrs. Richard Avedon, wife of the photographer) "in red-and-white gingham. I wore a white organdy and lace sleeveless dress designed by Norman Norell that had been on the cover of *Harper's* with a small veil and a white organdy babushka." Sondheim was one of the ushers, and another was Lemuel Ayers, who had designed the sets for *Out of This World,* among other productions, and had both designed and produced *Kiss Me, Kate.* Sondheim described him as tall and thin, almost translucent, with courtly Edwardian manners and the look of a piece of Byronic statuary. "He and his wife both, I think, prided themselves on a certain kind of elegance. Let me put it this way—they had an Afghan hound and it was hard to tell them from the Afghan."

Ayers was one of the few professional men of the theatre he had met so far, and Sondheim was delighted to find him highly cultured and serious-minded. Ayers had bought a play called *Front Porch in Flatbush* by two Hollywood screenwriters, Julius J. and Philip G. Epstein, who were also twins; they had won an Academy Award for their screenplay of *Casablanca.* In the intervening period Philip Epstein had died. *Front Porch in Flatbush,* their last play together, was a disguised portrait of their third brother, "a kind of raffish, lady-killing, cocksure gambler, sort of a Jewish James Cagney figure, I suspect," Sondheim said. "He had great social ambitions, at least according to the play."

The hero, who is leader of a group of lower-middle-class youngsters, is trying to make a killing in the stock market just before the 1929 crash. He is

Sondheim with Lemuel Ayers at the Ryans' engagement party

also ambitious to crash debutante parties at the Plaza. He does not succeed in this ambition but, outside the hotel, meets a rich girl with a southern accent. Sondheim said, "At the same time he takes money that has been given to him by . . . the gang to invest in the stock market. In a gesture of bravado, because he's intimidated by a landlord . . . [and] to impress this girl . . . he makes a down payment on the rent," using money from his friends that he had promised to invest. "It's the farcical and . . . I suppose you'd call it comic dramatic results of that, that spin the plot. The girl turns out to be as phony as he is and they realize that life should be blah, blah, blah. Julie and Phil had written a very popular comedy called *Chicken Every Sunday*, which was a period comedy about a boardinghouse. This was much closer to what their lives had been like than anything they'd written, but it had the same kind of warm, genial tone. It's a very sweet show."

Ayers had already approached Frank Loesser, because the play seemed exactly right for that composer, but Loesser was involved with another project. So after looking at Sondheim's early work, Ayers suggested that he try writing three songs. Sondheim did, Ayers and Epstein liked them, and Sondheim was engaged to write the score. John Barry Ryan had a gentleman's agreement with Ayers to co-produce the musical, to be called *Saturday Night*.

By then the newly-weds had moved into John's small apartment at 450 East Fifty-second Street, the same building in which Ryan's mother was living. D. D. Ryan said, "The apartment had originally belonged to Alexander Woollcott—he called it 'Woollcott's Wit's End'—and was cut up into a lot of small rooms. We removed walls and put two Steinway grand pianos from the thirties in the living room." She and Steve would talk every day and have wonderful conversations, and he would come to dinner. "When I think of the number of meals I made for them all!"

Sondheim was writing one wonderful song after another: "So Many People," "Saturday Night," "Isn't It?," "Class," "A Moment with You," "What More Do I Need?," "Love's a Bond," "All for You," "In the Movies," "I Remember That," and "One Wonderful Day." The Ryans and Ayerses were enthusiastic and made dates for eight backers' auditions. The first was held in an apartment belonging to Fairfield Osborn, the father of Shirley Ayers. And the second was held at Nin Ryan's. D. D. Ryan remembered the latter well, because it was the day her father died. Sondheim remembered it for another reason. He was the only performer—he played and sang the songs to an audience of about forty potential backers, who were not just unimpressed but actually hostile. Ayers was so discouraged he almost dropped the project.

Then Ryan and Ayers decided that they needed a cast. They signed up Leila Martin as the heroine, Jack Cassidy as the hero, Alice Ghostley in another leading role, Arte Johnson in a comic role, a singer named Dick Kallman, a girl named Robin Oliver, and Sheldon Harnick's brother Jay, who had a fine baritone voice. (In the course of the auditions Johnson dropped out and was replaced by Joel Grey.) The score, which shows a new assurance and a new level in Sondheim's development as a composer, is full of wit and varied pacing. It begins with "Saturday Night," which, as Professor Banfield says, incorporates ragtime piano and a jazzy keyboard style that set the musical in its 1920s period. Brooklyn comes in for its share of mockery in "It's That Kind of a Neighborhood." Brooklyn is the pride of New York, and has its own

> friendly golf course with greens
> And a friendly hash house with beans.
> There's a friendly clink whence
> Come juvenile delinquents,
> But they were born in Queens!

So sings the gang, using the comic parallels that Sondheim would develop so successfully in "America" in *West Side Story*. When the gang celebrates the life of the cop on the beat, who does his job with "pride (and a little graft on the side)," one hears the forerunner to the impudent sarcasm that informs "Gee, Officer Krupke!" If Sondheim's earlier attempts at humor sometimes seem forced, the score of *Saturday Night* scarcely hits a wrong note. He even uses the heroine's exaggerated attempts at a southern accent to point gentle fun at her, and it. In the song "Isn't It?" she is dancing with the hero and making small talk: "This is nice, isn't it? / Ah mean the music," she sings. "This is nice, isn't it? / Ah mean the beeeeyyyyaaaahhhhnd . . ." Songs that celebrate the hero's lust for the stock market, such as "Love's a Bond," have an appropriately tinny, cabaret sound. The score's sprightly and quasi-innocent tone of good-natured fun gives way to songs that describe a love affair in terms that are not only original contributions to a hackneyed theme but have an intensity that catches one off guard. In "What More Do I Need?," the heroine sings of the transformation that love has made to the way she feels about her grimy urban surroundings:

> My windowpane
> Has a lovely view:
> An inch of sky
> And a fly or two.
> Why, I can see
> Half a tree,
> And what more do I need?

But perhaps the most affecting song in the score is the moment in which the principals celebrate their love for each other, "So Many People." The mood is understated. The music even has an elegiac quality, but in spite, or because, of its quiet sincerity, it has an almost wrenching tenderness. Then there is "In the Movies," the natural sequel to "A Star Is Born," which pokes fun at all the films about girls from the wrong side of the tracks who end up as mistresses of rich men a week later.

> You can start with a bagel
> And end up with Conrad Nagel
> On the screen,
> But in life you wind up
> Right behind a
> Pillar in the mezzanine!

Given the score's freshness and charm, the reaction of the first set of backers is incomprehensible. Composers are notoriously bad singers and deaf to their own imperfections, as in the case of Leonard Bernstein, for instance. But Sondheim, while no singer, had a pleasing and accurate lyric baritone that he knew how to color so as to project his work to maximum effect. The only conclusion that makes sense is the one to which Prince pointed, that what they heard was something more sophisticated than the standard Broadway sound, so they naturally distrusted it.

Prince said, "It's amazing what that fellow put together so young. It may be a bit naive; he may have learned how to do things better, technically, but he'll never have learned to be any more unabashedly open than he was then. And so it's a very emotional and heartfelt show."

The arrival of a cast had the desired effect of arousing interest, and the team started to raise money. Sondheim thought that the cost of such a show in those days would have been about $300,000 and that perhaps $125,000 to $150,000 was pledged. The opening date was set for the spring of 1955, there was a postponement of a few months, and then disaster struck.

Much of *Saturday Night,* Sondheim said, was written while he was staying with Lemuel and Shirley Ayers in California. "Once a week a nurse and doctor would come to the house. I knew Lem was ill, but what I didn't realize was that he got a complete blood transfusion every Friday night." He was actually dying of leukemia, which he had contracted shortly after his first months as a producer on *Kiss Me, Kate,* something that was a closely guarded secret. "On Saturdays he would be un-visitable because he would be adjusting to the transfusion, and then on Sundays he would be okay." Then one day in August of 1955 Ayers died; he was just forty years old. The Ryans were left to pay the bills that had accrued so far, which were crippling, D. D. Ryan said, although she did not know the total sum. The project was dead. It was a sickening blow, and perhaps the lingering misery of the experience had something to do with Sondheim's reluctance to take up the project in years to come. If he had hoped that a Broadway production of *Saturday Night* would convince his father of the wisdom of a career in music, that hope, too, had been frustrated. His father's sixtieth birthday took place on July 2, 1955, and Sondheim gave him a copy of the score. It bore the inscription, "Hope I can give you one of these every year for the next forty years at least—All my love always." That ambition was expressed just six weeks before Ayers died.

CHAPTER 6

One Good Break

ARTHUR LAURENTS, the playwright and director who would play such a large role in Sondheim's life, met him that fateful summer of 1955. Sondheim was being handed around again, this time as a young composer and lyricist whose musical was about to have its Broadway debut—this, of course, before the death in mid-August of Lemuel Ayers. The enthusiast was George Oppenheimer, who had heard about another project from his friend Martin Gabel. Gabel had interested Laurents in the idea of creating a musical based on *Serenade,* the novel by James M. Cain. It was one in an honorable line of famous ideas that kept appearing in a new guise. Leonard Bernstein subsequently discussed making it into an opera with Roger Englander, an opera stage director who, at the time had ambitions to become a writer. Englander said, "The main character is a baritone who sings Escamillo, and Bernstein's idea for the opening, that the orchestra would strike up the Toreador song, I thought was brilliant . . ."

Bernstein was to be the musical's composer; Jerome Robbins, with whom he had already collaborated on *Fancy Free, Facsimile, On the Town,* and *Wonderful Town,* would choreograph the new work; the book would be written by Arthur Laurents, and Gabel, its producer. Although this would be his first musical, Laurents had risen to prominence in the previous decade for his screenplays, including *The Snake Pit,* and his plays, including *Home of the*

Brave, a wartime drama about a Jewish soldier, and *The Time of the Cuckoo,* in which Shirley Booth played a celebrated role as a warm-hearted teacher "on the wrong side of forty," Laurents said, who falls in love with an Italian and Venice. Bernstein had no sooner agreed to participate when he pulled out. Robbins would follow shortly thereafter, leaving Laurents and Gabel looking for a choreographer and also a composer/lyricist. Then Oppenheimer suggested Sondheim.

Sondheim came in for his audition with *Saturday Night,* and Laurents, whose reputation for speaking his mind is deserved, said he did not terribly care for the music but thought the lyrics were wonderful. But then *Serenade* changed shape once more, and became a Warner Bros. film displaying the talents of Mario Lanza, and that was the end of that. In the autumn of 1955 Sondheim and Laurents happened to meet again at a party after the opening night of a play called *Isle of Goats.* It was being held at the apartment of Ruth Ford and Zachary Scott, and Sondheim happened to arrive early. Seeing Arthur Laurents in a corner, he went over to make small talk. It transpired that Laurents, Bernstein, and Robbins were now in pursuit of a different idea, that of making a modern musical version of Shakespeare's *Romeo and Juliet.* Sondheim was curious to know who might be writing the lyrics.

"Arthur . . . smote his forehead, which I think is the only time I've ever seen anybody literally smite his forehead, and he said, 'I never thought of you . . .'" Sondheim said. Laurents invited Sondheim to audition for Bernstein. Like Laurents, Bernstein was not impressed with Sondheim's music, and besides, he was writing his own lyrics. However, it was clear that this young man had a gift. He offered him a position as co-lyricist. That was not what Sondheim had in mind. By now it was October, *Saturday Night* was dead, and the future looked empty. Hammerstein and also Sondheim's new agent, Flora Roberts, both argued that it was a chance to have his name on a prominent project and that he would gain valuable experience working with these talented men, so he allowed himself to be persuaded. "A true luck story," he called it.

A PLAUSIBLE CHAIN of circumstances had brought Sondheim to that post-theatre party, but it was mere chance that Laurents was the one person he knew in the room. It was luck that caused him to ask who was writing the lyrics, and sheer good fortune that Betty Comden and Adolph Green, Bernstein's collaborators for *On the Town* and *Wonderful Town,* who had been approached, decided to work on a film in California instead. "Thank God," Laurents said, "because this show wasn't for them."

If Sondheim's ambition to have a work produced on Broadway before he was thirty might have sounded wildly impractical to a businessman like his father, in the theatre it would have seemed an attainable goal. Although it is true that Broadway has been in a state of decline since those glorious years during the 1920s when there were over 250 productions a year, in 1950 its decline was not yet so marked that wiser heads would have shaken in despair at the notion that any full-time career was attainable. Musicals were flourishing—that year, Gertrude Lawrence and Yul Brynner were appearing in *The King and I*—and even in the less rosy field of drama, which was contracting more sharply, there were Tennessee Williams's *Rose Tattoo,* Louis Jouvet and his company performing Molière's *L'Ecole des femmes,* and Laurence Olivier and Vivien Leigh in alternating performances of Shakespeare's *Antony and Cleopatra* and Shaw's *Caesar and Cleopatra.* Those trends now so evident on Broadway were making themselves felt, but less insistently. The block of Forty-second Street between Seventh and Eighth Avenues, which had been badly hit by the Depression, had never recovered, and strip joints had taken up residence in the noble old buildings. The idea of constructing new theatres had become a thing of the past, since a theatre building, which much of the time was in use only at night and during matinees, paid taxes full time, making most uneconomical use of valuable land. Films on the West Coast had taken over the major role in show business once reserved for the theatre, and unlike in Britain, where the film and television industries evolved in physical proximity to the great stages, actors could not as easily supplement their modest salaries with the larger sums to be made via the screen. Television was an even more menacing competitor, since it provided entertainment without leaving one's living room, and it was free. By 1948, eighty percent of Broadway actors were unemployed, and the designer Boris Aronson remarked, "The theatre is an organized calamity."

All this was true, but even so, there were still eighty-seven productions on Broadway in 1950, the same number that had been launched during the 1899–1900 period. If a musical now cost something like $250,000–$300,000 to produce, individual backers could still be found who were willing to put up their shares, and there were still profits to be made. Sondheim said, "I think the smallest investment unit in the show was three hundred dollars. Because you could invest something like a tenth of one percent, and a big investment in those days was five percent of whatever the total cost was." This had the merit of diminishing the risks for everyone, although it did not make even seasoned professionals any more prescient. Sondheim recalled going to a backer's audition with Mary Rodgers for a musical that they both disliked and declined to support. It was *The Pajama Game,* one of the first of

Hal Prince's monumental moneymakers. Those were the days when a young man like Prince could get an introduction to a famous producer like George Abbott, evolve into a protégé, have huge successes while still in his twenties, and become almost embarrassingly rich. Ticket prices were still generally affordable. And in the 1950s, when anticommunism was at its height and Hollywood, with too much money at stake, was throwing out some of its best actors and writers to appease the McCarthyites, Broadway, with its historical tolerance for dissidence, was one of the few platforms left.

WHEN RECONSTRUCTING the genesis of any theatrical production, as William Goldman says in his unique study of Broadway, *The Season,* it's always *Rashomon.* That is because, in any group endeavor involving up to a hundred people, "on any given day you can interview the director, who will say that all is going blissfully, while on that same day the author will tell you of his agony with tears behind his eyes. Both could be telling the truth or lying . . . For when a show is shaping, no one can tell what the operative truth is at any given time." Fortunately, all the creators of *West Side Story* were aware of the fallibility of memory, and their stories, while differing in detail, do agree that without Jerome Robbins the musical would never have appeared.

Robbins said that some time around 1949 a friend of his was asked to play the role of Romeo. "He said to me, 'This part seems very passive. Would you tell me what you think I should do with it?' So I asked myself, 'If I were to play this, how would I make it come to life?' " Robbins began to think of the love story in contemporary terms and became enthusiastic about its possibilities. "So I wrote a very brief outline and started looking for a producer and collaborators."

Bernstein's recollection was that Robbins had explained his idea at a meeting with himself and Laurents. They all agreed that the setting should be New York's Lower East Side and involve, as the feuding parties, Catholics and Jews at the Passover-Easter season. Laurents recalled that Romeo would be Jewish, Juliet would be an Italian or Irish Catholic and Friar Lawrence would be a neighborhood druggist. Laurents did not remember having written anything and said so years later in a discussion about the origins of the musical. But it was clear that he was having second thoughts about the project at the time. He said it was *Abie's Irish Rose* set to music, and in any event he was committed to writing a screenplay. Bernstein did not like the dozen pages he said Laurents sent him and the "too-angry, too-bitchy, too-vulgar tone." So he used the demands of his conducting schedule—an invariable excuse—as a convenient way of dropping the idea. But the larger issue for them all was the choice of subject matter, since there no longer was a serious Irish-Jewish clash on the Lower East Side.

That was the end of the idea for the time being. Then, one afternoon in 1954 when Bernstein was in Hollywood to write the score for *On the Waterfront,* he happened to meet Laurents at the Beverly Hills Hotel pool. The papers were full of gang fights between Mexicans and Americans, and, Bernstein said, he and Laurents looked at each other and realized the moment had come to revive the idea of *East Side Story,* as the show was originally called. This version is contradicted by Robbins, who said that a year later, in the summer of 1955, he and Laurents went to visit Bernstein the day the news about *Serenade* was published. He wanted to know why Bernstein was wasting his time with such third-rate material when the noble idea of *East Side Story* was still waiting to be explored. Whatever the truth of the matter, the fact was that by transferring the contemporary setting to Puerto Rican gang violence on the Upper West Side, the creators had found their solution.

Working as a co-lyricist meant, for Sondheim, a close collaboration with Bernstein and, from the start, the match of personalities was far from ideal. Bernstein was capable of being intensely competitive, and Sondheim, who was twelve years his junior, was not quite young enough to fit into the category of artistic son and heir. Their personalities could not have differed more sharply, Sondheim's response to an unpromising situation being to withdraw to an impenetrable distance, and Bernstein's, to presume a superficial intimacy that Sondheim would have mistrusted, attuned as he was to any display of humbug. The immediate causes for disagreement were the lyrics Bernstein had already written.

"I had two street kids singing, 'Today the world was just an address, a place for me to live in.' Now, you know, excuse me, that's okay for Romeo and Juliet, that's a perfectly good line, but . . . That was Lenny's idea of poetry, very purple . . . He wrote a lyric for a tune, 'I Have a Love.' His lyric was—it's hard for me to do with a straight face—'Once in your life, only once in your life / Comes a flash of fire and light.' Wait for it! 'And there stands your love / The harvest of your years.' That was his idea of poetry." As for my words to "One Hand, One Heart," Sondheim said, "we used to break up laughing when they did it during the out-of-town tryouts. We had to leave the room. But one person stayed and wept over it every single time. That was Lenny." What he had learned from Hammerstein was that music amplified a song's emotional effect, and so a lyricist had to be extremely careful to ensure that the final effect was not the reverse of that intended.

"What I like in *West Side Story,* and people disagree with me all the time, is the dance music. The songs strike me as very up-and-down indeed, both musically and lyrically . . . The lyrics I like are 'Something's Coming' and most of 'Jet Song.' They have character and flavor, and I don't hear the writer at work. When you come to the so-called serious stuff, it's just extremely self-conscious." Disliking the tone, however, put Sondheim in a difficult position. Almost at once, he found himself at odds with lyrics that Bernstein, with his easy sentimentality and tendency to want to admire his own work, would have considered the peak of perfection.

Their working habits were equally at variance. Sondheim liked to work alone at night, mulling over an idea for hours. Bernstein, who had a full conducting schedule, had to work in the morning, and preferred to work together with short periods of concentration. So Sondheim, as the junior partner, tried to fit himself into Bernstein's schedule and make as many tactful changes as he could. Typically, he chose to approach the problem as an elegant game, a puzzle. "There's a great deal of joy for me in the sweat involved in the working out of lyrics, but it can lead to bloodlessness and I've sometimes been capable of writing bloodless lyrics," he wrote. "There are a number of them in *West Side Story.* You also have to know when and where to use rhyme. One function of rhyme is that it implies education. And one of the most embarrassing moments of my life was after a run-through of *West Side,* when some of my friends were out front. I asked Sheldon Harnick after the show what he thought, knowing full well that he was going to fall to his knees and lick the sidewalk. Instead he said, 'There's that lyric, 'I Feel Pretty.'

"I thought the lyric was terrific. I had spent the previous two years of my life rhyming 'day' and 'way' and 'me' and 'be' and with 'I Feel Pretty' I wanted to show that I could do inner rhymes, too. That was why I had this uneducated Puerto Rican girl singing, 'It's alarming how charming I feel.' You must know she would not have been unwelcome in Noël Coward's living room.

"Sheldon was very gentle about his criticism. I immediately went back and wrote a simplified version of the lyric which nobody connected with the show would accept. So there it is to this day embarrassing me every time it's sung, because it's full of mistakes like that . . .

"Words must sit on music in order to become clear to the audience. You don't get a chance to hear the lyric twice and if it doesn't sit and bounce when the music bounces, and rise when the music rises—" It was not just a question of placing the musical accent on the wrong syllable, which was bad enough, but if the lyric was too crowded and the words did not flow, then "the audience becomes confused. 'America' has twenty-seven words to the square inch. I had this wonderful quatrain that went, 'I like to be in

America / O.K. by me in America / Everything free in America / For a small fee in America.' The little 'for a small fee' was my zinger—except that the 'for' is accented and 'small fee' is impossible to say that fast, so it went, 'For a smafee in America.' Nobody knew what it meant!"

Apart from their conflicting ideas about lyrics, Sondheim and Bernstein hit it off extremely well. They discovered a common passion for word games and filled in the unproductive gaps by poring over the *Listener* crossword puzzle, to which Sondheim introduced Bernstein, and at the anagram table. "I drove him crazy because, to his dying day, he never beat me," Sondheim said. Even though he was dissatisfied with his own work he was having a wonderful time. And there was no doubt that they all knew something very good was happening. To Sondheim, the show's strengths had to do with its theatricality and the fact that a story was being told almost entirely in musical terms. "What the critics didn't realize—and they rarely realize anything—is that the show isn't very good. By which I mean, in terms of individual ingredients it has a lot of very severe flaws: overwriting, purpleness in the writing and in the songs, and because the characters are necessarily one-dimensional. They're not people. What lasts in the theatre is character, and there are no characters in *West Side,* nor can there be. It's the shortest book on record, with the possible exception of *Follies,* in terms of how much gets accomplished and with how little dialogue. It's more about techniques, not about people, and Arthur recognized the problem right away and instead of writing people he wrote one-dimensional characters for a melodrama, which is what it is. More happens in terms of plot of the show than in almost any other musical . . . and with less dialogue, which is how smart Arthur is and how he recognized that's the form it must take."

What Sondheim would call "cannibalizing" of the books of his musicals began then, with Laurents's willing cooperation. No longer was he in the position of a composer/lyricist who illustrates a play with music and words at polite intervals, as he had with *Saturday Night.* He was now embarked on the much more difficult process of integrating dialogue with thoughts that could be sung or even danced and mimed, an art that he saw being demonstrated on a daily basis by those infinitely more skilled than himself. "The entire prologue that is now danced on the stage was originally set with a lyric in which the gang was in a clubhouse and had a fantasy about taking a trip to the moon, and then Riff [leader of the Jets] came in. In the original version of *West Side* when we first started to write it, a number of characters were associated with specific musical instruments, Riff with a trumpet, and he came in and what is now the Jets song was a song called 'My Greatest Day.' That whole sequence, which took us about a month to write, was scuttled when

On the set of *West Side Story* in 1957: from left, Sondheim, Arthur Laurents, Hal Prince, co-producer Robert Griffith (seated), Leonard Bernstein, and Jerome Robbins

Robbins in consultation with Chita Rivera during rehearsals for *West Side Story*

Arthur Laurents made, I think, trenchantly and correctly, the observation that it would be better conveyed in dance and movement . . . and so all that work went for nil."

Laurents's willingness to have his own words appropriated was, for Bernstein, a highly unusual aspect of their collaboration that set it apart. He said, "The song 'Something's Coming' was a very late comer. We realized we needed a character-introduction kind of song for Tony. There was a marvelous introductory page in the script that Arthur had written, the essence of which became the lyric for this song. We raped Arthur's playwriting. I've never seen anyone so encouraging, let alone generous, urging us, 'Yes, take it, take it, make it a song.' "

That was the song for which Sondheim actually wrote some of the music. Speaking of Larry Kert, who played Tony, Sondheim said, "We thought we could launch it by having him sing a song early on, a specific kind of song called a 'two-four,' a very driving kind of showbiz song. Judy Garland and Larry were the champs at that kind of song—trolley songs. I thought we ought to write a two-four for him. Lennie Bernstein wrote the verse part and said, 'How do you make this into a two-four?' He knew what it was, but it's a showbiz term more than a musical term. So I started to ad lib with the thumb line (that is to say, the cello line, an inner voice). That's what I contributed, the two-four part of that."

With *West Side Story*, the writer Glen Litton observed, not only had the creators discovered a new flexibility and new opportunities in a form that had seemed hidebound but they had demonstrated that musicals, always thought to be vehicles for comedy, could also illustrate tragic themes. That was not entirely true, since with *Carousel* Rodgers and Hammerstein had already experimented with a flawed hero whose death is the central pivot of the plot. It is certainly true that the tone of *West Side Story* was bleaker and more tragic than popular musicals had ever been, including *Carousel,* and it was obviously very influential in Sondheim's later choice of subjects, which eschewed formulaic endings in favor of something much darker and more disquieting. Sondheim said that soon after he started work his father asked to read the script with the idea of investing in it, and he and some friends eventually did invest $1,500 and made a small profit. Sondheim remembered the day when his father brought the script back to his apartment, his face ashen, saying, "Not many laughs, are there?"

ONE OF THE REASONS Bernstein wanted help with the lyrics of *West Side Story* was that he realized that the emphasis being placed on dance as a vehicle for telling the story meant that a great deal more music was required of him than he originally expected. He was also in the middle of writing *Candide,* which he had begun in 1954 in collaboration with Lillian Hellman and the happy expectation that he could dash it off, as he had with *Wonderful Town,* in a matter of weeks. But by the end of the summer, he and Hellman had only written one act, other deadlines appeared, and they had both rejected the lyrics that had been written by John Latouche. (Bernstein first had approached Sondheim to write the lyrics, but he declined.) *West Side Story* intervened, and then, in May 1956, Bernstein went to Martha's Vineyard to work on *Candide* with a new lyricist, the poet Richard Wilbur, leaving Laurents, Robbins, and Sondheim to their own devices temporarily. Laurents had a new play in the works and used the time to complete *A Clearing in the Woods.* Robbins went off to direct *Bells Are Ringing,* and Sondheim found himself writing, besides *In an Early Winter,* a series on the English language for CBS called *The Last Word.*

Candide may be, as many critics believe, Bernstein's best score, but it was an experience fraught with setbacks and disappointments. Sondheim recalls that at the tryouts in Boston, things were going so badly that his advice was sought. That was very flattering, since he was only twenty-six at the time. He arrived at Bernstein's hotel to find everyone—Bernstein, Hellman, Wilbur, and the famous director, Tyrone Guthrie—awaiting his verdict, which naturally terrified him, although it did not make him mute. "I told them what I still think, which was that all the work was wonderful, except it didn't go together. The book didn't belong with the score, the score didn't belong with the direction, and the direction didn't belong with the book. I thought Lillian's book was wonderful, but it's very black. The score is pastiche, with bubble and sparkle and sweetness. The direction was wedding cake, like an operetta." He does not remember how they reacted, if at all.

West Side Story had other difficulties. It should have been seen as an attractive investment, because Robbins, Laurents, and Bernstein had had nothing but successes, but it proved surprisingly difficult to sell. Sondheim had tried to get Hal Prince involved, but he and his partner, Robert Griffith, had turned it down, as had George Abbott—he thought the score sounded like Prokofiev or some such "avant-garde" composer. Rodgers and Hammerstein were producing shows as well as writing them, so Sondheim approached his mentor, who thought it was an excellent idea. Hammerstein was choosing his moment to bring up the subject with Rodgers when, in a spectacular piece of bad timing, Robbins's agent referred to the deal as almost a fait accompli in a conversation with Rodgers. This made the composer suspect that "somebody had gone behind his back, which was exactly what Oscar didn't want to have happen," Sondheim said. "So that was that." When Cheryl Crawford and Roger Stevens eventually agreed to co-produce, the principals were devoutly grateful to have solved the problem, or so they thought.

Everyone remembered the famous night in the late spring of 1957 when a backer's audition was held at the apartment of a wealthy woman on East End Avenue. Laurents said, "It was before the days of air conditioning, it was hot, the windows were open, and you could hear the tugboats going up and down." Sondheim and Bernstein, singing and playing with a cast, gave it their all, and at the end, Laurents said, "No one offered a nickel." That was the final blow for Cheryl Crawford, who had expressed increasing dissatisfaction with the book, the score, and everything else. Sondheim thought that since she had recently had several flops, she could not risk having another. In any event, she called a meeting and announced that she was abandoning the project. Bernstein recalled that they all stood up gravely and left. But once they reached the corner of the street, "We all went to jelly, asking each other, 'What are we going to do now?' " Laurents found a phone booth and called Roger Stevens, who was in London. In those days, Stevens was financing shows but did not produce them himself. Stevens assured them that he would provide stopgap funding until they could find a new producing team.

That night Sondheim spoke to Prince in Boston, where he and Robert Griffith were working on a problem show of their own, *New Girl in Town*. Sondheim said, "I don't know whether I called him or he called me. They were not having too terrific a time, but I was much more miserable, and I was saying, 'God, it all fell apart, and now it can't be done, because Lenny has to take over the New York Philharmonic on September first,' or whenever it was." (Bernstein assumed his new post as joint principal conductor in the autumn of 1957 and left on tour the day after *West Side Story* opened in New York.) Sondheim continued, reporting his conversation with Prince, " 'There's nothing we can do and the show's down the tubes, a year and a half, whine, whine, whine,' and he said, 'Why don't you send it to Bobby and me?' and I said, 'I thought you didn't like it,' and he said, 'But you've changed it, haven't you?' and I said, 'Yeah, sure, but not essentially.' He said, 'Send it to us.' " Sondheim knew he had to get to Prince in a hurry, so he collated all the scripts and mailed them immediately. The response came from Prince almost at once that he and his partner loved the work and wanted to produce it. True to form, they would do nothing until their other show opened in New York. But also true to form, the day after *New Girl in Town* opened (to disappointing reviews) Hal Prince was at work on the new project, a way of dealing with success or defeat that became a lifelong practice. In the next two months they raised the money, finished the casting, and booked the Winter

Garden for September 26, 1957, with five weeks of tryouts in Washington and Philadelphia.

Sondheim said, "I'll give you an anecdote that will show you how strong Hal was. About a week before rehearsals—they'd already got the capitalization and posted bonds, they had spent money, and a week before rehearsals Jerry called a meeting in Hal's office and announced to us that it was too much work for him to choreograph and direct as well. He just wanted to direct. He wanted Herbert Ross to do the choreography. And there was a shocked silence around the room. I didn't know about this; Lenny didn't know about this; it was just announced.

"Hal Prince, then thirty years old, who had just had a not-successful show open and already, I am sure, had put in many thousands of dollars, said, 'I'll tell you what, Jerry. One of the reasons Bobby and I wanted to do this show, if not the main reason, was because of your genius as a choreographer, and if you don't want to do the choreography I'm not sure if we want to do the show. Let's all think about it, and come back here tomorrow.' And Jerry was turning bright red. A meeting took place the next day and it was wonderful. Jerry sat in Hal's seat at the desk and Hal had to stand, and Jerry was in a rage. But there was nothing he could do about it. And so he said, 'All right! I'll do the choreography *and* the directing. But I want an assistant choreographer.' Hal said, 'Fine,' and he said, 'I want eight weeks' rehearsal.' Now, these were the days when you never had more than four. Eight is doubling the cost. And Hal said, 'I think that will be okay,' and he said, 'I want three pianists.' Hal said, 'Why?' 'Well, I want one for the songs and one for the dance, and I just want to have another one around.' And Hal said, 'Well, why not wait and see.' In other words, Hal was that cool. He thought, 'All right, eight weeks is going to cost a lot of money, but I understand why he's saying it. An assistant—absolutely.' Peter Gennaro staged 'America,' and what's interesting, a wonderful lesson, is that we went to the rehearsal and it just didn't work. Moment by moment it worked, but something didn't come together. And then Jerry got his hands on it and reshaped it all and—suddenly, the number worked. He's a master artist."

Although Sondheim developed an enormous respect for Robbins, he agreed with the general verdict that he was a difficult man to work with. At one point Laurents, Bernstein, and Sondheim wanted to drop a song that Robbins had asked to have written and wanted to remain in the show. Laurents's view was that the song would tilt the show too far toward musical comedy, and the others agreed. Robbins, furious, rounded on Sondheim (Sondheim said he always attacked the person least able to defend himself) and made insulting remarks about his lyrics in front of everyone. Sondheim said, "It just froze me for twenty-four hours." Robbins was also known for his chronic indecisiveness and inability ever to be satisfied.

Sondheim said, "You'll write something and he'll say, 'That's fine. Now, couldn't you do it from *her* point of view?' The answer is, of course you could! You go home, you write it from her point of view. Then he'll say, 'Oh, that's very good, but maybe it should occur earlier in the day.' Everything is a possibility, and he wants to explore all the possibilities, because that's the way he choreographs. He sets his dancers going and then he says, 'Wait a minute! Try that again, but turn the other way, darling . . . No, that doesn't work. Okay, do that . . . No. Wait a minute! You put your hand up there. I know it's a mistake, but put it up again! I want to see that.' It can be done instantaneously. But a writer has to go home and write it."

On the other hand, he learned an absolutely invaluable lesson from Robbins early on, during rehearsals of "Maria." Robbins wanted to know what the hero, Tony, was doing.

Sondheim said, "Well, you know, he's standing outside her house and, you know, he senses that she's going to appear on the balcony."

Robbins said, "Yeah, but what is he doing?"

Sondheim said, "Oh, he's standing there and singing a song."

Robbins was getting testy. *"What is he doing?"*

Sondheim said, "Well, he sings, 'Maria, Maria, I just met a girl named Maria, and suddenly that name will never be the same to me.' "

Robbins said, "And then what happens?"

Sondheim said, "Then he sings . . ."

"You mean," Robbins said, "he just stands looking at the audience?"

Sondheim said, "Well, yes."

Robbins said, "*You* stage it."

Sondheim finally understood. "After all, it's not an art song, it's part of a dramatic action. There are certain kinds of shows which are presentational. You just get out there and sing the song. But that's not *West Side Story*. It's supposed to be an integrated musical. It's supposed to be full of action. It's supposed to carry you forward in the story, which means that every second should carry you forward in some way. Well, it's up to the songwriter to think those things up before you put the show in the director's lap. If you don't, you get clumsy staging or static songs and you end up throwing lots of things out on the road because they don't work." What he learned from that experience was that a writer actually had to "plot and plan" every bar, a lesson that was to prove invaluable in future. It was one more demonstration of Robbins's relentless perfectionism, that "black ferocity" he could display when he was at work, as the playwright John Guare described it. Then there is the story the playwright James Lapine tells about *Dybbuk,* the ballet written by Bernstein that was choreographed by Robbins and first performed in the summer of 1974. The story goes that as the curtain was about to rise, Robbins was in the wings with a pair of scissors, cutting pieces off the costumes, and the costume designer was crying and saying, "I'll never work with him again." Bernstein answered, "That's what we all say."

ONCE *West Side Story* arrived in Washington on an incredibly hot night of August 19, 1957, the collaborators knew they had a hit. Laurents said, "At some point we began to get a feeling and Jerry began pounding me on the back, saying, 'They like it, they like it!' " Bernstein remembered meeting Supreme Court Justice Felix Frankfurter, who was in a wheelchair, in tears during the intermission. Sondheim remembered that the only time "Something's Coming" ever stopped the show was that night. "We kept writing high, loud endings and low trail-off endings, and we finally just gave up." Then there was the charming letter he received from Bernstein that day, wishing him luck on his first opening night and expressing confidence in the brilliant career Bernstein was sure lay ahead. There was a touching letter from Dorothy Hammerstein to "dearest Steve," to say how delighted she and Oscar were. "Your good taste, your tenderness, your talent and your behavior are things which warm our hearts and make us proud to have known you since you were the little rabbit chaser that summer in Doylestown." The morning after the Washington opening Sondheim called his mother at dawn to read her the reviews. She promptly got Louella Parsons out of bed to boast about her son's achievements. All this must have compensated somewhat for the fact that neither Richard Coe, of the Washington *Post,* nor Jay Carmody, of the *Evening Star,* saw fit to mention his name.

Sondheim said, "I was completely ignored and I was very upset. It's much worse to be ignored than to get a bad review. And Lenny saw how glum I was, and as we rode back from a rehearsal to the hotel, he said, 'Look.' At that point the lyrics were credited to both him and me, and he said, 'You've done virtually all the lyrics—' What was left of Lenny's was mainly a line or two. And he said, 'The credit is yours. Take the full credit.' I said, 'Thank you very much.' He said, 'Of course we'll reapportion the royalties.' At that point, he got three percent and I got one percent. It would have been two and two. And like an idiot I said, 'Don't be silly. I don't care about the money.' The amount that single remark has cost me over the last forty years . . . !"

Opening night at the Winter Garden a month later was both wonderful and miserable. Wonderful, because he had made it to Broadway at the age of

Sondheim and Bernstein at the opening-night party for *West Side Story*

twenty-seven, comfortably inside his self-imposed goal of thirty. The advance sale was estimated at $700,000, there were the usual celebrities and television cameras, and the house was sold out. Robbins was mobbed by admirers and Bernstein was jubilant. "Cheer up. You're rich and we love you," Hal Prince and Robert Griffith wrote encouragingly in their opening-night telegram. Leonard Bernstein's was, "Tonight tonight may you be rich and famous like everybody else," a reference to two songs that had been cut. The chic crowd went from Sardi's to a huge party at the Ambassador Hotel on Park Avenue that was being thrown by the producers, where they drank champagne and danced to the music of *My Fair Lady.* Bernstein arrived fashionably late, his navy-blue coat slung carelessly over his shoulders, an affectation he had learned from his mentor the conductor Serge Koussevitzky, and carrying the morning papers. All the reviews were raves except that of Walter Kerr in the *Herald Tribune.* Sondheim recalled that the reference was a pan, but his memory was faulty: "The evening hurtles headlong past whatever endearing simplicities may be hidden in Arthur Laurents's text or Stephen Sondheim's lyrics," Kerr wrote.

During the evening someone edged up to Bernstein and commented that it was quite a nice little evening. It was Hammerstein, who had been filmed arriving with his wife, Dorothy, and Foxy Sondheim Leshin. Sondheim had gone to great pains to ensure that his parents would be separated for the opening-night festivities, which they were both determined to attend. Herbert Sondheim had arranged to entertain his friends at the "21" Club and arrive at the Ambassador Hotel about an hour later. The Hammersteins had agreed to take charge of Foxy, arrive at the party early, and, since they did not care much for any kind of big event, leave after a few polite greetings. The main point was to get Foxy home before Herbert and his second wife arrived. Sondheim did everything humanly possible but, he learned later, as the curtain fell his father, who had caught sight of his mother seated a couple of seats away, went up to her, murmuring words about what a wonderful moment it was and trying to embrace her. Foxy pushed him away.

Still, the after-theatre plans were flawless, or so he thought. "This is why you should never, never plan a murder!" he said. "Because, for whatever reason, the Hammersteins arrived a little late and stayed a little longer." They were on their way out, which involved mounting a curving staircase and arriving at a landing, which had been spotlit for the benefit of the cameras. Just as they arrived at the top, as if on cue, Herbert and Alicia Sondheim appeared. Sondheim said, "Oh, here comes Dave Garroway, *click, click*. Here come the Hammersteins, *click, click*. And Wilma Curley, who was a girl in the cast who was sort of hot for me, had been trying to get me to dance, and I'm a terrible dancer, I don't like dancing, I feel clumsy. And I said to her, 'Wilma, do you want to dance?' I just wanted to get into the other room. I didn't want to see the machine gun."

West Side Story's enduring reputation has come about, by general agreement, because of the film, which was made in 1961 and which won numerous Academy Awards, including Best Picture. The score became popular largely because of the film's expensive advertising campaign. Music the critics had pronounced interesting but not "hummable" turned out to be unforgettable because, Sondheim pointed out, people had had a chance to get to like it. If *West Side Story* had never become a film, its score would have languished in obscurity because, despite the reviews, the musical was not successful, as Prince and Sondheim have testified. "It got excellent critical press and people left in droves," Sondheim said. That, he thought, was because people did not go to musicals expecting experimental work. They went for an evening's diversion, and when a musical did not meet those expectations, audiences felt cheated. Sondheim recalled standing at the side of the aisle during the second night. "And I was so proud, you know, of my first show on Broadway. I'd been savaged and/or ignored in the reviews, but nevertheless, I had a show on Broadway! So I'm standing on the side, the curtain goes up, there are six guys on stage." He started snapping his fingers and humming the opening bars of the "Prologue." "About two minutes into the number I see a guy in the rear of the orchestra, 'Excuse me, excuse me.' And I think he's going to the bathroom, but he has a coat over his arm. 'Excuse me, excuse me.' And he came out to the aisle and caught my eye. He knew I must be connected with the show, because I was standing there instead of sitting in a seat, and he just said, 'Don't ask.'

"I had the whole picture. He's a tired businessman on his way home to Westchester, and he thinks, I'm going to stop and see a musical. The curtain goes up and six ballet-dancing juvenile delinquents in color-coordinated sneakers go, 'Da da-da da da,' with their fingers snapping. And he thinks, 'What—? My God!' And what he's expecting," and here Sondheim began to sing with animation, "is, 'As the girls go, so goes the nation . . .' I can't blame him. I can't blame him! But that's when I knew my career was in trouble."

CHAPTER 7

Coming Up Roses

A S IT HAPPENED, only one reviewer made a nostalgic reference to the days when a middle-aged man could settle back in his seat, knowing he was about to view "a score or so of cunningly constructed young women dancing merrily, all in a row," as Wolcott Gibbs wrote. One guesses that Sondheim was too elated, just then, by the attention they were all receiving to be deterred by a single theatregoer wending his way up the aisle.

On opening night Sondheim and Wilma Curley had danced to the music of *My Fair Lady* at the Ambassador Hotel, and *West Side Story* followed Lerner and Loewe's Cinderella story of the Cockney flower seller to London, opening in December 1958 at Her Majesty's Theatre in the Haymarket. The reception was, if possible, even more enthusiastic than it had been in either Washington or New York. At the premiere, the audience reacted with roaring applause. One reviewer said it was the greatest musical he had ever seen. A reviewer suggested that it was even more impressive than *My Fair Lady*, a serious concession since Lerner and Loewe's musical might have been expected to have the edge, based as it was on Shaw's play *Pygmalion*. Indeed, within three weeks of opening, *West Side Story* had won the London *Evening Standard*'s annual award as the best musical of the year, beating *My Fair Lady* by a vote of three to two.

"It struck London last night like a flash of lightning set to music, the most dynamic, dramatic, operatic, balletic and acrobatic of all those epics from Broadway," Cecil Wilson wrote in the *Daily Mail*. Keith Baxter, the British actor, then at the start of his career, was at the opening night. "There was no question in young people's minds that *West Side Story* was not only a far more shattering experience, but that it was a seminal evening in the development of musical theatre . . . *West Side Story* had been a success in America but in London its success was like a blaze. We had seen nothing like it." Baxter was introduced to Sondheim at a party afterwards and found him "holding a glass, slightly swaying, but from happiness not drink. There was a big grin across his handsome face . . . I suppose Bernstein was there, and Jerome Robbins too, but I don't remember them. I remember only Stephen and being aware that I had met someone of prodigious ability whose delight in language and the effortless manner in which he explored its nuances made his contemporary rivals sound lumpen and old-fashioned." The musical ran for over a thousand performances, still the record in London for the longest running Sondheim show.

Almost the only dissenting voice came from the drama critic of the *Sunday Times,* Harold Hobson. He began by describing his encounter with Noël Coward at the end of opening night. Everyone else had left, but Coward "remained in his stall, overwhelmed in the vortex of his admiration for the vibrant, tingling and clever show we had just been cheering," Hobson wrote, with a sly reference to *The Vortex,* one of Coward's early plays. "Gripping me firmly by the hand, 'Harold,' he said with a bittersweet smile" (another reference) " 'that was great theatre we've had tonight, wasn't it?' " Hobson did not agree. Coward was astounded. At least, he begged the critic, be gentle, advice that was not followed. ("It is Shakespeare pillaged in pidgin English.")

Given the overwhelming acclaim, it was possible to dismiss that kind of mean-spirited carping, as, in fact, Sondheim had dismissed the review that was published by *The Nation* after the New York opening the year before. Harold Clurman's review churlishly suggested that the authors were pandering to the masses by stooping to illustrate such material. Writing to Leonard Bernstein, who was then on tour in Israel with the New York Philharmonic, Sondheim thought it unlikely that Bernstein had seen the review since his secretary, Helen Coates, was famous for the fierceness with which she defended him against attack. Naturally, Sondheim said, he had canceled his subscription to the magazine. Otherwise, the news was all good, he wrote. The show was sold out for months, and would run for a total of 981 performances. There were theatre parties every matinee and evening for the next six weeks. Carol Lawrence's high notes had disappeared temporarily and her understudy had replaced her in the middle of a matinee. There were a few broken ankles, torn ligaments, and sprained wrists, but nothing serious. So far there was only one record of a tune from the show on the market, "I Feel Pretty," sung by Jill Corey. Others were planned; Rosemary Clooney and the British singer Vera Lynn had recorded "Tonight," although Sondheim had not heard them yet. Sammy Davis wanted to do "Cool," "Something's Coming," and "Tonight," and Mickey Calin, the actor playing Riff, had a recording contract and several movie offers.

The really important news was that the recording of the cast album had been made by Goddard Lieberson of Columbia Records and was being released on stereophonic tape as well as on monaural and stereo records. It had just gone on sale, with a first printing of 46,000 copies, and Sondheim wanted to know whether that was a good one. *Variety* had given the record a rave, and there was a good notice in the New York *Daily News* by Douglas Watt. The main problem they had encountered was that someone had badly underestimated the length of the balcony scene and the only way to cut it that made sense was to dispense with the dialogue, which had emasculated the scene. The prologue was taken at a faster tempo, mostly to make it more interesting. Larry Kert, possessor of a large and tuneful tenor voice, sounded a little tired in "Something's Coming," but by the time he sang it, he had been at work for nine hours. The girls singing in "America" and "I Feel Pretty" did not sound any better on the record than they did on the stage. One of the trumpet players played a wrong note in the final procession and no one heard it until it was too late, including Sondheim, who said he was out getting five minutes' sleep. He also slept during "America," since the recording session had lasted from ten in the morning until one a.m. the following day. There were bound to be other errors, but by and large Sondheim, who had acted as Bernstein's official representative, thought Bernstein would be pleased.

After working with Bernstein for two years, Sondheim knew that the best way to placate him was to warn him in advance. The letter was good-humored; and, in fact, the night of the opening, Sondheim sent Bernstein a hand-written letter of appreciation and slipped in a shy reference to their next project, whatever it might be: "Much as I want to write music, I'm not sure I like the idea of doing another show without you." But of course he would, he went on to say, and Bernstein would criticize his work, "and I'll be hostile and sarcastic about your criticism." It was as if he knew they would never have another musical on Broadway, and although they made one more attempt, they never did. Part of that had to do with Sondheim's growing stature as a composer/lyricist and his unwillingness to return to the old role of playing second fiddle to a composer. But Bernstein himself did not succeed in writing another musical until 1976. After making extravagant claims for the nature of their invention ("We . . . thought it might change the look of musical theatre as it is known in America"), Bernstein came to a creative halt, as if his grandly stated aims had presented a goal so lofty that even he felt inadequate.

As for his claim that *West Side Story* had signaled a new direction, Sondheim challenged this in later years. It was a unique experiment, that was all. "All Lenny was saying was, 'I wrote a great musical and nobody else can do it.' He was making that statement all the time. But he wasn't leading the pack at all. He was just blowing his own trumpet and it always pissed me off." Sondheim also thought *West Side Story* seemed dated nowadays, although it is still a popular choice for high-school and college drama departments and community theatres, and still provides royalties. The success of the record was a big surprise, and the popularity of the film an even bigger one, since originally no one had wanted to buy the film rights. Sondheim thought the selling price was about $375,000, then considered a bargain-basement sum. Prince managed to acquire a substantial share of the gross for the creative team, but Sondheim said they had been forced to sue over the years to get a proper accounting, which cut down on the profits. He would do much better with the film rights to *Gypsy,* and the stage royalties for *A Funny Thing Happened on the Way to the Forum* would provide his main income in years to come.

If his theatrical collaboration with Bernstein was over, his contacts with Robbins and Prince would be invaluable, and so would his growing friendship with Arthur Laurents. Sondheim wrote incidental music for a Laurents play, *Invitation to a March,* performed on Broadway in 1960: twenty minutes of music for trumpet, horn, clarinet, flute, and harp. Being unsure of his ground, Sondheim sought the help of Bernstein, who was happy to oblige and who supervised the scoring, the only orchestration Sondheim would ever attempt. At the end of the process Sondheim wondered whom he would get to conduct the work, since it was going to be recorded. Bernstein urged him to do it himself. Conducting was easy, he said; there was nothing to it. Bernstein would give him a few pointers and then he could go in and take charge. Sondheim received his lesson and then stepped into the recording studio, where several fine musicians were waiting for him. Five minutes into the recording, Sondheim realized he had no idea how to conduct an accelerando. The musicians tried to be helpful, but nothing was working. Finally, at the break, the suggestion was made that a professional conductor take over, and Sondheim gratefully agreed. He called it "a humiliating, awful experience" and never tried conducting again.

Sondheim was becoming known by a small but influential group of playwrights, composers, and producers who recognized his unique gifts. George Oppenheimer once again acted as matchmaker by introducing him to Frank Loesser, the versatile composer and lyricist of *Guys and Dolls.* Oppenheimer took him to Loesser's house at around noon one day, stayed for a while, and then left, leaving the two composers alone together. Loesser was writing *The Most Happy Fella* at the time, and Sondheim was enormously flattered when the composer played the score for him. Loesser was "also a drinker, at least in those days." Alcohol flowed freely and Sondheim, who had only been drunk once or twice in his life, found his head swimming as the hours went by. "It was a memorable afternoon in my life." A few years later, Loesser rang him up to ask whether he could become Sondheim's publisher. He had put together a group of young writers and had ambitions to "run an empire," Sondheim said. Sondheim's modest publishing interests were being represented by Williamson, the publishing company founded by Rodgers and Hammerstein. Loesser wanted Sondheim "in his stable." Sondheim said he would be thrilled.

Loesser asked who his lawyer was. Sondheim did not have a lawyer but supposed his father's lawyer could represent him. That would not do, Loesser said. He should have a lawyer who specialized in the entertainment business, and recommended Robert Montgomery, who was associated with a firm already familiar to Sondheim. Sondheim and Montgomery duly had lunch and the lawyer advised Sondheim not to join Loesser, because Loesser had a reputation for pushing his writers too far too fast. Montgomery said, "You're just beginning. You don't need a publisher yet, you don't need a promoter." Convinced, Sondheim called Loesser later that day to tell him what the lawyer's advice had been. Loesser said, "Didn't I tell you he was a good lawyer?"

AFTER *West Side Story,* Sondheim was determined to make his mark as a composer and not become identified as a writer of lyrics only. Roger Englander said, "The lyricist is at the low end in all musical theatre. No one ever remembers who wrote the words," and Richard Maltby, of the songwriting team of Maltby and Shire, recalled Sondheim saying that "the worst thing about being a lyricist is that everyone else is in rehearsal, whereas you are back at the hotel, trying to fix those two terrible lines." Then a new opportunity came along, one that looked even more promising than *West Side Story* had done in 1955: a project for a musical based on the memoirs of the striptease artist, Gypsy Rose Lee.

The idea originated with the producer David Merrick, who envisioned Ethel Merman in the central role of Gypsy Rose Lee's mother, Madame Rose. Merman's only failure on Broadway in a thirty-year career had been her most recent show, *Happy Hunting,* in 1956. Her most recent Broadway success, *Call Me Madam,* in 1950, had been choreographed by Jerome Robbins. Robbins was brought in to direct and choreograph *Gypsy* by Merrick's co-producer Leland Hayward. The team was being assembled, but Merrick was rebuffed in his attempts to recruit first Irving Berlin, who had written some of Merman's best songs, and then Cole Porter, who had done the same. Neither composer knew what to do with the idea, and Porter, in addition, was ill. Cy Coleman and Carolyn Leigh were asked to audition and prepared four songs, none of which Merrick liked.

In those days Betty Comden and Adolph Green were at the top of any producer's list, but they declined the offer to write the book. Then Merrick thought of Laurents, fresh from his success with *West Side.* Sondheim said, "Arthur talked to Gypsy Rose Lee and he realized from the things she said that she had made up most of [her memoir]. Every time he went back and talked to her she had a different account of how she got into vaudeville, how she got into burlesque, etc. So he decided he might as well make up his own story." Laurents said that even though he and Robbins had not been on good terms during *West Side Story,* Robbins nevertheless appeared to believe Laurents was the ideal choice as writer and said he would not do *Gypsy* unless he was hired. Laurents said his reply was, " 'Well, it's amusing, but it's not for me.' I was too grand for any of that trash—Gypsy Rose Lee's memoirs. Then one day I was at a cocktail party. Everybody was getting smashed . . . We all got to talking about our first loves, and one girl said, 'My first lover was Gypsy Rose Lee's mother.' That interested me." He discovered that not only was Madame Rose a lesbian, but she had once had a fight with a hotel manager who complained that there were too many people staying in her room. "So she pushed him out of the window and killed him. How can you resist doing a musical based on a woman like that?" he said.

Laurents's next step was to propose Sondheim as the composer and lyricist. All the omens looked favorable. But Merman had to agree. Although Sondheim said they had not met at that point, according to Merman's friend the late Benay Venuta, she took an immediate dislike to Sondheim. She wanted someone well-known, and Jule Styne, whom Merrick then approached, had written several hit shows, including *High Button Shoes, Gentlemen Prefer Blondes, Peter Pan,* and *Bells Are Ringing.* He was an old hand at tailoring songs to the singers who introduced them, including Judy Holliday. His musical versatility was legendary, as was his rapid-fire way of talking. Sondheim knew him slightly. They had met at parties, and Styne, who could always be coaxed to play the piano, was happy to perform the work of other men as well as his own compositions, which impressed Sondheim. Styne was, like Richard Rodgers, able to pull new ideas from a seemingly bottomless pit of possibilities. He was the most cordial of collaborators. So Sondheim was disposed to like the idea of cooperating with Styne. He did not want to be just a lyricist again and particularly did not want to work on a show-business story. But after Ethel Merman did not want him as a composer Laurents tried to persuade him to write the lyrics.

Again, Sondheim went to Hammerstein for advice, and Hammerstein once more argued that the advantages of writing for such a famous star outweighed the drawbacks. Sondheim said, "Instead of writing Madame Rose you write for Madame Rose as played by Ethel Merman. It turned out to be very useful, because when I wrote Joanne in *Company* I wrote for Joanne as played by Elaine Stritch. I wrote Mrs. Lovett as played by Angela Lansbury, and Sweeney Todd as played by Len Cariou, too. It's not so much that you tailor the material, but you hear the voice in your head whether you want to or not. I've often made the arch comment that I really don't want to write a score until the show's cast." In the days when shows traveled, the woods were full of hit songs that were written on the road: "You know the person who's playing the character, you know their strengths and weaknesses, and whether it's conscious or not, it filters into what you write." And, as Hammerstein pointed out, although *Gypsy* was interrupting work on another project that was closer to his heart, the delay would be brief, six months at most. So he allowed himself to be persuaded.

Gypsy's milieu was in hotel rooms and backstages at a time when vaudeville was dying and being replaced by burlesque. Until Arthur Laurents pointed it out, no one had seen that the story was really about Madame Rose. The title misled them, and Laurents said that was a concession to the author of the memoir, who was willing to accept the shift of emphasis so long as her name remained in the title. Madame Rose, who exhorts and cajoles and scrimps and battles her way through vaudeville in her heroic determination to make stars out of her daughters, is an unforgettable figure, by turns repellent, admirable, and, finally, full of pathos. For, as her creators also saw, the moment of Madame Rose's greatest triumph is also that of defeat and despair. Neither of her daughters, pushed and prodded into prominence, really wanted fame. She did, and it was something she would never have. Walter Kerr wrote, "There is always a faint chill around those warm and glowing alley doors—and 'mama' gives you the warmth and the chill in every roaring, unforgettable bleat.

"She brings us, too, to the only finale that is possible for this 'fable'— alone in a garish nightmare of neon, stomping out fresh confidence that can't help but break in the middle of a syllable, the king-pin of a world that has vanished beneath her feet. If you don't cry, I'm through with you."

SONDHEIM SPENT the autumn of 1958 working on the lyrics for *Gypsy* and spoke to Laurents at least twice a day for about four months. "Sometimes we talked about trivial matters, and sometimes it was about trying to form and shape the piece. This is apart from any meetings that the three of us would have or the meetings between Jule and me." Laurents said, "I'd read him some dialogue over the phone. We'd discuss it, and then Steve would say, 'Hey, wait, there's a song there.'" Sondheim gave Laurents all the credit for knowing where a song should be placed. "I realized after a long . . . time that it was his playwright's instinct for knowing when a speech should rise, when a speech should fall; when somebody should talk in an elliptical sentence and when they should talk in a complete sentence. He has a true dramatist's talent . . . I like to be able to justify . . . everything I do, because I think by being forced to justify it you discover what might be the danger in it. But there are times when you are reduced to saying, 'I don't know. It just . . . feels right to me.'"

Once again, fortune smiled on Sondheim as lyricist. The journeyman years of writing songs that were never going to be heard had honed his native wit and burnished his verbal facility; he was already coming into his own with *West Side Story;* and with *Gypsy,* his gift for sensing a scene's possibilities in terms of words and music was becoming increasingly acute. During the writing of *Gypsy* Laurents took Sondheim to sessions at the Actors Studio so that he could learn about the actor's perspective. "I thought a song should be like a one-act play, with a beginning, middle, and end. He's, I think, the only lyricist whose songs really arrive someplace. But more than that, in most shows almost anybody can sing any of the songs. His songs are very carefully crafted, and for that particular character. You can't shift them that way. I don't think there's any question he is the greatest lyricist there's ever been."

There is no doubt that Laurents and Sondheim, working in such close rapport, shaped *Gypsy* between them and that Styne was the malleable third man, perfectly prepared to throw out an approach and substitute another if it did not seem appropriate for that particular dramatic moment. They were all uncannily well matched: "One of the reasons I think the whole thing was so great is that we wrote it very fast," Laurents said. Robbins was not consulted at all and did not hear the famous song "Everything's Coming Up Roses" until late in 1958. Laurents and Sondheim went to England to meet with Robbins, who was engaged in tryouts of *West Side Story* in Manchester, and played him the tune. At the end of it Robbins said he did not understand the title. Sondheim said, "And I'm thinking, 'Oh my God, is it too poetic?' Because one of the problems was to come up with a phrase that means, 'things are going to be better than ever,' that isn't flat and yet isn't so poetic that you can't believe that Rose with her street jargon would say it. The point was to find a phrase that sounded as if it had been in the language for years but was, in fact, invented for that show. I was really proud of finding that phrase. And Jerry says, 'I just don't understand that title.' I say, 'Why not, Jerry?' And he says, 'Everything's coming up Rose's *what?*' " Laurents said, "We howl about it to this day."

Once she saw the lyrics Merman changed her view of Sondheim and became most appreciative. But, Laurents said, "She wasn't very much of a person. She was this—figure. She was not very bright. Steve called her the talking dog. And I wrote the stage directions 'louder,' 'softer,' and she would say, 'That's what it says here, so I'm doing it!' "

Ethel Merman was so pleased with the songs that she asked Sondheim and Styne to play them for her friend Cole Porter, who, as it turned out, had only a few years left to live. "So we went for dinner up in his apartment at the Waldorf Astoria Towers, Jule, myself, Merman, and Anita Loos," Sondheim said. "By then he was being carried around by his strong servant piggyback. My memory is that when we sang "Together," the song from *Gypsy* that has a quadruple rhyme, 'wherever I go, I know he goes. / Wherever I go, I know she goes. / No fits, no fights, and no egos, / Amigos'—and when I said, 'amigos,' I heard him go 'Ah!' right in the corner of the room. And it's a very Cole Porter line, because he would use these foreign languages for rhyme, for effect, and he didn't see it coming."

Gypsy moved toward its opening night at the Broadway Theatre on May 21, 1959, but the process was not entirely smooth. David Merrick, who was co-producing the musical with Leland Hayward, had a minor financial stake in the enterprise but was determined to have a major say in the proceedings, according to his biographer, Howard Kissel. He criticized the show so often in front of Robbins that Robbins threatened to stop work if Merrick came to the rehearsals. Laurents did not think Robbins was very interested in the show because it had far fewer opportunities for his talents as a choreographer. For his part, Sondheim had another disagreeable encounter with Robbins. He recalled that Merman said she would accept changes until a week before the opening. "So, we were in Philadelphia, and it was two and a half weeks before opening night, and I wanted a verse for 'Some People' in which she

Gypsy Rose Lee, center, watching rehearsals for *Gypsy* with Jerome Robbins at left, Styne at right, and Sondheim and Laurents in the background, 1958

Rehearsing for *Gypsy:* Robbins at left, Laurents, Styne at the piano, Ethel Merman and Sondheim

Robbins with some of the dancers from *Gypsy*

was telling her father to go to hell. And she wouldn't do it. The reason she wouldn't was because she didn't want, as Ethel Merman, to be telling her father to go to hell. So she used the pretext that the show was 'frozen.'." Merman appealed to Robbins, and Sondheim protested that she should live up to her agreement. He also voiced his private opinion about the reason why she did not want to sing that particular verse. "And Jerry said, in front of everybody, something to the effect that 'if you were half as talented as she is, there might be a point to this,' or 'more professional,' but the point was, he was saying, 'You're not worthy of . . .' And he was furious because he knew I was right, and he didn't want to face her. I was just stunned."

LAURENTS'S OUTLINE for the plot of *Gypsy* began at the end. He knew a moment would have to come when Gypsy Rose Lee would do her famous striptease, and that would presumably be the musical's high point. But since the story was really about her mother, he had to bring the focus back to Madame Rose and give her the moment when she would realize that her need for fame was a chimera that had destroyed her life. This had to become the final pivot of the play, but exactly how it was to be done had not been decided. Robbins suggested a nightmare ballet, one that would dramatize Rose's emotional crisis in terms of choreographed images from her past. The idea seemed promising, but after about a week of work Robbins decided it could not be done. It was going to have to become a song, and on it the fate of *Gypsy* would rest.

Sondheim said that the night "Rose's Turn" was written "comprised every Hollywood fantasy I'd ever had. We were rehearsing at the top of a decrepit theatre called the New Amsterdam. There was a small auditorium at the top of what had been a legitimate theatre, where in fact Ziegfeld had held his 'midnight frolics,' which were not as salacious as that sounds. Jule Styne was going around with our leading lady Sandra Church [who played Gypsy]. They had a date after rehearsal so Jerry said to me, 'Why don't you stay and we'll talk about the number?' I decided that what we should do is take all the songs of the show that were connected with . . . Madame Rose, and mash them up, just the way Jerry was going to do with movement . . .

"It was one of those things you dream of when you're a kid. You write a song with the star, only it was Jerry Robbins as the star. He started moving, performing a strip, sashaying back and forth on the stage, and I started to ad lib at the piano with the tunes that were already written . . ."

Jack Klugman, who played Herbie, Madame Rose's faithful suitor, recalled the moment, three weeks into rehearsal, when Sondheim and Styne arrived very late to announce they had just finished "Rose's Turn." The rehearsal stopped immediately. Styne sat down at the piano. Sondheim began to sing "with such feeling and such awareness of what it was about that I just fell apart and bawled like a baby. It was so brilliant. I will never forget that moment." There is a point in the song when Madame Rose, feeling increasingly bereft, has a psychological block on the word "mother." "When Steve did 'M-m-momma, M-m-momma,' and couldn't get it out, Ethel and I just burst into tears." Laurents said that Merman accepted everything about that scene except the line "I did it for me," which was a late addition. She had to be persuaded that, in a sense, that realization was the climax of the whole evening.

The evolution of "Rose's Turn" is a demonstration of the hidden turns and false starts that can lay in wait for any work involving people with conflicting opinions. Sondheim insisted that after Madame Rose ends her song, the audience not be allowed to applaud. He said, "A woman having a nervous breakdown should not get applause from the audience. To have a mad scene and then have a bow violated everything I thought I had learned from Oscar Hammerstein, who taught me to be true to character and . . . the situation. So I forced Jule not to put an ending on it, but to have it fade out with high scratchy violin sounds with those last chords when she's screaming—not singing, but screaming—'For me, for me, for me!' And there would be this chilling . . . moment in the theatre and then, as Arthur wrote it, the daughter would come out of the wings applauding her, and they would go on."

The scene was being played in this manner when they reached Philadelphia and Hammerstein came to see the performance. Sondheim and Laurents went "tremblingly" out for a drink with him afterwards to get his verdict. There were three problems, Hammerstein said. The first was that the kitchen doorknob kept falling off. A wave of relief went over Sondheim. As usual, his quick mind jumped several steps ahead: he concluded that the other two points would be equally trifling and that they had a hit. But then Hammerstein queried the placement of the song "You'll Never Get Away from Me." He thought that instead of being sung in the middle of a scene, it should go at the end. His third point was, "And you must give Ethel Merman an ending on 'Rose's Turn.'" Sondheim said, "I started to bristle, and I said, 'Why?' And he said, 'Because the audience is so anxious to applaud her that they are not listening to the scene that follows. Since the scene that follows is what the entire play is about, if you want them to listen, you must let them release themselves . . . I know it's dishonest, but *please*, fellows, put a big ending on that number if you want the rest of the play to play. Or bring the curtain down there.'" The ending was duly rewritten to allow for applause—Hammerstein had been right again.

The story of "Rose's Turn" was not yet ended. The first London production, fourteen years later (in 1973), was directed by Arthur Laurents, with Angela Lansbury playing Madame Rose. Once more, the famous moment received a small but pivotal revision. After the audience had finished applauding "Rose's Turn" and the house had grown still, Madame Rose should have continued with the scene. Instead, she remained where she had been standing and continued to bow. Laurents said, "It's very risky for an actress to keep bowing when there's no applause. You risk [having] the audience think that she's trying to milk [the scene]. But she did it absolutely brilliantly, and the audience realized she was as mad as a hatter when she was doing those bows." Not only had they gotten the applause they wanted, they had arrived at the chilling moment Sondheim knew was essential, but that the previous production had never achieved. Laurents said, "The principle is, if you think hard enough, there is a way to have your cake and eat it, too." Besides being a personal triumph for Sondheim, who imagined the number, assembled the music, and wrote the words, "Rose's Turn" was a pivotal moment in his development as a dramatist. He had found a way to show a human being at a moment of crisis who refuses to accept a realization that, at the same time, she cannot prevent from erupting to the surface, a moment that is revelatory and personally devastating. Someone caught in a vice of powerfully opposed feelings: this would become almost a blueprint for the quintessential Sondheim hero or heroine. The playwright John Guare said, "There is a moment when you realize the ground has gone out from under you. That's what Steve understands."

BECAUSE HE HAD FELT so frustrated at not being allowed to write music for *Gypsy*, Sondheim asked for a larger percentage for the lyrics alone than was usually given for both music and lyrics. That was better than two percent: "My guess is that I had two and a quarter, going to two and a half once the show made a profit. I don't remember what shows grossed in those days, but let's say it was $100,000. That amounts to $2,500 a week, or $2,250. That was a lot of money for those days, when theatre tickets cost four dollars and ninety cents," he said. *Gypsy* ran for a year and a half on Broadway and made a profit. That is not as long as Merrick thought it should have done; once the musical opened to glowing notices he became one of its most fervent admirers. It then sold profitably to the movies, and the film appeared four years later, with Rosalind Russell in the leading role. She played Madame Rose as a cross between a hockey mistress and a society matron and roared out "Rose's Turn" as if it were a moment of ramrod triumph. "We can say she wore black-and-white pumps and that's about it," Arthur Laurents said. Even though the film was a failure, Sondheim had proved he could make money, which did not prevent Herbert Sondheim from clinging to his belief that his son would never succeed as an artist. Finally the moment came when, as they shared a taxi, his father casually asked him how much money his son had earned the previous year. Sondheim told him, and there was "dead silence," he said.

For all his considerable artistic and financial success, Herbert Sondheim had never earned enough money to please himself, either, his son thought. As the years went by, his position became precarious. The ladylike look was going out of style, but he was too old, or too tired, to change his designs accordingly. He was loyal to his workers and kept them employed too long, his son said. "He still had his old cutter in the back room, who was now seventy-five or eighty years old and failing, and my father just couldn't let people like that go. Out of the kindness of his heart. I firmly believe that my father was one of the very few people in that cutthroat world whom everybody liked. Genuinely nice.

"That eventually contributed to his financial failure. My stepmother came down one morning saying, 'We've got to get your father to retire. He's literally screaming in his sleep.' " It transpired that the company was heavily

Herbert Sondheim on vacation at the Boca Raton Club with his old friends Milton B. ("Mickey") Eulau, center, and Lloyd Weill, right

in debt. Together, Sondheim and his stepmother persuaded Herbert to close the business. Stephen paid off his debts—about $100,000—"for Alicia's sake," he said. Herbert Sondheim, Inc., closed its doors in 1964, and Herbert Sondheim became an executive vice-president for Samuel Robert, maker of leather apparel, in the spring of 1965. He died just over a year later, aged seventy-one. Sondheim, who believed the cause was throat cancer, recalled visiting him in a Stamford hospital, the last time he saw his father. "He said two characteristic things. I remember that one was, 'It's going to be all right.' The second thing is, I have a slightly distorted memory but this is more or less right. He brought up the subject of his best friend, Lloyd Weill," whose company had never achieved the fame or stature of his own. "Then he said something like, 'But Lloyd Weill made a million dollars.' "

THEN THERE WAS OCKIE, who had been so generous of his time, so encouraging, and had gone to such pains to steer his surrogate son along the path he should take. *Gypsy* was the last performance of one of Stevie's works that Ockie would see—he did not live to see Sondheim's music performed on Broadway in *A Funny Thing Happened on the Way to the Forum*. When Sondheim celebrated his sixty-fifth birthday, Hammerstein's oldest son, William, gave him a pair of handsome black velvet slippers that had belonged to his father, with the monogram of O on one foot and H on the other. He was wearing them one day. It was interesting, a visitor said, that he and Hammerstein both wore the same size shoes. Sondheim said, "Oh, we don't. My foot isn't quite big enough . . . I have smallish feet, size nine. These are probably size ten." The shoes seemed to fit well enough, it was suggested. Sondheim said, "Not really. No metaphor there."

That same year, 1995, Sondheim spoke on a television spectacular, *Some Enchanted Evening*, in honor of the centenary of Hammerstein's birth. Sondheim said that Hammerstein had affected his life "in many profound ways, emotionally and professionally. He was a great teacher. He once had a line in *The King and I* that said, 'By your pupils you'll be taught.' Shortly before he died [in 1960], and we, the family and those close to him knew he was dying, he and Dorothy had a lunch, and we all gathered at the house.

"Oscar had two piles of formally posed photographs . . . and invited us to choose one. And I felt very peculiar, because he was a surrogate father to me, but I wanted to have one. And I asked him to sign it. And of course, because our relationship had been so close, he looked baffled as to how to sign it. And everybody else went into the dining room and he stood there trying to think, and suddenly he got a smile on his face like the cat that ate the canary. And he scribbled something on the corner of the picture, and then looked at me rather smugly and went into the dining room. And I read it, and it said—" here his voice broke, and there was a long pause—" 'For Stevie, my Friend and Teacher.' "

CHAPTER 8

Comedy Tonight

T HE LADY LIVING underneath his back apartment at 11 East Eighteenth Street used to complain. She claimed there was a city ordinance allowing neighbors to summon the police if assaulted by undue noise after ten at night. "No one ever did, in fact, call the police," he said, "but she would pound on the ceiling with a broom. At first I was annoyed, but then I thought, Geez, I can't blame her. If I were trying to go to sleep and somebody upstairs were playing the same phrase over and over again . . . It isn't like Rubinstein practicing Chopin. So I couldn't blame her."

This happened at about the time of *West Side Story.* Since he was earning money, he decided to look for a duplex apartment (in those days his top price was $400 a month) and found one on Fiftieth Street between Second and Third Avenues. He made a deal with the landlord then and there and they shook hands. "I had to go to Boston for the weekend with Arthur, to attend *West Side Story,* which had been on the road and was coming back to Broadway. And when I got back after the weekend the landlord had rented the apartment to somebody else." That was a blessing in disguise eventually. But it put him in such a bad mood that he talked to the business manager he had acquired by this time, who advised him to buy a house. Shortly after that, he attended a Democratic rally downtown and bumped into a friend in the crowd, the singer Anita Ellis. She had just seen a wonderful house with an upstairs apartment which she and her fiancé wanted to rent, and the house was for sale. Sondheim got the address in a hurry and managed to view the house before it appeared in the Sunday papers.

It turned out to be located in the Turtle Bay area of Manhattan, originally the site of nineteenth-century tenements that had become, by the twentieth century, fashionable row houses backing onto a communal garden full of trees and birds. It is a neighborhood concept still common in London but very rare in New York—Sondheim believed there were only three such areas left. The house Sondheim wanted had once been inhabited by the editor Maxwell Perkins. He subsequently realized he had been taken there for tea a few years earlier by his mother, when it was being lived in by her friends the broadcaster Charles Collingwood and his wife, the actress Louise Allbritton.

As soon as he saw the five-storey house he wanted it, even if he could only just afford it. The price was $115,000, which was deemed reasonable for that area; his father co-signed a bank loan, and the fact that his friends were on hand as instant tenants of the upstairs apartment brightened the picture considerably. (They lived above him for the next twelve years, and the rent paid his taxes.) In those days the house had front doors side by side off the street level. Access to the upper apartment, comprising three floors, was up two flights; Sondheim took the lower two floors. He said, "When I bought the house in 1960 it was on the grounds that *Gypsy* had just been sold to the movies and I was getting a lump sum. In fact, just before I signed the papers on the house the *Gypsy* deal fell through and I thought that not only would I not get the house but I would go to jail. But then *Gypsy* sold to someone else and I made enough money, over a period of a year and a half, to repay the loan to the bank."

There was a bedroom, studio, and bath upstairs and enough room on the ground floor for a kitchen and a spacious living room. The apartment was soon filled with records on shelves and the floor. By 1960 Sondheim had amassed a collection of some twenty-five hundred: operas, original cast albums, and works by Bartók, Stravinsky, Copland, and Ravel. He was trying to sort through and catalogue them; "If I don't," he told an interviewer, "I'll have to move out; they seem to increase and multiply each time I turn my back." He was adding to his collection of games and using them as decorative objects. "He showed me assorted board games, handsomely framed; antique ninepins; an elaborate contraption designed to make it easy for a princess royal to learn music; various fantasies of wood with carved figures ready to go into action of one sort or another. Spooky and surrealistic-looking these games," the writer Tom Donnelly recalled. "They put me in mind of the icily whimsical drawings of Edward Gorey. 'Ah yes!' said Sondheim. 'That's because these are mostly Victorian games and his drawings have Victorian settings.' "

There were few books on the shelves, and those in evidence were for reference. Sondheim had done his required reading in college, but since then, Arthur Laurents used to quip, he only read book reviews. He said, "I get hung up on style. Four sentences, and if I don't like the style I get impatient." He continued, "But the major thing is I am a slow reader, and nobody believes it. A quick mind and a slow reader, and I can't take the time. If you knew how much time it takes me to read the *New York Times* . . ."

There was, of course, his GI piano, which he eventually gave away after his friend Burt Shevelove moved to London in the early 1960s and left him with a Steinway spinet that looked more beautiful than it sounded. Eventually he gave that one to Alicia and his father. He also acquired an even more desirable instrument, a Baldwin grand that Leonard Bernstein, who had a promotional deal to play exclusively on Baldwin pianos, had used only a few times for his Young People's concerts. Bernstein wanted a larger model and was prepared to sell this one to Sondheim for the absurdly small price of $5,400, so Sondheim bought it and kept it ever after. (It went through a flood some years ago which damaged the sounding board, and had to be disassembled and repaired.) He also had another, a studio piano, which he eventually moved to an upper floor and kept in a semi-soundproof room.

That was in deference to his next-door neighbor Katharine Hepburn, who had not hesitated to make her views known once she discovered his fondness for a little night music. His Baldwin faced steps leading to a glass garden door and the story is that one night she was banging on the glass door in her nightgown and bare feet. She was away so much that Sondheim said he had lived there for ten years before he actually met her. The day came when he was trying to persuade a wonderful houseman and cook, Louis Vargas, a sort of South American version of Jeeves, who had worked for Jerome Robbins and Mike Nichols, to work for him. Sondheim said, "He came down and took one look—I was still living in the bottom two floors—and I could tell he was not impressed. And, you know, I tried to drop every name I could think of, and it wasn't until I pointed out who lived next door that he virtually said, 'I'll take the job.' The day he came to work he heard her voice out in the garden, and went out and was feather-dusting the flowers. They struck up a conversation . . . and became fast friends within ten minutes. She would bring him fruits and vegetables from the country and he would give her recipes."

Sondheim's pattern of working late at night, one he had formed while studying for exams at Williams, became unvarying. "My concentrative powers would start in midday and get quite intense by the early evening. I'd quite often go out to a diner or restaurant and work through dinner." He never minded if there was music in the background. He had started drinking bourbon in school and, unlike some authors, found that alcohol seemed to stimulate his mental processes rather than drown them. Jonathan Tunick, who would become his orchestrator, recalled their first get-acquainted dinner around the corner from Sondheim's house in an Italian restaurant on Second Avenue. "I remember he drank me under the table. I mean, he would've if he could've, but I stopped after three . . . I matched him Scotch for Scotch and we hadn't ordered yet. When the third one came, I said, 'I'd better stop here or else I'm going to be on the floor.' He said, 'I understand, but I'm going to go on and have another one because I *love* to drink.' As a result of my stopping at three, I think he's had it stuck in his mind ever since that I don't drink. Or maybe he's teasing me." After dinner, Sondheim would go back to the house and continue working. Since he was not interested in cooking, he rarely dined at home until Louis came into his life—he would occasionally broil a steak—and ate almost anything. In those days he smoked one or two packs of filter cigarettes a day. He still tended to stutter when his thoughts went too fast but never bit his nails, although he tried, just to see what it was like. In fact, because he was playing the piano he always made sure his nails were clipped short. "There's nothing more horrifying than having a fingernail hit a key. Oy!"

He still tended to be nonchalant about his personal appearance. When the writer Patricia Bosworth interviewed him she found him wearing faded khakis, "his hair hanging lankly across his pale forehead," looking more like a graduate student than a Broadway personality. He had become an ardent adherent of the puzzle contests posed by Ximenes in the London paper the *Observer* and used to do the *Listener* puzzle contests with Burt Shevelove.

Burt Shevelove's exquisite taste for clothes, furniture, books, and objets d'art was renowned. Perhaps his most famous apartment was just off the Marble Arch in Bayswater, comprising the top floor of a fastidiously detailed building, with a beautiful entrance hall, a huge living room and study, and two and a half baths. He had a collector's library of books along one entire wall, a Bechstein grand, china, glass, paintings, all of his possessions set against a background of black and beige: "Burt would have considered black and white too loud," his niece Judy Levin said. Ned Sherrin, the British man of the theatre, remembered Shevelove's amazing poster collection of dwarfs, Siamese twins, and hunchbacks, all life-size. Before he moved to London he had an apartment on Ninth Street in Manhattan that, even though it was just a single floor in a brownstone, was "one of the eight wonders of the world," Sondheim said.

Everyone loved his style, his humor, his taste, and his unique gift for friendship. Sondheim said, "He had a way of becoming part of your life. He lingers in everybody's memory. He was an enchanting raconteur. He was *wonderful* with children, although he never married; he had numerous godchildren, and the line in *Company* about 'seven times a godfather' is about Burt. He was extremely literary, extremely kind and generous, avuncular in the best sense." Sherrin remembered his lavish spending habits ("His money came in great jumps and then went away again") and his punctiliousness. Once Shevelove and Sondheim were served artichokes in a restaurant. Sherrin continued, "Burt, being very precise, had laid out every leaf. Stephen was trying to fight through to the center of the artichoke with a huge mess of leaves all over the table. And that was the sort of difference between them: the attraction of opposites, I suppose. Burt would have put every leaf beautifully around the plate, whereas Stephen would have turned it into a cabbage." There was also, so it is said, the time when, in another display of compulsive tidiness, Shevelove was passed a glass-framed game that was being handed around at a party. In his eagerness to show off the game, Shevelove turned it on end and neatly demolished the evening's supply of cocaine.

Before serving as an ambulance driver in the war, Shevelove had been at Yale as head of the Dramat, the student dramatic society, and had put on a performance of Aristophanes' *The Frogs* in the Yale swimming pool. After the war he proceeded to write more shows; he wrote the lyrics and some of the sketches, and directed as well, the successful revue *Small Wonder,* which introduced such future stars as the actor Tom Ewell and the dancer and choreographer Gower Champion. Then Shevelove wrote the book and lyrics for a show called *A Month of Sundays,* which starred Nancy Walker and Richard Kiley and opened in Philadelphia. Sondheim said, "I went down to see it and it was, in fact, a disaster, mostly because of the set by Jo Mielziner, which confined the action, but Burt was the director, so he was responsible for that." It was during the course of a similar fiasco, in which his help had been sought for a floundering play, that Shevelove, when asked how the show was coming, uttered the immortal words: "Well, I'm polishing a little here and polishing a little there. The trouble is, the more you polish shit, the more it looks like shit."

Shevelove had done a musical at Yale based on a play by Plautus, *Miles Gloriosus,* or *The Braggart Warrior,* and had always wanted to base a musical on the work of Plautus. Sondheim said, "Plautus was the first person to domesticize comedy. All comedy, Aristophanic, for instance, was about gods and goddesses. Nobody had ever written about husbands and wives, daughters and maids. Plautus is responsible for the situation comedy. In fact, when we offered *Forum* to Phil Silvers, he said, 'This is Sergeant Bilko. I've been doing this all my life.' Plautus wrote about domineering wives and braggart warriors and lecherous old men. At any rate, Burt said [to me], 'Here are some books, read these." So he read Plautus in translation and soon shared Shevelove's enthusiasm for making several of the short plays into a musical. So did Larry Gelbart, who became its co-author. They all began work in 1958, right after *West Side Story.* After finishing work on *Gypsy,* Sondheim went back to work on *A Funny Thing Happened on the Way to the Forum* and continued to work on it intermittently until the beginning of 1962.

"The problem was, we went to numbers of producers and directors. Jerry Robbins kept saying yes, then no, and then yes, and then no. We went to Joshua Logan, who wanted more naked boys and things like that. I offered it to Hal [Prince], and Hal said, 'Listen, kid, you know me. I hate farce.' Hal had two hates, which were my two favorite things, farce and melodrama. David Merrick agreed to produce. Then we were trying to get Jerry Robbins again. And Jerry said, 'Okay, I'll tell you what. I'll do it, but I will not do it with David Merrick. You have to get it away from him. I'll do it with Hal Prince.' So I went to Hal and said, 'If Jerry does the show, would you do it?' and he said, 'Sure.' So I went to David Merrick and I told a lie. Something I will go to my grave feeling guilty about. I said we were withdrawing the show for a while. We could give him back any advance we had taken—I think it was a thousand dollars. But the point is, I lied. Because the next day, I said to Hal, 'Okay, I got it away from David,' and I'm surprised David was ever nice to me again.

"And then of course Jerry, being the usual Jerry . . . They were trying to pin him to a date, Hal and Bobby Griffith, and he was off in Greece. They didn't hear from him, and the dates were getting closer and they had to put in bids for scenery. The show has to be designed and you have to put in bids for scenery way in advance." So Prince sent Ruth Mitchell, then Robbins's favorite stage manager, to Greece to track him down. "I can't remember exactly what happened, but when she came back it looked like he was going to do it. And then a letter arrived in the mail. As best I can remember, the letter was saying, 'I'm sorry, I just can't do it.' It was torn in four or eight pieces, and then he'd put it in an envelope. That was to show how tortured he was for having let everybody down."

Sondheim never did learn why Robbins was unwilling to direct *Forum,* ascribing it to his general inability to make decisions. He had caused them endless problems, but it is instructive to note that the world of musical theatre is so small that no one can afford to nurse a grudge. A few celebrated feuds to the contrary, partings are invariably gentlemanly, since everyone involved realizes that six months down the road, it may be in their mutual interest to be working on some other project. In fact, Robbins's help on *Forum* would be called upon once more, and he would come to their aid at last, with spectacular results. For the moment, however, "there we were without a director, and Hal decided to ask George Abbott," then aged seventy-five, with a lifetime's experience of directing hit musicals such as *Call Me Madam, Wonderful Town, The Pajama Game, Damn Yankees,* and *Fiorello!* Sondheim said, "Well, everybody in the theatre thinks Abbott is terrific. I don't. What he was great at was running a ship, but I found him a completely humorless person. Burt and Larry had to explain jokes to him. The best joke in *Forum* we had to act out for him in his office. But, you know, can you argue with statistics? He made his reputation directing some of the most successful farces and musicals in history." Personally, he liked Abbott very much. "He was a very reserved man, very commanding. He was always very nice to me. I just didn't think he had any talent."

Burt Shevelove, Sondheim, and Larry Gelbart at opening night of *A Funny Thing Happened on the Way to the Forum,* 1962

Abbott's first reaction was that *Forum* was too long: the obvious truth, since it would have run for about four hours as originally written, and they needed two and a half. Larry Gelbart wrote, "We were far too busy trying to get the piece right to take any time out to think about what some lucky marquee would one day read if we ever actually completed a final draft. There were to be ten drafts in all before we arrived at the last, merciful version of the book and score . . . It's not that we kept getting it wrong all the time. It was more a matter of never getting it right all at the same time." To satisfy Abbott, Shevelove and Gelbart cut with a ruthless hand. Then Milton Berle, who had agreed to play the leading role of Pseudolus, a conniving slave, claimed with some justice that some of his best scenes had been lost, and bowed out. Zero Mostel was the next choice. "I played the score for Zero," Sondheim said. "He gave out stories years later that he hadn't wanted to do it, but it wasn't true at all. He needed the work very badly and took it like *that*," he said, snapping his fingers.

Sondheim's score, which would be his first for a Broadway production, was subjected to the same agonizing review. Anthony Tommasini wrote, "For all the talk of *Forum* harking back to the days of good clean farce, theatrically it is an experimental work. It completely subverts the heritage of what is called the book show, handed down by Rodgers and Hammerstein, where the songs emerge from the plot. In *Forum* the songs purposely interrupt the farcical plot, giving the audience a needed break from the madcap hysterics." That, Sondheim said, was because he had yielded to Shevelove's argument that this particular musical needed the kind of songs that could be removed without making the slightest difference. Just the same, getting the right counterpoint and contrast took endless work and, he said later, he discarded more songs from the score than he ever had to do again.

Mostel had been hired, David Burns was to play Senex, a citizen of Rome, and Mostel's good friend Jack Gilford was cast as Hysterium, another slave. The musical was about to go into production when Sondheim became uneasy, typically describing that as a feeling in the pit of his stomach. "I thought maybe it was just the usual writer's neurosis, you know, 'Everything I write is terrible, everything everybody else writes is wonderful.' " So he asked a friend, the playwright James Goldman, to review the script and score. Goldman said that both were first-rate, but that Sondheim was right to feel uneasy because the whole tone of his own contribution was at odds with the book. Goldman said, "The book is written on a kind of low-comedy vaudeville level with elegant language, and you have written a witty score, a salon score." Sondheim saw the logic of that, and although it was far too late to change direction in the case of *Forum,* he was taught a valuable lesson, the golden rule of collaboration: "Make sure you and your collaborators are writing the same show."

This in no way affected his admiration for the work of Shevelove and Gelbart. He said, "I think that *Forum* is the best farce ever written . . . *Forum* is much more elegant than anything Feydeau ever wrote and much, much more tightly plotted. There's not a wasted moment . . . and the . . . test of it is that the play is just as funny when performed by a group of high-school students as it is when performed on Broadway. It is never *not* funny . . . It is based on situations so solid that you cannot *not* laugh."

He was so convinced of the work's superior merits that when out-of-town tryouts began in New Haven early in April 1962, he was completely baffled when the audience did not think it was funny.

Gelbart recalled, "The show didn't work because by the time we opened, we had . . . taken out a lot of complications in the plot, the subplot, the sub-subplot, as George Abbott suggested. But upon seeing it we realized we had done . . . a great deal of damage because a lot of fun was in the organized confusion. So we put it all back." People began to mutter what Sondheim suspected, that the book and score did not mix. Sondheim said, "I often say, if a play were going down, I would not be the one to rescue it. I think I'm a panicker." But Shevelove was no good in that crisis, either. "He got spiky and unpleasant and started blaming me. The numbers weren't working, which they weren't. But the whole show wasn't working. The only reason *Forum* came into town was because Hal, as producer, refused to close the show. I think any other producer would have closed it." Even Abbott, who was famous for his ability to rescue plays, was at a loss, and the only funny thing Sondheim ever heard him say was "when he said, 'I dunno. You had better call in George Abbott.' "

One of the bones of contention as the show was being rehearsed was its opening number. Sondheim's original composition, called "Invocation," was rejected by Abbott, who said it was not memorable enough, not "hummable." So Sondheim wrote something polite and charming called "Love Is in the Air," and audiences were not amused. When the show arrived in Washington on April 11 it was panned by Richard Coe of the Washington *Post,* who appeared to think that the kindest thing one could do for it was close it before it reached New York. One performance played before an audience of about fifty people.

Just after *West Side Story* opened in Washington, Sondheim recalled, he made a trip out to the airport with Robbins, en route to New York. During it, he made a lighthearted comment about what a shame it was that he had not had the fun of "sitting up until three o'clock in the morning in a smoke-filled

Brian Davies and Preshy Marker are a pair of dizzily star-crossed lovers and Zero Mostel the slave who is fighting for his freedom in *A Funny Thing Happened on the Way to the Forum.* Below, Mostel with Pat Fox

room rewriting the second act." Robbins looked at him in horror. "Take that back, don't ever say that out loud. Until you've been through it, you don't know what it's like." Now he was in just such a situation, and he had no idea what to do. As the New York opening crept closer, Sondheim, in desperation, suggested that Robbins be contacted. Prince was hesitant, because he knew that this could cause personal problems for his star. Robbins had acted as a "friendly witness" before the House Committee on Un-American Activities and one of those whom he had identified as a Communist was Jack Gilford's wife, Madeline. Although Mostel, who himself had suffered from the witch hunting of the McCarthy years, was indignant on Gilford's behalf, as Sondheim remembered it, his response was, "I don't have to have lunch with him." Gilford was also consulted and agreed to allow Robbins to be called.

Once the choreographer appeared, he quickly identified the problem. According to Sondheim, he said, "The opening number is killing the show. You open with a charming number and the audience does not know what they're in for, that it's a real farce. You've got to write an opening number that says baggy pants." Sondheim felt his face reddening. He said, "I did write that. I wrote a number that said, 'Forget war, forget woe, you're in for an evening of silliness.' And it had a nice twist at the end. It said, 'When you've laughed yourself silly and had a really good time, go home and resume war, and resume woe.'" This was "Invocation," the song Abbott had disliked because he could not hum it. Robbins agreed that it struck exactly the right tone. However, in the interests of diplomacy he suggested that Sondheim rework the idea in a slightly different form. "So I wrote 'Comedy Tonight,' which is roughly the same song in a new guise." Robbins took the idea and, in the course of a week, created an opening number that those who remember it agree is one of the classics of the American stage. Unfortunately, years later no one, including Robbins, could remember exactly how it went, and the production was never filmed, so Robbins's contribution lives on only as a confused impression of sight gags making use of prop arms and legs and mechanical stage effects.

Sondheim said, "And Jerry's reaction was, 'I could do this so much better if I had more time.'" This was why Robbins's reputation was so deserved. "I would work with him tomorrow even if he put me through hell, just because the result is so extraordinary."

Through all of the turmoil Mostel had behaved with exemplary fortitude, bringing his disciplined sensibility to the constantly changing demands of the script, alternating moments of broad slapstick humor with subtlety and nuance, and responding to Abbott's suggestions with impeccable concentration. By the time they arrived at the New York previews in the Alvin Theatre, however—the show was to open on May 8—Mostel was tense and under stress. Sondheim said, "We got to the afternoon of the first preview with our opening number, the one we hoped would change the show. And we were rehearsing and Zero kept screwing up on the lines." So once when Robbins stopped to consult with Tony Walton, the set designer, Sondheim went down to the footlights—"I never, never give an actor a critical note in front of other people"—to correct one of Mostel's lines. "Right, right, right," Mostel said impatiently. They began again, and again Robbins stopped. Mostel was still making mistakes. "And I said, 'Please, I know you've got a lot on your mind, but it's the plural, not the singular.' 'Yeah, yeah.' The third time, Jerry stops again—'Zero, it's the plural'—and Mostel says in a booming voice that fills the entire theatre and makes everybody start and turn around, he says, 'Well, maybe if you'd write me a funny line, you cocksucker!' In front of every-body." There was a silence that lasted perhaps four seconds. "And in the back of the house, Mr. Abbott went, 'All right, from the top please,'" and clapped his hands. "That's why he was great, because he . . . defused the tension like *that*." He snapped his fingers. "There was no chance for me to cry, no chance for me to run out hurt. George said, 'Back to business. Ignore it!' That comes from experience, and that's one of the things Hal has learned. If you want to fight, you do it *after* rehearsal. But you don't do it there. Very important."

Sondheim did not, however, follow Mostel into his dressing room, partly because he did not know what to say and partly because he thought it was likely to happen again. The success of the show hung on an opening number that had not been tested, and Sondheim believed he was being made the scapegoat for the anger Mostel really wanted to direct against Robbins. "And that night the show was a hit. It turned from black to white instantaneously. The audience loved the opening number so much. It's Oscar's old thing. He used to say, in essence, that if the opening is right you can read them the tele-phone book for forty-five minutes and they'll still enjoy the show. You couldn't have *not* enjoyed the show. The problem with *Forum* is that the first forty minutes prepare you for an hour and a half of screamingly funny farce. But it's all exposition. That's why there are so many songs in the beginning, because we're trying to sugar-coat the pill of saying, 'Now she thinks that he's done that. He wants this, but she wants him to do that. Meanwhile, this one is . . . And she's off there . . . And the Procurer thinks that. Now watch all the trains collide.' So if the opening number doesn't make the audience enjoy it, they just get bored."

Musically speaking, Sondheim's score has been described in measured terms, as "genial and felicitous," the work of a composer whose most distinc-tive contribution was yet to come. That it was the work of a polished composer/lyricist there was no doubt; the songs were impeccably constructed, with an absolute sureness of touch. What took them out of the ordinary was Sondheim's stylish humor. "Comedy Tonight" immediately sets the tone of the musical, with its sly juxtapositions—"Something appealing, / Something appalling," and "Something convulsive, / Something repulsive," and "Something aesthetic, / Something frenetic."—and its confident prediction of inconsequential chaos: "Nothing with gods, / Nothing with fate. / Weighty affairs will just have to wait." Sondheim gives credit to Robbins, but he deserves equal credit for the freshness and inventiveness of his own work, not to mention his ability to rise to the challenge at three in the morning. Then there is "I'm Calm," Hysterium's desperate attempt to hypnotize himself out of an attack of panic. There is the scatterbrained affability of the beautiful virgin Philia: "I'm lovely, / All I am is lovely, / Lovely is the one thing I can do." There is the song of the hen-pecked husband, Senex, who for one hopeful moment believes he will be getting Philia as a maid: "Tidily collecting bits of paper 'n' strings, / Appealing in her apron strings, / Beguiling in her blouse!" Only "There's Something About a War," to have been sung by Miles Gloriosus (it was cut before rehearsal), veers into satire:

> The rain may rust your armor,
> Your straps may be too tight,
> But decapitate a farmer
> And your heart feels light!

But for the most part *A Funny Thing Happened on the Way to the Forum* shows Sondheim at his most playful, poking fun at "tumblers, grumblers, fumblers" and "bumblers," "goodness and badness, / Man in his madness," bringing his quicksilver wit to a plot that, as one reviewer wrote, makes "virtue implausible, guilt impossible, and justice impractical."

New York reviewers were almost unanimous in their praise for the pace, wit, style, and farcical inventiveness of the work: "The affair is more than funny—it is highly hilarious fare for anyone with a taste for old-fashioned lowdown comedy," *Newsweek* declared. When the show opened in London a year later, with the comedian Frankie Howerd taking over the role of Pseudolus, Don Chapman wrote, "If only every adult pantomime were of such high pedigree, so beautifully contrived, so coherent in plot and production, so delightfully acted, so uproariously funny and so consistently entertaining from start to finish." In New York, Mostel received a chorus of praise: "a plastic-faced, rolling-eyed, Falstaff-like character," said Howard Taubman in the *New York Times*. Mostel "is, really, a whole road company all by himself,"

Walter Kerr wrote in the *Herald Tribune*. *Forum* went on to have a long string of successes, first as a movie, with Mostel, and with Phil Silvers (who had originally rejected the role of Pseudolus) playing Lycus; and then in numerous revivals, including a very successful one in New York in the spring of 1996 that starred Nathan Lane.

As for Sondheim's score, the Washington critic Jay Carmody called it "impish and mocking." Walter Kerr, while describing it as uneven, thought it was a success on the whole. Others were unenthusiastic, and the first really positive reviews came after the London opening in 1963. Despite his original disappointment, "at least I was going to earn some money," Sondheim said.

Then the Tony Awards came around. *West Side Story* had received several nominations, including one for best musical, which would have given Sondheim, as lyricist, an award, had it won in that category. It did not win. Only Oliver Smith, as scene designer, and Jerome Robbins, as choreographer, won awards. Two years later, in 1960, *Gypsy* received eight nominations, but it was competing against *Fiorello!* and *The Sound of Music* and lost in every category. *A Funny Thing Happened on the Way to the Forum* was the first Sondheim show to win in the category of best musical. But by the time this award was made in 1963, the categories had changed so that book and score were separate contests. George Abbott won in his category of best director. Zero Mostel won as best actor in a musical. David Burns won as best supporting actor. Shevelove and Gelbart took the top award for their book. Music and lyrics were not even nominated.

At the award ceremonies, Hal Prince, who had won as best producer, thanked George Abbott, Burt Shevelove, and Larry Gelbart. Shevelove thanked Gelbart. Gelbart thanked Shevelove. "They both thanked Mr. Abbott and Hal Prince, and nobody mentioned me on the program at all," Sondheim said. "As far as they were all concerned, my friends, my colleagues, I didn't exist. That's what really hurt. It hurt my friendship with Burt for about six months. Because the next day I called him on it, and he screamed at me over the phone. He said, 'Well, you were the problem out of town anyway,' or something like that. It was very unpleasant. Hal was the only one— Hal called me next day and apologized. He said, 'I'm sorry, kid. I should have mentioned you and I didn't.' " Flora Roberts, his agent, said, "Steve was so unhappy he wanted to kill himself." There was, however, an important consolation. Shortly after *Forum* opened, Sondheim received a letter from Frank Loesser making a special point of saying just how good he thought the score had been. Loesser wrote, "Sometimes even a composer's working partners, to say nothing of the critics, fail to dig every level and facet of what he is doing. But *I* know, and I wanted you to know I know." Sondheim was, after all, only thirty-two, and all three of his Broadway shows had been great successes. Shortly before he died, and before *Forum* opened, Oscar Hammerstein had run into Burt Shevelove and they started discussing Sondheim's future. "You know," said Hammerstein to Shevelove, "Steve won't really be a member of the working theatre until he has a flop."

CHAPTER 9

Anyone Can Whistle

B EING A LYRICIST HIMSELF, Oscar Hammerstein was aware
of the fate of most in his profession. Otto Harbach, his own mentor,
for instance, who had been responsible for a long sequence of musical hits,
had remained completely unknown. The field was "filled with hacks and gag
men who extended the tradition of ignominy attached to musical comedy
books." On the other hand, those with genuine talent were always sure of
work, which was more than could be said for ambitious young composers. So
it is not surprising that after *Forum*, "people were saying Sondheim was a brilliant lyricist but he couldn't write music," said the producer Robert Fryer. It is
a measure of Sondheim's determination that, far from being deterred by the
failure of his first score on Broadway, "I guess I felt I really wanted to prove
that I could do something that they would like."

Six months before *Forum* made its successful appearance, in May of 1962,
Sondheim and Laurents had already agreed to collaborate on a new musical,
one that would be highly experimental. Laurents had just finished directing *I
Can Get It for You Wholesale*, a satire about the predatory aspects of the garment trade, which served to introduce the talents of an unknown singer
named Barbra Streisand. Sondheim was anxious to explore the direction that
had been pointed out by *Allegro*, and his mood exactly matched that of the
playwright, who predicted, "This will be something very different in musi-

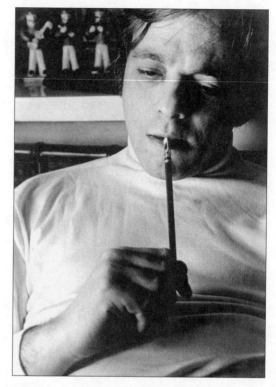

Sondheim in the 1960s

cals, very strange and zany. It will be contemporary, satirical and kind of far-out."

What Laurents called "a musical fable" had resemblances to the work of Jean Anouilh, with his gift for shocking the bourgeoisie. The scene is set in a town plagued by unemployment and run by a corrupt administration, the economy of which is revitalized when the mayor, Cora Hoover Hooper, seizes on the idea of a fake miracle to bring in the tourist trade. She immediately encounters the resistance of Fay Apple, a nurse in the town's mental hospital, called the Cookie (read "Kooky") Jar, and the nurse's handsome suitor, J. Bowden Hapgood, who is supposedly a psychiatrist but turns out to be just another mental case. As in all good absurdist theatre, the inhabitants of the Cookie Jar are the only sane figures. In the course of a complicated plot, during which the forces of repression are confronted and destroyed, *Anyone Can Whistle* takes on not only political corruption but such tempting targets as psychiatry, Madison Avenue, racism, the military-industrial complex, and stereotyped sex roles. The play's most important message, however, was that each individual had a duty to discover his or her potential.

Conformity as a psychosis, the importance of inner liberation: these would become well-worn themes, but, Sondheim said later, "In 1964 it was very daring, and the satire was very sharp and shocking." To take the example of the fake miracle, which would not cause a single raised eyebrow nowadays (at least among theatre-going audiences), spoofing the credulous masses was then considered a daring thing to do. Not surprisingly, the act of writing this manifesto had a liberating effect on the collaborators' imaginations. Laurents said, "We had a glorious time." Sondheim said that they "made a wonderful team. We thought very much alike and stimulated each other creatively. We were . . . able to finish each other's sentences and thoughts. One of the best times I had was working out 'The Interrogation,' the scene at the end of the first act," in which the Cookie Jar's patients have mingled with the crowd and the hospital doctor cannot distinguish between them and "normal" people. "It mingles dialogue, dance and music in a kind of surreal stew and there was even some spoken vocalise." Sondheim would map out the techniques to be used; then Laurents would read what he had written, "and he'd ad lib dialogue with me at the piano, and I'd start ad libbing lyrics to try to make a sort of seamless whole . . . It has one severe and not-quite-fatal flaw in it, which is the (title) tune isn't quite good enough. I was aware of it at the time and I couldn't find a good tune . . . But it's well worked out and . . . very effective

Herbert Ross

on stage." That kind of collaboration had been typical of their easy rapport from the first days of *West Side Story*, "truly fruitful, a fortuitous collaboration." Laurents also had vivid memories of writing the "Interrogation" scene, which still struck him as "remarkably fresh." He added, "I also will never forget the day [Sondheim] came running down here and played 'Everybody Says Don't.' I cried. I still think it's so moving. It's what the show is about."

SONDHEIM HAD DECIDED to base all of his songs on seconds and fourths and the relationships between a D and an E, a C and an F. That made it "sort of a music student's score," i.e., the kind of concept only an inexperienced composer attempts, under the misapprehension that the average listener will hear the relationships. However, he said that it helped him write the score. He also decided to use "nightclub language" for the mayor and the members of her administration: "Their songs are based on Kay Thompson and the Williams Brothers, which was all about jazzy arrangements and high style. It's absolutely heartless, and I thought that was the perfect kind of song to write for Cora and her cohorts, because they're perfectly heartless. The opening number, which is about a town that's starving, is a jazzy two-four number. It's a technique I also used for the characters in *Follies*, when they each talk about their psychological and emotional problems in traditional musical-comedy language, using pastiche for irony." Although the composer described his style as eclectic, with overtones of Ravel and Copland in his middle period ("a kind of wide open, rather gentle but gingery dissonance"), his use of familiar idioms was fresh and inventive enough that, to subsequent commentators, it presents a major advance over the music for *Forum*. The score's "main stylistic premises" emerge fully fledged, according to Stephen Banfield, and Sondheim's concern for a comprehensive musical structure distinguishes the work from its immediate antecedent. Sondheim added, "*Whistle* was also the first time I ever got to write the music I most like to write, which is highly romantic; for example, the title song and 'With So Little to Be Sure Of.' "

Not surprisingly, a musical with absurdist aspirations proved difficult to promote. The only precursor that had succeeded, in Laurents's view, was *Finian's Rainbow* of 1947, a fantasy about a leprechaun from Glocca Morra, and hardly comparable in tone with *Anyone Can Whistle*. As Angela Lansbury, who played the mayor, commented, "Arthur's premise that the 'cookies' in life are the only sane members . . . was rather heavy for a certain kind of audience. They weren't about to be made asses of." Producers were either uninterested or intrigued, but understandably hesitant. Eventually Kermit

Bloomgarden, who had just had a huge success with Meredith Willson's *The Music Man*—set in an imaginary midwestern town at the turn of the century, and with a lovable charlatan for a hero—became fascinated, and the drudgery of raising the necessary $350,000 began. That, Sondheim said, was when he got over whatever stage fright he had once had giving auditions. He said, "The big thing was, I had to raise money for it. I gave thirty-three backer's auditions. The first two, Arthur read a kind of synopsis, and he hated the audience so much, and the fact that we had to beg for money, that I said, 'You go home and let me do it.' So I did the rest myself. I did it for audiences of from two to full halls, and raised a good deal of money; not all of it, but a good deal of it. I remember doing one up at Yale and some professor came up to me afterwards and said, 'It's very interesting, to write an atonal show.' Atonal!"

Bloomgarden enlisted the help of other producers, including Robert Fryer and Diana Krasny, and Laurents began to cast: Lansbury as Cora Hoover Hooper, Harry Guardino as Hapgood, Henry Lascoe as Comptroller Schub, and Lee Remick as Nurse Fay Apple—three of them film stars who had never performed in a musical before.

Almost as soon as she had agreed to take part, Lansbury tried to bow out. She had no confidence in her own ability to sing or her potential gifts in musical theatre. But her main concern was the interpretation of the play-wright, who was also directing the show, with respect to her own part. "My feeling was . . . that there needed to be some vulnerability in a character like that, that would be far more interesting than playing her as an out-and-out bitch which would be merely a caricature . . . I was capable of playing a sullen bitch quite well, but that was something I had done on film and I guess they associated me with that. They thought that maybe I was that kind of woman. A lot of people do. But it's not in my nature."

Laurents thought that Lansbury was being unduly influenced to doubt herself by Henry Lascoe, for Machiavellian reasons. As Sondheim said, not only was the actress feeling insecure but Lascoe, in the role of Schub, was "wiping up the stage with her, because he knew his way around a musical and had been in a lot of them." Laurents and Sondheim were so dissatisfied that during the Philadelphia run, they invited the actress Nancy Walker to come to a performance, with the idea of offering the part to her. Lansbury found out about that, which did not improve her mood. "There was an awful lot of backstage gossip and carryings-on. It was a great show for people screaming up and down the aisles," she said. "I remember screaming my ass off at Steve once . . . yelling, 'I don't know what you want. What the hell do you want me to do?' "

Angela Lansbury and Harry Guardino in *Anyone Can Whistle,* 1964

"We all knew it was very special material and an immense gamble," said Harvey Evans, a young actor-dancer who had joined *West Side Story* some months after it opened and got to know Sondheim then—"he was so young, like one of the kids." But when it came to *Anyone Can Whistle,* "we scarcely saw him; he was locked in his hotel room." Everyone was miserable in Philadelphia. "It was the most neurotic, angst-filled time," he said. "Everything felt like life or death." He remembers drinking "an enormous amount of liquor at the Variety Club." The mood was not helped by the reaction of the audience. "One night someone stood up at the curtain and put his thumbs down. So Harry Guardino gave him the finger. I remember the costume designer, Theoni Aldredge, down in the basement spraying some costumes because they needed a new scene and they didn't have any money to buy new ones." Guardino, who had a natural singing voice, lost it, became depressed by the poor reaction, and began to drink. That was not all.

The dance numbers were being choreographed by Herbert Ross, who by general agreement was absolutely brilliant and did not get the recognition he deserved. But Ross's inventiveness led to the first catastrophe of the show. During rehearsal, Ross suggested that Tucker Smith, one of the dancers, step to the front of the stage and execute some steps during a ballet in the second act. Unfortunately, that night Smith, blinded by the footlights, misjudged the edge of the stage and took one step too many. Evans said, "We all saw it in slow motion." Smith fell heavily into the string section. He was not seriously injured, but the player who broke his fall had a stroke and subsequently died. The cast had hardly recovered from this spectacularly bad omen when they were called together to receive further terrible news: Henry Lascoe had had a heart attack in his hotel room and he, too, subsequently died. "We were just killing them off," Laurents said.

Everyone knew that too much time had been spent raising money and there had been too few rehearsals. Laurents said, "We knew it had faults and there was no time, because the dollars were ticking away." Laurents tried desperately to improve the musical's chances. When *Anyone Can Whistle* began a series of previews in New York in the spring of 1964, Laurents went to his producers in an effort to postpone opening night. Diana Krasny recalled that he and Bloomgarden got into a heated argument that ended in an actual fistfight in Shubert Alley. She had to stop them herself, she said. This version is contradicted by Laurents. "It's one of the legends," he said. "I don't doubt that we had an argument, but we did not come to blows. It reminds me of the *West Side Story* legend that I peed on the scenery, which I didn't. What happened was I was dissatisfied with the original sets and I said, 'If you don't take that off the stage I am *going* to pee on it.'"

Lascoe's death had the unforeseen effect of resolving the disagreement between Lansbury and the musical's creators. Evans said, "Lascoe's understudy, Gabriel Dell, took over, and proceeded not to know his first line and most of the rest. Angela Lansbury got angry and Arthur Laurents started laughing and broke the ice." From that moment on, everyone agreed that the actress came into her own. Laurents said, "She suddenly found out that all those lines that were supposed to be mean were getting big laughs, and she just sailed." As it happened, Nancy Walker did not like the part. "So, fortunately, we had to stay with Angie, who was wonderful." Evans recalled that the producers gave a cast party in Philadelphia to help restore morale, and they heard that Lansbury had telephoned Sondheim to ask if she could come: the rift was mended.

As the British novelist John Mortimer, himself a playwright, has observed in his autobiography, there is no way to explain why plays fail. Despite excellent notices they may fall victim to "various theatrical diseases such as the fact that it was raining, or too hot, or Holy Week, or the news was bad, or there was a bus strike, or it got dark at night." Even if all these explanations applied when *Anyone Can Whistle* opened on April 4, 1964, the musical's failure was nevertheless spectacular. Sondheim said later, "We were trying in a smart-assed, condescending way to be nonconformist and cover too many aspects of society." In tone, technique, and theme the musical was far ahead of its time, and only a few critics, including Norman Nadel of the New York *World-Telegram and Sun,* were enthusiastic: "It is exciting to encounter one so spectacularly original." The notices, as they say, were mixed, a euphemism that, "in the words of George S. Kaufman, simply means that they were 'good and rotten,' " Jean Kerr wrote. Laurents and Sondheim waived their royalties and even paid for an advertisement in the *New York Times,* but nothing helped, and *Anyone Can Whistle* closed after nine performances. It would be Sondheim's biggest disaster.

LEE REMICK, at age twenty-eight, was already a film star and took the top billing in *Anyone Can Whistle.* The character she played was that of a nurse, a disciplined rationalist whose sympathies are with the oppressed (read: her patients), who is not deceived by the so-called miracle and whose indignant speech of protest regularly brought down the house. It was so successful that the song following it, "There Won't Be Trumpets," was deemed superfluous by the director and was cut, over the reluctant objections of the composer. He was right to think it one of his best songs. Even though it was not on Broadway, it is frequently performed.

> There won't be trumpets or bolts of fire
> To say he's coming.
> No Roman candles, no angels' choir,
> No sound of distant drumming.
> He may not be the cavalier,
> Tall and graceful, fair and strong.
> Doesn't matter,
> Just as long as he comes along!

But behind her starched manner, Nurse Fay Apple conceals a vulnerable heart. She returns in the second act, looking meltingly fragile in a diaphanous gown, and plays a charming seduction scene in which she almost loses her inhibitions, becoming, Nadel wrote, "the total embodiment of sexuality."

Lee Remick as the temptress in *Anyone Can Whistle*, 1964

The critics praised Remick's dancing and acting and none found fault with her voice, although she was just as unsure of that as Lansbury was about hers; in fact, she was suffering from tonsillitis and subsequently had her tonsils removed. But that was Lee Remick. If she had private problems, she was not going to let them interfere with her work. "She was open, more like a funny, sweet girl than a movie star," Harvey Evans said. "She could have been the girl next door."

Lee Remick, born in Quincy, Massachusetts, was the daughter of a department-store owner and an actress. Her parents divorced when she was seven, her mother moved to New York, and she and her older brother, Bruce, grew up there. She went to an exclusive private school on the Upper East Side, took ballet and modern dance classes, and began her acting career at the

Laurents, Lee Remick, Sondheim, and Harvey Evans shortly after Sondheim met Remick

age of sixteen in summer stock on Cape Cod. That led to more theatre roles and a string of television appearances. After Elia Kazan spotted her and cast her as a seductive cheerleader in *A Face in the Crowd* in 1957, she was launched on a film career. She was highly praised for her performance in *Anatomy of a Murder*, and her role as the alcoholic wife in *Days of Wine and Roses* in 1963 brought her a nomination for an Academy Award. Although she had never studied acting, she seemed to have "a quality of truth exceedingly rare among Hollywood's young leading women," John Beaufort wrote in the *Christian Science Monitor*. There was something straightforward and uncompromising about her manner, something reproachful about her wide-set eyes, and a mobility to her beautiful features that conveyed delicate depths of feeling: the American ideal of a frontier woman. She said, "After *Anatomy*, in which I played a kind of tramp, I could have followed up with more of the same. Reinforcing my 'image' by becoming a sex symbol would have been one way to be more strongly identified as a star, but I had no interest in doing that. I can't be something I'm not." Clear-eyed, principled, unpretentious: this is the image of Lee Remick to which people turn again and again. Those who knew her well had yet another reason to admire her. When quite young, she had married a much older producer and director, William A. Colleran; they had a son and a daughter. Then, in 1960, while she was filming *Wild River* with Montgomery Clift, she learned that her husband had been involved in a car crash. It seemed he had been at a working meeting at Frank Sinatra's house one evening. On his way home, he was driving down a hill behind the Beverly Hills Hotel and made a sharp turn. His car hit an obstacle and went out of control. He was thrown clear but suffered broken bones, a terrible concussion, and complete amnesia. "He didn't know anyone," Mrs. Pat Packard, Lee's mother, said. The accident left him a semi-invalid. The family moved to New York and took a house on Sixty-fourth street. Lee Remick became the main breadwinner of the family.

Lee Remick's name was linked romantically with that of Elia Kazan, the director who had first seen her potential, and also with that of Herbert Greene, the musical director for *Anyone Can Whistle*. Sondheim first met her when he went to California to audition her and Angela Lansbury. "I flew in from Denmark," he said. "We had to do a quick one. Burt [Shevelove] and I were on holiday in Copenhagen, and then I had to fly back to London, where we were attending rehearsals for the opening of *Forum* there." (*Forum* opened in the West End on October 3, 1963.) "But I didn't get to know her until after *Whistle* had closed." He thought she had been on the point of leaving her husband when the accident occurred. Then, once Colleran's concentrative powers had gone, "she couldn't very well in all good conscience leave him." She was trapped in an unhappy marriage. He used to meet her secretly in the Village, Sondheim said.

Friends who saw them together during that period agreed they were in love. "If you could have seen the way she would look at him!" Lucy Beldock said. Laurents thought Sondheim adored her. "Absolutely. One night a year or so after the show, he and I were supposed to have dinner, and he called and said, 'Listen, Lee's in town. Would you mind very much if she had dinner with us?' I said, 'No, not at all.' So the three of us had dinner and the next day he called to apologize. He said, 'I know she's dull and boring.' I protested, but it was true. She was one of the nicest women ever. She always looked to me as though she had a lacrosse stick in her hand. I do not think she was feminine." Laurents conceded, however, that she was a beauty. "During our first rehearsal in New York Lee and I had lunch. And before we ordered a drink, which you did in those days, Lee said to me, the sweet and lovely Miss America, 'I want to tell you now: if Angela Lansbury gets the reviews in Philadelphia, I'm leaving.' That was something to say." But the reviews accorded the mayor stayed a respectful distance from those of the nurse. "A pretty girl's always going to get the reviews," Laurents said. "She was enormously personable and wonderful for a fantasy life. After all, she's not sexual, she's not challenging. And she's a movie star of sorts. She looked like Miss America. And she was mad about him. Insane about him. She would have given anything to get him." Sondheim would have liked to have a close relationship with her. "But, you know, she was married. And I'm a nice Jewish boy from the nineteenth century. And I think part of the fun of my relationship with Lee was how we had to hide all the time."

The British film director Kip Gowans, who married Lee Remick in 1970, readily agreed that his wife adored Sondheim. "I think she might have married him, but it was doomed from the word go," he said. "There is nothing she would have loved more. Lee knew that he was a homosexual, of course. There wasn't even a question of a sexual affair. I'd have known about that. We never had any secrets from each other." Her mother doubted, however, that her daughter would have married Sondheim. "Everyone knew he wasn't interested in girls in that way." She thought his mother, Foxy Leshin, whom she knew socially, was the source of the rumors. "She was dying to have it happen, and I said to Dr. Henry Ross, who was a mutual friend of ours, 'Doesn't she realize he's not interested in girls?' "

Besides Janet Long, who was his steady all through George School, and his friends Mary Rodgers, Nancy Ryan, Lucy Beldock, and Jill Schary, he seemed most at ease with girls who conveyed a sisterly, if not maternal, warmth. On the other hand, he had been known to compete for the attentions of a pretty girl, and it did seem important that she be beautiful. There was, for instance, Nancy Berg, a prominent, dark-haired model a year his junior who arrived in New York from Kenosha, Wisconsin, and was on the cover of *Vogue* six months later.

"We met around the time of *Forum* and *Anyone Can Whistle*," she said. "Through mutual friends, at a party, I believe, and saw each other for a couple of years. I thought he was quite a wonderful person, kind and generous. He and I shared the same love of language and he taught me to do word puzzles. We had another common bond: we both had the same Medea-like mothers, mothers out to kill their children. I knew he felt the way I did, lost and bewildered. We had this fury in common. I remember we talked a fair amount. It was a relief to be able to talk about it; one feels so alone." They went to a lot of parties together. She remembers a game he invented, "Objects in Plain View," in which, for instance, a carrot would have been carved so cleverly that it looked like a chess piece. They spent Christmases together. She owned a penthouse on Riverside Drive with a terrace overlooking the Hudson. When she told him her ambition was to swing out over the Hudson River, he had a miniature gazebo made with a swing and presented it to her.

"I guess it was a romance," she said. "I was quite mad about him. I was a glamour girl, the supermodel of the time. I had a lot of beaux, but no one as

The "supermodel" Nancy Berg

important as him." She never thought in terms of marriage, partly because he was doing a lot of partying and she would have preferred a quieter life. In any event, "I wasn't in shape for a real relationship. He was just a very sweet man and I adored him. I think he was quite mad about Lee Remick and I was terribly jealous."

There was Mary Ann Madden, whom he met through Bob Carrington, son of Elaine Carrington, with whom he had worked on the television musical *I Believe in You*. "Bob and I did a murder game at his mother's house in Bridgehampton, and Mary Rodgers and I were one of the couples," Sondheim said. "She was a divorcée when we met and had some money of her own. She did have a job, but I can't remember what." She had the same love of games and puzzles and a quirky, original mind; she would eventually invent literary competitions for *New York* magazine. She also worked for Mike Nichols, whom she met through Sondheim. "She was delightful," Sondheim said. Shevelove took "a great fancy" to her and they became a trio. Even though she hated to travel, they persuaded her to make a trip to London with them one summer. She was not a romance, just a very good friend, he said. Of recent years Madden has become reclusive and "lives in her New York apartment with her cats and computers and talks to Mike Nichols by E-mail," according to their mutual friend Larry Miller.

There was Hal Prince's wife, Judy, whom Sondheim has known since she was an adolescent, whose gift of the riposte is well known, and whom he considers a brilliant, if unpublished, writer, like Mary Ann Madden. Peter Stone, a friend of them both, called her "very complicated, terribly intelligent and very wry. Steve and Judy were very symbiotic for a long time; he almost could not function without her." In fact he completed a song for her called "Marry Me a Little," which he had written for *Company.* Sondheim said, "What happened was, I was playing it and I told Hal that I had started this song but thought I should not finish it" for reasons of the plot. "He said, 'I agree with you, it's too knowing,' but she was listening outside the door. She came in later and said, 'I don't care whether it fits or not, I just think it's fabulous.'" So when he was trying to decide on a Christmas gift for her, he thought of the song, finished it, had Harry Nilsson record it, and presented it to her.

> Marry me a little,
> Love me just enough,
> Cry but not too often,
> Play but not too rough.
>
> Keep a tender distance
> So we'll both be free,
> That's the way it ought to be.
> I'm ready!

Then there was Mary Rodgers. She remembers a conversation with Sondheim in about 1949 when they were sitting on the floor under her father's Steinway. He hesitatingly told her he thought he was a homosexual. "And I was heartbroken, for him and for me, because lurking underneath there was always the desire to be with him for the rest of my life, under any circumstances. Which is when I said, 'Well, gee, maybe you could go to a psychiatrist,' and he replied, 'I just don't know if I want to.'"

She married Jerry Beaty in 1951 and their first child was born a year later, when she was twenty-one. "And Steve was as excited about that . . . He was more excited than my husband!" Two more children followed in short order, although it was becoming clear that the marriage was fated not to last. "At one point my husband got really sore at me and said, 'You know what's the matter with you? You're not in love with me. You're in love with Steve.' And I said, 'That's the stupidest thing I ever heard in my life,' and as soon as I said it a bolt of terror went through me because I realized he was right." As it happened, she and Steve were writing their *Lady or the Tiger* (never produced) in

1953 or 1954. Sondheim said, "She suddenly fell in love with me on a given moment on a given afternoon, because she talked about it a lot afterwards. And it's the reason for the song, called 'Once I Had a Friend (Now I Have a Lover).' It's a song we wrote together. And at that moment she looked across the room and felt it happen. That's what she told me." That might have been a defining moment for them both but, she said, she felt him withdraw to their former friendly distance.

After her divorce, Mary Rodgers became engaged to someone else in 1960, but Sondheim was very insistent about her not marrying anyone. Soon after she made a short trip to New York from London, where her musical, *Once Upon A Mattress,* was in rehearsal, she received a phone call. Sondheim was calling to say that he had just bought a house, there was enough room for children, that he had thought about it and perhaps they should try things out for a year—an unofficial engagement, in effect. "So I broke my engagement to Paul Heller, who had already given me a ring, and I said, 'I'm in love with Steve Sondheim,' and he said, 'You must be out of your mind,' because everybody by that time had figured out Steve was gay. And I said, 'I suppose I am but I just don't have any choice. I just can't go on with you and here's your ring.' "

Sondheim has a different view. "She was more serious about me than I was about her," he said. He denied that they had ever been engaged, and if there was an informal arrangement it got off to a bad start. Rodgers remembers that the evening she returned from London, where her musical had just opened, they went to a big party together, "and we got inside the door and he instantly vanished!" She said, "I was left wandering around all by myself, not knowing anybody, and very tired, and a little unnerved . . . So then we spent—half a year, anyway—having the most uncomfortable time." Both agreed that the relationship never became a physical one because, she thought, of his need to maintain a safe distance. "He was terrified, not of giving love, but having to get it." After the experiment failed, Mary Rodgers married Henry Guettel. By then they had agreed to disagree and have remained good friends.

If Sondheim needed a failure in order to become a seasoned man of the theatre, as Oscar Hammerstein had said, *Anyone Can Whistle* was certainly a start in that direction. Hammerstein was perhaps referring to his own stalled career before the advent of Richard Rodgers into his life, which came at such a fortuitous moment. As if on cue, Rodgers appeared in Sondheim's life just as his future also seemed uncertain. There was just one small proviso: he had to go back to being a lyricist.

While they were working on *Gypsy* Laurents told Sondheim he hoped to have a musical made of his play *The Time of the Cuckoo,* which had opened on

Broadway in late 1952 and had a very successful run. It concerns an American tourist, not pretty, not young, unmarried, who takes a vacation in Venice, falls in love with a middle-aged Venetian, and then discovers to her horror that he has a wife and a large family. It is an unpretentious story with a delicate moral, Jamesian in its nuance and understatement, about what happens when American naiveté and romanticism meet European worldliness and disillusion. As performed by Shirley Booth and Dino Di Luca, they were a pair of utterly prosaic, middle-aged lovers with a human dilemma, and their very ordinariness gave a feeling of inevitability to the denouement. In the role of Leona Samish, the good-hearted, generous, and muddled American who is out of her depth, Booth gave a glowing performance. She "gathers all the good-will, emotional turbulence and chagrin of the character in an immensely dramatic performance," Brooks Atkinson wrote.

It might have been a case of a play depending for its unique effect on the qualities of mind and heart a certain actress brought to a role. In any event, the film *Summertime,* which followed in 1954, was an acute disappointment, not just because the Dino Di Luca role was now assumed by a handsome young Italian actor, Rossano Brazzi, whom no one could imagine falling for a dowdy tourist, but because Katharine Hepburn, as Leona, presented far too distinctive and sophisticated an image to be mistaken as one. What made the play seem so full of warmth and humanity seemed to have dwindled away.

Laurents originally thought Rodgers and Hammerstein would be the ideal team to write the musical and was duly introduced to Hammerstein by Sondheim. "Oscar said he'd like to do it, but he'd like Arthur to wait for a few years, because the movie had recently been made and he wanted more time to pass," Sondheim said. "And then he died. Before he did he said to me, 'I know you want to write music, but if you can see your way to writing with Dick, I would be thrilled.' So I said, 'I will try.' "

After that Rodgers kept sending him ideas. Sondheim said, "Oscar felt he was abandoning Dick. He thought Dick would be lost. I don't think he knew that Dick had ambitions to write his own lyrics." Indeed, Rodgers had taken a book by Samuel Taylor and written lyrics as well as music for *No Strings* in 1962. He also produced the musical, which ran for a year on Broadway. Interestingly, it, too, was a story about a European love affair that ends when the lovers part, but with a very different setting and mood. The book and characters were judged to be the musical's weakest element. The music was praised and Rodgers's lyrics were pronounced workmanlike if not outstanding.

That may have inspired Rodgers to agree that Sondheim should be approached for his next musical, now called *Do I Hear a Waltz?* Somewhere between the play and the film the concept of Leona had changed radically.

Perhaps it was no longer fashionable to have a plot revolve around a cultural gulf. Perhaps the theme of *Anyone Can Whistle,* with its emphasis on self-realization, inspired the playwright to declare that actresses who had played the leading role in the years since Booth were too old. He wrote, "The story of an aging woman who could not give herself physically is something small and rather dirty. What I wrote is the story of a woman who could not give herself emotionally, a woman young enough to have a chance at a future."

This shift of emphasis cleared the way for the casting of Elizabeth Allen as Leona, but it presented a new obstacle that Sondheim was quick to identify. This is a girl, he said, who, metaphorically speaking, "cannot sing," a real drawback in a musical. So he was not at all sure he wanted to work on this musical, something the famous composer naturally found irritating if not insulting. After all, Rodgers had known Stephen since he was twelve. In those days he was a charming little boy and he had grown into "a monster." That was said teasingly in Sondheim's presence in November 1964, once they were at work in Rodgers's East Side apartment, with its grand piano, and his Renoir, Chagall, and Matisse on the walls. But no doubt Rodgers had some lingering resentments, and so did Sondheim. He said that Mary Rodgers had begged him to do it because "it would make Daddy so happy." No one told Sondheim that Rodgers had become an alcoholic. "I was the sacrificial goat," he said. Arthur Laurents had also urged him to write the lyrics. Sondheim said Laurents had pointed out that nothing Rodgers wrote and produced ever lost money. Laurents denied having said this. But he added, "He is rightfully angry at me because he didn't want to do it and I talked him into it." He thought Sondheim had agreed purely out of loyalty and in the mistaken belief that to decline meant losing a friend.

Having committed himself, Sondheim went to Venice for ten days with his friend Larry Miller for the arduous task of soaking up the atmosphere. While they were there, there was an international display of fireworks on the Grand Canal. They hired one of the hundreds of gondolas, each carrying candles, and drank Strega while they watched the exquisite trails of color bursting all around them, "and I was sure we were going to get burned to death," Sondheim said. It was an unforgettable evening and the only thing he remembered about the trip. And if collaborating with Oscar Hammerstein's old partner was a moment of exquisite private pride, he did not comment on it. But he did say that the collaboration was easy and friendly, at first. Rodgers sometimes wrote a melody—especially the ballads—and Sondheim would then set it to words; but sometimes Sondheim wrote the lyrics first, as for the opening number. Rodgers said, "Steve will come in with a quatrain and that will be big enough for me to get going. A few days ago he handed me a complete chorus and I started off on a whole number. If I find myself going off from the set lyrics I'll confer with Steve, who will either rewrite or eliminate, if necessary. We get together whenever we have something to present to each other."

Work proceeded smoothly until the run-through in New York, just before the show was to open in New Haven and then in Boston in February 1965, when it was evident that something was wrong. Sergio Franchi was dreamily handsome as the married Venetian, but his performance was leaden. Elizabeth Allen was attacking her part as though she were Ethel Merman in *Gypsy*. John Dexter, the brilliant but abrasive English director, was alienating everyone with his temper tantrums. Rodgers wrote, "We found that instead of a musical we had a sad little comedy with songs." That was putting it mildly. Arthur Laurents said, "I just stomped out. I saw it was a disaster and I went out and bought a coat."

They decided they had to do something—anything—to bring the show to life, and Herbert Ross, who had added such a valuable dimension to *Anyone Can Whistle* with his choreography, was enlisted to create the dance numbers they originally thought they could dispense with. "That was especially needed in the first-act scene on the Piazza San Marco, where the heroine sits alone surrounded by tourists and Venetians," Rodgers commented. Rodgers's position was that casting the heroine as young and pretty had perversely made her less likable. He wanted to eliminate a crucial moment in the second act in which Leona "gets drunk and tells a young wife that her husband has had a dalliance with the owner of the *pensione*. I felt that this made the heroine unsympathetic." But Laurents refused to remove the scene, which was in the original play, and Sondheim supported him.

Rodgers and Sondheim had begun to appreciate the gulf that separated them because their basic approaches were so much at variance. Sondheim recalled that the words he wrote for "We're Gonna Be All Right" displayed a mildly cynical view of marriage, the suggestion that the wife and the husband might find consolation in an affair or two, including a homosexual one, and the lines

> We'll build our house upon
> The rock of my virility.
> We'd better scurry,
> We're gonna be all night . . .

Sondheim said, "I wrote lyrics which had some bite to them and Dick Rodgers thought the song was wonderful. Next day he called a lunch and kept slamming the lyrics against his forearm and saying, 'This will not do,

Rehearsing for *Do I Hear A Waltz?:* Sondheim, Julienne Marie (seated), Carol Bruce, Richard Rodgers, and Elizabeth Allen, the star of the show, 1965

Rodgers, Sondheim, and the playwright, Arthur Laurents, conferring on *Do I Hear A Waltz?*

Sondheim and Rodgers during rehearsals of *Do I Hear A Waltz?* with Laurents in the foreground

this will not do,' and I kept asking, 'Why?' The truth was, he'd shown the lyric to his wife and she did not like it. He probably showed it to her out of enthusiasm. But you know, it's got stuff about sexuality in it," and Dorothy Rodgers was known for being strait-laced. So he had to remove the offending lines, but they were subsequently restored, and these are the ones that are always heard. Speaking of Dorothy Rodgers, who was an accomplished interior decorator, as was Dorothy Hammerstein, reminded Sondheim that Burt Shevelove had been asked to arrange a party to celebrate the first anniversary of *The King and I,* which was being held in the famous old Astor Hotel. Shevelove's idea was that the two Dorothys would start redecorating at opposite ends of the room and "we'd see who got to the middle first."

Sondheim arrived in New Haven for the opening at the Shubert Theatre to be greeted by a barrage of telegrams, including one from Mary Ann Madden that was a gallant effort at humor, because his friends knew that the atmosphere between Sondheim and Rodgers was continuing to deteriorate. Sondheim said, "Jerry Whyte protected Dick from the world. He was, sort of, his keeper, and Dick would come to a meeting in New Haven and say, 'The trouble is the book and lyrics.' That's because they had kept the bad reviews about the music from him." Sondheim thought Whyte was afraid to show critical reviews to Rodgers because he would become extremely depressed and "go on a bender." Laurents said that during the Boston run Rodgers would disappear into the men's room at intervals and Whyte would stand at the door to prevent people from entering while Rodgers was in there drinking. And if Rodgers was in the wrong mood he would behave badly, drunk or sober.

Laurents recalled one occasion when Sondheim came on stage after having stayed up for thirty-six hours writing "Perfectly Lovely Couple" and handed it to Rodgers. "And Dick said, 'This is shit! I'm not giving this to my singers!' In front of the whole company," Laurents said. He continued, "Steve walked down the flight of stairs leading from the stage, came down the aisle to me, and said, 'I'm through. I'm absolutely through.' " Rodgers also threatened to quit. He accused Sondheim and Laurents of being in league against him. "He was always implying that we were having some kind of affair," Sondheim said. Rodgers was "the master of the imagined slight." They knew, however, that they were outvoted, because Rodgers, as producer, had the final word. The real problem, Sondheim believed, was that Rodgers was jealous of the close relationship he had had with Hammerstein. That to one side, *Do I Hear a Waltz?* was "what Mary [Rodgers] calls a 'why?' musical," he said. "I don't know if she did so in this case. It was a dead show. It was very well done; it just had no vitality, no life."

When the musical opened on Broadway on March 18, 1965, there were the usual witty telegrams. Maltby and Shire sent one saying, "Best of luck tonight. Now back to the piano." Another friend wrote, "Good luck to you and what's his name." Joe Stein, yet another friend, wrote, "I wish I could be with you on this important exciting and I am sure triumphant occasion but you didn't ask me." Larry Miller wrote, "I'm crossing my fingers and fingering my cross." Lee Remick wrote, "Very odd but I hear a sigh of relief," which was probably a quite accurate assessment of Sondheim's mood once it became clear that the musical was not the abject failure he had been expecting. In fact it had quite a respectable run of 220 performances, which made it a roaring success when compared with *Anyone Can Whistle.*

The failure of their daring experiment had not led to a cooling of the atmosphere between Laurents and Sondheim, but the aftermath of the Rodgers experiment did, at least temporarily. By mutual consent, as it seemed, they did not work together again until they collaborated, in 1973, on Laurents's play *The Enclave,* for which Sondheim wrote incidental music. Two weeks after the opening on October 30, Laurents wrote, "One of the loveliest things about this whole happy experience was working with you again." Richard Rodgers conceded later that the atmosphere had been tense—he blamed his co-creators for rejecting his ideas—and he told Keith Baxter, Sondheim's British actor friend, that he considered Sondheim brilliant but "a cold man with a deep sense of cynicism," Baxter said. However, the two remained on fairly good terms for several more years. After Sondheim's huge success with *Company* in 1970, Rodgers wrote him a letter of congratulations. Three years after that, when Sondheim appeared on the cover of *Newsweek,* he was quoted as saying that Hammerstein was a man of limited talent and infinite soul, and that Rodgers was the reverse. Naturally enough, that ended whatever friendship still remained. Sondheim must have found it ironic that this collaboration with Rodgers led to his first Tony Award nomination. He did not win.

SONDHEIM MADE his first attempt at undergoing psychotherapy in 1958 at the suggestion of Arthur Laurents. Laurents said, "At that time he was very defensive about sexuality. I mean, he introduced me to Burt Shevelove and one day I said to him, 'You know, there's something about Burt,' and he said, 'You're wrong.' And I said, 'What do you mean?' and he said, 'He's not homosexual.' It had never even occurred to me whether he was or he wasn't. But he was sensitive on that issue."

An informal portrait of Sondheim, circa 1965

Sondheim said, "I was never easy with being a homosexual, which complicated things." He agreed that social attitudes of the day toward what was considered deviant, if not criminal, behavior, made things very difficult. "I don't think I knew more than maybe four homosexuals in the fifties and sixties who were openly so. I'm guessing four. I'm actually thinking of one couple who were quite effeminate, so there was very little to conceal. I knew a lot of homosexuals who did not want it to be known. Everybody knew the theatre was full of homosexuals, but nobody admitted to being so."

Laurents had greatly benefited from therapy. "I went out of absolute desperation. The alcoholics say they've 'hit a bottom.' I'd hit a bottom." Sondheim went because he was curious. "I was just, sort of, unhappy. I didn't go for any reason and that's why it didn't take." For years, perhaps decades, almost none of his close friends, and certainly no family members, had any idea that Sondheim was attracted to his own sex. His half-brother Walter found out when the father of a high-school friend, a psychiatrist with a number of homosexual patients, casually remarked, "There's not a man in New York City who is more loved than your brother." Walter Sondheim said, "A lot of things fell into place."

The first really important man in Sondheim's life was a young man working on the administrative staff during *Do I Hear a Waltz?,* to whom he was very much attracted. They had a brief, intense love affair. "He was, I guess, the first person I had enough of an emotional crush on. We didn't know each other for very long, a few months maybe. When trouble in paradise struck, it wasn't anything specific, but it was my feeling of jealousy and possessiveness and his—I won't say flightiness, fickleness—I'm talking about it in a general way—that I got upset. I got terribly upset and we had a bad falling out. I don't necessarily mean a big scene, but it was an upset, angry falling out which neither of us was happy about. I can't say it was love," he continued. "But it was the first person apart from Lee that I thought I'd like to have a relationship with." The affair threw him into a turmoil, "and I thought, now's the time to go back into analysis."

IN *Anyone Can Whistle,* the title song was sung by Lee Remick. It is quite short, a straightforward, quiet melody in which Fay Apple laments her inability to express her deepest feelings. Tony Walton, who designed the sets and costumes for *Forum* and later co-produced it in London, was married at the time to Julie Andrews. He said, "I have a devastating memory of Sondheim singing 'Anyone Can Whistle' on the piano in our house. As a performer he is always very deeply embroiled in his own work. But this seemed so autobiographical. It made me think of Noël Coward on his seventieth birthday, singing, 'All I've had is a talent to amuse.' " The song expressed, Michael Billington wrote in 1986, "a heartfelt urge to join the human race." Sondheim sang it himself some years later during *Sondheim: A Musical Tribute* held in the Shubert Theatre. His moment came at the end of the program. He sat down at the piano and sang the concluding words,

> What's hard is simple,
> What's natural comes hard.
> Maybe you could show me
> How to let go,
> Lower my guard,
> Learn to be—

and here there was a long pause,

> . . . free.
> Maybe if you whistle,
> Whistle for me.

Laurents said, "I always thought that song would be Steve's epitaph."

CHAPTER 10

Being Alive

I T T O O K F I V E Y E A R S before another work of Sondheim's was seen
on Broadway. When that moment came, two of his musicals appeared
in rapid succession. Both were immediate successes, both solidified his position as a major composer, and both marked the real start of the collaboration
with Hal Prince. The team of Sondheim-Prince would be responsible for a
string of innovative musicals in the 1970s, culminating in *Sweeney Todd,* and
would become known as one of the most creative in musical-theatre history.

The five years between 1965 and 1970, however, were difficult ones for
Sondheim, full of false starts and sudden disappointments, of concepts that
kept changing focus, of disagreements, and of promises made and broken.
Sondheim's ability to endure setbacks, take criticism and turn it to advantage,
keep coming up with solutions to seemingly intractable problems, and medi-
ate between warring factions had already been tested. But during the next five
years that ability to keep an idea alive would be tried to its utmost.

After the disappointments of *Anyone Can Whistle* and *Do I Hear a Waltz?*
Sondheim was looking for a new collaborator, and decided to approach
James Goldman, a playwright who would have a great success with his Broadway play *The Lion in Winter* in 1966, and would win an Oscar for his screenplay of it in 1968. Goldman was the brother of William, the novelist and
screenwriter, who had been a friend of Sondheim's since *West Side Story* and

whose book, *The Season* (1969), would become famous for its insights into the inner workings of the business. Sondheim had admired another play of James Goldman's, *They Might Be Giants,* and the two met for dinner early in 1965. Sondheim, who was aware that Goldman had already tried his hand at a musical, asked whether he would like to collaborate with him. Goldman said he would think about it.

Goldman's idea, which went through a major transformation before it emerged as *Follies* in 1971, began with a newspaper clipping announcing a reunion of showgirls who had appeared in the Ziegfeld Follies. That famous revue had been modeled on the Paris Folies-Bergère and soon became known for its chorus line, its discovery of talented actresses like Anna Held, Billie Burke, and Lillian Lorraine, and the extravagance of its decor and costumes. It was also known for the topicality of its sketches and the audacity of its ideas. One early Follies introduced Lillian Lorraine in a sea of soap bubbles. She later climbed into a flying machine and scattered flowers on the audience while singing "Up, Up in My Aeroplane"—and that was 1907. The 1909 version featured a realistic impersonation of President Theodore Roosevelt on an African hunting trip. In 1910, singing as she went, Lorraine swung out over the audience to the accompaniment of eight showgirls ringing Swiss bells. The best composers of the day: Rudolf Friml, Victor Herbert, Jerome Kern, and Irving Berlin, wrote for Ziegfeld. Comedians like Will Rogers, W. C. Fields, Ed Wynn and Fanny Brice appeared in the revue at the Winter Garden. Beatrice Lillie appeared in the final Follies, in 1957, twenty-five years after the death of Flo Ziegfeld. Although the posthumous productions were accomplished and even handsome, it was conceded that nothing could match Ziegfeld's uncanny taste and flair; he had been a showman of genius.

As a phenomenon the Ziegfeld Follies were part of the recent past when Goldman and Sondheim began thinking about a musical in 1965. In fact, Jule Styne had just had a huge success as the composer of *Funny Girl* (1964), the musical about Fanny Brice that starred Barbra Streisand. Then there was a haunting photograph of about the same period that exemplified the kind of bittersweet nostalgia with which *Follies* would be infused. Sondheim said, "Hal [Prince] has always had an image of the show—there is a famous photo by Eliot Elisofon of Gloria Swanson standing in the rubble of the Roxy Theatre. The Roxy opened in 1928 with *The Loves of Sunya*, and when the theatre was torn down in 1960, some smart publicity man got her to pose in the daylight in all that rubble with her arms outstretched. And Hal said that's what this show had to be about—rubble in the daylight." And so *Follies* would evolve, with the image that Swanson, with her sure sense of the dramatic gesture, had made unforgettable.

Goldman started out quite differently, however, with the idea of a musical murder mystery, Sondheim said, "a 'who'll-do-it' rather than a 'whodunit.'" Goldman liked the idea of "a device Chekhov used for the curtain, at the end of the third act of *Uncle Vanya,* where people are driven by anguish to the point where someone fires a gun and misses." At the end of act 1, each of the four principals, two couples, had a reason to kill someone, and the second act posed the question of who would commit the murder. There was a duel, a gun that did not go off, and one of the girls locked the other in a phone booth. Goldman wrote a first draft, Sondheim composed several songs, and the resulting effort was titled *The Girls Upstairs.* Then the producers David Merrick and Leland Hayward were approached. When Merrick asked why Hal Prince was not involved, Sondheim replied, according to Merrick, that he thought Prince wanted to direct, and he did not think he was a good enough director.

Prince said, "I had more respect for his talent earlier on as a composer-lyricist than he had for mine as a potential director. So originally when he was doing *The Girls Upstairs* he offered it to me, but only as producer. He said, 'You're our fourth choice as director.'" Prince replied by saying he did not want to do it, not because of Sondheim's lack of faith in his talents but because he did not understand the show. "Steve was very encouraging when he saw *She Loves Me,*" the musical Prince directed in 1963, "and wrote me a lovely note which I got at the stage entrance saying, 'You've done a really terrific job.' But that didn't alter how he felt about my actually working with him as director. For quite some time. I think, maybe—I'm guessing—he didn't perceive me as audacious or creative.

"There's a story I do remember when I was just trying to get a foothold in the directing business. After I produced *Forum,* George Abbott was the first person who told me I was going to be a good director. Then *Forum* was a success—it was potentially not the happiest of marriages, and it turned out just fine—and George said, 'I don't want to go to London and do it,' and I was producing it with my London partners, the designer Tony Walton and the lighting designer Richard Pilbrow. So he suggested that I go over and direct his version. He made the recommendation to Shevelove, Gelbart, and Sondheim, and the three of them said, 'Absolutely not.' And that was—temporarily hurtful. But they were perfectly happy to have the stage manager go over and do it! No, it didn't lose me one moment's sleep. I'm a good one at figuring out why there is an advantage in what happens. The advantage is I should not have been on display redoing someone else's work. I ended up doing my own work and that in fact was better."

When asked about the choice of director for the London production of *Forum,* Sondheim said, "Gee, I had nothing to do with that, if that's true. I have no idea who turned him down. But I think he's right. I was reluctant to see him as a director." *She Loves Me* helped change his mind, he said. Prince obviously wanted to be doing more creative work, and he could visualize ideas, a gift Sondheim was aware of lacking himself. Be that as it may, Goldman and Sondheim's first choice for director was John Dexter, who had just directed *Do I Hear a Waltz?* Everything seemed set for the arrival of *The Girls Upstairs.* But then Merrick began placing obstacles in the musical's path and the idea collapsed. Goldman and Sondheim went back over their draft and sent it to Prince. "I found the script to be awful and I didn't know how to cushion how bad I thought it was." They wrote another draft and the producer Stuart Ostrow agreed to take on the project. Prince again read the script, again did not like it, and this time wrote three thousand helpful words on what he thought needed to be done. This advice was either ignored or lost. Prince subsequently learned that a new director, Joseph Hardy, had been engaged and that the musical would go into rehearsal at the end of 1969.

In contrast to Arthur Laurents, whose affinity was with what might be called the psychological realists, James Goldman had a poetic, metaphoric imagination that was stimulated by the challenge of writing, for instance, a historical romance or, in another collaboration with Sondheim, a modern fantasy set in a New York department store. Two years after they started writing together, in 1967, Sondheim and Goldman were invited to contribute an original work for a new, experimental television series called *ABC Stage 67.* Since they admired the short stories of John Collier, they decided to adapt "Evening Primrose." This is the story of a young poet who, wanting to work undisturbed, contrives to get himself locked in a department store after closing time. Once inside, he discovers that the store is inhabited by an odd assortment of people who have taken refuge there. One of them is a pretty girl who was "lost in hats" when she was six, now serves as a maid, and is barred from leaving. One is asked to accept the notion that the girl does not know the most elementary things about life, including what a kiss feels like, and that she cannot simply slip out of the door during business hours, because she will be captured and killed by the "Dark Men." Anthony Perkins, playing the poet, decides to rescue her, but both are murdered before they can find freedom. They subsequently appear (final irony) as mannequins in the store window, portraying a bride and groom.

That Sondheim, with his exquisite sense of the absurd, should want to adapt such a preposterous plot suggests that the work had an appeal on some other level, the very real issue of psychological survival. One can read a kind of symbolism in the concept of a child who is lost, or abandoned by parents, and is wandering in an airless world filled with beautiful objects, one that offers every kind of tempting display and consolation except that of human warmth. One of the most affecting ballads in *Evening Primrose* is the song the girl sings, "I Remember," full of vivid similes describing the life she longs for outside her prison.

> I remember snow,
> Soft as feathers,
> Sharp as thumbtacks,
> Coming down like lint,
> And it made you squint
> When the wind would blow.

Sondheim disclaimed any responsibility for these lyrical metaphors. They came from Goldman, he said, and he simply appropriated them for that particular song. "Jim started out with this lovely phrase, 'I remember snow,' and I kept trying to work with it, and I knew at the end I wanted to use the word 'die.' After some hours . . . I thought, 'It's called 'I Remember Sky,' and then I can repeat it at the end and rhyme it with 'die.' The light flashed on, and I was able to go ahead with it." Nevertheless, Sondheim set the words with exquisite sensibility, and the effect is not only sad but haunting. As the play ends, the image of two young people whose lives have been malevolently ended, and whose victimized bodies have been made into mannequins, implausible as it is, carries considerable emotional weight. In terms of mood, *Evening Primrose* inhabits a world of its own, somewhere between a hallucination and a nightmare.

Goldman needed to write *Evening Primrose* that year, Sondheim said, because "Jim's wife got pregnant with a second baby and they needed a larger apartment." Sondheim happened to know about the television series because Hubbell Robinson was its producer. The work "didn't pay that well, but it was enough to get them into a new apartment." After that, Goldman was working on *The Lion in Winter,* presumably the screenplay, and Sondheim was temporarily at loose ends. At just that moment Jerome Robbins made a curious reappearance in his life.

Robbins had always been fascinated by the work of Bertolt Brecht and was experimenting with Brecht's one-act play *The Measures Taken* at his American Theatre Lab, which had been established by means of a generous $300,000 grant from the National Endowment for the Arts. Sondheim did not admire the play and disliked most of Brecht's work. Robbins, undeterred, suggested turning another Brecht play, *The Exception and the Rule,* a polemic about the exploitation of labor of the 1930s, into a musical.

John Guare said that he was approached by Robbins shortly after the experimental workshop opened. Robbins and his troupe were working on improvisations, Robbins said, and needed a playwright to assess their ideas. Guare duly appeared and found they were "doing fantasies on the Kennedy assassination. Wonderful, but they were mainly dance," he said. "I didn't see how they needed me." Then Robbins asked Guare to make an adaptation of *The Exception and the Rule.*

Guare brought the play up to date by treating it as a play within a play that was taking place in a television studio. "It was supposed to deal with the idea that in 1968 having 'good intentions' was not enough and that it was presumptuous and hilarious to expect that *showing* man's inhumanity to man would change anything in the world. I guess we still had illusions . . . And it was odd, because when we were in the middle of writing it, Bobby Kennedy was killed." Robbins was excited by Guare's treatment, Zero Mostel agreed to take the leading role, and Bernstein, who was in his final season as music director of the New York Philharmonic and looking for the chance to return to Broadway as a composer, agreed to write the music.

Guare said, "Socially, Jerry can be the most charming person. He said, 'Tonight you have got to come to my house. Steve is coming and we have to convince him to write the lyrics.'" Guare was a great fan of Sondheim's work and knew he had not been seen on Broadway for the past three years. "So that night I went to Jerry's. He said, 'Okay, he's upstairs. If Steve says no, Lenny is out and there's no show.' He opened the door and pushed me in and left me alone with Steve. I said, 'This is a nightmare, a set-up!' We talked and I told him about the show and he agreed to do it. I said, 'Why haven't you all worked together since *West Side Story?* and he said, 'You'll see.' We began work and continued for about eight months."

Speaking of that collaboration with Sondheim, Guare said, "Strangely enough, what I remember was how much we laughed. It was like being in college; we talked and talked." Robbins became a relentless supervisor. Guare recalled one weekend when Robbins rented a house from the pianist-writer team of Gold and Fizdale outside Nyack, New York, and shut him up in a room. Robbins told him that he could not come out until he had finished. He was required to pass his pages under the door, rather like Colette being imprisoned by Willy. "Ah!" said Guare. "Until you have been in that room with Jerry you don't know what a taskmaster is." As for Sondheim, "The reason for his comment 'You'll see' began to dawn on me. Bernstein only worked at midnight, and Robbins only worked bright and early in the morning." It was a lunatic experience, and Guare came to depend on Sondheim to "decode and decipher their crazy way of working," he said. Besides, Bernstein's score, which ought to have been lighthearted and modest, was weighed down by the composer's feeling that he had to make "a major musical statement," Guare said.

The producer Stuart Ostrow, who would appear and disappear in Sondheim's life in connection with *The Girls Upstairs*, agreed to produce the Bernstein-Robbins-Guare-Sondheim musical, now titled *A Pray by Blecht*. An opening date was set. They were in the middle of auditions and a new actor had just arrived on stage with his accompanist. Guare continued, "Robbins said, 'Excuse me a moment,' and he left the theatre. Minutes went by and he did not come back. So I went backstage to see what was happening. The doorman told me, 'Oh, he got into a limousine. He was going to Kennedy Airport.' I had a feeling of horror and relief. Lenny burst into tears and said, 'It's over.' "

That was typical of Robbins, said Laurents, who had been called in to give advice. Not only was it almost impossible for him to make a decision, but he could not bring himself to tell his colleagues when he did. "So he just walked out into the night." Sondheim was not in the least upset. "I was ashamed of the whole project. It was arch and didactic in the worst way." He had written one song and half of another, the only works he ever threw away. When Robbins and Bernstein made a brief effort to revive the project eighteen years later, Sondheim refused to contribute any lyrics. Guare said, "It's a real curiosity piece."

DURING THOSE YEARS when Sondheim was struggling to bring to fruition projects with a slippery tendency to shatter without warning, Hal Prince was forging a new career as a director. His production of *Fiddler on the Roof*, directed by Jerome Robbins, ran for seven years and closed after three thousand performances, giving him the financial security to experiment in new directions. That he was doing throughout the 1960s. He directed the musical *Baker Street*, based on Conan Doyle's Sherlock Holmes stories, early in 1965, and although reviews were mixed, the experience only increased his determination to become a director. He went on to direct *It's a Bird . . . It's a Plane . . . It's Superman*, the musical Sondheim would find hilarious when it was in its early stages in Philadelphia. That, too, was less than a resounding success, but the innovations he introduced, which included transforming the stage into a series of comic-book boxes in which scenes progressively appeared, were praised. Then came *Cabaret,* the musical based on Christopher Isherwood's stories about Berlin in the decadent and anti-Semitic thirties, and Prince's new position was secure.

Prince had been thinking for some time about the isolating and deadening effect of city life on contemporary marriage. By that happy convergence of forces which providence sometimes allows, an actor named George Furth was struggling with the very same subject matter; he happened to be a friend of Sondheim's. Sondheim said they met in 1963 when Furth was appearing in a revue called *Hot Spot* with Judy Holliday and he was contributing lyrics for songs for which Mary Rodgers was writing the music. Then Furth moved back to California and had an active career in film as a supporting actor, the person whose face everyone recognizes, since he appeared in so many films, among them *Sleeper, Blazing Saddles,* and *Butch Cassidy and the Sundance Kid.* Furth's analyst had suggested he write plays as part of his therapy. So he wrote a series of one-act plays examining various aspects of relationships between couples, not necessarily married ones. The plays turned out remarkably well and were to be produced on Broadway as an evening with Kim Stanley, John McMartin, and Ron Leibman. Just as the show was about to open, the producer announced that he had not been able to raise the money. In January 1969, Furth called Sondheim in despair. Sondheim said, " 'Let's ask Hal Prince. He's the person whose advice I would most respect.'

"I showed them to Hal and he said, 'I think we should make a musical of these.' It was a fascinating idea. And although James [Goldman] and I had been writing a nonlinear piece, this was nonlinear in a different way. George came to New York and we spent a few weeks in Hal's office talking about how to shape these disparate pieces into a large form. Because some of them were sketches rather than plays. As we talked we realized that what the plays had in common was a couple and a third person. And gradually it dawned on us that the third person should be the same person." It went without saying that Prince would direct.

When the idea for *Company* began, Sondheim was confidently looking forward to the opening of *The Girls Upstairs.* Then he lost his producer, Stuart Ostrow, his director, Joseph Hardy, was calling for further revisions, and so the future looked bleak in July of 1969. Sondheim contacted Prince and asked him to postpone *Company* while he pulled together his forces in an attempt to launch *The Girls Upstairs* once more. Prince refused, saying, "I'm working, I'm ready, my set is designed, my costumes are designed, you haven't written any god-damned music, but my show's ready." Sondheim replied that he was too discouraged and upset to work on *Company*. Prince agreed to review *The Girls Upstairs* one more time. Then he told Sondheim that he would take it on, but he wanted to direct *Company* first. Delighted and relieved, Sondheim went to work.

In *Company,* Robert, a bachelor-around-town, is about to be given a surprise thirty-fifth birthday party by a group of his friends, five married couples. As the evening develops, the audience meets each couple in turn: Sarah and Harry, who bicker about the fact that although he supposedly is no longer drinking, he is still sneaking to the bar, and about her attempts to diet; the scene ends with a wrestling match, as Joanne sings:

> It's the little things you do together,
> Do together,
> Do together,
> That make perfect relationships.
> The hobbies you pursue together,
> Savings you accrue together,
> Looks you misconstrue together
> That make marriage a joy.

Then there are Jenny and David, who try to smoke pot with Robert, and Susan and Peter, who intend to go on living together even though they are getting a divorce. There are Paul and Amy, who are about to be married when she has an attack of panic. Finally there are Joanne and Larry, perhaps the most spectacularly mismatched couple, whose rage at themselves and each other is expressed in an unpleasant drunken scene. The women feign concern about the fact that their attractive bachelor friend is not married, while undercutting any interest he has in a girl; the men are merely envious. Robert wants nothing to do with marriage, but, as Walter Kerr wrote, "He's willing to listen to—he cannot escape—the finger-wagging advice, in buzzing overlapping rhythms, of his matchmaking friends. Only trouble is, when he asks how any of them feels about being married, he gets an at best ambiguous, and at worst despairing answer. 'You're always sorry, you're always grateful,' a trio of furrow-browed husbands carols to him (in quite a nice little lazy-beat song), ending with a dying 'you're always alone.' The mood is misanthropic, the view from the peephole jaundiced." Sondheim's view was, "*Company* says very clearly that to be emotionally committed to somebody is very difficult, but to be alone is impossible."

To create a musical that simply explored an issue, the state of marriage in modern urban society, was an avant-garde idea in tune with the times. The 1960s had been filled with experimentation as novelists and poets, having jettisoned what they considered anachronistic notions of structure and form, even the shape of the sentence itself, wrote plotless novels or themeless poems. Music had soared into the realms of higher mathematics with the establishment of the tone row. Even dance was being taken ever further in the direction of gymnastic abstraction, as if choreographers were ignoring what was meant by the very name of the art. It was felt, however, that audiences for that most conservative of forms, the musical, would not accept any tinkering with a formula that had been successful for decades. Would people who arrived at a theatre expecting escapist entertainment accept a free-form exploration of a theme that challenged all their preconceptions? Sondheim wanted his audience to laugh uproariously and then go home and not be able to sleep. He hoped the musical would have that effect, because "it kept me awake for six months."

How to approach such a score presented a major problem. Unlike Goldman's, whose descriptive passages seemed to beg for lyrical expression, Furth's writing, Sondheim said, was antithetical to singing. "Every time I tried to develop a song out of dialogue it didn't work. Which is why all the songs in *Company* are either self-encapsulated entities or Brechtian comments on what is happening. In the score of *Company,* nothing comes out of the play, nothing. It's absolutely the reverse of what Oscar taught me. And it is, for lack of a better word, Brechtian, in the sense of comment songs like 'Another Hundred People,' 'The Little Things You Do Together', and 'You Could Drive a Person Crazy.' Others are soliloquies, like 'Someone Is Waiting,' 'Being Alive,' and 'The Ladies Who Lunch.' Then there are things like 'Barcelona,' which is a musical scene." He disliked the whole idea of stopping the flow of the action to make an authorial comment, but it seemed the only solution in this case.

Company and *Forum* had certain similarities in that the songs in both musicals were complete in themselves. "The difference is that in *Company* you can't take the songs out and have a show left. Not really. Because the songs are used for emotional transitions, as in 'Being Alive.' And if you don't have the attitude of the couples towards Bobby, as in 'Side by Side by Side,' or 'Poor Baby,' you don't have any perspective, and it becomes a series of disparate playlets. So the score is much more integral than in *Forum*, where, as I say, you could take out the songs and you'd still have the show."

On the difficulty of translating Furth's dialogue into music, Sondheim gave as an example an idea he had for a song in which Bobby introduces

Hal Prince, Sondheim, and George Coe, who plays David, discussing Coe's song "Sorry–Grateful" from *Company*

Jenny and David to pot. "I had an idea for a song called 'Wow,' which would just be space, essentially, and then someone saying, 'Wow.' If you've ever smoked pot you know that time takes on a different dimension. What actually is about three seconds seems like five minutes because you drift. It's a kind of wooziness; it's taffy-pull relaxation. So I thought it would be fun to have a song in which you'd go . . . [*pause*] . . . 'Wow!' Meanwhile it was all filled up with music. And then they start to say things they think are profound and it would come out in sudden bursts: 'Oh my God, do we have the spaghetti ready yet?' "

It sounded wonderful, "and it didn't work! I never finished it because I could tell it didn't work. That was the hardest song to find, as a matter of fact. I think it was the last song I wrote because I couldn't figure out how to get a song into that scene."

What helped Sondheim immensely was the arrival of the set design. "I wrote the opening of *Company*, as a matter of fact, after having seen a sketch by Boris Aronson, the set designer. It showed me what I was writing for." Frank Rich wrote, "The designer's emerging concept was . . . sparked by the paintings of Francis Bacon. In Bacon's pictures of anguished, contorted figures sitting alone in abstracted cages, Aronson found an image that expressed the bleak mood of alienated contemporary New Yorkers who are at once

The cast begins work on *Company*. Prince is at the end of the table and the playwright, George Furth, is to his left. Stephen Sondheim is at the piano in the background. And below, Sondheim at the piano with the cast: from left, Furth, Dean Jones and Elaine Stritch, Prince, Barbara Barrie, and choreographer Michael Bennett

trapped and exposed in their glass enclosures." Aronson's design, a chrome-and-glass abstraction with various levels and compartments, could be viewed as apartments, or as the Manhattan skyline symbolically rendered, or as a spare, perfectly realized piece of sculpture. Aronson added some sliding panels, moving platforms, a revolving door, and, in a final stroke of genius, two elevators.

Prince's choice of Aronson—who had also designed the sets for *Fiddler on the Roof*—was inspired, as was his choice of Michael Bennett as choreographer. Up to that point Bennett had not been particularly successful, but *Company* and *Follies* showed that he had the makings of a major choreographer, and *A Chorus Line* would solidify his reputation. He and Sondheim worked together closely, if only because, based on his experience with "Maria" in *West Side Story*, Sondheim had acquired the habit of precisely timing everything that would happen while the character was singing his song. "The director is free to change it or not but he has a blueprint," Sondheim said. "He never has to turn to me and ask, 'What am I going to do here?' I always give him more than enough . . . If you want the character to cross from here to there, or he has to pick up a coffee cup and drink it or whatever it is, I time those things here in my studio. Then I say, 'Okay now, during these beats or in between, he empties the coffee cup.' The director may say, 'I don't want a coffee cup in the number' and that's all right. But that's the idea and almost no other composers do this. When I first worked with Michael Bennett and I did the opening number for *Company* he couldn't believe it . . . He'd always had to invent out of nowhere . . . I staged that entire number in my head around the elevator. I asked Boris how long it would take the elevator to get from the top to the bottom so that I knew I could get the people off the stairs and onto the stage level and that's what that climax is about."

If the New York critics had formerly reacted with coolness to the idea of Sondheim as composer, this was no longer true. The musical was so brilliant it passed over one "like a shock wave," Douglas Watt wrote in the *Daily News,* and the critics at *Time* and *Newsweek* both praised *Company* as "a landmark." London critics, as exemplified by Harold Hobson of the *Sunday Times* in 1972, were equally admiring: "There are no native composers in this city of the varied brilliance of Stephen Sondheim, who is responsible for both music and lyrics—lyrics that are sometimes sharp as an icicle, and that at others set the mind achingly dreaming of unforgotten joys and irrational sorrows . . . It is extraordinary that a musical, the most trivial of theatrical forms, should be able to plunge as *Company* does with perfect congruity into the profound depths of human perplexity and misery."

Above, Sondheim at the piano. Below, conferring with the musical director of *Company,* Harold Hastings

Unfortunately, the influential critic of the *New York Times,* Clive Barnes, while admiring Sondheim's "sweetly laconic cynicism," found his sophisticated style to be slick, clever, and eclectic rather than emotionally stimulating. "It's the kind of musical that makes me say, 'Oh yeah?' rather than 'Gee whiz!' " That was a real blow, even though another *Times* critic, Mel Gussow, was full of admiration: "On re-hearing, Stephen Sondheim's elegantly intricate score deepens in sophistication, intelligence and lyrical and musical inventiveness." The song about April, the airline stewardess, who gets out of Robert's bed in the middle of the night because she has to go to Barcelona and who, after much coaxing, agrees to stay (to his horror), was an instant classic. Then there was the moment when Joanne, who is drinking vodka stingers, those symbols of urban dissipation, sinks into self-pity as she describes herself as "too young for the old people and too old for the young ones." "Here's to the ladies who lunch," she sings scornfully:

> Everybody laugh.
> Lounging in their caftans and planning a brunch
> On their own behalf.
> Off to a gym,
> Then to a fitting,
> Claiming they're fat.
> And looking grim
> 'Cause they've been sitting
> Choosing a hat—
> Does anyone still wear a hat?
> I'll drink to that.

There was Amy's headlong scream of desperation as she, in her wedding dress, explains that she cannot get married after all:

> It isn't only Paul
> Who may be ruining his life, you know,
> We'll both of us be losing our identities—
> I telephoned my analyst about it
> And he said to see him Monday
> But by Monday I'll be floating
> In the Hudson with the other garbage.

Part of the success of the work has to be credited to Sondheim's new collaborator, the orchestrator Jonathan Tunick, who entered his life at this point and stayed. Tunick said, "I had just started to have a career as a Broadway orchestrator. I'd finished *Promises, Promises,* a show I did with Burt Bacharach. I had met Sondheim socially through a mutual friend, and when *Company* was announced, I was eager to work with him. I knew his music and was *very* enthusiastic. I remember a friend bringing over the album of *Forum,* saying, 'You've got to hear this,' and I said, 'Oh, Stephen Sondheim. Isn't he the guy who wrote the lyrics for *West Side Story?* He writes music?' I made the discovery that he was a composer immediately. The first few notes of the overture I practically hit the ceiling. That descending scale that keeps going down and down . . . And I agreed with my friend. 'This is terrific stuff!' "

Tunick took his courage into his hands and called Sondheim asking for the job on *Company* and was subsequently hired. "Not knowing Steve very well, I just assumed he had a close relationship with Leonard Bernstein, and so I was very intimidated, unnecessarily, as it turns out, because every note I wrote I felt Bernstein leaning over my shoulder. Bernstein showed up for a preview and I was introduced to him. But that leads to a story. When I was orchestrating 'The Ladies Who Lunch,' there is a reference to Mahler and two bars of vamp. That was an open invitation to a quote, so I started going through the Mahler scores and would reject one idea after the other, thinking it was too obvious. I went through agonies over this. I finally put a quote from Mahler's Fourth, which is still there.

"We played the number at the orchestra reading in Boston and nobody said anything. Steve heard it, Hal heard it, and Michael [Bennett] heard it. Nobody was getting it! So I said to myself, 'When Lenny hears it he'll get it.' We played it through the entire Boston run. Bernstein came to see the show in New York. The night he did, the flute player missed his cue and didn't play it."

Sondheim said he liked to give Tunick a complete piano copy of each song. "I was trained as a pianist and I don't know much about orchestration. I mean, I know what the instruments are, but I don't really know anything about the techniques of blending them . . . But virtually every note that is in the score is in the piano copy when I write it. Jonathan will sometimes add lines—I won't say fills, because I always do those fills that occur between the vocal lines myself—but, for example, he will put a high string line on because he'll feel that something has to hold it together." When they discussed orchestration, Sondheim never gave Tunick specific directions but spoke in general terms about the effect he wanted, leaving Tunick considerable latitude about how to achieve it. The composer David Shire, who met Sondheim when he came to see the first off-Broadway show he wrote with Richard Maltby Jr., *The Sap of Life,* and became a friend, thought Tunick would be exactly right for Sondheim. Shire said, "I unhesitatingly recommended Jonathan. Because Steve's music is written with a Ravelian transparency; if it gets thickened too much it loses the wonderful interplay of lines. Jonathan makes it come out orchestrally with the same texture, feeling and sensibility of Steve playing it on the piano."

THE CREATORS OF *Company* readily conceded that the central character of Robert was the least well defined. Michael Ratcliffe wrote, "This exceptionally energetic show fizzes around a large question-mark and an empty space: a hero who is too indecisive to move. Who is he?" Prince and Sondheim had originally engaged Tony Perkins to play Robert, which would have enhanced the role with someone whose film personality was well established. But then Perkins, pleading that he really wanted to direct rather than act, dropped out, to be replaced first by Dean Jones and then by Larry Kert. The latter had originated the role of Tony in *West Side Story* and was a good friend of Sondheim's. His sister was Anita Ellis, who rented Sondheim's upstairs apartment with her husband, and Kert often stayed with them. Kert is the author of a memorable line, in connection with *Company,* that is often

Three of *Company*'s stars: Elaine Stritch, Dean Jones, and Barbara Barrie

quoted. It is said that when the musical was being prepared for its London opening at Her Majesty's Theatre early in 1972, after a technical dress rehearsal that dragged on into the small hours, Kert became exhausted and then exasperated. "He came striding toward the front of the stage, looked out balefully across the orchestra and said, 'Who do I have to screw to get out of this show?' " said Ned Sherrin, who would create a successful revue of Sondheim's songs a few years later. "Shocked silence at Her Majesty's. I mean, it's not . . . the way they put things in England. The silence was finally broken by a small Sondheim voice from the back of the stalls saying, 'Same person you screwed to get in.' "

Both Jones and Kert received respectful reviews, but because their personalities were not as well established as Perkins's, the missing dimensions of Robert may have seemed more evident. Sam Mendes, artistic director of the Donmar Warehouse in London and director of a successful revival of *Company* in 1996, believed that the root of Bobby's crisis was not emotional indifference or complacency, but loneliness. Since the audience is given such a scant description of his inner life during the course of the evening, it is hard to empathize, let alone understand why he seems to have such a magnetic appeal for all those people. And in fact Furth and Sondheim had a great deal of trouble arriving at an ending. It was agreed that a song was needed. Bobby, making his first clear statement of the evening, comes out with "Happily Ever After," in which he concludes that marriage is to be avoided at all costs:

> Someone to need you too much
> Someone to read you too well,
> Someone to bleed you of all
> The things you don't want to tell—
> That's happily ever after,
> Ever, ever, ever after
> In hell.

The musical played with that ending in Boston, but, Prince said, "It was the bitterest, most unhappy song ever written, and we didn't know how devastating it would be until we saw it in front of an audience." Something had to be done before the show arrived in New York. Fritz Holt, a young stage manager, remembered taking a scene he had just typed as a lead-in to the new song, "Being Alive," and handing it to Sondheim at his hotel door. "He looked *terrible*. That was the first time I realized the agony Steve goes through on a show. It's painful and horrifying."

"Being Alive" had some resemblances to two works with which Sondheim had been associated a few years before. In the climactic moment of *Anyone Can Whistle,* J. Bowden Hapgood tells Nurse Apple that she is too complicated to enjoy being alive, and that is why she cannot whistle. Then, in *Evening Primrose,* the heroine has a wonderful ballad called "Take Me to The World," in which she sings:

> Take me to the world that's real,
> Show me how it's done.
> Teach me how to laugh, to feel
> Move me to the sun.
>
> Just hold my hand whenever we arrive,
> Take me to the world where I can be alive.

What is interesting about the ballad is the entirely passive role the heroine plays. Her very existence depends upon her being rescued by someone else, as if she were under a sorcerer's spell. Something of the same sort happens to Robert, trapped in his isolation. In a very interesting sleight-of-hand, Sondheim, with a minimum of alteration, completely turns around the actual phrases from "Happily Ever After" to come to the opposite conclusion. In the original there is

> Someone to hold you too close,
> Someone to hurt you too deep,
> Someone to bore you to death
> Happily ever after.

That thought evolves with breathtaking economy into

> Someone to hold you too close,
> Someone to hurt you too deep,
> Someone to sit in your chair,
> To ruin your sleep,
> To make you aware
> Of being alive,
> Being alive.

Nothing actually has changed. Marriage is still the same smothering relationship, full of vain regret, unsolved antagonisms, and annihilating resentments, but its existence spells the difference between a submerged, half-dead kind of life and true awareness. The implication was that barriers that were self-imposed could only be removed by the arrival of someone else, but it was a debatable point, given the marriages on display here. If Robert had learned anything by the end of the show, it was not about the ideal of marital harmony or wise maturity. All his friends had rotten marriages, but he knew that already. If nothing had happened to the hero, how could he have a change of heart? Artistically speaking, "Happily Ever After" was the only valid ending, even if, as Prince said, it seemed to frighten audiences. But "Being Alive" it was, and it became one of Sondheim's best-known songs. Years later, while listening to an orchestral reading for a revival of *Company* by the Roundabout Theatre Company on Broadway in 1995, Sondheim was observed afterwards leaving his seat, walking away and wiping his eyes.

Sondheim said he had always been aware that "Happily Ever After" was the logical song for Robert to sing, and he had never felt comfortable with the substitution of "Being Alive." "There was one time when I saw the show where it worked, and I can't tell you why, but it was an off-Broadway production at the York Theatre some years ago. Susan Schulman directed it, and the leading part was sung by a guy, now dead, named David James Carroll, and somehow, when he turned front and sang that song, it was as if the whole evening had led to it. I don't know how he did it, but it was completely fulfilling. I thought, My God, we don't need a transition if the right actor's playing it.

"Now maybe if I saw it again I wouldn't think so, but that is the way it seemed that night, and it was the one time the song moved me. I don't mean that I don't get touched or moved by it. But the thing that moves me is a line that was written by George, not me. It's when Amy says, 'Blow out your candles and make a wish. Want something. Want *some*thing!' I get chills listening to it."

CHAPTER II

Broadway Baby

S ONDHEIM HAD ACCOMPLISHED what he set out to do with *Company*: he had started a debate that would continue for the next twenty-five years. When *Company* arrived in London in January 1972, it "was discussed with a seriousness normally extended only to new novels and plays," Michael Ratcliffe observed. Writing in *The Independent* twenty-five years later, what Michael White called "the disturbance factor" in Sondheim's musicals was still being argued, i.e., "the lingering, after-hours emotional fall-out" that identified the work of a mature artist. Not surprisingly, his work inspired strongly opposing reactions.

Cameron Mackintosh, then at the start of what would be a distinguished career as a producer, said that when *Company* arrived at Her Majesty's Theatre it was the first American show he had seen with an original American cast. "I was infatuated with musical theatre and beside myself because I couldn't yet afford to see a Broadway show or go to America, and this was the first time a whole company had come over since the original cast of *Oklahoma!* had come to Drury Lane straight after the war. So I fought my way to opening night. I'd stood and cheered three times during the performance, absolutely hysterical, and yet I hadn't liked the show!"

After holding the composer at arm's length, the Broadway community made up for past omissions. Sondheim and Furth took a New York Drama

Critics' Circle Award. There were fifteen nominations for the Tony Awards, then a record, and seven awards given in 1971: for best musical, best music, best lyrics, best book, best scene design, best producer, and best director. The awards to Hal Prince were in recognition of the role he had played in *Company's* creation. He would play an equally pivotal role in the evolution of *Follies*, which abandoned the original Goldman-Sondheim concept of a murder mystery involving two couples and centered around the image of Gloria Swanson standing in the rubble of the Roxy Theatre that had haunted him ever since he had seen it in 1960. *Follies*, Prince thought, ought to be something larger, more ambitious and impressionistic than the story of four lives. Like a waking dream, it should gather up the miragelike qualities that the photograph represented. *Follies* would come to signify the death of a certain kind of musical theatre and its evolution into one that was going to be more sophisticated, more knowing, more nuanced and entirely devoid of sentimental illusions.

To fully understand why *Follies* was such a landmark, one had to appreciate what Prince and Sondheim were reacting against. For instance, *On the Town*, Bernstein's musical about three sailors on twenty-four-hour shore leave in New York, which now seems far too naive and picture-postcard pretty, was almost a classic statement of the mood of the times when it was produced in 1944. Betty Comden and Adolph Green, authors of the book, explained that it held a mirror to the poignant feelings of people who were "trying to cram a lifetime of experiences into a day." Once the war was won there was a rosily optimistic view of what the future had in store: "some kind of marvelous expansion of life as it was before the '30s, before the Depression, combining the latest technological advances with the old pioneer spirit, and the sweetest, most sentimental moral traditions of the 19th century—home, family, success—all the desired rewards of individual get-up-and-go . . ." *Oklahoma!* in 1943 had been successful precisely because it expressed hope for the future and sentimental nostalgia for the past. So if musicals of the postwar years seemed cloying, with their pots of gold at the end of every rainbow, they were at least reflecting the mood of the times, with its faith in "progress" and the ethic of success. An abandoned theatre would present the ideal background for an era in which the dream had faded and old problems had been supplanted by new ones that seemed even more intractable. At the end of every rainbow was a pile of rubble. It was not pat, and it was uncomfortable, but it certainly was daring.

Sondheim and Goldman were intrigued by Prince's concept, which would require "something like" their thirteenth draft since *The Girls Upstairs* had first been envisioned in 1965. As before, the ostensible reason for the

The poster for *Follies*

gathering would be a reunion of old showgirls, invited to one last evening in the theatre before its demolition is complete. Two couples emerge. Phyllis and Sally met during their youth when both appeared in the Follies. The men they married, Ben and Buddy, were courting them in those days. Sally and Buddy have a conventional marriage and children and are outwardly content. But Sally has never recovered from the love affair she had with Ben when they were young. Phyllis has become bitter and self-pitying. Ben is outwardly successful and inwardly tormented with doubt. "The Ben I'll never be, / Who remembers him?" he sings in "The Road You Didn't Take." Their sorry adjustments to what has become of their lives are juxtaposed against snatches of scenes in which they are played by actors representing themselves when young, full of verve and optimism. Weaving in and out of the present are the towering ghosts of the past, the black-and-white, insistent images of the Follies in their heyday, peopled by exquisitely beautiful girls. They conjure up a portrait of the past everyone wanted to remember, even if it never existed. T. E. Kalem, writing in *Time* magazine, called *Follies* "the first Proustian musical."

Although *Follies* bears a superficial resemblance to *Company* in its portrait of contemporary marriage, its context is larger: "the death of vaudeville as a metaphor for the death of American innocence," Frank Rich wrote. Nevertheless, the delineation of the principals makes it clear that Goldman has taken his characters a step further than Furth did in *Company.* Each of them is fleeing from self-knowledge. It transpires that the source of their unhappiness is not so much their slavish adherence to false values, although they have fallen into the familiar trap, as it is some basic character flaws. Phyllis cannot surmount her angry disappointment and desire to get even. In the light of conflicting signals from Ben, Sally convinces herself that he is about to divorce his wife and marry her. Buddy is emotionally unable to want anyone who wants him. Coming face to face with the past forces Ben to confront the bitter truths about the present. He is the one who learns most, but he is also the one who has a breakdown at the climax of *Follies.*

If *Follies* is a kind of monument to failed hopes and blasted dreams, it is also, in its way, a bittersweet Valentine to the great musical traditions of the past. Something irreplaceable has been lost, something worth celebrating. So *Follies* is as much a revue as an exploration of wasted lives, deserving of elegiac reflection as the principals leave the stage and the ghosts of their pasts steal back onto it. As Milan Kundera wrote in *The Book of Laughter and Forgetting,* "The past is full of life . . ."

WORK STARTED ON *Follies* soon after *Company* opened in the spring of 1970 and involved months of discussion. Then Prince went on holiday to Majorca, and Boris Aronson began to design the set with the approximate guidance of a script that was about to change radically and a recording of four songs Sondheim had written for *The Girls Upstairs:* "Don't Look at Me," "Flowers," "Waiting for the Girls Upstairs," and "Pleasant Little Kingdom / Too Many Mornings." (There would be twenty-three musical numbers eventually.) Aronson had agreed to send photographs of a model to

Prince by the summer, and to incorporate the director-producer's suggestions into final sketches and models by Labor Day. That the set had to be designed first was unavoidable, and Prince had warned Aronson that the final version would bear almost no resemblance to the script he had. In fact, the original script called for theatrical dressing rooms and a box office, among other scenes, none of which would eventually be needed. Aronson did know that he had to portray an empty stage in the process of being dismantled and also, that near the end of the show, there would be a recreation of a Ziegfeld Follies type of number.

Aronson decided to emphasize the grandeur, even the monumentality, of the building's scale. "I wanted it to be more than just a music hall." And since memories arrived in fragmentary form, he wanted to extend the concept of disintegration to everything on the stage. "If you see a statue and a hand is missing, or the nose is broken, it leaves so much more to the imagination than if it were complete." As with *Company*, he gave his director infinite flexibility in staging by creating several units of open scaffolding that could be moved around at will, making for a variety of platform heights, entrances and exits. For the surrealistic Follies sequence, Aronson designed a fan-shaped and lacy collage reminiscent of a Victorian Valentine, "a flash of color amidst the doom," he explained. The moment when a bare stage becomes an elaborate, kaleidoscopic setting into which the ghosts of showgirls pirouette and prance would be the musical's most famous sequence. At the end, on a sunny morning, the characters take their leave of the empty theatre, beyond which, for the first time, one can glimpse the street scene outside.

While Aronson was refining his design, Sondheim, Goldman, and Michael Bennett, who had become co-director as well as choreographer, thrashed out the script in Prince's house in Majorca. "The trouble there," Sondheim said, "was that Hal's a day person and I'm a night one. He starts off the day on high and drops off after a few hours. It takes me a few hours just to wake up. But there's a minute or two as we pass each other when ideas flow." There are tantalizing clues that, in their incipient approaches to their work, Prince and Sondheim were, in some respects, mirror images of each other. When Sondheim was cautious and full of self-doubt, Prince would be expansive, imaginative, and enthusiastic. But Sondheim had an amazing ability to find solutions at the eleventh hour, and Prince had a way of despairing just as everything was going well. For instance, he was capable of coming down with what looked like hepatitis before rehearsals began, with symptoms of fatigue, stomach ache, and yellowed eyes, as he did in the case of *Follies*. "I had lots of tests taken. All negative. It was panic. I always panic. It usually lasts twenty-four hours. When Michael Bennett asked me what I had, I told him the

Alexis Smith and John
McMartin in rehearsal
for *Follies,* 1971

Boris Aronson's set
design

Showgirls in the Love-
land sequence

truth—fear." And *Follies* engaged him in a way that it does not seem to have done for Sondheim; Prince confessed later that he became so closely involved with the drama, and particularly the character of Ben, that "I put myself through a whole emotional crisis." The fact that their qualities of mind were complementary, even compensatory, had a great deal to do with the enduring strength of their relationship. Most of all, each deeply respected the other. Prince said, "Until Steve broke through, there was a great reluctance to appreciate the nature of his talent. It isn't all that unusual, either. Because it is a unique talent." Sondheim said of Prince in 1975, "There isn't anybody else."

George Abbott, a man with a well-deserved reputation for taking charge and keeping everyone focused in the right direction, had been one of Hal Prince's mentors in the difficult act of conveying authority, one he soon learned, as Sondheim has described. Even the formidable Jerome Robbins, said to take over every project in which he was ever involved, had had to come to terms with Prince. It is perhaps only a coincidence that while still in his twenties, Prince grew a beard, which helped to add an air of authority to his youthful features, and also just a coincidence, perhaps, that he would address Sondheim, his junior by only two years, as "kid." Prince's pattern of speech was more measured than Sondheim's, but he showed the same level of restless energy, pacing back and forth in rehearsal, occasionally rubbing his forehead in an effort to think. He dressed well, if conventionally, his sole gesture toward bohemianism being an occasional refusal to wear socks. Photographs of him at work invariably show a pair of glasses perched on top of his balding head. An interviewer wrote that while rehearsing, Prince could be effusive and demonstrative but also blunt, "expecting egos to be as sturdy as his when often they're not." The playwright Terrence McNally put it even more forcefully, calling him "a screamer and a yeller. Hal only negotiates from force," he said. George Hearn, who would play the title role in *Sweeney Todd*, said, "Hal has, it seems to me, an inner film of what he wants to see. It's not my favorite way to work as an actor because it doesn't start from within and work out . . . The gratification with Prince is working with someone so bright, so fast, and so generous. He's going like wildfire all the time. It's exciting to be around that mind."

The partnership split naturally, Prince taking charge of the overall shape of the production, Sondheim concentrating on the integration of book and music. He would spend a good deal of time working with the music director and his singers, on diction and motivation; decisions about whether a song should be dropped or replaced, or a new one written, seem to have been arrived at jointly. But there were curious gaps in their easy relationship. Referring to the divorce of Sondheim's parents and its aftermath, Prince said,

"I have to tell you something—for people who are as old, good friends as we are, we never talked about any of that stuff. Never talked about—a hell of a lot. Which people might construe as not much of a friendship!"

If Prince's strengths were invaluable to Sondheim, there were other reasons why Sondheim was valuable to Prince. Thanks to his experiences while auditioning the scores for *West Side Story, Saturday Night, Anyone Can Whistle, Forum,* and so on, Sondheim had developed a faultless auditioning technique. As his tapes show, he was an accomplished pianist and able, because he thought with such dizzying rapidity, to accompany himself, sing the most demanding of patter songs, and insert stage directions all at once. While in his twenties he sang in a youthful baritone, which darkened as he aged, made all the more engaging by the lack of any attempt at polish. If he could not make a high note, he cracked on it. If he was running out of breath, he just trailed off at the end. None of this seemed to matter. He had absorbed some valuable lessons in those evenings when Lloyd Weill sang and his father accompanied at the piano, launching himself into his songs with such fearlessness and singing with such expression and conviction, that he was his own best proselytizer. No musical-comedy hopeful ever put across his songs as persuasively as Sondheim did himself on these tapes, and, as has been noted, he was cheerfully prepared to repeat the performance as often as necessary.

As with people who have to work in close quarters for hours on end, they had their disagreements. It was a source of continual irritation for Prince that Sondheim took so long to write, and as the latter often said, in his ideal world no song would be written until he knew who was singing it. Sondheim was late with his music for *Follies,* but that could hardly be helped, given the amorphous nature of the script and the fact that "we hadn't decided what the end was going to be," he said. And then *Follies* was subject to the usual eleventh-hour decisions about songs that had to be replaced because something did not "work," a common theatrical generalization that can mean anything or nothing. "Directors tend to judge the effect of songs by the amount of applause they get," Sondheim said. "If they don't stop the show—out. Performers quite often do, too. If the song doesn't get a huge hand they worry that it's no good, never mind what it contributes to the texture of the whole evening."

Given the valedictory nature of the theme, Sondheim had the particular challenge of writing, as he said, "for something I've never known: the pastiches in *Follies* have come from listening to records and playing the piano." In a television interview about the history of musical theatre which was made at about this time, he said he thought that the evolution of the genre had something to do with living in New York, "and the fact that everything is tumbling all the time, and it needs some kind of wild and poetic expression. And I think that the musical is poetic; even when you are dealing with something . . . like *Hello, Dolly!*, there's something magical about it that just does not exist in films and television." He concluded, "It's not about being smart; it's about being alive."

Hal Prince, who had acquired a well-deserved reputation for his skill at careful budgeting, felt he had no alternative but to allow the immense budget, for those days, of $800,000. Not only was an adjustable set expensive, but so were the one hundred and forty fantastic costumes designed by Florence Klotz. They were "marvellously foolish," Walter Kerr wrote. There were headdresses of black and white willow ostrich three feet high, headdresses of crystal chandeliers, of wedding cakes, birds' nests, and galleons riding billowing manes of curls. In order to further the effect, showgirls were picked who were six feet tall and then given platform shoes. Some of the costumes were so immense and so encrusted with ornamentation that they had to be lowered onto their owners moments before they appeared on stage. The showgirls imparted, one reviewer wrote, "a strangely poetic quality to the show, like Fates in an ancient tragedy, plumed and glittering, looming over . . . mortal men." Prince held his final two weeks of rehearsal on the actual set at a scenic studio in the Bronx. Finding that the stage was too steeply raked for any kind of dancing, Prince had alterations made then: "It saved a great deal of money adjusting there, instead of in Boston with stagehands and orchestra hanging around."

By then they had assembled a first-rate cast, with Dorothy Collins playing Sally, Alexis Smith as Phyllis, John McMartin as Ben, and Gene Nelson as Buddy, along with Ethel Shutta, Fifi D'Orsay, Mary McCarty, and Yvonne De Carlo in cameo roles. Alexis Smith was considered a surprising choice for the role of Phyllis, since her career had been made in Warner Bros. films, usually playing secondary roles, and no one knew how well she could sing and dance, although she had been on tour and in stock. However, Smith took a crash course in voice and movement and made a special study of the song that was generally agreed to be the most difficult, "Could I Leave You?," before she came to New York for her final audition. No one worried about the singing ability of Dorothy Collins, who had been a television star on Lucky Strike's *Your Hit Parade* in the 1950s. Yvonne De Carlo, who once played in *Salome Where She Danced* (1945), was logically cast as an aging movie star. Then there was Fifi D'Orsay, a well-known musical-theatre performer from the 1920s, who made such an impression at the auditions that "Ah, Paris!" was written for her. An equal impression was made by Ethel Shutta, who would begin her fiftieth year on Broadway when *Follies* opened in the spring of 1971 at the Winter Garden, the theatre in which she had made her debut in *The Passing Show of 1922*. Prince had once asked her for an autograph and had gone to Horace Mann School with her sons. Sondheim wrote a song just for her.

> I'm just a
> Broadway baby,
> Walking off my tired feet,
> Pounding Forty-second Street
> To be in a show . . .

When she sang that song, "jabbing a rhythmic finger at us as she thrusts one foot forward," Kerr wrote, "she is giving an object lesson in what it is to *place* a song." Another surprise was Yvonne De Carlo's vocal ability; she had, Sondheim said, "a very large range." She was doing well with "Can That Boy Fox Trot!" but not quite well enough. The song was "supposed to be done by a lady standing at the piano with a drink in her hand," Sondheim said. "One chorus and off. I wasted some time trying to build the number in Boston . . ." But the song simply refused to develop, and Sondheim replaced it with one that was even better. Theodore S. Chapin, who acted as a production assistant on *Follies,* said that Sondheim took the trouble to sit down with De Carlo and listen to the story of her life (she was then forty-nine). He came back with the incomparable song "I'm Still Here."

> Good times and bum times,
> I've seen them all and, my dear,
> I'm still here.
> Plush velvet sometimes,
> Sometimes just pretzels and beer,
> But I'm here.
>
> I've stuffed the dailies
> In my shoes,
> Strummed ukeleles,
> Sung the blues,
> Seen all my dreams disappear,
> But I'm here.

As Brooks Atkinson observed, "No one would undertake the intricate, painful, gargantuan, hysterical task of putting on a musical play unless he had

more enthusiasm than most people have about anything." One of the reasons
why Prince may have had a moment of panic as rehearsals began was that for
all the months of advance planning, the musical was in a highly fluid state,
not just because so many songs and the Loveland sequence remained to be
written, but because of the complexity of the design itself. As past mingled
with present, cinematic effects could be achieved. The action could shift from
the present day (in color) to the past (black and white) in seconds. Similarly,
images from the past could glide and intermingle, interjecting comments, acting as silent commentary on what was being said, weaving a kind of perspective and dramatic emphasis that would be impossible (or at least very difficult)
with conventional stagecraft. All this was thanks to the accommodating
nature of Aronson's set. But having so many options meant that decisions had
to be made by the minute by a director who, at the same time, had to maintain a coherent vision if the final effect were to be convincing and not just
confusing. Actors found it bewildering. Gene Nelson said, "I couldn't make
heads or tails of it. It was all in Hal's mind. This was a whole new kind of theatre, multiple scenes and overlapping lines, a story in reverse."

Chapin said, "A lot of moments that went into *Follies* were rewritten in
rehearsal. By everybody. Michael Bennett did three versions of the prologue
in Boston. A lot of songs were changed even before going into rehearsal.
'Bring On the Girls' was changed to 'Beautiful Girls,' for instance. I do
remember, in the daily log that I kept, saying as a sort of observation that
somebody seemed to be miserable all the time. I can't remember exactly
who it was, between Steve and Hal and Michael and James Goldman.
Putting on a musical is an astonishing amount of work. In the early days,
when the choreographer would be with his dancers in one room doing one
thing, and the musical director would be teaching music to somebody else
in another room, and Hal would be staging things in the big room, you
had to make certain everything was coordinated and there was enough coming in from the choreography to take into the big room and put it all
together."

Another essential figure, the orchestrator, was always hovering in the
background, taking notes. His work had to come last, for obvious reasons.
Jonathan Tunick well remembers the night he orchestrated "I'm Still Here" in
a Boston hotel room. He called it "one of my overnight wonders," with a
whole copying staff across the hall snatching up each page as it appeared.

The problem was the sheer volume of the music. "There were stacks of
the stuff. And some very involved production numbers. There were some
tricky moments for the orchestration of 'The Road You Didn't Take' and
'Don't Look at Me.' I remember, in the latter, that Steve had written glis-

sando passages that I had to change to something, so I wrote some arpeggio passages for woodwinds." Then there was Ben's aria toward the end of the show, "Live, Laugh, Love," when he sings about how happy he is and has a nervous breakdown. "I wanted the instruments to reflect this, and it was Michael Bennett's idea to have the orchestra gradually fall apart. So I conceived the idea that the orchestra would be tooting along and then would start splitting apart. First it would split in half, then the two halves would split in half, and so on, until at the end everybody in the orchestra was playing a different tune. And they were playing the wildest things. One trombone was playing Rimsky-Korsakov's *Scheherazade,* another is playing 'Gettin' Sentimental Over You,' somebody is playing 'The Stars and Stripes Forever,' somebody else is playing 'Begin the Beguine,' somebody else the Brahms Violin Concerto . . . organized chaos. It was a marvelous success. Something Charles Ives would have appreciated."

Sondheim has said he dislikes attending rehearsals, often because he finds fault with what he has written, or he had imagined the song for a soprano and has had to settle for a mezzo, and also because his tendency is to want to stay somewhere in the back row, not down front and center taking notes. But in this particular case he was at home "for hours, because he had a great deal of work to do," Chapin said. "He would come in at the end of a day and play a song. One particular day when he came in, he handed me a lyric to type, went into conference, and came out saying, 'You wasted your time. They've just cut the song.' " (Chapin thinks it might have been "The World's Full of Girls," an instrumental version of which was used in the film *Stavisky.*)

"The song 'Losing My Mind' was originally written for Phyllis and Sally, not for Sally singing alone. The song 'You're Gonna Love Tomorrow' was not [yet] written, 'Love Will See Us Through' was not written, 'The God-Why-Don't-You-Love-Me Blues' was not written, 'Live, Laugh, Love' was not written, 'The Story of Lucy and Jessie' was not written, and neither was its predecessor, 'Uptown Downtown.' So he had his hands full during the rehearsal period writing all those songs. It was January in New York, and I was proud owner of a Volkswagen, a bright red convertible, and was taking people back and forth to rehearsals on the set in the Bronx. One day I picked up Judy Prince and then Steve. He got into the car and said to Judy, 'Oh, I just had a rhyming fit' (he was writing a song), and proceeded to tell her the rhyming scheme that is in 'Uptown Downtown.' I remember driving thinking, Whooooa—this man is unbelievable!"

Chapin greatly admired Sondheim's ability to continue improving songs that already seemed polished to a high gloss, as in the case of "I'm Still Here." "There was one lyric originally, 'I got through three commercials and I'm here,' he changed to 'I got through five commercials,' partly because 'through three' is hard to sing. Then that was changed to 'I'm almost through my memoirs, and I'm here.' I thought, There are very few lyricists who can do this. There was one about Greer Garson, 'should have been Greer, but I'm here,' that got cut. Steve has always been an extraordinary editor of his own work."

They were all dealing with false starts and problems for which there seemed to be no solution. *Follies* simply did not lend itself to an intermission and in the end was played without one. But Prince and Bennett kept trying to find a logical break. "I remember one time the action stopped right at the end of the song 'Who's That Woman?' " Chapin said. "As Michael Bennett conceived it, the older women started the song, lined up with mirror images of themselves. So the idea was, bam, the curtain came down. Then it came up again at the beginning of the second act and all the ghosts were gone. That didn't work. They tried it at the end of 'Too Many Mornings' and that didn't work." These changes were being made during the New York previews in early spring. "The creative staff would stand at the back of the theatre, listening to the audience and how the show played, and they didn't get the audience response they were looking for."

Prince has said that a producer's biggest asset is his ability to say no. "If you're having trouble casting, and at the same time the theatre you want in Boston is booked, or if the only way you can get the theatre you want in New York is by coming in earlier or later than you want, get suspicious. You tell yourself you're running into bad luck, which translates as something is wrong . . ." Prince's superstitious sensibilities may or may not have been aroused as *Follies* made its way toward an April opening at the Winter Garden. He must have had some qualms, partly because of the audiences, which went on refusing to respond in the overwhelming way a producer must see if he is to have a hit.

The problem seemed to be, as with *Company,* that the ending was too somber for the kind of person who goes to a musical. Opera audiences expected it, and would have felt cheated if their leading characters had not expired by the end of the third act. Theatregoers, who had been exposed to the nihilism of Samuel Beckett's *Waiting for Godot,* Peter Weiss's *Marat/Sade* and Harold Pinter's *The Caretaker, The Birthday Party,* and *The Homecoming*—all plays of the 1950s and 1960s—were intellectually, if not emotionally, prepared for more of the same. But the people who went to see a musical did not want to be shaken up or challenged, and that, William Goldman theorized in *The Season,* had to do with the kind of theatre they wanted to see. "Whatever you call it, the thing that characterizes Popular Theatre is this: it wants to tell us either a truth that we already know or a falsehood we want to believe in." Speaking of plots in which love is triumphant, he continued, "I cannot believe . . . in light of our divorce statistics, that Americans actually believe any longer that love really will find a way, that Cary Grant is just around the corner. But they want to believe it . . . The Popular Theatre . . . whatever else it may be, *can never be unsettling.*"

In fact, the Cameron Mackintosh revival of *Follies* in London in 1987, which was a critical success if not a financial one, was extensively reworked by James Goldman with Sondheim's cooperation and also given an intermission. Mackintosh said, "What I didn't like was that there was no change in the characters from beginning to end. I don't like going into the theatre and feeling the same after two-and-a-half hours as I did in the first ten minutes. I feel you've got to take the audience on a journey." In the London production, he said, "The characters come to understand each other. It doesn't have a happy ending, but . . ." Sondheim said, "It's not so much that it's more optimistic as that what Cameron described as some of the 'down' moments have either been excised or smoothed over." He did not think the London script was as good as the original, but "there was one wonderful thing that was added, which is that at the end of the first act, the principal characters recognized their younger selves and were able to acknowledge them throughout the last thirty minutes of the piece, whereas in the New York production they never did. I wish we'd thought of that. It seems so obvious now."

The whole tone of the New York production became a bone of contention for the late Michael Bennett, his assistant, Bob Avian, said. "Michael had this mercurial quality. If he thought something wasn't working, he would say something like, 'Let's do act two first.' " In his opinion, the book was the problem, so he argued that Sondheim should rewrite the whole musical as an opera, because he thought that would be easier for the audience to accept. Avian said, "I thought it was a good idea. But Steve, diplomatically, couldn't do that, you know. You can't just take over an author's work and write him out of the picture. But Michael was saying, 'Oh yes you can,' and he couldn't. Hal knew that. You have to commit yourself to the project at hand." Bennett also suggested they bring in Neil Simon, another idea Prince vetoed. "Michael in his frustration got angry at Hal, and Hal was annoyed at Michael's childish impracticality." They never worked together again.

SONDHEIM INVARIABLY CARRIED a flask on opening nights, drinking as a way to combat the tension. But starting with *Company,* Larry Miller would hire a capacious limousine, which would be parked at the curb like a welcome wagon, Sondheim said, and at intermission they would repair to the limousine to drink champagne and smoke pot. Whatever the reviews, opening nights were always big occasions, with an official party at some place like Sardi's or the Rainbow Room, with plenty to eat and drink, followed by a smaller party at Sondheim's or the Princes', where everyone went on drinking. Both of them were polished hosts, although Sondheim recalled that after the disappointing Clive Barnes review came through for *Company*, and after everyone had arrived at the Princes' apartment, Prince had "a small breakdown," Sondheim said. He went upstairs to his office and gave way to tears. Then he dried his eyes, came down to greet his guests, and no one knew how much it had cost him.

Any celebration could be ruined once the reviews arrived, usually in the middle of the party, and everyone was on edge until they did. Howard Erskine, who by then was producing and directing his own plays on Broadway, said, "When notices were due you would go upstairs [at Sardi's], where the press agent had an office in the building, and everyone would get on the phone, and the press agent would call the critic at the *New York Times*, who would read the review to you." Some time after eleven in the evening Vincent Sardi would have copies of the early editions for everyone unless, as Keith Baxter said with a smile, your show was a flop, in which case, the moment you appeared the proprietor would whisk them all away. On the opening night of *Follies*, Sunday, April 4, 1971, the party was held at the Rainbow Room. Baxter said, "First-night parties are often remarkable for displays of duplicity and dissembling, but the unaffected enthusiasm of the throng . . . was unmistakable. I heard no whisper of criticism, not one cavil or quibble. The lukewarm reactions in the papers . . . were dismaying . . ."

Then, as now, what the leading *New York Times* critic had to say carried the most weight. Since Barnes had been less than enthusiastic about *Company*, in a desperate attempt to divine his mood, Ted Chapin gave himself the task of watching him watch a performance, not that it was much help. Barnes liked *Follies* better than *Company*, but only marginally. His complaint seemed to be that Goldman had frittered away his talents writing about the lives of four annoying people, and as described by him they do sound tiresome. All the old showgirls, he wrote, "get out of the graveyard and the geriatric ward . . . for one final bash. They sing a few of their old numbers and open up a few of their old sores." Although it was heartening to see the musical being taken seriously as an art form, all that effort, he implied, had been lavished on worthless material, and Mr. Sondheim's music had not helped: "The pseudo-oldie numbers . . . sound like numbers that you have almost only just [sic] forgotten, but with good reason. This non-hit parade of pastiche trades on camp, but fundamentally gives little in return . . ." When this review was read to the assembled guests by Prince, the audience chanted, "Send him back to England!" Arthur Schlesinger Jr., chairman in the humanities at the City University of New York, put it slightly more politely. Barnes, with his particularly British perspective, was not perhaps the right person to see the virtues of a work that, "with its complex and sardonic commentary on the American theatre and American mores in general, is a peculiarly American show," he wrote. It was a charge that Barnes, naturally enough, denied. He must have taken comfort from the fact that Walter Kerr, his colleague at the *Times*, did not like the work either, finding the plot trivial and hopelessly attenuated. Nothing the directors had done in the way of "platforms bearing jazz bands gliding in and out of the dark, curtains made of candy-box lace raining down from the skies, [and] the ghosts of showgirls past" could disguise its deficiencies.

Fortunately for the authors, other critics had a far greater appreciation for the audacity of the experiment. "*Follies* is a pastiche show so brilliant as to be breathtaking at times," Douglas Watt wrote in the *Daily News*. "It struck me as unlikely that the tools and resources of the Broadway musical theatre have ever been used to more cunning effect than in this richly imaginative work." Jack Kroll wondered how many theatre people had the "talent, taste, inventiveness, resourcefulness and high professional standards" of Hal Prince. He called *Follies* "a brilliant show, wonderfully entertaining, extraordinarily intelligent, and having both a stunning direct appeal and a rare complexity of feeling and structure." T. E. Kalem, in *Time* magazine, stated that "the frontier of the American musical theatre is wherever Harold Prince and Stephen Sondheim are," and called their work "a daring act of creation."

Frank Rich concluded some fourteen years later that *Follies* was in advance of its time in indirectly mourning the death, not just of its characters' deflated dreams, but the world that created them. "It's not merely a theatre that's being torn down but what that theatre represented—the classic Broadway musical and the values it propagated to a faithful public during the glory years of Gershwin and Porter and Rodgers and Hammerstein. 'New York's all changed,' says one of the *Follies* girls when she arrives at the reunion. 'I couldn't even find the theatre tonight.' In 1971 such sentiments seemed hyperbolic," Rich concluded, writing in 1985. "They don't now."

A bootlegged tape of *Follies,* recorded in the middle of its New York run, reveals the kind of shuffling of feet and coughing in the audience that strikes dread into the heart of a producer. Even so, the show ran for over five hundred performances. Audiences were large enough to keep the doors open but not large enough to do more than cover weekly expenses and start repaying the backers. As a result, *Follies* lost its entire investment of $800,000. The musical went on to win the Drama Critics' Circle Award as best musical of the year and to take seven Tony Awards in 1972 for best music and lyrics, best director, best choreographer, best scene design, best costumes, best lighting, and best actress (Alexis Smith). Then it began what was to have been a national tour in Los Angeles but closed on the road. One might believe, with Cameron Mackintosh, that it was "one of the most brilliantly flawed shows ever written," or a classic example of William Goldman's dictum of having made a cardinal error: telling audiences what they did not want to hear. John McMartin, who played Ben, said that Sondheim is always accused of being unsentimental, but after the last night of *Follies* he was in his tiny dressing room, just large enough for two people, when Sondheim knocked on the door. "He said, 'Can I sit with you?' We both sat there and cried for about ten minutes."

SHORTLY AFTER *Forum,* Sondheim and Burt Shevelove were looking for a new subject and had the idea of writing a musical based on *Sunset Boulevard,* the famous film starring Gloria Swanson and William Holden. Had the work ever been realized, it would have appeared almost three decades before Andrew Lloyd Webber's ambitious musical on the same theme. Sondheim and Shevelove had made an outline and were writing the first scene. Then, as luck would have it, Sondheim happened to meet the film's director, Billy Wilder, at a cocktail party and shyly described what he was working on. In decided tones Wilder told him he was quite wrong to think of the story as a musical. It could only be written as an opera, because "it's about a dethroned queen." Sondheim decided he had to be right. "It's such a flamboyant subject you can't do it as a musical. The minute they would talk you would scream with laughter because they're such bigger than life figures, and you can't go swanning around that stage the way the lady would have to, and then sit down and have camp dialogue." He agreed with Wilder that it might make an interesting opera, but that was not what he wanted to write, and he held to his view when, in 1981, Hal Prince approached him about writing *Sunset Boulevard* as a vehicle for Angela Lansbury.

As far as his mother was concerned, Sondheim had long since concluded that screaming with laughter was his best defense. While living in California, Foxy Sondheim claimed to have worked for Jane Wyman and Barbara Stanwyck as an interior decorator. Her son remained on distant but reasonably cordial terms in those days. He recalled that not long after she went to live on the Coast and had a big birthday, "one of her round numbers," his stepfather bought him a plane ticket and he went to the celebration. Then, after about a decade of marriage, Leshin died, and Foxy Sondheim returned to live in New York. She actually wanted to live with him, Sondheim said, in horrified tones. Instead, she took an apartment on the East Side at Sixty-fourth Street and York Avenue.

He had known as a teenager, he said, that his mother was a fabricator, but he "couldn't face it." Once she was back in New York, however, it became too obvious to ignore. He said, "She'd make up anything. My mother was the type of woman who lied for the sake of it. If it was raining out and you actually looked out of the window and said 'What's the weather like?' she would say, 'Sunny.' For no purpose. It was a quirk. A truly compulsive liar."

His deep distrust of his mother was not shared by her friend Benay Venuta, who took a more benevolent view of Foxy Sondheim's character traits and shortcomings. She found her "gay and animated, and she knew something about art. And she was very good at interior decorating, although she was never a big success." Venuta once helped her sell some of her possessions. There was a Matisse drawing she had given Sondheim; it was in storage in his basement and needed restoration. Venuta sold it for a large sum; the proceeds went to Foxy. There were a couple of Rodin drawings: "Everything she had was very good. The little pillows on her velvet couch were exquisite. She had some very good jewelry and wore very chic little black dresses; she was always conscious of her figure." Venuta would see Stephen and his mother together from time to time. "But there was no warmth. I always had the feeling he couldn't wait to get away from her." Even so, Foxy Sondheim went to all of his musicals, boasted about him constantly, and although their friends knew the relationship was strained, "She had his picture by her bed and would always say he had just been there." She added, "And I helped her finish the needlepoint pillows she made for every show, *West Side Story, Gypsy,* and so on. I wonder where they are now?" Foxy liked to reminisce about those days in the farm in Bucks County and listening to Stephen playing the piano hour after hour in the living room. "She'd say she had told him, 'Stop playing that goddamn piano!,' and laugh," Venuta said. The subject of Stephen's homosexuality was never discussed; "she would never have admitted it," Venuta said. "And I used to go right along with it. She always pretended. Everything was fine!"

Foxy had cocktail parties where one met interesting people and she would get a little drunk. If you brought up someone's name she would always say casually, "Of course, I know her very well." And she would talk about her hair and clothes and nails and all the lovers in her life, which one tended to believe, because she had been very attractive. She was vain and silly and

Foxy Sondheim Leshin, far right, at the wedding of her niece, Joan Barnet, in 1961, with her sisters Frances Fox Persky Arculis, left, and Marienne Stutz

sometimes difficult, and yet one felt sorry for her because one knew, some-where far in the background, that she was a very unhappy woman.

> Here's to the girls who just watch—
> Aren't they the best?
> When they get depressed, it's a bottle of Scotch
> Plus a little jest,
> Another chance to disapprove,
> Another brilliant zinger,
> Another reason not to move,
> Another vodka stinger—
> Aaaahh—I'll drink to that.

—"The Ladies Who Lunch," from *Company*

Many of the stories with which Sondheim would regale his friends had to do with his mother's attempts to make him feel guilty. These attempts invari-ably centered around her health. One of his mother's close friends was the actress Glenda Farrell, who was married to a prominent doctor, Henry Ross, a friend of Lee Remick's mother. One day Sondheim went to visit his mother and knocked on the door. "I say, 'It's Steve,' and she says, 'One minute,' and I hear kind of tumbling sounds, like somebody getting something out of a closet. After about a minute she opens the door and she's got a neck brace on with an elegant scarf over it. I said, 'Jesus Christ, what happened to you, Mom?' and she said, 'Just something with my spine. It's all right, don't worry about it, darling,' and 'Hank just told me I have to wear this neck brace.' So we go inside and talk for a bit and the doorbell rings. She opens the door and there is Hank Ross. He said, 'Listen, Foxy, Glenda wanted me to return this lampshade . . . What the hell is wrong with your neck?' She'd gone through this elaborate charade because it was one of those days when she wanted to make me feel guilty."

Foxy Sondheim made yet another clumsy attempt to arouse those around her to expressions of concern, if not remorse, in the summer of 1970 when she was staying on the island of Majorca. Hal and Judy Prince had just bought an elegant house on top of a mountain called El Calvario outside Pollensa with a spectacular view from all directions. The house stood in a tiny cluster of buildings, hardly big enough to be called a village, and next door to another, less elegant house, owned by Margaret Stark, a painter. That particular summer Sondheim rented the Stark house for the months of July and August and his mother had talked him into letting her use it for the month of July. She was entertaining friends, who included a young doctor, Benay Venuta, and the Charles Collingwoods—he had just returned from a tour of Cambodia.

Foxy Sondheim was drinking too much at night and being very difficult, Venuta said. She was emotionally involved in some way with the young doctor. Sondheim said, "He wanted to get out and she wanted him to stay." Venuta and the doctor went off for the day together. When they returned that evening, Foxy threw a scene and Venuta decided to leave. "I made up a story that I'd bumped into some friends and was going to join them in Ibiza. Then I borrowed a hundred dollars' worth of pesetas from Hal. I ordered a limousine and I left!"

The doctor had been supplying Foxy Sondheim with sleeping pills. Sondheim said, "He, knowing better, had given her placebos, with just a few sleeping pills." That night she took the whole bottle. Prince said, "He knew she had taken an overdose because she waved the container in his face." But because so many of them were placebos, "she took eight to twelve sleeping pills instead of forty, which would have killed her," Sondheim said. Next morning the doctor left early. He slipped a note under the Princes' door saying, "She's sleeping easily." Later that morning, Louise Collingwood appeared, looking very concerned, saying that Foxy could not be roused. She knew there had been a big fight but she did not know what about. Prince said, "We all came over. Judy ministered to her and got this local doctor, who sent a nun as a nurse. But when the nun found the lady was a potential suicide she ran back down the mountain with her skirts flowing behind her."

That same morning Prince called Sondheim in New York. Sondheim said, "In those days the phone system was not very sturdy and so there was a lot of crackle on the phone. He said, 'Listen, I think you'd better come over.' I said, 'What?' He said, 'Your mother tried to commit suicide last night.' I said, 'What!' He said, 'Your mother—' and the line went dead. I tried to get him on the phone: the line was busy. He tried to get me on the phone: busy. About fifteen minutes later, the phone rang. 'It's Hal again. Did you hear?' I said, 'Yeah, what happened?' He said, 'The Collingwoods came over this morning, and—' crackle. The phone went dead. After a few phone calls I found out that she had taken a fistful of pills but that they thought she would survive." Prince added, "And he called back and said, 'There's a direct flight, but it's all night, and then there's a flight through London.' And I said, 'You're not going to take the direct flight?' And he said no, and arrived in his own good time, about twenty-four hours later."

Sondheim continued, "When I finally got to the house I got out of the car and my mother came towards me wearing a large gardening hat. She looked up at me tearfully and said, 'Oh, Steve, I'm so grateful-sorry.' She'd rehearsed the line and fucked it up," since the title of the song to which she was referring is "Sorry-Grateful," from *Company*. "I said, 'Mom, excuse me.' I ran next

Foxy Sondheim Leshin on holiday in Majorca, photographed shortly before her suicide attempt that day

door to the Princes' and burst in, and they were looking at me kind of stark, and I said, 'I have got to tell you the most hilariously funny thing you have ever heard in your life.' " Sondheim believed his mother had made her dramatic gesture to make the doctor feel guilty and get him to fly to her side, but her inability to stage a convincing scene had frustrated her efforts once more.

"She was *completely* inept, even when she was trying to commit suicide. Actually, she said something that is perhaps ambiguous but could be quite tragic. As she was coming out of her twilight sleep, she said, "All my life, since I was a little girl, I've wanted to do this.""

The Boy in the Bubble

T HE COMPOSER NED ROREM recalled meeting Sondheim at a party in about 1965, one at which "I got really drunk. As I left, Steve did too, and we went down in the elevator together. Then we shared a taxi downtown and he invited me in for a drink.

"Something happened, I don't know what it was. Something bad. I do remember I said to him," and here he laughed, " 'Oh, are you a composer?' Thinking vaguely that he had written a few lyrics here and there. He was not amused. I also remember he had some records of mine, which flattered me, and I pretended to be blasé about it. I know nothing sexual happened. But there might have been something like me teasing him and being rude and generally awful. All I remember is that a couple of days later I was at a party at Gloria Vanderbilt's and there he was, and he nodded, that was all. Coldly." Another laugh. "And the one or two times I saw him after that, I nodded coldly."

As time went by, after Sondheim made a name as a composer, their paths crossed again; once again he was invited to Sondheim's house. Upon entering, Rorem said, "Before we go any further, you know I've been here before." Sondheim replied, "Yes, I know." Rorem said, "Shall we leave it at that?" They had an amicable discussion and became good friends. Sondheim says of Rorem's prodigious output of beautifully crafted essays and other writings,

"He is one of the best writers about music that I have ever read and that is no easy thing to do." Rorem continued, "Steve and I don't exchange confidences, although I did ask him if he was going to write a homosexual opera and he replied that he did not know what that meant, and got a little bit defensive. I feel that of the four people who created *West Side Story* [Bernstein, Laurents, Sondheim, and Robbins] there is something very sexy about Steve still. There's something about his huffiness that kind of attracts me . . ."

That certain quality, what the British consider a mundane reserve, is the one most often mentioned. Shirley Rhoads Perle, a lifelong friend of Rorem's and Bernstein's, thought he always seemed "surly and noncommunicative, and had a reputation for hating women." One music critic thought everyone around him walked on eggshells and that he was "really scary"; Robert Brustein, director of the American Repertory Theatre at Harvard, thought he was "very bristly and sensitive." Yet another interviewer called him secretive and a man about whom little was known. "He's always feuding with someone," the same person said, "and bitter about the theatre, for which I don't blame him." One of his closest friends agreed that most people were scared of him. When told that college classmates at Williams had found him formidable, Sondheim stammered with surprise. "I've always been very smart, is that what they mean?" he asked. It was suggested that the phrase used was "He didn't suffer fools gladly." He replied, "Impatience. It's certainly possible. When Judy Prince first met me, and she's very, very smart, she thought I was obnoxious. It may have to do with some kind of snappish intolerance . . ."

The remark revealed how unaware Sondheim was of what others saw as a compulsive need for distance, however much they might "adore and worship his mind," as Roger Englander, a television producer who worked closely with Bernstein, expressed it. Nancy Swift, who worked with him extensively on record albums, and liked him, said, "He was aloof and I never felt I knew him any better. I always had to re-establish contact with each new album." Martin Richards, a producer who also worked with him and admired him, found him so inhibiting that if they met by chance in an elevator he would be unable to say hello. Robert Fryer, another producer, confessed to being frightened of him. He said, "Steve has this wall. I would never tell him this, but there is a remoteness to him. He keeps his distance and I found that . . . intimidating." Elaine Stritch said, "He's scary . . . I think he's very close to a genius, if not a genius, and it's hard to be around people like that. They're mind-boggling, their talent is so explosive and there's a kind of dangerous quietness about them." Susan Woelzl, a press officer who worked with him when the New York City Opera did a new version of *Sweeney Todd*, said, "He's crazy. He's so bright he's in orbit. Every so often he touches down. He is horribly perfectionistic, with his own stuff as well. At the dress rehearsal I saw him curled up in a chair as if it were very hard for him to watch."

Those meeting him for the first time invariably described the way he would flutter his eyelashes, holding his head to one side, speaking with eyes closed (his way of thinking, he explained), and looking anywhere but at that person. In that regard, the British playwright Alan Ayckbourn had an amusing encounter.

The two men met once in an Oxford restaurant to discuss a possible project. Ayckbourn said, "He speaks very, very fast and very, very quietly and he tends, certainly with people he doesn't know, to stare anywhere but at the person. I talk very, very fast and very, very quietly and don't stare at people either. So there were two guys—one of us could have left the table and the other would never have known it." His longtime agent, Flora Roberts, said that Sondheim was simply shy. In a profession where hugging and glad-handing were the rule, not to do so could seem like evidence of ill will. "So he'll go to a play and then pass by people and quietly think they won't notice, and of course they do."

Even if it were being used as a defense, Sondheim's quick wit was often the first quality to be appreciated. Before they worked together, Jonathan Tunick recalled attending a Philadelphia preview of *It's a Bird . . . It's a Plane . . . It's Superman* with his friend Ed Kleban and having Sondheim pointed out in the auditorium a couple of rows ahead of them. Tunick said, "*Superman* had a lot of typical glitches in it, a lot of things that didn't quite come together, but it was screamingly funny and it had a very good score too. But nobody laughed except Steve. Something funny would happen, the audience wouldn't laugh, Ed and I would chuckle, and Steve down in front would be going 'Haw, haw, haw!' So Ed went off to smoke during intermission. When he came back he said, 'I've just heard two ladies talking. One of them said to the other, "Who's that strange young man in front who laughs in all the wrong places?" ' "

Arthur Laurents thought there was something comically endearing about Sondheim as a young man. He seemed gauche, awkward, bumbling, the kind of person who is helplessly unable to deal with the practicalities of life. Laurents later modeled one of the characters in his play *Jolson Sings Again* on some aspects of Sondheim. "I've described this character—in this case, a misfit in Hollywood—who would wear shorts with black socks to the beach and walk as though he were carrying the Manchester *Guardian* under one arm. And not be playing tennis. That's a description of Steve." Laurents was referring to Sondheim's characteristic walk, head slightly tilted to one side, right shoulder dropped, as if weighted down by what he was carrying, but with a rolling quality, a jolly nautical gait. He could do anything with his voice, which had a rich, melodious quality. There was the actor's finely honed ability to suggest infinite nuances of feeling with an economy of means, as well as a faultless sense of timing. His friends claimed to be able to read his mood as soon as he answered the telephone.

Sondheim believed he was a difficult person to describe, because "I just don't have an awful lot of colors. I don't say that with pride or anything. I've lived an isolated life. I'm virtually the boy in the bubble. Once you've stated the boy is in the bubble, there's not a lot more to say until he leaves the bubble. And because I've been protected by money, meaning I've come from an upper-middle-class family, and was well educated, and because of the peculiar circumstances of my parents, I lived all my life in school. And when I got out of school and I got the job right away, and I started to earn money right away and I had my own apartment right away, I didn't have to share things, I didn't have to knock on doors . . . I did some knocking on doors, clearly . . . but it was hardly what most people go through. By sheer luck, when I was twenty-five, *West Side Story* happened. From then on it's been, you know, very easy to be isolated.

"So that's one of the reasons I have not lived a very colorful life. I wasn't responsible for anybody . . ." He referred to an old friend, married, with children, who had a terrible personal and career crisis and recovered with great gallantry. "And he's by nature gregarious, which is another thing, and so he gets involved with people." He conceded that he was also gregarious, "but not on an intimate level. Never. So I never . . . got into real trouble with people. I was able to maintain all my friendships, because that's all they were. Where it caused difficulty was with people like Mary [Rodgers] who got fixes on me." Laurents and Bernstein were two others. He was not speaking of romantic involvement, but the degree of friendship. "Intimate-friendship jealousies," he said. "My relationship with Arthur was completely nonsexual. When I say he felt rebuffed by me, I don't mean sexually. I mean, I wasn't doing everything he wanted me to do. I wasn't dancing attendance on him the way he might have wished. And so on. One of the reasons I had such a smooth relationship with Burt [Shevelove], except for *Forum,* was that he didn't make any demands, either. He was also somebody who lived alone and didn't want to be responsible to or for anybody. And so we were a perfect couple!"

Laurents thought Sondheim took a kind of pride in being the person who did not love, for whom others meant little, the one who was not going to get hurt. Sondheim gave lavish presents, Laurents once told him, "because he could not give himself." He also seemed to think that Sondheim's ability to rationalize his feelings sometimes misled him about what he really felt. By a curious paradox Sondheim was extremely sensitive to evidence of insincerity and pretense in others, or what he perceived as such. "Oh, come, you don't know it," he said when someone made noises of recognition about a particular part in a play, and he was right. This unwillingness to accept a polite social lie sometimes spilled over into derision when his view of the world was questioned, that of society as hopelessly corrupt, the view of someone who cannot be caught out being hurt any more. Not that his friends took his occasional flashes of cynicism very seriously. Mia Farrow, his friend for almost twenty-five years, said, "He's not cynical. He might think he is, but he is not the best judge of that." She added, "He has retained the sense of wonder that grownups lose. He doesn't get over how amazed he is. Sometimes I wonder how he gets through the week, his feelings run so deep." That emotional volatility beneath the surface was remarked on by many of his friends; because he was more vulnerable than others, he therefore had had to erect more elaborate defenses, Susan Blanchard believed. For the fact was that others' opinions mattered a great deal, and not very far below the surface, making him vulnerable to criticisms that others could shrug off. And there were times when, for all of his rapid responsiveness, he tended to jump to conclusions and misconstrue what was actually meant. Ayckbourn thought that Sondheim created from "a highly, nervously charged energy. He is very, very intense, more so than any of us." Most of his friends were protective of his privacy, knowing how much he needed to be left alone. The British actress Julia McKenzie, a Sondheim favorite, talked to an interviewer and was reproached by Sondheim for having done so. There was a sweet-sour aspect to him, she said. On the eve of her fiftieth birthday in London, Sondheim took her out to a restaurant for drinks and a lavish dinner and lingered until midnight, so that, he said, he could be the first to see her now that she was fifty. He was rather gleeful, she thought.

William Goldman mentioned Sondheim's particular abhorrence of public embarrassment, which no doubt stemmed from one too many incidents with his mother in adolescence. Sondheim recalled that he stopped playing in bridge tournaments for this reason. He entered one tournament with Larry Miller at a club on Fiftieth Street in New York. Unfortunately, one of them picked up his hand a fraction of a second too soon, and an opposing player called foul. Sondheim said, "The entire room turned around . . . My friend hadn't done anything bad, and neither had I, but it was some breech of etiquette or protocol, and I thought, never again."

The playwright John Guare said, "With Steve you always know he is telling the truth and not exaggerating," a view held by other friends. In fact, Sondheim's determination to be honest with himself and candid with others was cited as one of his most admirable characteristics, sometimes allied with a tendency to nurse a grudge. Flora Roberts thought "he had a little list." He could think about "marvelous dark vengeful things to do with people who have done him in, but not go through with them." For the most part he avoided confrontations, although he could be goaded into displays of anger that terrified some people. One friend was so unnerved that he went into therapy to learn how to defend himself. Roberts had never felt intimidated by Sondheim, but she thought he sometimes got angry "about the wrong things."

Perhaps his most poignant fear was of being at someone else's mercy. He said he was always tense when being driven in a car and that in earlier years he disliked flying, presumably for the same reason. Ned Sherrin recalled one occasion when they were en route to Canada for an opening and Sondheim smoked marijuana all the way to the airport. Perhaps it was just an interesting coincidence that dramas about characters who controlled the fates of others were often found in Sondheim's lexicon; there was Madame Rose in *Gypsy,* the slave Pseudolus in *Forum,* and Robert in *Company,* to be eventually joined by Sweeney Todd, the homicidal barber, a galaxy of presidential assassins, and Fosca in *Passion,* who used love as a weapon. He saw characters in musicals as puppets, through whom an artist could talk.

Sondheim was back in analysis, this time with Dr. Milton Horowitz, whose particular interest is the relationship between creativity and neurosis, and continued as his patient for the next twenty-five years. He found the experience extremely valuable, "to find you're not the only one in the world, which is of course what everybody goes through. You think, I'm the only one who likes to suck eggs, and you find out everyone likes to suck eggs. I'm the only one who's never fallen in love . . . Every time I would tell Milton something I'd expect him to be shocked, and he'd say, 'Yes . . .' And after about five sessions I realized, He's heard everything! And I'm just another ordinary neurotic fellow." Even after the sexual revolution of the 1960s, Sondheim said, "I realized the trouble was a lot different. It included homosexuality, but, you know, it was about not being open to let somebody else into my life. I had thought it was all about homosexuality, but when homosexuality became the lingua franca it didn't affect me at all."

MANY PEOPLE SAW Sondheim in terms used to describe the English artist Mark Gertler by Michael Holroyd: "There was indeed something striking and unforgettable about his presence—the shock of hair, the amazing vitality, the versatile gift of mimicry and extravagant humour, and the romantic excitement he communicated was given depth by a contrasting look of profound suffering in his eyes . . ." Sondheim's view of himself was prosaic. He saw himself simply as a playwright-actor, with a gift for composing music and juggling words. "And when I write songs I become the actor, and that's why actors like my stuff. It isn't a conscious effort to put a subtext in—it's just that I approach it as an actor." If, as Isaiah Berlin quipped, the world were divided between foxes, who knew a great many things superficially, and hedgehogs, who knew one thing well, he would have to consider himself a fox. He was a pragmatist, with a schematic imagination. That he could be, however, equally intuitive about his work was made clear by Jule Styne, the composer of *Gypsy.* Shortly after writing the music for "If Mama Was Married," the song near the end of the first act in which the two daughters of Madame Rose hope their mother will settle down so that they can leave show business, Styne played it for his collaborator. "And Steve analyzed it perfectly," Styne said. "He felt that the music already established that Mama was not going to get married. He pointed to a certain measure in the score and said, 'You know what that note means? It ain't going to happen.' "

Sondheim saw himself as lacking self-confidence, which was a real handicap when the time came to assess his own work, because he would be persecuted by doubt. Did he like it because he wanted to like it? Did he reject it because he was too insecure to see its merits? At a certain vulnerable moment, he was in danger of "throwing the baby out with the bathwater," which was why he valued the opinions of his collaborators. He added, "I really don't like to play anything to anybody until it's polished, because songs are such short forms that unless you polish them well, the smallest flaw is a mountain." Could this tendency to magnify his own imperfections, what Hal Prince called his "negativity," have anything to do with his habitual ennui? Sondheim said of that, "I've always been a low burner. I'm just slightly down." He toyed with the idea of the four humors, phlegm, blood, choler, and melancholy (thought to be the types of fluids in the body responsible for one's mental attributes), as a way of describing how he felt. He did not have an explanation. "That's just who I am."

If Sondheim were frequently depressed, feeling enisled in the sea of life, as Bernard Berenson wrote, he seemed less conscious of his own expansive moods, and the exuberance that his friends witnessed. His only memory of the creative process might be the acute drudgery involved. Others described times when his speech could hardly keep pace with the ideas that were tumbling one after the other out of his imagination. They recalled the energy that carried him forward, the humor, the optimism, and, most of all, the delight. To see Sondheim's face light up as he discovered a new word or a rhyming scheme was to begin to understand what work well accomplished meant to him. Elaine Stritch said, "When you get it right, no one is ever as happy. And that's where you get to have a real relationship with another artist. He really lets you have it. He's terrible when you're not with it, but when you get it right he is so overjoyed by the material being interpreted the way he saw it that he makes you feel like a million bucks." Tunick talked about creativity as an act of deliverance. He recalled from as far back as 1970 seeing "Steve standing at the back of the house during a runthrough or a tech, his face bathed in tears. When you make that kind of investment in a piece, as I can witness in my more limited way, there is something metaphysical about it. All that energy and all that feeling gets stored on paper, and when it's released by human energy, there is an enormous sense of personal relief, catharsis if you will."

However, to see Sondheim struggling with an intractable problem was to see the pit of despair into which an artist could fall when a work refused to take shape. At such moments, Hector Berlioz wrote, "It is difficult to put into words what I suffered—the longing that seemed to be tearing my heart out by the roots, the dreadful sense of being alone in an empty universe, the . . . disgust with living, the impossibility of dying . . ." At such moments Edgar Allan Poe would write pleading letters to his friends: "Write me immediately. Convince me that it is worth one's while—that it is at all necessary to live, and you will prove yourself indeed my friend . . ."

In *Touched with Fire,* a fascinating study of the lives of artists, poets, composers, and writers, the psychiatrist Kay Redfield Jamison states that profound swings of mood, from euphoria to despair, are commonly found among creative people. She quotes the Danish writer Hans Christian Andersen, who suffered from recurrent depressions, to the effect that "I am like water. Everything moves me, I suppose it is part of my poetic nature, and it often brings me joy and happiness, but very often it is also a torment." Dr. Redfield does not suggest that neurosis or psychosis is a precondition for successful creative work but only that there is an association. She cites William James, who himself suffered from melancholia and disturbing swings of mood, to the effect that when someone possesses a mutable temperament and a superior intellect, "We have the best possible condition for the kind of effective genius that gets into the biographical dictionaries."

SONDHEIM AND BURT SHEVELOVE were working together often in those days. Sondheim sent him an urgent appeal for help in the spring of 1973 when the first evening of tribute to his work was running into difficulties, and in grateful exchange Sondheim agreed to help Shevelove. The least he could do was go back to acting. Shevelove was directing a television production of a play about Tin Pan Alley by George Kaufman and Ring Lardner called *June Moon,* with Susan Sarandon and Jack Cassidy, and wanted Sondheim in one of the roles. There is a photograph of Sondheim in the part, with a fedora perched on top of his head and the look of a man who cannot quite decide why he is there. He later confessed that the whole experience had embarrassed him; he did it for Burt.

He also agreed to contribute words and music to a revival of one of Shevelove's early successes, his prewar version of Aristophanes' *Frogs* in the Yale swimming pool. The original production had been such a success (the *New York Times* even wrote an editorial about it) that there was some talk about taking it to Broadway, but the war intervened. When Robert Brustein, who was then artistic director of the Yale Repertory Theatre, asked Shevelove to do it again, Shevelove in turn engaged Sondheim's help to rewrite it. By then Sondheim was already late with the score of the film *Stavisky,* directed by Alain Resnais, and at work on *A Little Night Music* with Prince. So he barely had a month to write *The Frogs,* and turned to his first idea for the overture to *Forum,* which he had called "Invocation." This became "Invocation and Instructions to the Audience" and got the evening off to a flying start. "Don't take notes / To show us all you know the famous quotes," he wrote.

> And when you disapprove, don't clear your throats
> Or throw your crumpled programs, coins and coats,
> Or tell your neighbor scintillating anecdotes,
> And please—
> No grass.
> This is a classic, not a class.

Writing about it later, Brustein observed that a modest production grew far past its originally agreed-upon size, since Shevelove was the one who insisted upon a composer, which meant hiring Jonathan Tunick as well, and also a larger orchestra than had been planned. "The small cast on which we agreed . . . had now swelled to include not only our eighteen-member company but also a singing and dancing chorus of twenty-eight, a swimming chorus of eighteen, an orchestra of twelve, and a support group backstage of thirty-five. With over a hundred people involved . . . the production had mushroomed into a spectacular extravaganza." Both Brustein and Sondheim agreed there was not enough rehearsal time, and even though the show only ran for a week, Shevelove and Sondheim were still rewriting and revising three days after the opening. Under such conditions it was a miracle the work ever got performed. But Christopher Durang, who would have a successful Broadway career as a playwright and in cabaret, was in the chorus, along with the future movie stars Sigourney Weaver and Meryl Streep, and thoroughly enjoying himself. "Members of the chorus sat at the side of the Yale swimming pool, a cast of undergraduate swimmers played the frogs in green mesh and jock straps, and the star, the late Larry Blyden, was in a rowboat surrounded by frogs as he was about to make his descent into Hades." Singing in a swimming pool, especially with a chorus at one end and an orchestra at the other, led to some unavoidable reverberations and the loss of words, especially when the song involved a lot of patter. One song originally meant for the chorus was given to Larry Blyden when the words disappeared into the echoing hall. While Blyden sang, the chorus "was supposed to be dancing around madly, but since we weren't dancers it wasn't going very well," Durang said. When the swimmers got out of the pool, "they dripped water all over the stage and the dancers kept falling and I was trying not to laugh." Everyone kissed everyone else at the black-tie opening night, and the show played to sold-out houses all week.

Burt Shevelove in consultation with the choreographer Carmen de Lavallade for *The Frogs* at Yale, 1974

Perhaps because of the pressures and the lack of time, Sondheim was in a prickly mood. Brustein recalled himself getting up at one point and thanking the singers and cast but—shades of *Forum*—forgetting to say anything about the orchestra. For Sondheim, the memories must have been all too vivid. He no doubt remembered that Brustein had criticized his music in a review of *Forum* in *The New Republic*. Sondheim told Brustein, "I know you don't like my work, but the least you could do . . ." Brustein was very embarrassed. It had been an unfortunate oversight, and "he's had me down as someone who is hostile to him ever since." Brustein concluded, "No artist is ever able to have enough skins to protect himself against the outside world."

Even so, his friends thought that Sondheim had grown far less likely to take offense as the years passed. Howard Erskine said, "Before Steve went into psychoanalysis I can remember times when something would happen that would annoy him and he would just blow up. We had a big party at my house up on Eighty-sixth Street given for my partner, Joseph Hayes, when [Steve] was writing *Gypsy*. There was a piano in the dining room and Steve sat down at it and said, 'This is what we did today.' Then he began to play 'Rose's Turn.' He got about halfway through and someone or other of Joseph's drunken friends came over and said, 'Do you know "Melancholy Baby"?' It's a joke. And Steve said 'Yep' and went right into 'Melancholy Baby' and played the whole thing. The guy said 'Thank you,' and Steve went right back into 'Rose's Turn,' and I knew then that the analysis was working. A couple of years before, Steve would have exploded, or walked out."

ANOTHER OF SONDHEIM'S close friends in those days was Anthony Perkins, who had played the leading role in *Evening Primrose* and had been Sondheim's first choice to play Robert in *Company*, an actor whom Mary Rodgers described as "immensely bright, thoughtful, and literate." Perkins had first attracted national attention as the sensitive student at a private boys' school in *Tea and Sympathy*, with Joan Fontaine in the role of the understanding older woman. He then went on to play sensitive youths in Hollywood and achieved fame as the schizophrenic killer in Alfred Hitchcock's *Psycho*, a part that inevitably put one in mind of that of Danny in *Night Must Fall*, which Sondheim had played with such elan at Williams. Although he had become well known as an actor, Perkins was not satisfied and was looking for opportunities as a director and writer. He had a little-known but well-developed sense of humor, a love of intricate games, and an instinct for dramatic development that was not lost on Sondheim.

Perkins was living with Grover Dale, a dancer and choreographer who had played in *West Side Story:* "one of the gang," Sondheim said. They came to know each other better after they acted as co-hosts for an ambitious treasure hunt on Halloween night in 1968 that took place all over Manhattan. The two men spent a month planning it. They hired four limousines, split a group of friends into four teams of five, and sent them chasing all over the city. Sondheim said, "Some of the clues were pictorial and some participational, and all of them had to do with inductive reasoning. And my advice when everybody gathered at the house before they went off in their limousines was, 'Keep talking to each other. Do not try to solve these things individually.' " The creators had found some posters in Perkins's basement left over from a forgotten political campaign, and these were distributed to specific sites; the discovery of a poster told the teams that they should start looking for a new clue. One such clue was planted at a town house on the East Side where they were offered tea and cake by, as it turned out, Tony Perkins's mother. A few people remembered the cautionary advice that they could not have their cake and eat it. They assembled their individual slices and discovered that a new clue had been spelled out by the icing. Lee Remick's team ate their cake and lost. Herbert Ross's team won and were each given a bottle of champagne.

In those days the choreographer was constantly suggesting that Sondheim write plays and Sondheim would respond that he had nothing to say as a playwright; the only kind of plot that would interest him would be a murder mystery. "So when Herbie Ross became a successful Hollywood director, he called me and said, 'Would you like to do a murder mystery movie?' and I said, 'Well, I'll plot one for you, but I won't write it.' . . . So I outlined a plot about a group of people in a small Long Island community when they're all snowed in, so it had that surrounded, Agatha Christie feeling. Then he said, 'I love this plot, but you've gotta write it,' and I said, 'I tell you what, I can only collaborate.' " At that point Sondheim called Perkins, because he knew he was a murder mystery fan, "the trick kind, John Dickson Carr and people like that." Sondheim suggested they join forces and Perkins agreed with alacrity. "We wrote it, and then went to California to give Herbie the so-called treatment, and he said, 'It's terrific, but I don't know why you're putting it in some dreary place like Long Island in the winter. Why don't we set it on a yacht in France and we can all have a wonderful time?' It never occurred to me that movies were set in places where people wanted to go. So we switched it to a yacht in France . . ."

Working on *The Last of Sheila* was one of Sondheim's happiest experiences: "Not having to write lyrics made it like a vacation." And Tony's letters were such treasures ("the kind of letters you wish you'd written") that he knew the result would be entirely satisfactory, and it was. "We divided up the scenes alternately—I did the plotting. It was a real lesson. It's been my observation that most of the great playwrights from the Greeks on have been actors. I think there is a good reason, and I found it out when I was working with Tony. I would write what I knew, classically, a scene with a beginning, a middle, and an end, which character had a motivation, an action, it went from point A to point B, and it had character conflict, it had subtext, so that there were things to act, et cetera . . . And he'd say, 'It isn't a scene. I can't explain it to you.' And I'd say, 'But . . .' He'd say, 'Let me read it to you.' And he'd read it as well as he could, but you could see there was a dead-fish aspect about it. Then he would go off and rewrite it and it would be a scene. It's because he had an actor's point of view. So it was a very good and easy collaboration . . ." They co-authored two other projects. One was an elaborate, ninety-page treatment with dialogue called *The Chorus Girl Murder Case,* which, Sondheim said, "had a really good gimmick in it," and the other was called *Crime and Variations,* written for Home Box Office. Neither was produced.

The Last of Sheila revolves around an unsolved hit-and-run murder of a Hollywood producer's wife after a party at their home. The producer arranges for a yacht party and invites all the guests who were there the night his wife was killed. He has all kinds of unsavory information about each of his guests which he plans to use as blackmail in the attempt to solve the murder. A distinguished film director, played by James Mason, secretly molests children; a film star, played by Raquel Welch, has a compulsion to shoplift; and yet another guest, happily married, it would seem, has had a homosexual affair. But before the producer can force his wife's murderer to confess, he himself is murdered. Then one of the guests dies, and the plot eventually resolves itself in a last-minute confession, the unlikeliest person in the group being, naturally, the most calculating and cold-blooded of them all. Sondheim was longing to do his own version of the *Thin Man* series that starred William Powell and Myrna Loy. "I always loved the moment . . . when it's just before they unveil the murderer and they have everybody to a dinner party or something like that, and . . . she turns to him and says, 'Do you know who the murderer is?' And he says, 'No, but it's going to be interesting.' So by cross-questioning everybody and pointing things out, he gets them all to reveal things and then he says, 'You are the murderer.' " What fun it would be to write a sequel and lead the hero of Dashiell Hammett's enduring series to a terrible discovery: that the murderer had to be his own wife. The idea of having a charming hero and heroine who could not possibly be guilty, but were, teased and confounded Sondheim. This was what he really wanted to write, but it could only be done when there were real movie stars, and now they were all actors.

Sondheim, foreground, in Cannes before a billboard advertising his film, *The Last of Sheila*

Anthony Perkins with Sondheim during the filming of *The Last of Sheila*

Richard Benjamin in *The Last of Sheila*

Perhaps Lee Remick might have been possible, but even she did not have a firmly established personality as a charming innocent, since she had played "a lot of neurotic parts."

So the casting was far from ideal. Sondheim thought that Richard Benjamin and Joan Hackett, who took the leading roles, were, as excellent actors, looking for dimensions that were not in the script he and Perkins had written. The characters were strictly stick figures, and the only thing that mattered was how well the plot twisted and turned and kept one step ahead of the cleverest member of the audience. "When we had our first reading, everybody was talking about . . . what the motivation was . . . In Herbie's mind it was a satire on Hollywood. And it was a murder mystery . . . period. And nobody would take it as such except James Mason, who raised his hand and said, 'I have one question. I don't understand why the piece of wood is in the robe.'" Sondheim did not say so but thought that was the one intelligent question of the day.

The film received mixed reviews when it was released in 1973. Some critics thought the plot unnecessarily complicated and the delineation of the characters so cool as to seem heartless; but other critics praised its ingenuity, and it went on to gain a cult following. It is one of Sondheim's favorite memories. "It is boys' work, not man's work, I'm sorry to say. But it was a wonderful time."

CLUES FOR THE FAMOUS Halloween party were concealed not just on the icing of cakes and on bowling pins but in envelopes pasted under benches in blacked-out parks, "dangling from strings in deserted alleys overhanging the East River, and various other clandestine message drops made familiar from the evidence in spy trials . . ." Writing for the *Sunday Times* of London, Alan Brien described the trials and travails of the likes of Jerome Robbins, Hal Prince, Arthur Laurents, Herbert Ross, his dancer wife, Nora Kaye, and others as they matched wits with the resourceful Perkins and Sondheim that fateful evening in 1968. Sondheim told Brien later, "Tony and I were planting one poster in a street full of warehouses where no sane person would be found alone after dark. Two minutes after we arrived an alarm rang and our way out was blocked for an hour by fire trucks and police cars."

Be that as it may, Murder was one of their favorite games during the evenings when Sondheim's friends came to the house in Turtle Bay. He started the dinner parties, he explained, to keep his houseman, Luis Vargas, happy—Luis grew wan and wistful if there was not a steady stream of guests through the house. And guests came in great numbers, because Lou was such a spectacular cook. Patricia Sinnott, who served as Sondheim's personal secretary later on, said, "If Steve couldn't boil water, as he claims, with Lou around you wouldn't want to. He could cook any type of cuisine, and Steve only had to tell him he was having a party and everything would be handled in perfect taste." After this Lucullan fare, guests would settle down to the serious work of the evening: "charades, anagrams, arithmetical puzzles, double-acrostic crosswords whose rules I cannot even understand," Brien wrote, "three-dimensional noughts and crosses, four-handed chess, jigsaws constructed from abstract paintings or cut out of black-and-white circles . . . elaborate toy mazes, boxes and trays and jars of coloured marbles, numbered bricks, geometric shapes, which must be arranged in sequences of patterns . . . late-night 'Truth or Forfeit' sessions, group therapy seances designed to inflame rather than relax tensions . . . knock-out tournaments of pencil-and-paper competitions, like 'Dictionary' or 'Bartlett's' where the object is to invent the most convincing false definition or quotation." It was all very bracing, Brien concluded, and quite wearing.

Sondheim had followed up his outrageous "Stardom" game (where the object was to sleep with an imaginary movie queen and the cards were full of "unprintable, and largely accurate, studio gossip," Brien wrote) with a game called "Analysis," in which the pieces you played with were tiny, intricately upholstered couches. Then there was the game invented specifically for Hal Prince, with overtones of Monopoly, in which players had to tackle the pitfalls of negotiating Broadway plays, from raising the money to keeping the play from closing, the object being to take over all the theatres and bankrupt everyone else. It was a game Prince always won.

Sondheim invented an even more elaborate present for Leonard Bernstein, to whom he gave a game in three parts for his fiftieth birthday. Each was an aspect of "The Great Conductor Hunt" and took its cue from the fact that Bernstein was about to retire from the New York Philharmonic to devote full time to composing. "So the players are competing to see who is to replace him," Sondheim explained. "First you have to graduate from music school, which is actually a very good game and a very nice principle. The second game is called 'Itinerary,' in which you try to track him down all over the world, so that he will hear you conduct. But he's very elusive. And the first one who wins is the one who conducts the shortest program, because of his attention span. The third game is in the form of a Plexiglas maze, in which you try to track him down at the Philharmonic, and you can go into various rooms and find friends, cronies, and associates, some of whom subtract from your score and some of whom add to it . . ." Brien wrote, "As a game its originality lies in the use of an unpredictable, moving target who flits around the globe, protected by secretaries and agents, unanswered telephones and locked dressing rooms."

In its elaborate design and convoluted complexity, the "Great Conductor Hunt" could have served as a metaphor for the interior that Sondheim was building, item by item, around himself in those days. After Sondheim decided in 1973 that he needed the whole house, it underwent extensive alterations, the front door to the upstairs apartment was removed from the façade, and Burt Shevelove was consulted. The result was to transform what had been essentially a nineteenth-century interior to one befitting a Prospero, and to display his bewildering collection of games, in cabinets, on walls, tables, chests, and in every drawer, to their best advantage.

One entered through a low passage, with Lou's domain, the kitchen, on the left, leading into a kind of foyer cleverly lit so as to display a single exquisite potted plant on a perfect antique table. The living room, crammed as it was with trophies of the game hunt, was in muted tones of forest green and beige. Beyond that was a dining room, full of tropical plants in huge pots, grouped around a large table and overlooking the communal garden at the rear. One was likely to be served coffee in delicate Limoges china, tiny black stripes on a white ground, edged with gold.

The staircase, now filled in and stuccoed so as to present a single sinuous curve, rose to the second floor. The office in the front of the house was full of photographs, of Bernstein, Mostel, Sondheim, Prince, Laurents, Rodgers, and many others, and over the fireplace there were two survey maps of Turtle Bay Farm, one dated 1881. Where the house now stands, there were farms in the nineteenth century, and a stream, now presumably underground, crossed the property and descended to the East River. The shelves were full of reference books, about quotations, proverbs, slang and modern English usage, acronyms, initialisms and abbreviations; there were *Johnson's New Rhyming Dictionary and Poet's Handbook,* foreign dictionaries in French, German, Spanish, Italian, and Latin, Oxford Companions to American and English literature, the theatre, and the American theatre, a dictionary of British folk tales, and the like. Where the banister rail might have been there was a long, useful countertop that might well hold several neat piles of papers, letters, photographs, and underlined lists of coming events. The landing was decorated with nine identical panels, gold-edged, with black backgrounds, enclosing wonderful archaic playing cards, perhaps an old French set, or an early variety of the British game "Happy Families." The bathroom was partly devoted to display a case of delicate old china, each piece decorated with a puzzle story, or rebus, in which the tale was told partly in words and partly in symbols. And then, at the back of the house, overlooking the gardens, was the room Sondheim used for his study, with a handsome desk, a grand piano, a cocoa-brown carpet, and banks and banks of scores, everything arranged with amazing neatness and precision. There, beside a handsome stained-glass window, was the daybed on which the composer would recline while writing, with plenty of razor-sharp pencils and lined yellow pads close at hand.

Within his own walls, Sondheim had taken on the trappings of a magus or wizard, perhaps even a puppeteer, since trying to match wits with someone as skilled in the art of misdirection was bound to leave the average player at a helpless disadvantage. Some found the challenge intensely stimulating. The playwright Anthony Shaffer came to tea and was immediately intrigued by the game that had so delighted Nancy Berg, i.e., how to camouflage an object so well that it could not be detected, even though it was in plain sight. Shaffer incorporated the game into the climax of a play in which one of the protagonists is aware that his life hangs on his ability to discover what has been so cleverly concealed by his devious opponent. The play, *Sleuth,* opened on Broadway in 1970, starring Sondheim's friend Keith Baxter and Anthony Quayle, won a Tony award, and was subsequently made into a film starring Laurence Olivier and Michael Caine. The play was briefly titled *Who's Afraid of Stephen Sondheim?,* which was complimentary, but not the playwright's idea; it had been invented by the producer, Morton Gottlieb. However, the character of Andrew Wyke, who takes a diabolical revenge on his wife's seducer, was partly modeled on Sondheim. In the play Wyke describes himself as a games-playing man; "the complete man—a man of reason and imagination; of potent passions and bright fancies." He is "joyous and unrepent-ing. His weapons are the openness of a child and the cunning of a pike and with them he faces out the black terrors of life."

Sondheim was willing to concede a certain resemblance to himself. "To me, the connection between puzzles and detective stories is all about order and solution. The nice thing about them is that there's a solution and all's right with the world—as opposed to life."

CHAPTER 13

Applause for the Clowns

A LITTLE NIGHT MUSIC began in the imaginations of Harold Prince, Arthur Laurents, and Stephen Sondheim years before it reached the stage, with the idea of making a musical from *Ring Round the Moon,* Jean Anouilh's play of 1948. Prince said, "We wanted to do something based on the kind of material that's called a 'masque.' Something that deals with encounters in a country house, love and lovers and mismatched partners. Such masques frequently have people of all ages from a child to an old lady who's seen it all, and there are lots of foolish crises. Love and foolishness tied in with age."

They approached Anouilh after *West Side Story* and were rejected; nothing daunted, they tried again and were again rejected. Even before *Follies* closed, Sondheim and Prince were looking for a subject that, if not exactly crass and commercial, might stand a better chance of pleasing the public than another hugely admirable flop.

Sondheim arranged screenings of Jean Renoir's *Rules of the Game,* from 1939, and Ingmar Bergman's *Smiles of a Summer Night,* made in 1956. The Swedish film director, better known for films like *The Seventh Seal* and *Virgin Spring,* had shown an unexpected gift for romantic comedy. As the title suggests, the action took place in a country house one summer weekend, and its atmosphere had something in common with Shakespeare's *Midsummer*

Night's Dream. As if bewitched, the main characters appear, separate, pursue one another, fall in love with the wrong people, and, in short, behave in the manner of normally befuddled human beings groping through an emotional maze. Everything eventually gets resolved, but not before some huge misunderstandings.

That Harold Prince, after decades of success in musical comedy, should feel the need to rehabilitate his reputation could be taken as an indication of the fickleness of audiences and backers, or of the colossal uncertainty of any such enterprise. Both were probably true in this case, and it was happening at a time when William Goldman wrote, "As far as money is concerned, today . . . is the golden age of musical comedy . . . The runs of the great hit plays are becoming shorter . . . while the runs of musicals are growing longer and longer." That was published three years before, but was still relevant. The rewards were huge, but so were the obstacles. Something like a hundred and fifty new productions were planned at the start of every theatrical season. Of those, only about fifty opened, and less than a dozen became established hits. Prince calculated his costs and estimated that $650,000 would be needed to bring *A Little Night Music* to Broadway. That was considerably cheaper than *Follies,* but to his intense chagrin, not attractive enough to backers on whom he had been able to rely in the past.

"My little investors just didn't have the money to put into the new show since they hadn't earned any on the old one," he said. Meantime, other faithful backers had died. Prince thought he might be reduced to the indignity of holding backer's auditions, something he had not been obliged to do since he produced *The Pajama Game* in 1954, but the money finally appeared. He began work knowing that the new show would have to gross $61,000 a week to cover its operating costs. Since the musical was booked for the Shubert Theatre, with almost fifteen hundred seats, its theoretical weekly gross could be $108,000. (*Follies* needed $84,000 a week to break even, and never did.) It was a reasonable gamble. And if *Night Music* played to capacity houses, it could begin paying off its backers in about twelve weeks. As for the money a composer-lyricist in those days stood to make, assuming that he had the usual 4 percent share, a gross of $100,000 a week would give him about $200,000 a year. Then there were the touring companies, the recordings, and the stock and amateur rights. And if a song became a "standard," i.e., one that was still being recorded after five years or so, a composer could easily make $250,000 from that single song, such as "The Impossible Dream" from *Man of La Mancha.*

The plot of *Night Music* centers around the problems of Desirée Armfeldt, an actress who has decided to settle down and marry lawyer Fredrik

Egerman, the father of her child, only to discover that he has just married a charming eighteen-year-old. She maneuvers him and his wife, along with Count Carl-Magnus Malcolm, her own extremely jealous lover, and his wife, and sundry other characters, to the country house of her mother, Madame Armfeldt, and the complications begin. Sondheim had suggested an ambitious variation on the Bergman plot in which Madame Armfeldt would become a kind of deus ex machina, perpetually shuffling a deck of cards and thereby changing the fates of the hapless lovers. The action would pause, the group would reform and begin all over again with a new dénouement. To take the original film into the realm of fantasy was a daring idea, and Hugh Wheeler, a British playwright who had written some successful plays and had a previous career as a mystery novelist, was approached to write the book. Wheeler persevered, but his imagination was not sufficiently stimulated by the challenge of what might have been, or never was, and he returned to the original outlines of the Bergman plot.

Sondheim wrote several songs based on the film itself, all of them more Strindbergian than the musical Prince had in mind. Sondheim said, "And of course he was right. I usually love to write in dark colors about basic gut feelings, but Hal has a sense of audience that I sometimes lose when I'm writing." The idea that they wanted the effect to be "whipped cream with knives" crept into the discussions and is often cited, although Ratcliffe observed, "I don't find its delicious astringencies in the least fattening: hardly a sentiment remains untested by the ironies of doubt . . ." As for the knives part, that would imply "blood in the mouth," definitely a more sinister atmosphere than is conjured up by *A Little Night Music.* What Prince said he wanted was warmth and compassion. The title came from Sondheim and is a reference to Mozart's *Eine Kleine Nachtmusik,* which further suggested an operatic light-heartedness, although, ironically, Sondheim did not much care for Mozart. It was a comedy of manners, and Sondheim started thinking in terms of "fughettos, canons, contrapuntal duets, trios" and the like, "all composed in three-quarter time and multiples thereof," and developing a score that Clive Barnes would describe as "an orgy of plaintively memorable waltzes, all talking of past loves and lost worlds."

Auditions began in the spring of 1972. True to past practice, Prince was not looking for musical-comedy stars with huge voices—in any event, stars with the stature of Ethel Merman were rapidly dwindling in number—so much as actors who could sing if they had to. The shift, which had become pronounced with the casting of Rex Harrison, talking his way through the part of Professor Higgins in *My Fair Lady,* was in general use once the era of microphones and, later, the undetectable body mike took over. If it were a choice between a singer with a glorious voice who was a wooden actor or vice versa, directors would always choose the latter. If all else failed, the right actor could croak his way through his songs. This made casting much easier, although it made the work of the composer harder, since a song that had been written before it was cast might have to be extensively revised in order to disguise the shortcomings of the actor who would eventually sing it. In the sub-specialty of tailoring melodies to fit individual voices, Sondheim became something of an expert, although it did make for more than the usual false starts and revisions. *Night Music* went into rehearsal with only ten (of its final complement of sixteen) songs written, and two of them, "Two Fairy Tales" and, "My Husband the Pig," were immediately cut. Prince said that going into rehearsal this way was "sheer lunacy. It was maddening and I'll never allow it to happen again with anyone!"

The role of Desirée Armfeldt was reasonably easy to cast. Prince and Sondheim considered Tammy Grimes, well known for her success in Meredith Willson's *The Unsinkable Molly Brown* a decade before (1960), but decided upon the English film actress Glynis Johns, she of the uptilted eyes and chin, blurry smile, and bruised features. Walter Kerr wrote, "Miss Johns, that cousin of bullfrogs and consort of weary gods, is more or less the catalyst of the piece, the not-too-aging actress whose easy bonhomie helps soothe the ruffled feathers and unrequited lusts of men constricted by their celluloid collars and the Martin Luther mores of well-dressed Sweden, 1900."

Casting for Madame Armfeldt was more difficult. The distinguished British actress Hermione Gingold wanted the part so badly that she even auditioned for it, something she had not done for years. Prince thought she would be entirely wrong for the part because she was a comedian and he "wanted the humor to flow from the character." Gingold was so sure she was right that she actually appeared at an audition unannounced. She said, "I went down and sang a song I remembered vaguely . . . and Steve said, 'Now would you sing something else . . . and don't speak it quite so much . . .' And I said, 'I'm sorry but I only know one song. I'll sing it again if you like.' " So she did, and got the part. In a career spanning four decades, she had often performed for royalty but never had been so nervous. "Steve Sondheim and Hal Prince were too much for me. The only one who frightened me more was Noël Coward."

That was not the experience of the actress Charlotte Moore, who was appearing in a play in Hartford when she was invited to audition for *Night Music.* So she bought a piece of sheet music, a song she thought she knew. "I walked out onto the set of *Follies,* handed over the music, and began to sing the song from *Carousel* 'If I Loved You' into this black hole." The more she

Glynis Johns and Len Cariou in *A Little Night Music,* 1973. Below, Cariou with Victoria Mallory

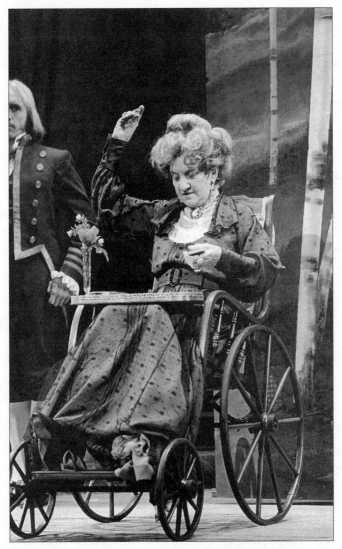

Hermione Gingold in *A Little Night Music*

sang, the more unsure she became. Her voice finally trailed off and she burst into tears. "Two people rushed up and comforted me, Prince and Sondheim. The first thing Steve said was, 'Why on earth did you pick the hardest song in the English language?' They were incredibly kind and sweet." They invited her to try again in a couple of weeks, but she decided against it.

Len Cariou, who would take the role of Fredrik Egerman, had been following the careers of Sondheim and Prince with interest for some time before he ever thought of auditioning for them. "When *Company* opened, I thought it was quite wonderful. Primarily the wit—a totally different attack to the musical-comedy form. And you could see Prince's stagecraft taking shape and bringing in other elements, taking dictation, for instance, from the set design. They were very much the front runners, and everyone wanted to be a part of what they were doing."

He always thought Sondheim was difficult to know. "I think he's very shy. I find artistic people tend to be that way. There's always a little thing that sits on one's shoulder saying, 'I know I am good, but am I really that good?' Someone who would worry about what others thought of him even when it didn't matter." But Cariou and Prince were friends, and after he had appeared in *Applause*, the musical version of *All About Eve*, with Lauren Bacall in the Bette Davis role of Margo Channing, Prince told him that he was the best leading man he had seen for a long time. Cariou had been cast to play Oedipus at the Tyrone Guthrie Theatre in Minneapolis when he was asked to audition for *Night Music*. He said, "The role I was being considered for was Desirée's lover, Count Carl-Magnus. I didn't want to play that, but I didn't want to miss singing for Sondheim and Prince." He thought the script read as well as an Anouilh play and was first-class, even without any music. He was very nervous during the audition. "No matter who it is you feel like a fool. You forget the lyrics. Getting up on stage and going blank—I was famous for that." Next day Prince called and asked him to play Fredrik Egerman, the part he secretly wanted. He was so eager that he worked out a way of juggling his performances in Minneapolis with rehearsals in New York, and never regretted it. As Egerman he seemed, Clive Barnes wrote, "delightfully and jauntily battered as the husband whose wife doesn't even know him, let alone understand him."

Once they had decided that the whole musical, even its bedroom scenes, could be set in a forest—"They would be metaphorical trees, not literal trees," Sondheim said—the designer, Boris Aronson, went to work. He was inspired by a painting by René Magritte called *Blank Signature* (1965), in which a woman on horseback in a forest can be seen in full outline because the artist has sliced up the image into vertical segments and inserted them between the gaps in the trees; the effect is to suggest, in an unsettling way, that the image is in motion. A whole forest of trees, divided into sections, was painted on silk and then mounted on huge plastic panels that were moved around by motors. The advantage of the huge panels was that a complete scene, with its own furnishings, could be hid behind it, or panels could part to reveal hidden pairs of lovers.

Very precise engineering was needed to ensure that the scenery stopped and started at exactly the same point each time. The first problem was with the panels themselves. "The sound they made in their metal tracks was picked up and amplified by the production's microphones," Frank Rich wrote. "It's a little night music, all right: rattle, rattle, clank, clank," Prince said. The problem was solved by replacing the metal tracks in the floor with wooden ones. Then there was the furniture itself, which had to glide across the stage on its own tracks. Halfway through the first dress rehearsal in Boston in January 1973, a banquet table at which Hermione Gingold was seated, which was supposed to slide to the center of the stage, took off with such alacrity that it sent cutlery flying, broke all the china, and destroyed a pair of antique candelabra worth $350.

By the first run-through Sondheim had written fourteen songs, but two more remained, one of them "A Weekend in the Country," which serves as the finale to act 1. That turned out to be an advantage, because by then the staging had been completed and the song could be tailored right down to the last semiquaver. Then there was Sondheim's best-known song, the one in which Desirée Armfeldt confronts life's missed chances with genuine despair.

Len Cariou said, "The song in the show was meant to be for Fredrik, only Stephen couldn't write it, so we didn't rehearse it." Finally the scene was restaged so that the focus was on the actress. "I was salivating," Cariou said, "because at last he was going to write this goddamned song. Two or three days later Hal said, 'Steve is bringing the song.' That's all he said." Then Sondheim arrived. "He had stayed up all night and we had come in to rehearse at ten the next morning. He looked as if someone had hit him with a hammer, with big, huge circles around his eyes. He looked like death. But I think he needed the pressure to make him function." They all gathered around the piano and then Sondheim said, 'I'm sorry, Len, you don't sing this one. It's for Desirée." It was "Send in the Clowns." Cariou said, "I've dined out on that story quite a bit."

Prince said, "We were doing a run-through for an invited audience at the Shubert, and we met early in the morning and Steve delivered the song. *Very* apologetically. He said, 'I don't know what I think of this,' and then muttered to me, 'Sounds like a piano bar song.' And he played it in front of Glynis Johns and myself, and we adored it. And, talk about the guts of a jailbird, Glynis said, 'If you'll put the lyrics on a piece of paper I'll sing it in front of the audience today.' And she did. She held it and sang it. Steve always suspected it was too pretty, too easy to remember, too whatever. It's certainly one of his biggest successes." When he and Prince began thinking of Desirée Armfeldt, they decided they would probably not be able to find a leading lady who could sing, so Sondheim thought of it as a nonsinging role. But then he discovered that Glynis Johns was rather musical and had a small, silvery voice, but could not sustain a phrase, so he deliberately wrote a melody with a lot of pauses for breath. "One of the reasons I like the song is that nobody can sing it as well as she." When it became a hit and was recorded by Cleo Laine, Frank Sinatra, Judy Collins, and others, who were real singers, they tended to lengthen the phrases but the song lost some of its rueful, biting quality. One had to be able to throw away the first line, "Isn't it rich?," and that is why he used the closed-off consonants of *ch.* He said, "You don't use open vowel sounds. You use little cut-off things so that the audience doesn't think it is the actress's fault. And that makes the song specifically for someone who can't sing."

Another pivotal song in *A Little Night Music* was "The Miller's Son," written for the one levelheaded, earthy member of the group, the maid Petra. Sondheim said, "*Night Music* is about how people play at love and about flirtations and about how people who are sexually attracted to each other put on masks and clothes and faces and get caught up in the games instead of the business in hand and as time goes by they've lost everything." He wanted to give Petra a song that would sum up what the playwright was conveying but could not, given the conventions of a musical, write as a speech. "But you can do that in a song because you can clothe it in so many costumes. Rhymes and playing around, that can make it fun." Petra's view of marriage is entirely practical, but she sees no harm in taking advantage of whatever life has to offer. Sondheim said that the song came about as the result of a comment made by the daughter of a friend of George Furth when she was six or eight years old. Her birthday coincided with Christmas and she was asked which occasion she wanted to celebrate. Her reply was, "I just want to celebrate everything that passes by." And Sondheim thought, " 'Boy, that's a sentence!' And so the song is based on the little girl's sentence."

> It's a very short road
> To the ten thousandth lunch
> And the belch and the grouch and the sigh.
> In the meanwhile,
> There are mouths to be kissed
> Before mouths to be fed,
> And a lot in between
> In the meanwhile.
> And a girl ought to celebrate what passes by.

Sondheim began thinking about the song at an early stage but had only written the first verse when the show was cast. "We cast a girl who was primarily a dancer who could sing the verse." She was Garn Stephens, and the show's choreographer, Patricia Birch, said, "From the time I first read the script I said, 'That's Garn.'" But the song continued to develop, "and I let it go the way it wanted to go and it became this rather bravura piece and Garn couldn't handle it," Sondheim said. So Stephens was fired in Boston, which was, Birch added, "a terrible shock to the company." Cariou made a similar comment. "It hurt morale," he said. "Theatre is a collaborative art. You form a team. The whole piece has to work as a concept," and to lose one of the principals at a late stage, by implication, threw everyone else's contribution into question. "Steve wanted people to know it was his decision. He said to me and most everyone that it just needed to be sung better, but I don't think the problem was solved with her replacement. I think he thought the song was more important than it was."

It was a disruption they could have "done without," Cariou said, and there were others. The day of the show's opening in Boston, with critics expected that night, Sondheim was in his hotel room reworking one of the lyrics for "Remember?," which is sung by the group of lieder singers. One line, "The way taboos we knew were old-fashioned / Fell with a crash and / Sank" did not please. It took eleven hours before the line emerged as "The wine that made us both so merry / And oh, so very / Frank." Prince decided that one of the props, the invitation to the country weekend, was so small that it looked "like an invitation to a party in Queens," and insisted that a larger one be made. That night, everything went wrong. Instead of arriving with a bang the banquet table left with one, throwing the actors standing around it into their chairs. Hardly had they recovered than one of the panels of trees collided with a piece of scenery and had to be untangled by a stage-hand in full view of the audience. At yet another pivotal moment, part of the set jerked into place between Glynis Johns and Barbara Lang (playing Mrs. Anderssen) with such abruptness that Lang shouted "Heads up!," the inter-national danger code for actors.

The critics gamely refused to be put off: "a lovely show, a civilized enter-tainment, elegant and amusing," Elliot Norton reported in the Boston *Her-ald American,* and other Boston critics were just as admiring. Then, on February 20, in the middle of New York previews and five days before the official opening, Glynis Johns was hospitalized with exhaustion and Lang, her understudy, took over. The columnist Earl Wilson reported that Tammy Grimes might replace her, and perhaps this was the incentive Johns needed to get well: she was back in her part before the big night of Sunday, February 25. Ethel Merman was there, Alexis Smith, Nancy Walker, and a host of other famous friends. Opening nights are deceptive, but there seemed to be more than simple goodwill in the air. The show was a hit: "A production possessing style and imagination," said Richard Watts in the New York *Post,* and Clive Barnes called it "heady, civilized, sophisticated and enchanting. It is Dom Perignon. It is supper at Lasserre. It is a mixture of Cole Porter, Gustav Mahler, Antony Tudor and just a little of Ingmar Bergman. And it is more fun than any tango in a Parisian suburb . . . Good God!—an adult musical!" The news had already reached Anouilh's agent, the one who had twice refused the team of Prince and Sondheim. He sent a telegram saying that the rights to *Ring Round the Moon* were available, oblivious to the obvious fact that by now they had their "masque."

Here was a musical that seemed to have found the right balance between subject matter likely to please a wide audience and a sensitive and tasteful adaptation. Musicals are sometimes so much a part of their epoch that when the moment has passed, recreating their appeal is impossible. But *Night Music,* set in a comfortably remote time and place, making its wry commentary on the absurdities of love, was as successful during the next twenty years and numerous revivals as it had been in 1973. Then in 1995 the Royal National Theatre mounted yet another revival in London. Sondheim had not approved of the Olivier Theatre, which has a huge, open apron stage, arguing that the musical needed a proscenium arch, and he was right.

That to one side, the music, lyrics, the snap of the dialogue, and the polished acting style more than made up for the staging; it seemed as if *Night Music* had just been written, and it was a perfect jewel. Charles Spencer wrote in the *Daily Telegraph,* "Sean Mathias's supremely elegant staging . . . leaves no doubt that this is one of the great musicals. He dextrously balances the work's humour with its affecting moments of heartfelt humanity without ever letting the piece cloy into romantic mush." As for Dame Judi Dench in the leading role, she was "in devastating comic form as the raddled actress Desirée . . . From her first entrance in the most preposterous of hats, she has the audience eating out of the palm of her hand, and her waspish asides as her old lover rhapsodizes about his new wife are brilliantly delivered. But Dench also suggests a desperate vulnerability behind the bright facade, a woman who knows that her time is running out, and in her marvellous performance even the hackneyed 'Send in the Clowns' becomes almost unbearably moving . . ." As Ingmar Bergman explained, his film had been based on the realization that it was possible for people to go on loving each other even though they found it impossible to live together. But *Night Music's* great virtue is that nothing is solemnly underlined and everything ends frothily, much like the dénouement of Richard Strauss's *Der Rosenkavalier* after the Marschallin has

Sondheim, Ruth Mitchell, and Hal Prince at the London opening of *A Little Night Music* in 1975

made her poignant renunciation. "Ah, how we laughed," the *Liebeslieder* singers recall ("Remember?"). "Ah, how we cried. / Ah, how you promised and / Ah, how I lied."

IN THOSE DAYS a production booked into the Shubert Theatre was required by union contract to employ a minimum of twenty-five musicians, which usually became the maximum, and adequate only if the orchestrator used great care. Since *Night Music* was turn-of-the-century and romantically Viennese in feeling, Tunick decided to use an operetta orchestra with the traditional combinations of strings, woodwinds, brass, and percussion. He wrote, "The score is so delicate that I was tempted to disperse with the trumpets and drums, but decided to include them for safety's sake. It was, after all, a Broadway musical, a field in which no one has ever suffered due to lack of subtlety." Sondheim's general directions were that he wanted a perfumed atmosphere, with the smell of musk, and Tunick's response to that was "plenty of strings." He thought of the musical in terms of a scherzo, "light, fast, playful, mysterious and in triple meter," as the proper accompaniment to

Wheeler's precisely plotted book, in which, as in *La Ronde,* the famous play by Arthur Schnitzler, every figure in a liaison is in love with someone else. The composer responded by the use of trios, when characters were separated ("Now," "Later," "Soon"), and duets in which someone else was being described. "These songs of alienation and yearning for cohesion and balance all represent the unstable number three drawn to the stable two—the triangle yearning to be reconciled to the proper couple," Tunick wrote. Although there were some variations, most of the score used permutations of triple time, such as the waltz ("You Must Meet My Wife"), the mazurka ("Remember," "The Glamorous Life"), the sarabande ("Later" and "Liaisons"), the polonaise ("In Praise of Women"), the étude ("Every Day a Little Death"), and the gigue ("A Weekend in the Country"). Since Sondheim invariably avoided using the conventional melodic, harmonic, and rhythmic solutions of most Broadway composers, orchestrating his score presented special problems. There was, for instance, "the cross-hand étude pattern in the accompaniment of 'Every Day a Little Death.' The syncopated eighth-note pattern was originally assigned to the clarinet [players], who quickly retitled the piece 'Every Page a Little Breath,' due to the complete absence of rests in their part," Tunick wrote.

The critics unanimously admired the score—*Time* magazine called it "a beauty in an exceedingly distinguished career." The discipline imposed by the forms used "seems to have released something in Mr. Sondheim; his music has never been so eloquent before. Individual melodies lilt, soar, tantalize, dazzle, but never descend into lushness. The effect is of an overwhelming romantic sense held in check until the very last moment," Robert Cushman wrote. That, Sondheim said, was intended: "I generally like . . . to keep things dry, keep them from getting mushy. Also because music has such a direct emotional force . . . you're able often to give enormous color and depth to something if you play a subtext in the orchestra that belies or undercuts the lyrics and vice versa. It keeps songs alive."

This characteristic technique helped to convey a mood of ambivalence, which Sondheim called his "favorite thing to write about, because it's the way I feel, and I think the way most people feel. It wasn't dealt with very much on the musical stage. People had an emotion and sang about it. That was the Rodgers and Hammerstein tradition, although the 'Soliloquy' in *Carousel* is a study in ambivalence. It allows for dramatic contrast and of course is really about that old devil subtext, which is talked about all the time in the theatre these days," he said in a television conversation with the conductor-composer André Previn in 1977. "The best actors always find a subtext, something that leaves the audience something to discover, or smell—it gives body, like body in wine. Take all the songs in *Company* that Bobby sings—he's supposedly happy with his unmarried life and what we have to discover without being told is that underneath, he's screaming."

Others found that the dominant mood behind Sondheim's work was not so much rage, desperation, or even ambivalence as it was a kind of hopeless longing. There seemed to be a continuing conflict "between suppressed romanticism and intellectual control," Michael Billington observed, adding that it was just this quality that gave the writing its fruitful tension. And there was no question about the quicksilver wit being displayed, "brilliantly funny, seeking out improbable and inspired syllabic pairings which would have brought pleasure to [Alexander] Pope." There is the song "Now" at the beginning of *Night Music*, in which Fredrik Egerman, whose year-old marriage to his wife, Anne, has yet to be consummated, tries to decide whether he should seduce her by the use of charm, take her by force, or just take a nap, using a lawyer's plodding logic:

> Removing her clothing
> Would take me all day,
> And her subsequent loathing
> Would turn me away—
> Which eliminates B
> And which leaves us with A.

Or there is the song "Liaisons," Madame Armfeldt's trip down memory lane, in which she recalls her many affairs with dukes and counts that, when played according to the rules, led to such delectable consequences, and of their sad disappearance:

> What once was a rare champagne
> Is now just an amiable hock,
> What once was a villa at least
> Is 'digs.'
> What once was a gown with train
> Is now just a simple little frock,
> What once was a sumptuous feast
> Is figs.
> No, no, not even figs—raisins.
> Ah, liaisons!

Sondheim was being called a poet of the theatre. His brilliance as a musical dramatist bound the show together. In his musicals the dialogue almost acted as a kind of operatic recitative: that is, it was a necessary bridge that advanced the plot to the next song. "Sondheim's numbers in a real sense *are* the drama," Tom Sutcliffe and Paul Sheren argued in an illuminating essay. "They can be duets, mixtures of events presented together, ballads, self-portraits, personality type analyses. Above all they are poems for the theatre." If Sondheim's skill as a lyricist merited any reservation, "it would be that the wit—so characteristic of his time and milieu—is indulged almost as an automatic reflex, as a defusing element, in the face of emotion nakedly and truthfully presented . . . Yet this sad, almost zany humor with which pain is turned away, this attribute of Feste the Clown who is Sondheim's cultural ancestor, should rather be noted as a characteristic of the art than questioned. It is as much part of the game as breaking into a number at a moment of climax. Musical comedy, however deeply it delves into feeling is, after all, entertainment."

A Little Night Music ran at the Shubert Theatre on Broadway for seventeen months and six hundred and one performances. With his usual caution, Sondheim pronounced it "the least poorly received of all our shows at the time," and it made a comfortable profit for its backers. It was being cited as an example of the way in which art and commercialism could coexist on Broadway. It was no great surprise when *Night Music* received twelve nominations for the 1973 Tony Awards. Its main competitor was *Pippin,* with eleven nominations. This work, with music by Stephen Schwartz, began as a quiet allegory about a young man's search for identity and was transformed by its director, the choreographer Bob Fosse, into a kaleidoscopic salute to show business. During the ceremony each musical took five awards. Glynis Johns won as best actress, Patricia Elliott (in the role of Countess Charlotte Malcolm) was best supporting actress, Hugh Wheeler took the award for best book, Florence Klotz for her costume designs, and Sondheim, his third Tony in as many years for best score, then a record. Then Rex Harrison opened the evening's final envelope, for best musical, and announced that *Night Music* was the overall winner.

The next step, Prince decided, was to turn his successful production of *Night Music* into a film. Films that became musicals, then films again, were becoming common enough; one thinks of Shaw's *Pygmalion,* a play that became a film that became a musical that became another film, as perhaps the most famous example of a concept that triumphs no matter what the medium. Both Prince and Wheeler were "desperate to make it," Sondheim said later. He was opposed because of the basic difficulties implied in translating a work for the stage into cinematic terms. He said, "I think the only way musicals work on screen is [if they are] performing musicals—the Astaire-Rogers pictures which are obviously . . . frothy confections that are excuses for a series of songs and dances or . . . René Clair kinds of musicals, which are not about character or anything we care about but an excuse for stylish ways of presenting musical numbers. It is style over substance and the kind of musicals I've been connected with, and most musicals since Rodgers and Hammerstein . . . have been about character, about story."

Night Music, he said later, was too static a story to lend itself to film. "It's all about savoring moments." No doubt Prince would have disagreed. As a director of musicals, he had been extremely influential in furthering the idea of staging that jumped from scene to scene effortlessly, as in *Company, Follies,* and *Night Music.* But paradoxically, once he went to work behind a camera his theatrical instincts took charge, and what ought to have been fluid became stiff and lifeless. Or so the critics seemed to think. There was much carping about casting, with the exception of Hermione Gingold, repeating her role as Madame Armfeldt; and there was particular sniping at Elizabeth Taylor in the role of Desirée. She might have been forgiven for not being able to sing or act, it seemed, but the fact that she was overweight was the ultimate offense. "Liz Taylor as actress Desirée Armfeldt, all calories, cleavage and camp," was pitifully miscast, according to *Cue* magazine, and another writer cuttingly observed that she looked like "a raunchy barmaid." But the main criticism was reserved for Prince, and the static photography and routine editing did not help matters. Every staging decision was almost suicidally wrong-headed, Vincent Canby wrote.

The film quietly disappeared but did nothing to dim Sondheim's reputation. Craig Zadan, who would become a successful theatre, record, and film producer, recalled being assigned to interview Sondheim for a magazine when he was just out of college. His article subsequently attracted the attention of a publisher, who wanted him to write a book about "the new Cole Porter." So he brought up the matter with Sondheim, who turned him down with the comment "Who will buy it, my mother?" He did not want a biography written, but thought it might be interesting to put together a history of the making of his musicals from the verbatim accounts of those who had worked with him. That became *Sondheim & Co.,* a best-selling book that was first published in 1974 and was updated in 1989 to include Sondheim's output through *Into the Woods* (1987).

Just as *Night Music* was being readied for Broadway, the American Musical and Dramatic Academy, in cooperation with the National Hemophilia

Foundation, was preparing its annual fund-raising event in the form of a trib-ute to Harold Prince. When Prince declined, Sondheim was approached. He agreed, thinking that he "wouldn't have to do anything, listen to a few songs, eat your chicken à la king and get up and blush and you've done your bit." That was the start of "Sondheim: A Musical Tribute" on the stage of the Shu-bert Theatre on Sunday, March 11, 1973, with thirty-three performers, a direc-tor, an orchestra, a recording crew, a choreographer, and a packed house—the first of many such celebrations. Zadan, as one of the producers, made all the arrangements for taping the evening and recording the songs as a two-record set. Burt Shevelove flew in from London to direct. Donna McKechnie, who had performed in *Company*, was choreographer, and Sondheim took final responsibility for the whole affair. "Putting this thing on was like organizing a peace march," he said. For Zadan, it took nine months of work but con-vinced him that he wanted to become a producer and changed his life.

Ethel Merman, who was to have sung some of her most famous songs from *Gypsy*, decided she would rather visit her daughter in Florida instead. Phil Silvers, who was to have performed songs from *Forum*, had a stroke. Lee Remick, who had planned to sing some of her songs from *Anyone Can Whis-tle*, including the title song, called two days before the performance to say that she could not get away from filming in London. Zero Mostel, who was originally enthusiastic, wanted so much time devoted just to him that he could not be accommodated. But so many others did appear that it hardly mattered: Larry Blyden, Len Cariou, Jack Cassidy, Hermione Gingold, Lau-rence Guittard, Glynis Johns, Larry Kert, John McMartin, Chita Rivera, Ethel Shutta, and Alexis Smith. Angela Lansbury flew in from London, where she was rehearsing for her performance as Madame Rose in the first West End production of *Gypsy*. Nancy Walker came in from the West Coast to belt out "I'm Still Here." Glynis Johns was gamely prepared to sing even though suffering from laryngitis. Jonathan Tunick wrote an overture for the occasion, which the conductor, Paul Gemignani, and his orchestra, did not get until the morning of the benefit. Gemignani did not have all of his singers on stage together until that afternoon, and there were more than forty songs to rehearse and record. The recording engineer, Phil Ramone, who had been hired a month before, called from Las Vegas to announce that he would not be able to be there after all; his replacement was found on a California golf course. By the time the performance began, the orchestra pit was so full of men, music stands, and microphones that there was no more room for one of the cellists and his instrument, and he had to be sent home.

The tickets, at $100, $50, and $25, had been sold out for weeks, and even standing room was overbooked, in defiance of fire regulations. Dozens of socialites and Broadway figures were in the audience, according to Eugenia Sheppard: Dina Merrill and Cliff Robertson, Amanda Burden and Steve Paley, Adolph Green and Phyllis Newman, Sybil and Jordan Christopher, and many others. Hal Prince, Anthony Perkins, Jule Styne, Sheldon Harnick, Jack Cassidy, Burt Shevelove, and Leonard Bernstein all appeared on stage, introducing aspects of Sondheim's career and adding their reminiscences. Bernstein sat down at the piano and talked about their collaboration on *West Side Story.* Some early songs were included. "Class" from *Saturday Night* gave no hint, Arthur Bell of the *Village Voice* thought, of the brilliance that was to come; but there was also "There Won't Be Trumpets" from *Anyone Can Whistle,* rendered by Alice Playten with such style and conviction that the critic wondered why it had ever been cut. Other highlights of the evening were Nancy Walker's "I'm Still Here" and Ethel Shutta's wonderful rendition of "Broadway Baby." Finally, Hermione Gingold, Nancy Walker, Angela Lansbury, Alexis Smith, Glynis Johns, and Dorothy Collins, all seated on little gold chairs, got up to sing songs they had made famous. When Collins finally rose to perform "Losing My Mind," the evening had reached a fitting climax. As usual at such moments, Sondheim was overwhelmed when he tried to express his gratitude to everyone, and particularly to Shevelove and Prince: "and above all, to Hal Prince, without whom I would not be . . ." he began to say, but the rest was lost.

With Bernstein following the performance of *Sondheim: A Musical Tribute* in 1973

At the supper party afterwards at the Pub Theatrical he was photographed talking to Alexis Smith and seated beside Angela Lansbury, whose hand he held in a tight grip. His black tie was somewhat askew by then, and he was moving from room to room with a glass in hand, kissing and hugging his friends and well-wishers. At one point a young man approached him, said he was a good lyricist and wanted to send his work to Sondheim for review.

Sondheim explained apologetically that he did not set other people's lyrics to music. That was not what he had in mind, said the young man. He did not want Sondheim to set his lyrics to music; he wanted to set Sondheim's lyrics to *his* music. "Your lyrics are everything; your music is not much." Sondheim had hardly said "That is a matter of opinion" before a guest, sensing a gathering storm, swept him up and bore him away.

CHAPTER 14

Someone in a Tree

W HEN THE TIME CAME to describe a certain moment in his life—their social fortunes suddenly rose and they were feted and invited everywhere by rich and powerful people—the late art historian and author Kenneth Clark called it "the Great Clark Boom." It lasted for a few years, was entirely inexplicable, and one could only say, he wrote in his enchanting memoir, *Another Part of the Wood,* of himself and his wife, Jane, that "it had as little to do with talent as Australian gold shares have to do with the precious metal in a mine." It reminded him of the word coined by Bernard Berenson's brother-in-law, Logan Pearsall Smith, when he underwent a similar experience: "a swimgloat." He continued, "Absurd as it sounds, I think that the real explanation was our innocence."

One can date Sondheim's great boom almost as neatly as Lord Clark managed to identify his own, and although it may have had something to do with innocence, one cannot say in his case (although Clark was being characteristically modest) that it had little to do with talent. The success of *A Little Night Music,* hard on the heels of *Company* and *Follies,* had made it plain to the meanest intelligence that this was a musical dramatist of rare stature. Magazines discovered him as a fresh, unsullied subject for leisurely dissection and analysis. Here was a rumple-haired musician, still dressing "like a ragamuffin," with a house full of puzzles and games arranged like artifacts in a museum of his own invention, being described as "the most important force in the American musical theatre" by no less than Leonard Bernstein. He pedaled around Manhattan on a bicycle, and his idea of a really good meal was a steak washed down generously with Scotch. He freely admitted he was in therapy and, to general surprise, was as animated in conversation as his works were on the stage. And no less than the great Oscar Hammerstein had spotted his gifts when he was a mere adolescent.

Robert Kimball, former curator of the musical theatre collection at Yale, stated that Broadway's eviscerated tradition was being revitalized by Sondheim and Prince. "If there's not an audience for *their* shows, there's no audience for adult, intelligently crafted musical theatre," he observed. But, at a moment when ambitious musicals like *Dude* and *Via Galactica* were opening and closing within days, *Night Music* was doing a sell-out business, and that proved there was an audience for work that was sophisticated, full of urbane humor, and genuinely contemporary. And Sondheim's reputation grew with every new work.

"You've got to understand," William Goldman said, "when Steve happened, we didn't know it then. But nobody really ever had a stronger debut in terms of quality: *West Side Story, Gypsy,* and *Forum! West Side Story* is now everybody's old horse but it was a revolutionary show then, and so was *Gypsy.* He was different and the lyrics were different; they were conversational. He was so gifted, and I think Steve wanted to be thought of as brilliant. I think that was very important for Steve when he was younger."

He might grumble that he was being overworked: " 'You ask about my life-style,' he cried aloud. 'I'll tell you about my life-style. I have no life-style. Since 1969 I have done nothing but write, write, write. I mean, I haven't even had a game party in my house in three years.' " He might claim that "all I ever really wanted was to make enough money from the theatre to be able to write for the theatre." He might believe that he could go to Christo's, his favorite steakhouse, as anonymously as before, or drop into the Turtle Bay Chemists on the corner of Forty-Eighth Street and Second Avenue just like anybody else. But if he were in the company of Leonard Bernstein and Katharine Hepburn, as he was one evening, several pairs of eyes were watching him buy fancy soaps and bath preparations, according to Stanley Herman, a pharmacist who used to work there. And he was even beginning to be recognized by maîtres d'hotel and restaurant owners—the ultimate accolade.

Howard Erskine said, "We've had an ongoing lunch at the Four Seasons restaurant since the 1970s, and we all sit at this terrible table. The first time we" (meaning himself, Charles Hollerith, and Sondheim) "had lunch, I said to Steve, 'Where do we go?' And he said, 'Some place where they wear big hats.' So I suggested the Four Seasons. I remember calling and making the reservation. They didn't know me from Adam, so they gave us this table in the Grill Room. You walk through where all the powerhouse people sit and up to a little stairway with a balcony of tables running across, and there's one table to the right. It's just the end of the world, and there's a room behind it where people walk back and forth, past you all the time, and it's just the *worst* table. So when we sat down for lunch the owner came by and said, 'My God, Stephen Sondheim! What are you doing here? I'll move you,' and so on. And Steve said, 'No, no! You're going to stick Howard Erskine at this table, so we'll just stay here!' And we've been there *all* these years. I always ask specifically for that one."

There was no doubt that the effort of working on three hugely successful musicals in something like four years had taken a toll. His eyes were smudged with dark shadows, his cheeks sometimes looked puffy with fatigue, and he could "lumber like a benumbed bear shaking off a winter's sleep," *Time* observed. His hairline was receding slightly, there were some gray hairs among the brown, and he had the beginnings of a paunch. His friends agreed that he tended not to take care of himself. Sondheim said, "Unfortunately I had, and still have, a great capacity for liquor, which is not good for the health. I wish I didn't but I do. I found it loosened me up a great deal, helped me get past the mental censors when I started work. You try putting 'I love you' down on a page! Marijuana also helped a lot. The only thing I've ever written without the use of anything at all except water was the music for the film *Stavisky*. Because it didn't involve any lyric writing. The problem of marijuana with lyrics is that when you get to the precision part of it, marijuana is useless. It's all about drifting, and when I've got to have a two-syllable word . . . But it's swell for starting." He would try to start without it and then, if he felt blocked, he would take a puff or two.

He was smoking one or two packs of cigarettes a day, always filters, but trying to give them up, since he realized that smoking had control of him. "I was not enjoying it. My mouth was dry and that sort of stuff. I didn't develop a cough or anything like that. I just thought, I've got to get out of it! I tried three times to give it up, separately, six months each time, and then I would get under pressure, like rehearsals or something like that. When I was working with Dick Rodgers I was smoking cigars, because you don't inhale. But eventually I'd take one puff of nicotine and I'd get it back again." He finally succeeded with SmokEnders and has become an enthusiastic adherent.

Cocaine was very chic, the drug of choice, and, unfortunately, like nicotine, easily became a habit. "I found it an easy one to break by simply not having any around the house." He continued, "It's very good if you're tired, if you want to get a little jump start of energy." He never took a really expensive grade, so his was probably cut a great deal with sugar. And he started to experiment with psychedelic drugs in the 1970s. "I couldn't wait to try them. I loved mescaline and acid (LSD)—I had about a dozen over a period of six years and never had a bad trip. I tried [psilocybin] mushrooms three or four times but it never worked at all. That's the one I would have liked to use because it's natural, it's organic. The trouble with both mescaline and acid, particularly acid, was that it [is cut] with speed [amphetamines] and speed is not my drug of choice. I do not like the feeling of speed at all; it makes my nerves jangle."

Some people had very specific visions. "I had none of that. Do you remember the paintings of Peter Max? The Yellow Submarine? That's what mine were like. This ceiling looks white to me right now. But to an artist, as with Seurat, how black your hat, how red to me. Peter Wooster [a close friend] could look at this ceiling and say, 'No it's not white, it's yellow, it's green, it's blue . . .' I don't see that. But taking a psychedelic drug heightens your senses that ordinarily don't operate. And so I would lie on the floor quite often and stare at the ceiling and be aware of the sensations of textures and shapes. All the senses that I don't employ much, namely, sight, taste, and touch. The one thing that was hardly ever affected was music—well, that's not true. The way I like psychedelic drugs is to play something and stare at something equally intensely at the same time. And it just opens up your mind and you see all these wonderful, kind of trippy patterns. The only time it didn't work was when I listened to my own music. I sobered up immediately! As soon as I heard anything of my own I'd say, 'Oh God, there's that terrible B-flat again,' and, 'Gee, isn't that a great chord change!' But I could trip out listening to anybody else, from Beethoven to Kander and Ebb. I just couldn't do it with my own work—it was too close to me, I think."

SONDHEIM WAS FOND of saying, "I hate throwing things away. I feel the same way about people. I have a small circle of friends whom I enjoy seeing over and over again, year after year." That was quite true, except that the circle was being expanded rapidly as new friends joined it and became *unser einers,* along with Dominick Dunne, James Goldman, Hal Prince, Arthur Laurents, Mary Rodgers, Howard Erskine, Chuck Hollerith, Ford Schumann, Mary Ann Madden, Lee Remick, Larry Miller, and so many others. He had a gift not just for making his friends feel at ease but cared for. He wanted them to enjoy other people they had yet to meet and share his enthusiasm. His invariable introduction would be how much they would all like each other, and he was usually right. In a world where casual intimacies were the rule, his were not easily given, but they were hard to dislodge.

In those days Diane Johnson was married to Lee Wright, who met Sondheim in the 1970s when he was working as an actor. Then he turned to men's fashions and began giving Sondheim clothes of his own design, suits, jackets, shoes, and pajamas, as lavish Christmas presents. "Lee had a really good eye for color, and his clothes were sophisticated, yet functional," she said. "He didn't make any special point of choosing colors for Steve but just gave him the clothes he liked himself, usually in tones of tan, brown, and green. Steve particularly liked the silkier knit shirts with polo necks and the sports jackets. Everything coordinated so it was easy to assemble." Before long, "Steve was becoming more aware of his appearance. At one time he never bothered to go to a store."

The Christmas parties were wonderful, she said. Louis Vargas knew all the best recipes. His turkeys had cornbread stuffing and were basted with ginger ale. Peter Wooster, a talented architect and interior designer, took a gourmet's interest in side dishes like beets with parsley and creamed onions. Guests usually brought the desserts and, while the turkey was cooking, would drink syllabub, wine, and champagne, and nibble on the homemade bagel chips toasted with herbs that Louis had made, the cheese sticks and nuts. "It was a very warm, homey feeling," she said.

Chuck Hollerith, who foresook his banking career to become a successful theatrical producer as a result of his friendship with Sondheim, said that their Christmas parties had begun in the 1960s. "At the time it was Mary Rodgers and her husband, Ford and Caroline Schumann, my wife and myself, and Steve. Mary Ann Madden very often came. Judy and Hal came a couple of times." One of the highlights of the party was the annual grab bag, small gifts worth one or two dollars contributed by Steve. A string would be attached to each present and guests would take turns pulling on the strings. The idea was to see how imaginative one could be for very little money. After dinner they would open the big presents. Hollerith said, "My Christmas shopping, the first concern was 'What *will* I give Steve for Christmas?' " It had to be just right. Some years he would spend months making a gift, something personalized that was, if possible, funny as well. "I think Steve gave a train to Henry Guettel one year that played one of his songs. He was always terribly generous. Even when he wasn't making money he'd go to the best store on the East Side and find some wonderful antique for you." And Sondheim went on inventing special games for his friends, particularly if he thought they needed cheering up. The actress Phyllis Newman, who had been in the cast of a musical that closed out of town, returned to New York feeling depressed, so Sondheim invented a game for her.

He said, "The old game of Murder is so boring. It's just a lot of people groping each other in the dark, which is fun but not a game." So he came up with the idea of a murder mystery that could be played by a dozen people or so in a large apartment or house with a minimum of six rooms. He said, "We played it up at Jerry Robbins's house in the country and it was a terrific success. Everybody has to go searching for clues in rooms lit only by candles. Along the way there's a murderer let loose. The clues are photographs, all over, in bathrooms—all over the place. It's quite suspenseful. People really get scared in this game. It's really nice."

There were all the game parties and invitations from people like Lenny and Felicia, who might have a Japanese dinner with everyone wearing kimonos, or Jerry and Arthur and Adolph and Betty, a whole group of people who called themselves "the Blob," the director Mike Nichols said, "a community of like minds." Or they might be grand affairs, like the night Truman Capote gave his black-and-white masked ball in honor of Katharine Graham, publisher of the Washington *Post*. Sondheim was surprised but delighted to be invited. The costume designer Florence Klotz made him a mask out of music paper, and "I was one of the people who closed it up," he said. Or there might be country-house invitations, as when he visited Julie Andrews and her first husband, Tony Walton, in the Channel Islands and he was photographed with his head in her pregnant lap. Then there was John David Wilder, an actor whom he met in 1971 and who was the first boyfriend his friends could remember seeing with Sondheim. Some thought they had lived together, but Sondheim said he would just occasionally stay overnight. For a revival of *Forum* starring Phil Silvers on March 30, 1972, Wilder sent him a telegram that said, "Then we'll just have to learn to be happy without it," and when reminded of it, Sondheim laughed. "That's a quote from *Forum*." It is Philia's reply to Hero, the young romantic lead, when he laments that they will never know happiness. Sondheim and Wilder bought an English sheepdog together, which, when the relationship ended, was left with Sondheim and used to skid around the floor.

"I remember that Steve introduced us just after *Company*," D. D. Ryan said of Wilder. "He became a great friend of mine and stayed in our house in Nantucket for a long time. He was a real charmer. He called me day in and day out and I was absolutely charmed by his wit and humor, but he was one of those fly-by-night people who stay for a whole summer and somehow did more to create turmoil within our family . . . I had this almost-crush on him, because he was giving me such companionship, affection, and attention—my husband wasn't always around. But then I realized he was a real 'mixer,' as the English say. He was a very peace-at-any-price kind of person, but he just couldn't help stirring the pot."

Laurents, who was staying with Tom Hatcher in his house on Long Island, recalled inviting Sondheim and Wilder there for a week. At some point, another friend was having a cocktail party and Sondheim did not want to go, but Wilder did, and he got into the car with Laurents and Hatcher. "No sooner are we in the car than he said, 'Oh, you two are wonderful, not at all what Steve said.' The next thing is, over the weekend he made a pass at Tom." Later, Wilder rented a small house they had on the property and "made trouble between Steve and me. He told lies. He also went around later saying he wasn't gay and that he'd never been to bed with Steve, and turned on him. The ins and outs of that I don't know. All I know is that I didn't like him at all." Wilder subsequently died of AIDS.

Foxy Sondheim continued to be in the background of his life and made her periodic demands for attention, consideration, and love, using the maladroit methods that had long ceased to prompt any reaction from her son except derisive laughter. She was seen around town, often at dinner parties given by Jo Copeland, according to Barbara Barondess MacLean, an interior

Sondheim with Julie Andrews, who was pregnant, on the island of Alderney, 1962

designer and clothes designer who knew her well; she always was wearing something fashionable and was prepared to boast about her son at the slightest opportunity. Oscar Hammerstein's biographer, Hugh Fordin, recalled riding in a car with her and Dorothy Hammerstein after attending a matinee of Michael Bennett's hit musical *A Chorus Line* in 1975, and hearing her declare "in no uncertain terms" that her son had been plagiarized by the composer or lyricist and that she was going to tell him to sue. No one took her preposterous claim seriously.

Some time in the 1970s she was to go into the hospital to have a pacemaker installed. Sondheim did not remember exactly when. Although it was just a pacemaker, his mother somehow convinced herself, or wanted him to believe, that it was open-heart surgery. Could they have had some kind of argument before the event that caused her to feel her son did not care whether she lived or died? What Sondheim remembered was that she wrote him a letter and had it hand-delivered, "because she thought she was going to die and wanted to make sure I got it. She said, 'The night before I undergo open heart surgery'—underlined three times. Open parenthesis. 'My surgeon's term.' Close parenthesis. 'The only regret I have in life is giving you birth.'"

He continued: "As quickly as my hand could cross the paper I wrote her a three-page reply. Everything I'd felt, that I'd never expressed up to this point. It wasn't hard. I just said, 'I don't want to see you any more. I'll continue to support you, and just call my business manager.' That was all. I must say even that is a little startling to me because, as my shrink pointed out, not all nice Jewish boys support their mothers. But I told him, 'You know, I have the money. What am I going to do—let her starve on the street?' She had no money of her own; she'd spent it all and was no longer capable of earning a living." To keep his mother in reasonable comfort cost him $80,000 a year.

That incident caused a rift that lasted until the death of Janet Sondheim Leshin in 1992 at the age of ninety-five. Once the full significance of what she had done dawned on Foxy, she tried desperately to make amends. She sent friends like Colleen Moore to plead her cause, and wrote letters. He realized that "she had no idea what she'd said. She was not burning the bridges consciously." It was her pattern to become irrationally angry, say the most hurtful thing she could think of, and then be amazed when the other person bore a grudge. "She was actually baffled, because I got a couple of letters from her after that saying, 'I don't understand what you feel. Why can't we have fun the way we used to?' And I just, literally, photocopied the letter she had sent and sent it back to her. She was an impossible person."

In later years Foxy Sondheim Leshin had an apartment at 27 East Sixty-fifth Street, in "a strange blue ceramic building on the corner of Madison Avenue," as Prince described it, where she was cared for by a registered nurse named Constance. Then, some time in the 1980s, when it became evident that her health was failing, Sondheim moved her to a nursing home—eventually, the Actors' Nursing Home in Englewood, New Jersey—and sold her apartment. In that connection, Hal Prince remembered a funny story. "After she got to the nursing home she decided she wanted to go back to her apartment and sent Steve a message to that effect. And he said, 'I'm afraid you can't. Hal's living there. Hal's rented the apartment,' and she never asked any questions. She never said, 'How come? What happened to Judy and the two children?' " He laughed. "I thought it was hilarious. She accepted this crazy explanation of why she couldn't go home, as he probably knew she would."

Prince said, "I don't think anybody in the world would defend Foxy, not anybody." But Patricia Sinnott, who was Sondheim's personal secretary for nine years, starting in 1978, liked her, and so did Louis Vargas. "Lou was very kind and would go to see her often and take her little gifts he knew she loved, like a particular Estée Lauder nail polish, lipstick and slippers and little dressing gowns and stuff. One day he said to me, 'Ah, come on, Patricia, come and take the trip.' So I called and invited her to lunch on the 'outside,' because she was better there. Her health improved. We found a lovely little restaurant that was near a Lord & Taylor or something because she wanted so badly the joy of going to the cosmetic counter and telling the salesgirl, 'They don't make red the way they used to!' We went to lunch. I ordered a glass of wine and she belted down two really fabulous vodka martinis! And she was eighty-something if she was a day. She was beautifully groomed and charming and the waiter hardly said a word to me, and hardly looked at Lou, because he was so charmed by her." So whenever Foxy called, even though she could be demanding and dictatorial, and would want to know what had happened to her pearl ring, "things that long ago were gone," Patricia Sinnott would humor her. "Steve used to come in and hear me on the phone with her and look *annhh,* but be curious enough to want to listen. But he wouldn't want to get involved. And then other times he'd be jealous and complain she was wasting my time." As she aged, Foxy's mind began to wander. Once Ronald and Nancy Reagan, old pals from Hollywood days, were in the White House, she was so sure she was about to be invited that she packed a suitcase. The fact that an invitation to dinner never came did not trouble her in the least, and the nurses left it there because it made her happy.

Then one time, perhaps it was her birthday or a special occasion, Steve went with Lou and Patricia to visit his mother. "And I realized that all her attention was on him. She was being as animated as she could be, and I looked at his face—enraptured—and I felt I did not belong in that room.

"Lou drove us home—normally, Steve would drive—and he had all the barricades up, as I like to call them. He had some music, he had his *New York Times,* and he would look out of the window. He scowled all the way back. And I thought, Um-hmmm! I think he had actually enjoyed being with her and did not want to admit it."

Sondheim was in London when his mother died and did not return for the funeral. Alan Ayckbourn recalled the occasion and remembered Sondheim saying that he did not want the usual expressions of sympathy because he did not need them. His feelings had not changed since the time when, writing to Henry and Mary Guettel, he had said, "Thanks for the plate, but where was my mother's head?" Arthur Laurents said, "Shortly after she died somebody asked him about his mother and he said, 'She's the same.' Then he added, 'Oh, I forgot. She died.' "

Susan Blanchard said, "The awful part is I am sure she was deeply unhappy. She must have been sure Stevie would never love or forgive her, because it was too late for that." And how awful it was for someone with as kind a heart as his to be carrying such a burden of hatred. "One has to forgive for selfish reasons. It is like acid if you can't forgive; it eats away at you." Dominick Dunne thought the time had come to be reconciled. "It's happened a lot of times in my life where I have known friends who despise their mothers. And yet, their friends have a totally different picture of the same person. So, you know, the older I get the more tolerant I get. I know that Steve's hatred of Foxy exists to this very day. I love Steve and he is one of the great friends of my life. And about Foxy, I used to say, 'He's got everything. He's famous, he's acknowledged, he's rich—ease up on the old lady. Ease up!' "

AMONG THE NEW FRIENDS of the 1970s were Mia Farrow and her husband André Previn, who were living in England and had just become the parents of twins. Previn was doing a television series on individual musicians and interviewed Sondheim at length about the methodological fine points of his work. In the interview Previn was quietly appreciative and Sondheim ebullient, smoking occasionally and illustrating a definition with a flick of the wrist. He was wearing a rust-colored jacket, well-tailored pants, and a polo-neck sweater in beige, a coordinated look that doubtless owed something to Lee Wright. His fine brown hair had been neatly trimmed and he sported a beard, an effect he apparently liked, because he continued to wear one ever afterward. The effect was to give a look of definition to features that formerly seemed almost too mobile, plastic, and unformed, and also draw attention to his eyes, with their darting gaze and ability to seem full of delicate intuitions.

Previn asked him whether he had ever written poetry—he replied he had tried it in college, just to see what it was like—and whether he had ever set prose to music. He said, "I'm very bad at prose writing, which I do not say with any false modesty. I tend to be verbose. One of the things I like about writing lyrics is that they restrict me from getting too verbal." As a young composer, had he set out to be self-consciously different? He allowed that he had. "Richard Rodgers once made a remark about me saying that I wrote—" and here he hummed a familiar theme—"tiddly um tum, tum. And indeed, when I first started to write, as in *Forum*, I deliberately would take little unexpected notes." Then, gaining confidence, he realized it was "okay to be what you might consider banal," since what made a song effective was not just a single surprise but the total framework of rhythm, harmony, and mood.

He was asked whether there was anything he would have liked to rewrite and immediately responded with *West Side Story*. "It was very young work and I was persuaded to try to be poetic, because Lenny really wanted the show to have size and substance, and what I learned from Oscar and from that show was, 'I just kissed a girl named Maria' is poetic because of the way it sits on the music. Lyrics don't exist by themselves. It's what happens when there is

Sondheim being interviewed for André Previn's television show, *Previn and the Pittsburgh*, on WNET/13 in 1977

music. 'Oh what a beautiful mornin'' is a line I'd be ashamed to put on paper, but when you hear it—that's known as poetic."

Making the lyrics sound natural rather than contrived became one of his main interests. "Quite often one is acutely aware of the lyric writer, as in the case of people like Ira Gershwin and Lorenz Hart, where the accents and stresses are off almost constantly, and where the effortfulness and the twisting of syntax points up the problem. On the other hand, in those days prior to Rodgers and Hammerstein, conversational lyrics were not at a premium. That is to say, the characters were not characters in the shows; there were block comedy scenes and then songs, and the songs themselves were playful and therefore didn't have to sound natural . . . People like Fred Ebb, Sheldon Harnick, and Jerry Herman make the lyric sound natural: the rise and fall, the stress, the inflection sound much more like speech and much less forced and there's much less inverted grammar and syntax, and that's because our generation was affected by Hammerstein whose primary concern . . . was that lyrics should sound natural and not written."

Getting to that point, as he has said, took agonizing work. His method for achieving the proper state of mind had some similarities with that of Leonard Bernstein, who liked to lie on the floor in a darkened room, clear his mind of extraneous information, and wait for ideas to float to the surface. Sondheim had a slight variation on that, since moments of relaxation, almost of meditation, were accompanied, as he has said, by alcohol or drugs and might be interrupted by a brief nap; but the outlines were the same. He emphasized that when making a start, one had to suspend one's critical faculties. "Whenever I tell students about writing, I always say the real problem comes between the time you pick up the pencil and put it on the paper. Don't censor anything." He repeated that for emphasis. One little phrase might lead to a better one, "little nuggets from which thoughts and lines will grow." One began, thinking one could not face the work, but once one had "a tiny little breakthrough," it started to get interesting. "And unless things go really badly, you have a very good time. Getting absorbed."

As for which came first, sometimes he had a snatch of a musical idea, but for the most part he observed the method followed by Hammerstein and Porter and wrote lyrics with a specific rhythm in mind, but without knowing how the melody would eventually evolve. Putting words to music was almost easy compared with the infinite toil of finding words in the first place. He had evolved a method of writing backwards. "You start at the bottom of the page and preserve your best joke for the last. The ideas should be paced in ascending order of punch. And another thing, the last word ought to be singable. It's best to end with an 'ow' or 'ah'—open sounds that the singer can go with. Two of the most useful words in the language are 'me' and 'be,' but unfortunately they have pinched sounds. I tried desperately to fix the end of 'The Road You Didn't Take' in *Follies*. The line I wanted to use was, 'The Ben I'll never be, who remembers him?' but 'him' is a terrible sound for a singer to hold and expect to get any kind of applause." Rhymes had to be crafted with equal care. "Most people who write lyrics don't understand why rhyme is used. They just rhyme at the ends of lines to neaten it out, like tying up a package, without giving proper thought to the fact that a rhyme gives point to a word. If you don't want that word pointed up, do not rhyme it . . .

"Rhyme will often get in the way of sense. In fact, one of the problems I find in lyric writing is that the thought will give you two words that don't rhyme but are closely allied in terms of vowels, such as 'home' and 'alone,' and you can't use them because it sounds as if you were trying for a rhyme. So you try to find words so distinctively different that the ear knows that this is not what's meant." Inner rhymes had yet another function. "They speed up a line and give what might be an ordinary line brilliance. It's like a high gloss, a polish. I love the lyrics to 'Where Is the Life That Late I Led?' from *Kiss Me, Kate,* because the inner rhymes help the lines speed up, and perfectly okay jokes like 'She gave a new meaning to the leaning tower of Pisa' are suddenly hilarious, because of the rhyme between 'meaning' and 'leaning.' If you take out the rhyme, the joke has lost half of its sheen." Taking an example from his own work, he cited some lyrics from "The Ladies Who Lunch": "Here's to the girls who play wife— / Aren't they too much? / Keeping house but clutching a copy of *Life* / Just to keep in touch." He said, "The 'clutch' is hidden, there's no musical pause there, no way of pointing it up, but it's there to help make the line terse, the way the character is."

Needless to say, "It is always better to be funny rather than clever, and much harder to do. There are very few times when you laugh out loud in the theatre at a lyric joke. One laugh per score is a lot for me, and I think most of my shows have one laugh. In *West Side* there's the section in 'Gee, Officer Krupke' that uses a favorite technique of mine, parallel lines where you just make a list:

> My father is a bastard,
> My ma's an S.O.B.
> My grandpa's always plastered,
> My grandma pushes tea.
> My sister wears a moustache.
> My brother wears a dress.
> Goodness gracious, that's why I'm a mess!

"That's not exceptionally funny on its own, but it brought down the house every night because the form helps make it funny."

One of the easiest lyrics he ever wrote was a song for Countess Charlotte, wife of the philandering Count Carl-Magnus Malcolm in *Night Music,* whose anger, frustration, and desire for revenge needed to be expressed. Sondheim's original solution was to begin with a song called "My Husband the Pig" (which was dropped from the original production). Prince asked to be allowed to move the bridge of the song to a new moment in the plot and divide it between the two wives. Sondheim agreed, and the decision led to a flood of new ideas.

One morning when he was staying with the Princes in Majorca, he got up at dawn and went outside to look at the commanding view and watch the sun rise. He had a pad of paper in hand, "because I was way behind on the score." "Every Day a Little Death" was written in about an hour, "one of the quick lyrics of my life." It was easy, once he had the concept; getting the right approach had been the hard part.

As he had noted, his songs were tailored for a specific situation, which was, according to the opinions of many reviewers, both their greatest strength and their greatest limitation, since many of them could not be isolated from their context without losing some of their effectiveness. The reasons for that had to do with his playwright's sensibility but also, perhaps, with the changed circumstances of the show tune itself. As Jesse Green wrote in an article titled "The Song Is Ended," for forty years, until about 1968, Broadway shows were the principal sources of American popular music. Some of the most enduring and successful songs, the kind now called "standards," songs like "Night and Day," "My Funny Valentine," "Easter Parade," "Ol' Man River," and "Begin the Beguine," and hundreds of others, came from shows (and later, films), to the plots of which they were only dimly connected. Long after the musicals were forgotten the songs they enshrined had endured, and they shared the common traits of high sophistication and superb craftsmanship. John Kander thought the shift away from songs of Broadway origin began after the Beatles "showed people in the music business that they could keep a lot more money for themselves if they didn't depend on professional songwriters." A whole new generation of "garage guitarists" sprang up who not only sang their own music but did not sing the work of other composers. At the same time, many of the forces that had once helped disseminate popular songs by frequent repetition, such as the big bands of the 1940s and '50s, slowly disappeared, along with their audiences. Rock-and-roll changed the whole tone and mood away from elegance and restraint, and the making of the Broadway show brought about the further disappearance of the intimate song. Bad popular art had driven out good, and the result was not so much that Broadway songs were no longer "hummable," but that the public was not listening. Kander said, "What was the point of trying to lay in a bunch of hit songs if there was no one willing to record them? When popular music seemed to stop caring about theatre music, people who wrote for the theatre stopped trying to write for that market. The musical naturally became a lot more experimental."

Since he recognized the particular problems the Broadway composer now faced, Andrew Lloyd Webber took the precaution of releasing his music on records months before his shows were due to open, yet even despite this attempt to familiarize his music with the buying public, his only real hit has been "Memory" from *Cats*. Describing Lloyd Webber's "through-composed" scores, Jesse Green wrote, "At best, one discrete musical noodle will rise up from the soup and announce itself as the show's big number." Sondheim's songs did not invite popular acceptance for a different reason, the same writer thought: "The songs are so customized to the action and tone of the narrative that their structure defies reinterpretation." Of the more than eight hundred songs he had written during a long career, only one, "Send In the Clowns," had been an unvarnished hit, after it was recorded by Frank Sinatra in his album *Ol' Blue Eyes Is Back* in 1973. Judy Collins recorded the same song two years later and made it a best-seller; the record did even better when it was rereleased in 1977 and won a Grammy for song of the year. Collins went on to record a version of "Green Finch and Linnet Bird" from *Sweeney Todd* in 1980; Sinatra recorded another Sondheim song, "Good Thing Going," a year later, and Carly Simon sang "Not a Day Goes By" on her album *Torch*. But when, in 1985, Barbra Streisand recorded *The Broadway Album*, which included six songs with music and lyrics by Sondheim, along with two more from *West Side Story*, Sondheim had a huge success. *The Broadway Album* reached first place on the Billboard chart and sold over three million copies. Many of Sondheim's cast albums have also made large sales, including that for *Company*, which has sold over one and a half million copies. *West Side Story*'s original acclaim as a cast album and soundtrack has already been noted; *Follies, Into the Woods, Sweeney Todd,* and many others have been similarly successful. Many well-known singers, including Mandy Patinkin, Julie Wilson, Cleo Laine, Julia McKenzie, Sarah Brightman, Geraldine Turner, and Dawn Upshaw, have recorded Sondheim songs. Modern jazz and even symphonic ensembles have made arrangements of his work, and the list is expanding. Every cast album ever issued is still in print on CD.

As performances of his work multiplied, Sondheim became known for the meticulousness with which he oversaw recordings and edited the accompanying texts of his lyrics. Words had to be reprinted exactly as they had been written, and a comma out of place would lead to an instant request for a correction. The idea that a singer might rewrite one of the songs to please herself ("I'm Still Here" being a particular favorite for female singers of a certain age group) would cause the kind of response to be expected of any creator whose canvas has been touched up by alien hands. If permission were asked in advance, however, Sondheim could be generous, as in the case of Streisand. She seemed to think that a certain passage in "Send In the Clowns" did not express the singer's dilemma clearly enough for the average listener. So in addition to the poetically allusive line "Just when I'd stopped opening doors," Sondheim added a verse which, while making the singer's dilemma crystal clear ("Why only now when I see that you've drifted away"), did so at the expense of the delicate understatement that is the song's great strength. And, surprisingly, he did not object to the use of his songs for commercial purposes. "Comedy Tonight" from *Forum* went on to have a lucrative afterlife in a number of commercials, and "Putting It Together," which he would write for *Sunday in the Park with George,* was used in a Xerox commercial.

Despite his lack of a string of hit songs, Sondheim has probably done better financially than many songwriters on Broadway, because of a fortunate business decision which was made early in his career. Acting on advice from Hammerstein and Rodgers, who were astute businessmen with their own production company as well as Williamson, their own publishing company, Sondheim was encouraged to form a publishing company of his own when he was just twenty-nine. Most successful songwriters of the day would sign contracts with a big publishing house, such as Chappell, to split the proceeds from sheet music and recording sales on an even basis. For every dollar that accrued, the publisher received fifty cents and the author fifty. It was a traditional division of the spoils that still pertains. However, a songwriter might often have to give up ownership of his copyright and would have no control over how his work was used and to whom it was sold. Rodgers and Hammerstein had formed their company precisely for this reason, and convinced Sondheim that he should establish a holding company to protect his copyright. The move would also mean that the publisher's share would be further divided to include his company, resulting in a higher percentage of profits for him. The original arrangement included Williamson as administrator, and the company he had founded in 1959 continued to protect the rights to his work for the next decade. (His *West Side Story* rights fell into another category, being administered under the terms of an earlier contract with Chappell.)

Publishers typically do far more than issue sheet music, being, if they are successful, promoters and impresarios. In the late 1960s, following the death of Hammerstein and his own unsuccessful collaboration with Rodgers on *Do I Hear a Waltz?*, Sondheim decided to go into partnership with the late Tommy Valando, who was representing all the important musical songwriting teams on Broadway at the time. Burthen remained in existence, and Sondheim established a new company, Beautiful Music Inc., to protect his copyright for *Company* and *Follies,* as well as *A Little Night Music,* in partnership with Valando. Finally, he established a third company, and since he was writing *Pacific Overtures* at the time, and the way the Japanese pronounce their "l"s was on his mind, named it Rilting as a private joke about American racism. The company now has its own office within Warner-Chappell, and its chief executive officer, Paul McKibbins, is responsible for promoting Sondheim's work and furthering his musical cause. There are Sondheim mugs, T-shirts, and other miscellany, and the Sondheim page on the Internet, McKibbins said, is visited so often that he had to remove his address. A few years ago Sondheim said, "I've always wanted to have a smash, but I rather doubt that I ever will. My kind of work is caviar to the general. It's not that it's too good for people; it's just that it's too unexpected to sustain itself very firmly in the commercial theatre."

OF ALL SONDHEIM'S unlikely investigations of the form, *Pacific Overtures,* his next musical, has to be considered "the most bizarre and unusual musical ever to be seen in a commercial setting," as he described it just before the show opened in 1976. The idea came from a play written by John Weidman, son of the novelist and playwright Jerome Weidman, who was studying law but found himself irresistibly drawn to the theatre. He had written a play about Commodore Perry's visit to Japan in 1853, ostensibly to deliver a letter to the Emperor but actually to force Japan to open trade negotiations. Up to that point Japan, a feudal society, had been completely closed to the outside world, but Perry's gunboat diplomacy would be followed in short order by similar visits from the British, the French, the Dutch, and the Russians, and within a few decades the old order would be crumbling, for better or worse.

Prince tried for two years to mount the play but decided it was not theatrical enough. It was, as has been pointed out, essentially a Brechtian polemic about what happens when capitalism and industrialism invade an ancient and poetic culture. But after looking at graphic art by Japanese artists describing Perry's historic appearance, showing the Commodore with Oriental eyes and in Japanese costume, Prince began to wonder what it would be like to change the viewpoint. Instead of the Rodgers and Hammerstein approach to *The King and I,* written from the perspective of an Englishwoman who enters a Siamese culture, what if *Pacific Overtures* were to show Perry's arrival from the perspective of the Japanese?

Jonathan Tunick said, "We were all dragged into it kicking and screaming by Hal, including Steve. Because it's such an outlandish idea. And the excitement, the charm, and the delight you take in the show is the challenge it presents: what are they going to do with this?" As in other musicals with Prince, much depended on the work of Boris Aronson—it would be their final collaboration with him—and once more, he did not disappoint them. "In Japan, the West of today combines with the ancient traditions. How do you have such a synthesis of cultures?" he said. "I say they are not combinable. That was the problem in the play. How do you present the conflict between an ancient, traditional society and a foreign, mechanized, modern approach to life?" Aronson decided that the set had to look pleasing, a Japanese garden as imagined through Western eyes. It would recreate a light, ephemeral world, and against a white surround and bleached hardwood floor the actors' outlines would stand out in sharp relief. As in a Japanese print, everything would be controlled, exquisitely elegant and fragile, but there would also be a collage quality to the sets, a visual indication that a world made of "rice paper, origami, kites, bamboo" was being shattered by the invasion. There would be no heavy scenery. Individual scenes would either float onto the set from above or be assembled by stagehands and actors. One of the most successful of Aronson's creations was Perry's ship, which moved with "the fragility and delicacy of a paper dragon," Howard Kissel wrote. The ship came to symbolize what was meant by the ironic title as the vessel, gliding toward the audience, towered over the scene, with its fire-eating eyes and menacing, masklike prow. Whatever could be done in visual terms to imply fracturing and disintegration would be done. Many of Aronson's most ingenious ideas, which took their cues from origami and children's toys (in which paper flowers bloom magically in water), had to be reluctantly abandoned because of their complexity and cost. Nevertheless, his set designs gave Weidman, Sondheim, and Prince the spatial reality they needed, into an alien world.

Sondheim said, "Hal had . . . decided that John's play needed a kind of epic theatre expansion, which meant music. And so he asked me. I couldn't have been less interested in politics or in this particular kind of theatre, Japanese theatre, which I'd always found just silly and screaming and slow and boring." However, he made a start, and at the end of three months he was completely fascinated. "I decided I would attack the musical aspect of it first, and I thought, Now what kind of sound is going to work here? For a month I just kind of fiddled and did some research into Japanese music. And I made the, for me, remarkable discovery that the Japanese pentatonic scale (which is unlike the Chinese pentatonic scale) has a minor modal feeling and kept reminding me of the composer de Falla, whose work I admire a lot. A Spanish guitar principle or modality that underlies his music was precisely the Japanese modality. I know de Falla's music, so I just started to imitate him. I took the pentatonic scale and bunched the chords together until they resembled that terrific Spanish guitar sound. And then I was able to relate to it, because suddenly it had a Western feeling and at the same time an Eastern feeling. I became excited. I had seldom written in minor keys . . . but because I had to have the feeling of Japanese tonality, this afforded me the opportunity to do it."

Working with an extended theme would result in "Someone in a Tree," which he was proud of for its success as a "developed" composition. So much was happening musically and verbally, and yet it held together as an idea. That would be the song to which he always pointed with the most pride. Finding the right lyric style was also more successful than he had imagined. He used "a kind of translator-ese, parable sentences, very simple language with . . . simple subject-predicate structures and very little in the way of rhyme." One of the most delightful numbers, "Please Hello," in which the British, the French, the Dutch, and the Russians make their obsequious entry, is set in rhyme and is a hilarious imitation of the kind of patter song that Gilbert and Sullivan made famous:

> Please
> Hello, I come with letters from her Majesty Victoria
> Who, learning how you're trading now, sang 'Hallelujah, Gloria!'
> And sent me to convey to you her positive euphoria
> As well as little gifts from Britain's various emporia.

The remarkable quality of the work, Tom Sutcliffe, music critic of the *Guardian*, wrote, was its certainty of tone and the confident way in which both Japanese and American elements had been fashioned to illustrate the dramatic points being made. The opening song itself conjured up a timeless world in which, serenely buttressed against all that was happening outside, the inhabitants planted rice, or traded bows, or painted screens; it set exactly the right mood. Just as the music would, by imperceptible degrees, become increasingly Westernized, until the final number, "Next," which would sound like the promotional song for a commercial show about this year's automobile, Prince decided to work within the framework of kabuki and bunraku staging techniques. These would act as metaphors not just for the fine aesthetic sensibility of the old order, but also its insularity and rigidity. He gave pride of place to the "reciter," who acted as a one-man chorus on the course of events. Masks, face paint, fans to represent various objects or actions, even a runway through the audience, which the actors would use to make their entrances: all were calculated for their contribution to the final vision, of an American invasion as described by a Japanese playwright. That caused the critic Edwin Wilson to wonder whether it were possible for a Westerner ever to see his own culture through a foreign sensibility. Wilson wrote, "Are we seeing a Japanese work through Mr. Prince's eyes, or are we seeing an American musical through the eyes of his imaginary Japanese counterpart? It cannot be both, though Mr. Prince seems to want it that way. Brecht understood this. When he incorporated oriental settings and techniques in his work, he still wrote from his own perspective."

There were other reservations, having to do with the way the two main characters, a shipwrecked fisherman and a samurai, end up at odds over the desirability of accepting Western ideas. The creators agreed that the first act was a success but that the second petered out in a series of scenes that repeated, but did not advance, the thesis. Finding himself at a loss, Weidman agreed that Hugh Wheeler, the playwright with whom Prince and Sondheim had already worked, should be consulted. Wheeler thought the play was too obviously a political tract and tried to interject "more humanity" into the characters, he said. Neither Prince nor Sondheim liked his major reworking of the plot. Sondheim said the musical was an attempt "to tell a story that has no characters in it at all, that is entirely about ideas." Weidman's concept carried the day (some of Wheeler's additions were retained), but the lack of characters one cared about would be another reason for critical disapproval. Once *Pacific Overtures* was revived by the York Theatre Company in 1984 on a smaller stage, the new production was praised for correcting what had been seen as another flaw: Stephen Holden wrote that the original production had smothered the show's "reflective delicacy" under "spectacle and bombast." And *Pacific Overtures* had originally been mounted on a large stage, that of the Winter Garden. Prince said that after it opened early in 1976, he and Howard Haines, the general manager, stood on the street in front of the theatre looking at the huge billboards and realized that the show looked like "a limited engagement of a Japanese show" rather than an American musical. He turned to Haines and said, "What do we do?" and the latter replied, "I don't know." Audiences were less than enthusiastic, and the show closed after 193 performances, having lost its entire investment of $650,000.

It would take time for reviewers to see that the traditional musical had been replaced under the more comprehensive heading of "music theatre." Mark Czarnecki wrote, "In the experiments of such composers and lyricists as

A scene from *Pacific Overtures,* 1976. Below, a recording session for *Pacific Overtures,* 1976: from left, music director Paul Gemignani, producer Thomas Z. Shepard, Sondheim, orchestrator Jonathan Tunick, and Jay David Saks, associate producer for the RCA album

Stephen Sondheim and Philip Glass, the new ways of uniting music and theatre—whether in drama, musicals or opera—are yielding kaleidoscopic patterns which may serve as blueprints for [the] future . . ." That was in 1985, when reviewers and audiences were beginning to appreciate the merits of such an approach, which would have been cold comfort to the composer at the time. Then there was the interview he had given Clive Hirschhorn, theatre critic of the London *Sunday Express* years before, in 1976. Hirschhorn had made him seem condescending towards Orientals while (the critic wrongly asserted) employing an Oriental servant, defensive about criticisms of his work, and unenthusiastic about Michael Bennett's *A Chorus Line,* which the critic appeared to admire extravagantly. Since Bennett's musical was then in direct competition with *Pacific Overtures* for the Tony Awards, and subsequently won most of them, Sondheim's comments seemed graceless. Sondheim said he had been badly misquoted. "It seemed that the article was meant to damage, and meant to wound, and that's what it did." As a result, he decided to give no more interviews, and perhaps after that, the impression began to form that he was eccentric and reclusive, "a taciturn, withdrawn man." As Kenneth Clark also discovered when he was virulently attacked for having made a questionable attribution in his role as director of London's National Gallery, a "swimgloat" can be a mixed blessing.

CHAPTER 15

Dies Irae

Ingemisco tamquam reus;
culpa rubet vultus meus;
supplicanti parce, deus.

THE FREQUENTLY HEARD complaint that Sondheim's tunes
were not tuneful was one that would have been familiar to Leonard
Bernstein, since his work was criticized for the same reason. *Wonderful Town*
played to packed houses in 1953, but his agreeable songs, which included
"Ohio," "A Little Bit in Love," "A Quiet Girl," "My Darlin' Eileen," and "It's
Love," were not being heard on radio, television, or even Muzak. That
inspired Bernstein to write a mock dialogue in which a composer's manager
was complaining that his client's musical had been running for five months
and lacked a single hit. Bernstein, like Sondheim, had set himself the task of
creating a complex intermeshing of mood, theme, and dialogue and then felt
let down because none of his songs were hits in Tin Pan Alley. As Bernstein
found out, once the film of *West Side Story* made his tunes familiar, they were
suddenly tuneful, after all. Sondheim liked to point out that audiences at *A
Little Night Music* would invariably come out at the end of the first act humming the melody to "A Weekend in the Country," which proved his point,
because "they had just heard the same refrain repeated sixteen times."

He was not likely to hear that criticism in London, where the qualities of his work that were cause for reproach on Broadway (his shows were too experimental, too intellectual, too bracing for popular consumption) were the very attributes that tended to be admired. Here was an artist who had sustained his uncompromising vision despite all the pressures to squeeze his ideas into well-worn commercial formulae. If his musicals were sophisticated, demanding, and lacking in pat endings, British playgoers were likely to listen with greater concentration and attentiveness. His delight in sentences full of wit and verve seemed tailor-made for audiences trained in the language of Shakespeare and Sheridan, Shaw and Wilde. Since the British have always enjoyed musical anthologies, like *Cowardy Custard* and *Cole,* perhaps it was just a matter of time before someone thought of doing an evening of Sondheim songs.

Ned Sherrin said that he became involved when David Kernan, then performing as Count Carl-Magnus in a London run of *A Little Night Music,* and Millicent Martin, then in a long-running play by Alan Ayckbourn, contacted him with the idea of doing a Sunday-night concert. Sherrin had already staged some charity shows for a small country theatre in Wavendon, near Milton Keynes, run by Cleo Laine and her husband, John Dankworth, and since he had met Sondheim through Burt Shevelove and admitted to a "nodding acquaintance," received his limited permission. Sherrin arranged the "rolling order" because Millicent Martin had no idea what Sondheim had written and did not even know that the song by Mary Rodgers that was in her cabaret repertoire, "The Boy From" (from *The Mad Show*), had lyrics by Sondheim. "Nor did she know he'd written 'Everything's Coming Up Roses,' which she would have wanted to sing (over Stephen's dead body)," he said. "And she had terrible trouble seeing 'I'm Still Here' as the final number because she had only heard Yvonne De Carlo's recording and did not see its possibilities until she heard Nancy Walker's recording." The actress and singer Julia McKenzie, then appearing in another long-running Ayckbourn play, knew exactly who Sondheim was and "said she would commit suicide if she couldn't sing 'Broadway Baby' and 'Losing My Mind.' David's original idea was that the three of them should come on wearing red noses and singing 'Send In the Clowns,' " Sherrin added. "So we had to get rid of that."

Dankworth and Laine had converted the stables behind their home into a charming little theatre that held about two hundred, and there Sherrin and his three singers tried out their revue, originally called *A Sondheim Songbook,* one Sunday night, with Sherrin, providing spoken commentary. "It was rather disconcerting the first night," he said, "as half the audience left at intermission. It turned out they were all old-age pensioners, and their bus had arrived." Then he and the singers "sort of got a taste for the idea" and took the show to Brighton. One producer rang him up and said he wanted to take it to London, but could he replace the three singers with young talent, as London critics loved that? Sherrin replied with some asperity that the idea of having eighteen-year-olds singing Sondheim was too ridiculous to consider. They went back to Wavendon, then on to Bury St. Edmunds. Burt Shevelove came to that engagement and suggested the title *Side by Side by Sondheim*, which took hold. Bury St. Edmunds is just off the fens in Suffolk, so one very cold night when "fog was practically coming up in the theatre," Sherrin said, when they got to the song "Side by Side" from *Company* and the lines "Isn't it warm, isn't it rosy, / Side by side?" everyone was "shivering away." That night the prominent British theatrical producer Michael Codron was in the audience. He said, "I've never seen three more wonderful musical comedy performers on the stage," and the actors thought that meant he was going to "bring it in." But Sherrin knew it was his diplomatic way of saying "he wasn't going to do it."

Finally, in desperation, Sherrin seized the chance of having the show be seen somewhere in London by taking it to the famous old London hospital, Guy's. He said, "The legend has it that somebody at Guy's had a lot of money and kept saying they must build a theatre there, which was interpreted as a performance theatre, whereas he probably meant an operating theatre." Their performance in the hospital's small theatre was seen by the Honorable George Borwick, heir to a baking-powder fortune, who used to invest small amounts in plays. "He got very excited and grandly said he would 'back it,' which I knew meant a few hundred pounds at most."

Meanwhile, Cameron Mackintosh, then a young producer who had yet to make his mark on the international stage, had been contacted. Mackintosh said, "I had done *Trelawny,* which had had very good reviews, which was a big musical in London, and I'd done *The Card,* which had medium reviews but didn't quite make it." When he was contacted by Sherrin, "I thought, Well, if he wants *me* to come and see it, it must mean that no one else is buying. So I decided to go to a performance in Wavendon. For some reason I got it into my head that Wavendon was on junction 12 or 13 off the M1 motorway. And I was told it was *just* off the motorway. So at twenty past seven I turn off the motorway, can't see any signs for Wavendon, and pull up by a police station. 'Where is Wavendon?' 'Oh, no Wavendon, zur,' " he said, imitating a West Country accent. " 'Don't know Wavendon! I'll ring through.' So he rang through and they said, 'Well, zur, don't know how to tell you this, Wavendon's just off the M1. You're on the M4!' I'd gone down the wrong motorway! And I was two hours away. I couldn't have got there in time.

"As it happens, at that point I was booked on the very first trip I could ever afford to America, you know, my triple Apex fare, lashed to the back of the plane. I was to stay with an American producer named Arthur Cantor, who had become managing director of H. M. Tennent after Binkie Beaumont." They met when Mackintosh, who had seen his picture in the evening papers, chased him down the corridors of a hotel until Cantor had agreed to hear a song from *The Card*; he subsequently co-produced the show. Then Cantor invited Mackintosh to manage the touring company for *Godspell*, which he did for the next five or six years. "So I was in the middle of doing this at the time," and went to the United States without having seen *Side by Side*. "I sent an actor to see it named Christopher Biggins, who is quite a well-known personality in England and a very good friend of mine, and George Borwick.

"So I'm in New York, I've been to see my first show on Broadway. I'm deliriously happy, I go to sleep and at seven in the morning I'm woken from my stupor by Arthur in his underpants to tell me I have a phone call, rather crossly. 'It's some drunken friends in London.' So Christopher Biggins, who's very larger than life, is going 'Darling!' on the phone, and 'George here!' and I could hear this bedlam in the background, and it's a postperformance lunch party. They're having a whale of a time. And George is saying"—he imitates the voice—" 'Cameron, it's absolutely marvelous! Marvelous! You must do it. Tell them you'll do it!' And I'm saying, 'What's it like?' And he said, 'Well, it's the four of them on stools with two grand pianos.' And I said, 'Is that all?' 'And some slides,' he said." Mackintosh laughed. " 'Tell them I'll do it.' And George said, 'And I'll put up *all* the money. Well, half the money.' " Somewhat to his surprise, Borwick did eventually invest a thousand pounds. The rest came from H. M. Tennent, for a modest total of six thousand pounds sterling. "I thought, the worst that can happen is that it will get very good reviews and not make any money. So I won't be any worse off. And I'm going to be doing something of quality." The show opened at the Mermaid Theatre for a limited run on May 4, 1976. It subsequently transferred to the larger Wyndham Theatre, ran in London for three years, and made a huge profit, as did the cast recording. Harold Prince took it to Broadway, where it opened on April 18, 1977, and ran for 384 performances.

Every review on both sides of the Atlantic was extravagantly complimentary. The revue demonstrated, Mel Gussow wrote in the *New York Times,* that despite the conventional wisdom, Sondheim's songs could be extracted from their settings very satisfactorily and that, while no sentimentalist, Sondheim had written lyrics full of delicate feeling and nuance. Even the redoutable Clive Barnes called it "a dream of a show." The verdict in London was that

Sondheim was the best lyricist, the most adventurous composer, and the most accomplished of musical dramatists, even "the greatest lyric poet of contemporary world theatre," as Sheridan Morley wrote. Some twenty years later, Patrick O'Connor of the *Daily Telegraph* thought it was this revue that established Sondheim's preeminence in Britain. Sherrin said, "What people began to realize was that here was a unique voice."

THE ENGLISH PLAYWRIGHT Christopher Bond, who would write a play about the Demon Barber of Fleet Street, believed that nobody was able to establish that Sweeney Todd ever existed. True, there was a Jacobin barber in revolutionary Paris who cut his customers' throats, "though whether for profit or because of political differences is unclear," he wrote. There are accounts of someone named Sawney Bean, head of a family of robbers in seventeenth-century Scotland who ate their adversaries. As a theme, cannibalism has a long and respectable history, e.g., Shakespeare's *Titus Andronicus*, who tricks a mother into eating her sons, served up in meat pies. But of Sweeney Todd, the Victorian mass murderer who was unjustly imprisoned and returns to wreak vengeance on his enemies, there was no trace in real life. He appeared on the London scene in the 1830s as the invention of George Dibdin-Pitt, a writer for penny dreadfuls, who described his deeds in blood-curdling detail. The novel was an instant success and attained a kind of horrible plausibility in its readers' minds. It sounded so true that it must be true, bringing about a suspicion that Sweeney Todd is an historical personage that continues to this day. Meantime, Dibdin-Pitt had adapted his novel for the kind of theatres known as "blood tubs," and it played all over England. Then Christopher Bond decided to try his hand at rewriting it.

He thought the play needed to retain "the title, the razors, the pies and the trick chair . . . Fortunately it wrote itself. I crossed Dumas's *The Count of Monte Cristo* with Tourneur's *The Revenger's Tragedy* for a plot; added elements of pastiche Shakespeare in sort of blankish verse for Sweeney, the Judge, and the lovers to talk . . . remembered some market patter I'd learnt as a child; and adapted the wit and wisdom of Brenda, who ran the greengrocer's shop opposite my house, for Mrs. Lovett's ruminations on life, death and the state of her sex life."

In 1973 Sondheim was in London while the new production of *Gypsy* starring Angela Lansbury was in rehearsal; by coincidence, Bond's play, *Sweeney Todd, the Demon Barber of Fleet Street,* was being performed at Joan Littlewood's Stratford East Theatre. It was creating a stir, and Sondheim, who had always wanted to see Grand Guignol, went with the actress Sheila Reid. (She would end up playing the part of the Beggar Woman in the London musical production.)

Sondheim said, "It turned out to be not Grand Guignol but this charming melodrama, and melodrama and farce are my two favorite forms of theatre because . . . they are obverse sides of the same coin. Next day I had lunch with John Dexter and asked him whether *Sweeney Todd* would be the basis of a good operatic piece. He had always been pushing me to write a through-composed piece. He said it would be perfect." Sondheim was enchanted by the transformation Bond had made of what was, basically, a dreadful Victorian relic. "This new version is . . . still a melodrama, but also a legend, elegantly written, part in blank verse which I didn't even recognize till I read the script," he said in 1978, once he was working on the musical. "It had a weight to it and I couldn't figure out how the language was so rich and thick without being fruity; it was because he wrote certain characters in blank verse . . . He was able to take all these disparate elements that had been in existence rather dully for a hundred and some-odd years and make them into a first-rate play."

The Stratford East production had interspersed scenes with street songs of the period. When Sondheim expressed his interest, he discovered that the producers Richard Barr and Charles Woodward had already optioned Bond's play for Broadway, using barroom songs. But when they were approached by Sondheim, the producers asked the playwright if he would allow Sondheim to do a musical version once work was finished on *A Little Night Music.* (As it transpired, it took four years for *Sweeney Todd* to open, and the two producers would be joined by Robert Fryer, Mary Lea Johnson, and Martin Richards, in association with Dean and Judy Manos.) After meeting with Sondheim's agent, Flora Roberts, Bond agreed, partly on the basis of the composer's reputation and also because he had met him and liked him. He remembered a meeting at Granada studios in Manchester, where *Side by Side* was being filmed for television in about 1976. "I was moving house at the time, and, since I was driving a large lorry full of furniture, was sober for once. We talked about the play in some detail and what struck me most forcibly was his complete lack of bullshit. 'What a lovely bloke,' I remember thinking. 'What's he doing working in the theatre?' "

Sondheim's first impression of Bond was less sanguine. At their first meeting, he said, "He came in wearing work boots and a kind of lumber jacket and I thought, Gee, he must be lower-middle-class. He put his feet up on the table and treated me with real condescension. He clearly thought I was Mr. Broadway, come to tread on art. Then he thought, Oh, what the fuck, and said all right, and so I was insulted but not deterred." When the time came for the musical to open, on March 1, 1979, Sondheim, not knowing the Bonds were wealthy, paid for their air fare. Bond and his wife appeared at the opening-night party forty-five minutes late. They were "dead drunk, and insulted Hal, and were just dreadful. I called the next day and absolutely bawled them out. Bond said, 'Well, we were nervous.' " What Sondheim did not realize at the time was that Bond was an alcoholic and remained, as he himself wrote, in that "semi-permanent state until 1984 when I knocked it on the head and joined A.A."

Sondheim's first thought was that he would not need a collaborator and would be able to do his own "snipping and trimming." But he soon realized that the work was so intricately constructed that he was afraid of damaging it. And even though it seemed short, if he intended to set every word of Bond's play the musical would run for hours. The impeccable Hugh Wheeler was engaged to cut the play to a manageable length. It tells the story of Benjamin Barker, a barber who is unjustly imprisoned by a judge who has lecherous designs on his wife. Fifteen years later Barker escapes and returns to London with a new identity, that of Sweeney Todd, his one thought that of revenge. After meeting Nellie Lovett, a most unsuccessful pastry cook, he learns that the judge raped his wife, that she subsequently took poison and died. The judge has brought up Todd's daughter, Johanna, as his own child and now has designs on her as well. But when, at the crucial moment, Todd has his persecutor in his chair and loses his chance to slit his throat, he turns in vindictive frustration on the world at large and proceeds to carve up customers, one after the other. Meantime, Mrs. Lovett's business is flourishing.

Sondheim said, "I was only worried about how the audience would take the murders, whether they'd think them silly or not. And then, when Mrs. Lovett gets the idea for making the meat pies, what would the audience's reaction be? In America nobody's ever heard of Sweeney Todd . . . So they were seeing this wild plot for the first time, and there was a loud gasp at the first murder, which was staged very violently with a great swash of blood. Then when Mrs. Lovett got the idea for the pies and the audience realized what was up, there was a satisfying laugh, the like of which I've rarely heard."

The only moment that presented real difficulties was the moment when Todd turned from being "a private murderer into a serial or public murderer. In Bond's version the idea is 'I have tasted blood and now I shall go on.' I thought that wasn't strong enough. Hugh wanted to have a religious reason, which I thought was not right, so I made up the whole thing and that took me about a month. After that it was easy." Wheeler contributed some valuable ideas, and the only thing about the collaboration that irritated Sondheim was that "Hugh, being Hugh," as he said, removed Bond's fine dialogue in favor of his own; Sondheim made sure to go back to the original play when he wrote his songs. Wheeler put the matter slightly differently in an interview with Craig Zadan before he died. He said he had encouraged Sondheim to "cannibalize" his script and tell the story almost completely in terms of music. From his point of view, even Bond's adaptation was too melodramatic. The challenge had been to turn an old potboiler into something approaching tragedy. "The hardest thing of all was how to take these two really disgusting people and write them in such a way that the audience can rather love them. And I think people did love Mrs. Lovett—yet she doesn't have a single redeeming feature."

Sondheim said that as a piece of music, *Sweeney Todd* leapt into his mind almost fully formed. "All I wanted to do was sing it." Its content dictated the operatic form, but the style took longer to hammer out. He said, "The end of *Sweeney Todd* is something we argued out for quite a while. It had to do very much with tone. Once that was decided on, there was a whole last-minute rescue, a humorous moment for Anthony and Johanna, that we wrote and . . . actually put on the stage. It didn't quite work." But his idea that all the musical ideas would "collide" at the end was always there. "I determined that it would be fun . . . to start each character with a specific musical theme and develop all that character's music out of that theme, so that each song would depend in the true sense of the word on the previous one." That "handy compositional principle" served him well, so that even though he did not write the last twenty minutes of the musical until they were in rehearsal, for once no one was panicking, because "all . . . the groundwork had been done."

He wanted the music to set the mood of foreboding immediately, "because in most horror films what really scares you, apart from the lighting and makeup, is the music." He told Tunick that he wanted him to use electronic sounds and a loud crashing organ because that was "as scary as anything and also has a wonderful Gothic feeling." He was writing in the hope that Angela Lansbury would play the part of Mrs. Lovett, cheerful, chatty, cozy, and without a single scruple. This she eventually would do, her Cockney eyes as large as saucers, her topknots dancing on her head, wiping her greasy fingers and slapping roaches off the table with inimitable flair and panache. Almost as soon as Wheeler and Sondheim have introduced Todd, and the audience has learned his bleak history, Mrs. Lovett is wheeled in to provide comic relief with the song "The Worst Pies in London," a masterpiece of sardonic humor. She sings,

I know why nobody cares to take them—
I should know,
I make them.
But good? No,
The worst pies in London—
Even that's polite . . .
If you doubt it, take a bite.

Angela Lansbury said, "I'll never forget the first time he sang it and made all the noises and banged the dough and exhaled his breath and did all those things . . . I mean, we were really screaming hysterically on the floor."

At the end of Act One, Mrs. Lovett has just had a sensible idea. The price of meat being what it is, why waste the corpses Mr. Todd's razor is about to provide? In a song without peer for its black humor, they debate the gustatory merits of the various victims-to-be. "What is that?" Todd sings. Mrs. Lovett replies, "It's priest. / Have a little priest." "Is it really good?" he asks. She says, "Sir, it's too good, / At least. / Then again, they don't commit sins of the flesh, / So it's pretty fresh." He is doubtful. "Awful lot of fat," he remarks. "Only where it sat," she says briskly.

If *Sweeney Todd* is dominated by the tragedy of its main character, it is full of gentler moments. There is the moment when Anthony, who (in the best tradition of musical comedy) has only to look at Johanna to fall in love, sings,

I feel you,
Johanna,
I feel you.
I was half convinced I'd waken,
Satisfied enough to dream you.
Happily I was mistaken,
Johanna!
I'll steal you,
Johanna . . .

The love song has a quality of aching tenderness, one that is matched by "Not While I'm Around," the song the orphan Tobias, whom Mrs. Lovett has befriended, sings to her when he suspects Todd of foul deeds, assuring her that he will protect her. The fact that he is ignorant of the true state of affairs gives the song genuine pathos. However, there is no doubt that the towering moment in the plot comes when Todd, thwarted in his attempt to slit the Judge's throat, goes on a murderous rampage ("Epiphany"). By turns fren-

Angela Lansbury in her award-winning role as Mrs. Lovett in *Sweeney Todd, the Demon Barber of Fleet Street*

zied, piteously despairing, bitter, frantic and demonic, Todd's final declaration that "the work waits, / I'm alive at last / And I'm full of joy!" has to be one of the most chilling moments in modern theatre.

SONDHEIM SUBTITLED his score "A Musical Thriller" and made use of the traditional setting of the Dies Irae, the sequence of the Catholic mass for the dead. The text for "Day of Wrath" is thought to have been written by the Franciscan monk Thomas de Celano, but the Gregorian chant itself is of unknown origin. Sondheim said, "I always found the Dies Irae moving and scary at the same time. One song, 'My Friends,' was influenced by it . . . It was the inversion of the opening of the Dies Irae. And although it was never actually quoted in the show, the first release of 'The Ballad of Sweeney Todd' was a sequence of the Dies Irae—up a third, which changed the harmonic relationship of the melodic notes to each other." He was proud of the fact that this was the first musical he had worked on, perhaps "the first musical ever," not to need an orchestra call between the first preview and opening night, "because we never had enough new material going into the piece to warrant any changes that we weren't able to dictate . . . What that means is that the show—in spite of its being overlong and in spite of some clumsinesses that we wanted to fix up—was the show that we were going to open with . . ."

Besides the Dies Irae, his music was also influenced by Bernard Herrmann. He said, "It's an open secret that the music for *Sweeney* is in homage to Herrmann's language," which he thought had a way of making a mood of suspense "lushly musical." His harmonic style, Sondheim decided, "was just right for *Sweeney*. I didn't consciously copy him but it was *Hangover Square* that started that kind of thought process in my head." That snatch of score which he had memorized in 1945 had surfaced more than thirty years later as a musical idea of such importance that it influenced Sondheim's most brilliant work. But George Harvey Bone, the gentle, kindly, socially correct composer with the guilty secret who feels compelled to kill without knowing why, has been replaced by the desperate, vengeful Todd, who is past all hope of redemption; his life has become a kind of witness to the annihilating power of vindictive revenge.

That this was the musical's major theme appears to have come slowly to Sondheim. He also said, "I never start with subject matter . . . I always discover the subject I'm writing about as I write." After he had written the first seven songs, which were easier to write than anything he had ever done, he rang Judy Prince. She usually wanted to hear everything he wrote, but he had not heard from her and wondered why. "Finally I said to her one night over the phone, 'You know this is the first show . . . I've been working on it for over a month now and you didn't even ask . . .' She said, 'You know me and murder mysteries.' I said, 'It's not a murder mystery . . . I've misled you, it's not that.' Well, she came down and I played two bars and she fell off the chair and she said, 'Oh God, I didn't know this was what it was about.' I said, 'Yeah, it's Grand Guignol.' She said, 'It's nothing to do with Grand Guignol. It's the story of your life.' " Sondheim continued, "It never occurred to me! It's never been brought up in any article. Everybody always says, 'Oh, he's interested in murder.' They're missing the point entirely."

SONDHEIM NATURALLY WANTED Hal Prince, who had gone from producing to directing full-time, to direct *Sweeney Todd*, but the man who had played such a major role in shaping the concepts of *Company, Follies, A Little Night Music,* and *Pacific Overtures* was reluctant. The role of hesitant one had most often been played by Sondheim. Here was the composer brimming with ideas and enthusiasm and now Prince was full of doubts. He said,

"I found the nature of the material so hard to live with, because I couldn't find it inside myself. The show is, of course, about revenge, and I do not have a vengeful nature. Thank God for that! You know, it eats at you. I don't feel that. I'm much more into denial. So I don't remember bad reviews; I deny them . . . But I had to commit to what *Sweeney Todd* was about," and it became hard to face. He would wake up every morning thinking, Why do I have to do this?

What helped was his decision to take his own approach to the subject matter. The main characters in the play were, after all, people who had been driven to acts of extreme desperation at a time when the Industrial Revolution was dehumanizing British society. Since Bond had drawn a distinction between his upper-class characters, who spoke in blank verse, and the proletariat, that led Prince to see the actors as personifying various stages of helplessness and impotence. From there he jumped to the idea of presenting the action, much of which remained on a small, not to say intimate, scale, within a larger social framework. The set would look like a gigantic machine, part prison, part factory, part cathedral; as Jack Kroll would write, it showed the Industrial Revolution as something that had dwarfed and degraded whatever it touched. Eugene Lee's eventual design, which would fill the huge stage of the Uris Theatre, actually used parts of old foundries which the designer found in Rhode Island and had shipped to New York. "There was a peaked roof of grimy glass panes supported on steel trusses and rusted iron beams. Stairways and platforms filled the sides of the stage. The back wall was made of corrugated tin and rose to reveal a painted drop of nineteenth-century London. There was also a catwalk bridge suspended from a traveling girder and there were all sorts of moving parts that did little but create an atmosphere." The decision was subsequently criticized—Arthur Laurents thought the set was about social significance, while the composer's score described a black comedy—but it seemed to free Prince to find the strengths in the work. "I realized what a romantic story it really is. And what we did was swell. I *loved* what happened on that stage."

Sondheim had not agreed with Prince's approach. He said later, "I meant it to be done as a small piece because I wanted to just scare people, but Hal Prince . . . who is very much influenced by Meyerhold and Piscator, said, 'I know what you want, and you'll lose some of the scariness but I'll give it a large, epic feeling. Perhaps that will serve the piece in a different way.' I thought, 'It can always be done small, but things can't always be done big, so let's try it.' " He would decide that he liked it both ways. One of their few disagreements had to do with a controversial song the Judge sings. He is sexually aroused while spying on Johanna, strips to the waist, flagellates himself, and has an orgasm as the song ends. Prince said, "I took it out. We did it at the first preview, and I said, 'It's gone tomorrow.' I don't get it; I don't know how to do it, and every note of music is with the beating of the thing, boom! boom!—and I thought, Oh God, I can't work that way! And furthermore, I don't *like* it, so it wasn't there." Prince did not add that the scene was restored when he directed *Sweeney Todd* for the New York City Opera version in 1984 and is routinely included in productions nowadays. As such scenes went in Sondheim's work (there is one with whores in *Pacific Overtures,* for instance) this was the most graphically sadomasochistic statement, although references to similar themes could be found buried in his work. For instance, in *Company,* the song "The Little Things You Do Together" includes the verse:

> It's sharing little winks together,
> Drinks together,
> Kinks together,
> That make marriage a joy . . .

Three years before *Sweeney Todd,* in 1976, he wrote "The Madam's Song" for the film *The Seven-Per-Cent Solution,* in which Sherlock Holmes and Freud collaborate on a murder case. (The title refers to the solution of cocaine that Holmes is using.) "There's a scene where they visit an elegant brothel," Sondheim said, "and they wanted to cast Régine as the singer-proprietess, and so they asked me would I write a song . . ." In "The Madam's Song" the singer silkily explains why she will never undertake the same experience twice and makes studied references to a baron with a riding crop and chains, an abbot bearing a hammer and nails, and a captain of the guard accompanied by a St. Bernard. Patrick O'Connor observed that, like the lyrics of Cole Porter, Sondheim's were "littered with obscure and sometimes slyly obscene references," which, he thought, added to their charm for the intelligentsia.

The Judge's song, his version of "Johanna," offers an even more explicit set of references (he sings, "Deliver me, Johanna, from this hot red devil") and as a plot device Donal Henahan found the song "repellently cheap." Nevertheless the song stands as the one statement in Sondheim's work of the tormenting mixture of emotions that presumably accompanies incestuous desires, emphasizing as it does the degree of guilt and also some kind of genuine remorse, the only moment in Wheeler's book in which a character demonstrates such feelings.

The play's ending makes the dimensional failure particularly clear. Todd has only just been prevented by circumstance from murdering his own daughter, who is disguised as a sailor, and, as one would kick away a roach, has slit the throat of the beggar woman, only to find that she is his long-lost wife, Lucy. His staggering realization—"What have I done!"—is quickly buried by Mrs. Lovett's patter song of explanation about why she has never managed to tell him what she knew, that his wife is still alive. Barely has he received this news than Todd, in a flash, takes revenge on Mrs. Lovett by hurling her into her own furnace. Even when Todd lies prostrate over his dead wife's body, crooning about how beautiful she used to be, the audience lacks any sense, as in that parallel moment in Verdi's *Rigoletto,* for instance, when Rigoletto is cradling his dying daughter, that he realizes what damage his obsession has done. Rigoletto sings, of Gilda, "She has been struck by the arrow of my righteous vengeance!" Wheeler gives no such moment of remorse to Todd.

Robert L. McLaughlin wrote, "This is Sondheim's darkest statement of the problem of love in contemporary society: like Sweeney, we respond to the forces that victimize us by becoming like them, by victimizing others." "*Sweeney Todd* is brilliant, even sensationally so, but its effect is very much a barrage of brilliancies, like flares fired aloft that dazzle and fade into something cold and dark," Jack Kroll wrote. "This 'musical thriller' about a homicidal barber, a tonsorial Jack the Ripper in Dickensian London, slashes at the jugular instead of touching the heart."

It is worth noting that in revivals in New York and London, the directors Susan Schulman and Declan Donnellan both said it was crucially important, as far as they were concerned, to have Todd come to such a moment of realization, in order to give him his full dimension as a tragic hero. What Wheeler had not supplied somehow had to be made clear. That both directors managed to bring this about added a further refinement to a masterwork, as reviews of their productions subsequently showed. Frank Rich noted of the Schulman production that Todd's longing for his lost wife and daughter becomes "an overwhelming obsession, finally to reach a rending catharsis in his sobbing embrace of his wife's corpse." William A. Henry III of *Time* magazine also noted that Todd had been transformed from a monster into a human being. He "howls piteously over the body of his beloved wife, lost and too late found. As corpses pile up in the apocalyptic finale, this version urges spectators not only to think but also to feel."

WHEN PRINCE AND SONDHEIM told him they wanted him for the part of Sweeney Todd, Len Cariou said, he thought "they had both lost their minds. How are they going to make a musical out of that?" He read the play and decided it was "bizarre, but it might work." That was in the autumn of 1975. But in the summer of 1976 the film of *Night Music* was being made, and the project kept getting postponed, "and I thought it was never going to happen." He had hesitated because "melodrama is very hard to act. If you go over the line, it's bad theatre." What was the line? "You must play it absolutely seriously. I just thought he had been wronged. I didn't think I could make him likable. A pretty scary guy bent on revenge. After he had his chance at the Judge and botched it, he snapped." Cariou believes everyone who acted in it was surprised at the musical's success. "We were all wondering if the audience would get it." Prince had decided not to have out-of-town previews because the set was too large and expensive to move around, but that meant they were taking a big chance. Cariou added, "I remember during the first New York preview we were having a terrible time with the set. The barber shop was directly above the pie shop, and the whole thing was supposed to be made of aluminum so that it could be pushed around, but they had made it out of steel. It weighed a ton and nobody could move it."

The technical problems continued. "Every run-through we had to stop. We hadn't gotten to the end for a week and I said to Hal and Steve, 'I have forgotten how this fucking thing ends.' We finally got an audience and we knew it was twenty minutes too long, but the audience loved it. I remember Stephen standing in front of my dressing room with his hands on his head saying, 'They understood it! They fucking understood it!' And he gave me a bear hug. He was so afraid no one would get the point of the show."

After Sondheim did thirteen backer's auditions and "didn't raise a cent," the producers, Woodward and Barr, took the unusual step of advertising for backers in the *New York Times* and got a total of two hundred and seventy-one, then considered a record. The show was being capitalized at $900,000. (It eventually cost a little more than $1 million.) Among the investors were Gregory and Veronique Peck and their two children, the novelist Tom Tryon, and Robert Fryer. He was a friend of Hugh Wheeler's and "just fell in with it." Like Martin Richards and Mary Lea Johnson, Fryer wanted to be part of the venture even though he was convinced it would be a failure and did not know how they could fill the Uris Theatre, which had almost two thousand seats. In fact, preview audiences in February 1979 gave a mixed reaction, and numbers of people walked out during intermission. It was clear that something had gone wrong: "The show got lost in its set and did not come through strongly," Richards said, so a meeting was arranged. When the point was put to Hal Prince, he responded, "Give me forty-eight hours and don't anyone come into the theatre." Richards said, "We all agreed, and two days later the whole thing had been restaged. From then on it got better and better."

Keith Baxter had gone to the first preview at the Uris, "one of the most bleakly forbidding houses in New York, a concrete structure of vast proportions," and sat with Shevelove and Shevelove's godson, Peter Wooster. The preview went as might have been expected. There were problems with the light cues. The sound system was occasionally unbalanced, and some of the scenes did not quite come together. None of them discussed the show during intermission. Baxter knew that no one wants unsolicited advice at this stage. But in any case, he had personal objections to the huge, and in his eyes inappropriate, framework that had been placed around the intimate drama. "There are many things you can see from Fleet Street—St. Paul's, Waterloo Bridge, the wharves of Ludgate; what you can't see is the Manchester ship canal with a factory belching smoke; there never were any mills or heavy industrial plants at the centre of London." The references in the score to "a city on fire" surely could not mean the furnaces, which you could not see, either, since these were in Islington, Camden, and Kentish Town, and anyway, the last fire in London had been in 1666. He knew these were subjective objections and did not want to burden anyone with them. "There seemed to be an uneasy balance at the Uris; on the one hand Todd was a kind of Avenging Angel . . . on the other, he was a figure of hilarity with his fright wig and lolling tongue," he wrote.

The three went to dinner at Joe Allen; Sondheim was to join them later. He appeared as they were halfway through their meal. "He was in that exact state one would have expected; exhilarated, proud, pleased, nervous. Absolutely exhausted. Living on the last squeeze of his adrenaline. And very, very touchy. Just as anyone might rightly be after a first preview . . . As he threaded his way towards us some idiot touched him on the arm and said condescendingly, 'I loved what *you've* done!' with the implication that everything else was rubbish. It may have been the last straw for Stephen. He swore furiously as he sat down and sloshed some white wine into his glass. And then Burt, attempting a bantering tone, said, 'Well, do you want the good news or the bad news?' It was a terrible error of judgment. Steve slammed down his glass and glared at his friend. 'There is *no* bad news, Burt! Do you understand? No bad news!' Burt, taken aback, attempted some badinage. Stephen would not be placated. 'There is NO BAD NEWS, Burt!' He then delivered a tirade, bred from his exhaustion, entirely understandable. But nevertheless cruel. Peter and I toyed with our food. People at the tables nearby were agog. Burt's eyes filled with tears." The friends papered over their differences, but Sondheim, for whom any intense creative effort might bring about a volatile mood, was not to be dissuaded. He even made the suggestion to Baxter that the actor's reason for going to the preview had been so that he could spread the bad news around London. The idea was so "dotty," Baxter said, that they were able to laugh him out of it. As the composer David Shire discovered when Sondheim was in the middle of writing the score for *Sweeney Todd* and played him excerpts, even the most measured comments and suggestions could bring forth a heated response that was almost irrational in its vehemence. And he so much wanted to have this latest bold experiment succeed. It had been his idea, after all. He had managed to overrule Prince's doubts. They both knew from bitter past experience what rejection felt like. Besides, a first preview was always an ordeal. "It was awful. I hated it because all the professional bitches come . . . and tell their friends how terrible it is."

Sondheim need not have worried. "A triumph of audacious theatricalism," one critic wrote after the show opened. "In sheer ambition and size, there's never been a bigger musical on Broadway," said another. "Total theatre, a brilliant concept and a shattering experience," said a third. "There has been no musical as dark, savage and shocking as Stephen Sondheim's *Sweeney Todd* in sixty years," was typical of the kind of comment that came later from London. If the Prince-Sondheim collaboration had seemed on occasion to venture further into the realm of experimentation than Broadway reviewers wanted to go, this was not the case with *Sweeney Todd*. They almost vied to find adequate superlatives for the daring involved in the choice of subject matter, the effectiveness of Prince's direction, the admirable qualities of the acting, the wit of Sondheim's lyrics and the brilliance of his music.

Richard Eder, writing for the *New York Times,* found the work's musical and dramatic achievements so multifaceted that they almost defied adequate praise: "There is more of artistic energy, creative personality and plain excitement in *Sweeney Todd* than in a dozen average musicals," he wrote. He admired the way Sondheim and Prince had taken "this set of rattletrap fireworks" and turned it into "a glittering, dangerous weapon." Schuyler G. Chapin, commissioner for New York City's Department of Cultural Affairs and former general manager of the Metropolitan Opera, said that when he went to the opening night, Harold Clurman, then the dean of theatre critics, "came charging across the lobby at me and said, 'Why didn't you put this on at the Met?' And I replied, 'I would have put it on like a shot, if I'd had the opportunity.' And I would have. There would have been screams and yells and I wouldn't have given a damn. Because it is an opera. A modern American opera." Hal Prince restaged *Sweeney Todd* for the New York City Opera at Lincoln Center five years later (1984), and there was an even more successful revival at the Royal National Theatre in London in 1993, directed by Declan

Donnellan (the co-founder of the much-admired theatrical company Cheek by Jowl), whose work on *Sweeney Todd* was called "transfixing." What had begun as a noble experiment even Prince thought was doomed to fail ran for 558 performances and, although it still lost money, did repay more than half its investment. More important, by general agreement, it was the crowning achievement of the Sondheim-Prince collaboration. *Sweeney Todd* won eleven Drama Desk Awards, the Drama Critics' Circle Award for best musical and eight Tony Awards, including that of best musical. It would be their finest moment. There was one more encomium that Sondheim particularly valued, however, and it came from Jule Styne. He remarked, "I think the most unbelievable job of music writing, and I say this with deep reverence and envy . . . is *Sweeney Todd*."

CHAPTER 16

Old Friends

S TEPHEN SONDHEIM HAD a heart attack a little more than three weeks after *Sweeney Todd* opened, and five days after his birthday. It was March 27, 1979, and he was forty-nine years old.

He was awakened in the middle of the night with a terrible pain in his chest. The first five minutes were absolute agony. "Oh!" he said. "You don't know what pain is until you've had one." It did not render him unconscious, but he started sweating heavily and called his doctor. "I just thought that I wanted it to stop, just let it stop. It just hurts too much. Just let me get to the hospital . . ." His doctor dispatched an ambulance and told him they would meet at New York Hospital, but the ambulance took him to Lenox Hill instead. "Luckily, as I was being wheeled in I said, 'I think this is the wrong hospital.' Because I'd been to New York Hospital before. So they got me there. Ten minutes late. I suppose I could have died in those ten minutes."

However, it did not occur to him that he might die. He said, "Apparently, in many cases, when you die of a heart attack you have a sense of impending doom . . . Not always, but you get a sense that it's all over . . . I was real nervous and scared but it didn't occur to me that I would die . . ." He was taken to intensive care and given morphine and other drugs to ease the pain, and "I felt not bad the second day. I mean, I didn't feel terrific, but—I found out later they were worried about me for two days. Much more worried than I had known they were. Which is just as well because I'm a hypochondriac. If I'd known they were worried I would have died of terror. If I have a pain in my toe I immediately think of cancer.

"But you know, there are people who don't care. Hal Prince is a great example. I've seen him pretend to himself that he doesn't have a 104-degree fever, and guess what: he got over it. I'll tell you an anecdote about Hal. This takes place in the intensive care. Hal and Judy were away and came back to New York the day after the heart attack and I was allowed to use a phone the second day. And I called him and told him I had something to tell him. And he and Judy were burbling about Majorca or wherever the hell they'd come from. I said I'd had a heart attack. Pandemonium. I said, 'I'm okay, I'm in the intensive care unit.' 'We're coming right over.' I said, 'It's not necessary. I just wanted you to know because you would hear.' They insisted on coming. Now, Hal refuses to admit that death exists, so his idea of hell on earth is to go into a hospital. He was not happy being in the hospital, but he came out of dearness, and I decided to play a truly sadistic trick on him." He laughed. "I was lying in bed and the monitor was going up and down, the way you see it in the movies. I discovered that if I moved my arm it would make the thing jump. So Hal and Judy are sitting at the foot of the bed, and Judy of course is looking at me. Every now and then I would see Hal's eyes go to the monitor. And I'd say, 'Listen, I'm feeling fine!,' jiggling my arm, and he's trying not to let me know that something is very wrong. But he's thinking, Do I call the nurse now? And I'm saying, 'Tell me about Majorca,' jiggling my elbow again." Sondheim agreed that he was in a pretty good mood. "Little did I know that they were worried I wasn't going to survive."

By then his household had been expanded by Patricia Sinnott's arrival in the summer of 1978. She remembered the first day she went to his Turtle Bay house, "because when the door opened there was Louis Vargas, this very smiling Latin man, and Steve, and right behind me was someone with a huge delivery, and flowers all over the house and in the kitchen, because it was Lou's fiftieth birthday." They went upstairs and talked. Sondheim looked at her resumé and said he could not imagine that someone with her background in arts management would want to work for him. Then he said, "By the way, I write music for Broadway shows." She replied, "Yes, I know." She said, "He wasn't putting it on." Now, of course, Sondheim is very well known, but he really thought then that people would not know who he was. And he was still riding his bicycle in traffic because it was easier and faster and good exercise. It was always standing just inside the front door, and often she would see the bicycle chained to one of the stanchions outside a Broadway theatre or Radio City Music Hall and know that he was inside. When she was hired, Sondheim was just starting work on *Sweeney Todd*. Hugh Wheeler dropped off the script and Sondheim asked her to type it up. She did not know the story, and it was "a true Gothic thriller," so she sat and typed away, because she did not want to peek at the end.

She learned he was in the hospital when "Lou . . . called me about four or five in the morning because he was a nervous wreck. Peter Wooster came in from Brooklyn. And I called his doctor, because no one seemed to know anything." That led to her suggesting that she visit Sondheim. His response was, "I don't want anyone to see me," and she was not sure she should go anyway, because she did not feel she knew him well enough. "He's a very stand-offish person, again because I think he is very shy, there's that invisible wall. But if anyone asks me why I stayed as long as I did [nine years], I think it was the Steve I met at New York Hospital, whom I came to care about a great deal.

"The person I met was very scared and alone. He was very poignant, and very sweet, and *very* honest and candid."

Sondheim was in the hospital for two weeks. He talked to Burt Shevelove, who had suffered a heart attack himself. Shevelove said, "I just want to prepare you. You're going to get very depressed." Sondheim replied, "Okay, thanks for the warning." He said later, "Well, I wasn't happy, but I certainly wasn't depressed. I got home, started to recover, and about five days later I woke up one morning and understood what depression was. I thought, 'There's no point in going on. I just want to die.' It wasn't pain. It was the intimation of mortality, a glimpse into the chasm." Sondheim said that he had no religious beliefs—"I was brought up in a pragmatic world"—and thought that death was, as the song goes, a long, long sleep. As for that moment when he stared into the abyss, "I'll never forget it. It's weird, because not one moment of the day has any meaning or makes any sense. It's what true depression is, and many thousands of people suffer from it. I don't know how they can get through the day."

The feeling was gone a day later and he did not know what had caused it. Perhaps it was a dream. "As George [Furth] said in *Company*, once you've been married you can never not have been married again. So I can never believe entirely what I believed before the heart attack, which was that I could go on living any way I wanted, and that nothing bad would happen." His friends attest to the dramatic change in Sondheim after his heart attack. From being someone who never noticed what he ate, he went on a low-calorie, low-fat, low-salt diet, thanks to the faithful Louis, whose ability to cook delicious meals without these aids was described with awe by everyone who ate his food. Sondheim, whose exercise had been limited to bicycling through traffic, began sports training. He bought himself a stationary bicycle and, to relieve the boredom, pedaled his way through dozens of old movies. He lost weight and limited his alcoholic intake to wine. "The doctor did all kinds of tests and found out, luckily, very little of my heart was damaged," he said. "There was just a tiny, tiny bit of scar tissue there."

"I had eaten eggs every day of my life and now I only ate them once a month. I'd eaten lots of meat—I've had maybe one piece of steak a year during the last fifteen years. I thought I would never get to like fish. Guess what, within a week I loved fish. I eat vegetables most of the time nowadays. I could live on soup, vegetables and fruit, so my diet is pretty healthy." Jamie Hammerstein said that within three months, Sondheim looked better than he had for years. William Goldman agreed that "he is far fitter than he was." He looked what he was, a handsome man. Goldman continued, "He had a wonderful phrase. We were talking recently and he said, 'I didn't like my work because it's not what's in my head. There are two things in forty years that I am proud of.' Then he said, 'You have to learn to forgive yourself.' I love that phrase. The Steve I knew when he was young would not have said that."

Jay David Saks, an associate producer for RCA Records who had worked on the cast albums of Sondheim shows, recalled that the album for *Sweeney Todd* had been recorded just before Sondheim's heart attack. Saks said, "I didn't see him at the time because I was buried doing two records, but when he was home recuperating we cut some test records and Tom Shepard [the album's producer] took them over to him. Sondheim listened to the records and was moved to tears." The record won a Grammy Award for best original show album and became a best-seller. "Steve got on the phone to me and said some of the sweetest, nicest things. I was so touched."

IN 1979 CRAIG LUCAS, the future playwright, was in the chorus of *Sweeney Todd.* Lucas said, "I had seen *Company, Follies,* and *A Little Night Music* while I was at Boston University because I was a musical comedy aficionado. I happened to have a big, bright, untrained voice, so I was singing, acting, and doing creative writing while I was doing chorus work in New York." He met Sondheim and they would talk at rehearsals. "He threw parties for the cast and would come to ours." Sondheim happened to mention that he had written a number of songs that had never been performed.

"While we were doing *Sweeney Todd,* I gave Sondheim a draft of my first play. Then I went to his house and he had a lot of suggestions and notes. He's very opinionated and a natural mentor. He wants to pass on lessons he has learned, which are sometimes particular to his experience, so his advice can be liberating, helpful, and sometimes not. And I gave every word of his such weight." He thought of Sondheim as a modern master. So when Lucas was invited to write a late-night cabaret for an up-and-coming Off Off Broadway group called the Production Company, and asked permission to use Sondheim's songs, the composer sent him away with forty-five songs to look at, seventeen of which were eventually chosen. Three of the songs came from the never-produced *Saturday Night;* "Pour le Sport," from *The Last Resorts,* the musical that was to have been made from Cleveland Amory's book; and the music for "The Girls of Summer," the first Sondheim work to be heard on Broadway. "Your Eyes Are Blue" was cut from *Forum;* "There Won't Be Trumpets," Lee Remick's song, was cut after the first preview of *Anyone Can Whistle;* the title song and "Happily Ever After" came from *Company.* "Uptown, Downtown" and the double duet "Little White House" and "Who Could Be Blue?" were dropped from the Loveland sequence in *Follies.* "Can That Boy Foxtrot" was another *Follies* song that did not survive. Then there was "Two Fairy Tales," written for the first act of *Night Music* and dropped during rehearsals, as was "Bang!," originally written to be sung by the Count and Desirée Armfeldt.

Lucas put the songs into the framework of a man and a woman living in the same apartment building—his apartment is directly above hers—trying to fill in the time on a lonely Saturday night. They have not met. She is doing household chores; he is a writer at his typewriter. The scene is set for them to invent a variety of romantic situations in the course of their solitary evening. The last song is "It Wasn't Meant to Happen," and each of them climbs into a solitary bed.

As he was developing the idea with Norman René, the director, Lucas said, "Sondheim was very helpful, although he didn't always agree. He wanted 'Pour le Sport' [which is set on a golf course] cut because it didn't fit in tone. It was the only dicey moment in the show. We didn't cut, and I could tell he wasn't happy. He didn't pull rank and say 'You can't do this,' although he had every right. In retrospect, what probably damaged the show most is that I am not a fabulous performer. I cast myself as the boy because I was so eager to perform, and Sondheim said in a very nice way that I was only okay as a performer. He may have used the term 'mediocre.' But he called me a promising writer."

The title of the cabaret, *Marry Me a Little,* from the song of the same name that was also cut from *Company,* seemed exactly right, and the late-night show was an immediate hit when it opened in the autumn of 1980. It was designed to take place on the set for a play that was running at the same time, called *S.R.O.,* about single-occupancy hotels. The theatre was small, the atmosphere informal, and the players—Suzanne Henry, a singer and actress, took the part of the girl—modest and engaging. William B. Young, himself a playwright and budding producer, attracted the interest of another producer, Diane de Mailly, and they decided to move it to Off Broadway.

Young said, "We made the mistake of assuming we had a hit and didn't take the precautions we should have. We could have used more rehearsal time, and [we] kept the previews to five days. In those five days we were selling out, but after it opened and the reviews were not as good as they might have been, audiences fell off." *Marry Me a Little* closed after three months without making back its advance. But Tom Shepard, the indefatigable producer at RCA, managed to convince his superiors that a record should be made. The show served to arouse interest in some unappreciated songs, among them the title song, "There Won't Be Trumpets," and "So Many People." Several more unknown songs by Sondheim would shortly be heard in New York. "Invocation and Instruction to the Audience" and "Fear No More" from *The Frogs,* "Isn't It?" and "What More Do I Need?" from *Saturday Night,* "Poems" from *Pacific Overtures,* and "Echo Song" and "There's Something About a War" from *Forum* were among the Sondheim works heard during an evening of his music produced by the Composers' Showcase and performed at Sotheby's in the spring of 1983.

BY THE TIME Craig Lucas was working on his late-night cabaret, Sondheim had recovered from his heart attack and was working on a new project. It was a musical based on *Merrily We Roll Along,* the George Kaufman and Moss Hart play that opened at the Music Box Theatre in the autumn of 1934, and ran for only 155 performances, a succès d'estime that, as Kaufman once said, "ran out of steam." Its protagonist, Richard Niles, a playwright at the peak of his fame, has left his sense of integrity behind. His life story is told as a morality play in reverse; the play begins with the sordid present and returns by degrees to the rosy past when Niles and his friends Julia Glenn, a writer, and Jonathan Crale, a painter, were united in their love for each other and dedication to their muses. The play had been very much admired by Brooks Atkinson, who wrote, "You are likely to hold your breath from fear and horror when you see by what normal cupidity a cynical playwright can descend from a fervent college idealist. Mr. Kaufman and Mr. Hart have reminded us of the exalted impulses we lose when we connive to keep alive." The significant word in that sentence is "connive." *Merrily's* conclusion would have seemed particularly apt to a nation not yet recovered from a catastrophic depression, causing vast numbers of people either to look for escapist entertainment or to reflect, in a high-minded sort of way, that things could be worse: they might be down and out but at least they had not sold their souls. It was a theme the playwrights would treat two years later, this time in a much more lighthearted vein, with that amiable tale about a muddle-headed family pursuing individual artistic visions, *You Can't Take It With You*. What had seemed to impart a salutary lesson to Atkinson when he saw the play in 1934 had become something else to the critic by the time he came to write his panoramic history of Broadway in 1970. *Merrily*, he wrote, "was not a contribution to thought or literature, and it came with ill grace from two of Broadway's most successful playwrights. It is best remembered by an ironic comment Herman Mankiewicz, one of their friends, made after the opening performance: 'Here's this wealthy playwright who has had repeated successes and earned enormous amounts of money, has mistresses as well as a family, an expensive town house, a luxurious beach house and a yacht. The problem is: How did the son of a bitch get into this jam?' "

It is safe to say that such thoughts were far from the mind of Hal Prince when Judy Prince suggested he and Sondheim do a show about young people, a kind of *Babes in Arms* brought up to date. Prince immediately began casting his mind back to familiar works that would seem appropriate for the age group of his adolescent son, Charley, and daughter, Daisy. He thought briefly of Thornton Wilder's *Our Town* but rejected the idea. Then one morning as he was shaving he recalled *Merrily*, in which his former producing partner, Robert Griffith, had once played a small part. It seemed like the perfect solution. Prince immediately called Sondheim. Prince said, "It was the first time he ever said yes on the phone."

Sondheim expressed his usual aversion to stories about people in show business. And he thought the main character was a cipher, not that this was an insuperable obstacle, since he saw him as representing a kind of collective shortcoming: "what this country is always in danger of . . . which is expediency." In tackling *Merrily*, Sondheim was returning to the theme of failed hopes and blasted expectations that he had first seen explored in *Allegro;* had tried to develop in *All That Glitters,* his musical version of Kaufman's play *Beggar on Horseback;* had carried through with singlemindedness in *Climb High;* and which had appeared again as one of the themes in *Follies. Allegro's* influence had cast a long shadow on his life, perhaps because Hammerstein had always wanted to revise it, so that it was no longer misunderstood and dismissed as a corny story about a rich doctor, but was seen as he intended: what happens when an artist loses sight of his or her goal. But the fact that this was a theme to which he returned time and again had to mean that it had an even more personal significance. Perhaps one could trace a certain Ariadne thread all the way back to his childhood wish that there never had been a divorce, that he never had been sent away, and that his parents, who loved him after their fashion, had not set him adrift emotionally for their own self-absorbed reasons. If so, it was a desire so blasted, so trampled on, and so subterranean that it could only appear in its disguised, reverse image, as a morality tale about regret, disillusion, and the vainness of hope.

Prince and Sondheim approached George Furth, who had collaborated with them so successfully on *Company*, and a musical version of *Merrily* began to take shape. Obviously, *Merrily* would need a modern setting. Furth toyed with the idea of making the playwright a politician before settling on that of a composer who sells out to the movies because, he said, "it's much easier to show the first-class talent of somebody if he's a composer." The choice of métier seemed a curious one since, as Banfield pointed out, there was never any idea of presenting the conflict between, say, the demands of writing opera and symphonic scores for no money versus the easy money to be made in commercial theatre. From the start, the renamed Franklin Shepard wrote only popular music, and, as Banfield observed, "Popular music's first duty is, presumably, to be popular." But the play's biggest problem, in retrospect, was the Kaufman and Hart decision to tell the story backwards, robbing the trio of character development and sapping the audience's empathy, as *Variety* noted. "They were introduced at their worst—jaded by success, embittered by rejection, and so the suspense was over."

Jonathan Tunick said he wondered whether Prince and Sondheim were following their own dictum, which was to make sure they were all writing the same show. The one that was described to him "was this happy, upbeat, accessible show. I think Prince even used the word 'commercial.' He said it was going to be like a Jule Styne or an Irving Berlin musical. And then what was presented to me was a show full of anger and ill will, pessimism and hurt. It was supposed to be all about this youthful idealism, but to me it was a show about how important friendship is in life, and what a tragedy it is when a man destroys every friendship he's ever had . . . As for the plot, in which our hero writes a couple of musicals and then becomes a movie producer, I don't think the average playgoer understands that the highest aspiration of mankind is to write Broadway musicals, and anyone who doesn't is contemptible!"

In retrospect, Prince and Sondheim agreed that it had been a catastrophically bad idea to imagine that a cast of starry-eyed adolescents would be equal to the task of portraying dissipation and disillusion. For youngsters to tackle the Kaufman and Hart play would have been difficult enough, but because it was a well-developed version of the theme, even that would have been more forgiving than the truncated version that is all any book musical can be.

Eventually, only caricatures of Kaufman and Hart's original characters would be recognizable in Franklin Shepard, the antihero at the pinnacle of his disreputable fame; Mary Flynn, still a writer, but now a flailing alcoholic; and Charley Kringas, the artist character, now turned lyricist, who is the one person who has not sold out. The time frame would begin in 1980 and return to 1955; in the final scene, the intrepid trio are deciding to write a revue, one that will start them off on the downward path to wisdom.

> It's our time, breathe it in:
> Worlds to change and worlds to win.
> Our turn coming through,
> Me and you, pal,
> Me and you!

George Furth was joined by Eugene Lee as set designer; Paul Gemignani was serving again as music director, as he had ever since *Follies;* Jonathan Tunick was in his usual role; and Ron Field, who had worked with Prince on *Cabaret,* was choreographer. As soon as they began work, Prince explained his idea of the play. It was on the question of what constituted success. "I wanted to show that success is not necessarily measured in bank deposits," he said. "I like Franklin a lot, but I'm sorry for him, because success is very seductive . . ." It was easy to lose track of the pleasure one received from doing the work itself. He was at pains to state that no one should draw parallels between *Merrily's* characters and its producing team. "But it certainly would have been about our times . . ." That there was an identification on some level, however fleeting, is suggested by the fact that a television newsman called Hal and a newswoman named Judy make cameo appearances. As for Sondheim, he said that "Opening Doors" was the one consciously autobiographical song he ever wrote. Sondheim realized recently just how much the artless verve and optimism of *Merrily's* characters mirrored his own youth, after friends sent him copies of his letters of that period. They are full of zest and almost incoherent in their eagerness to describe all that is happening and how avidly he is reacting. It was an aspect of himself that he had almost forgotten.

Whether adolescent actors could deal with Furth's dialogue was very much on Prince's mind when he returned to New York—he was overseeing worldwide productions of his hit musical *Evita*—for the casting sessions in May 1980. Among those auditioning was his own daughter, Daisy, then fifteen (she was sixteen by the time the musical opened), whose sole experience had been to act in some productions at the Dalton School. She was cast as Meg, wearing white, a pretty ingenue who is about to become Franklin Shepard's next wife as the musical opens. As her final audition, Daisy Prince decided to sing Gershwin's "Someone to Watch Over Me." Despite her stage fright ("My entire life flashed before my eyes"), she was aware that tears were rolling down Sondheim's cheeks.

Prince cast James Weissenbach, the son of a college friend from the University of Pennsylvania, in the role of Franklin Shepard, but replaced him during the tryouts with Jim Walton, aged twenty-six, who had been cast in a smaller role. The part of Mary went to Ann Morrison, aged twenty-five, because of her big voice, one that reminded Prince of the young Judy Garland. The plum role of Charley was given to Lonny Price, aged twenty-two, a former office boy in Prince's office who had become an actor Off Broadway and had already won an acting award. Prince said one of his biggest problems was that the rawness of his cast of twenty-six, many of them in their late teens, seemed so engaging. "I was charmed by the beginnings of their artistry, by the roughness of their craft, their inexperience. I was charmed as hell by that . . ." Prince had overlooked how difficult it would be for the actors themselves. Lonny Price said, "Hal's initial idea was that we weren't telling our own stories, we were telling adult stories. That's the way he directed it, but it's a hard concept to get, and there was something very raw and young about the results." Jim Walton had, as the oldest male in the cast, the most acting experience. Although he liked the book, he thought: "You are supposed to come away with a feeling of ironic sadness, but the problem was we were all too young to have the right emotional frames of reference. I began as a forty-three-year-old man having a nervous breakdown," a challenge to which he hardly felt adequate.

Merrily was setting up some strange reverberations in their lives. The young Franklin Shepard gets married to Beth when she discovers she is pregnant, and divorces her quickly. During the run of *Merrily* Walton was living with Janie Gleason, who was also in the cast. They discovered she was pregnant, so they were married at City Hall one afternoon and had a wedding party onstage after the performance that night. Janie wore Beth's wedding gown for a lark. Two years later, Jim and Janie were divorced. Walton said that the parallels continued after *Merrily* closed. He and Lonny Price, a fictional songwriting team, went on to collaborate in real life. They wrote a one-act musical called *Daisy Abbott,* a project that took them two or three years. It was never performed. "It was life imitating art," he said.

REHEARSALS WERE to have begun in late 1980, but Sondheim had not yet finished the score and they did not start until September 1981. It seems evident, since Prince characterized *Merrily* as like "a Jule Styne or Irving Berlin musical," that he never intended anyone to take the musical's moral seriously. In his mind it was simply a way to introduce a company of fresh young faces. Music, dance, and charm would count for much more than plot, the way they always had. Although Prince continued to resist commercial pressures, he seemed to think that the moment had come to launch something with natural box-office appeal, and that *Merrily* was it. (Although he had not produced *Sweeney Todd*, he did put money towards *Merrily*'s budget of $1.5 million, along with Lord Grade, Martin Starger, and Robert Fryer.)

Sondheim's job was to write a popular score, something, Prince observed, that he had not done for a long time. "Obviously, 'Send In the Clowns' was a very successful song, but the score was not that type of score. In this show we've got the Sinatra record and the Carly Simon record, and my mother can sing the songs first time out, so that makes her happy." Prince was referring to the fact that, although the show had not yet opened, Sinatra had recorded one of its songs, "Good Thing Going," and Simon had recorded another, "Not a Day Goes By." The omens were all good.

Sondheim said he was writing "real thirty-two-bar songs," making use of contemporary harmonies. But, Sondheim being Sondheim, it was not quite that simple. He wanted the songs to be based on the interrelationships of the principal characters, alternately forceful or fragmented, depending on the script. He got the idea of building the score in thematic blocks. Instead of writing transitions from one song to another, or interweaving themes, as he had in *Sweeney Todd*, he would move sets of ideas around in more or less recognizable groups. "You take a release from one song and make that a verse for a different song, and then you take a chorus from a song and make that a release for another song, and then you take an accompaniment from yet a different song and make that a verse in another song. So that it's like modular furniture that you rearrange in a room . . ." Thus the release in the song "Rich and Happy" becomes the refrain for "Our Time," the melody of "Old Friends" becomes the accompaniment for "Opening Doors," and the chorus of "Like It Was" becomes the interlude for "Old Friends." All of Franklin Shepard's songs share the same theme. "The Hills of Tomorrow" is closely related to "Opening Doors," which in turn becomes "Good Thing Going." The composer who had disdained the reprise found himself, by accident or design, bringing back the same themes in different guises, as if determined to have something linger in the memory once the curtain came down.

If the sound is big and brash and the overture makes the conventional references to the main themes in the score, the songs themselves demonstrate

From left, choreographer Larry Fuller, Sondheim, librettist George Furth, Harold Prince, and, in the front row, cast members Jim Walton, Ann Morrison, and Lonny Price at the premiere of *Merrily We Roll Along*. Below, members of the cast

Sondheim's ability to "place an individual signature on a basically familiar form," as Clive Barnes wrote. The songs for Charley Kringas and Mary Flynn are particularly sympathetic and display a feeling for their human qualities that are lacking in the book. They agonize, they exult, they sing of their disappointments, large hopes and small triumphs. It is clear that Ann Morrison, in the role of Mary, with her strong, bell-like voice, is the one real singer in the group, but Lonny Price's ability to express feeling more than compensates for any vocal shortcomings, and Jim Walton's pleasant tenor adds its own coloration, eager, approachable, and basically nice. If *Sweeney Todd* was about despair and revenge, *Merrily* celebrated the death of hope in a mood of longing and regret, rather than one of disillusion. There are the infectious rhythms of "Merrily We Roll Along" itself and the sardonic humor of "Franklin Shepard, Inc.," another of the patter songs Sondheim does so well. Then there is Mary's song "Like It Was," which directly follows an early scene in which Franklin Shepard and all of his coterie have behaved abominably, as she has herself. She sings to Charley:

> Charley,
> Why can't it be like it was?
> I liked it the way that it was.
> Charley,
> You and me, we were nicer then.
>
> We were nice,
> Kids and cities and trees were nice,
> Everything . . .
> I don't know who we are any more,
> And I'm starting not to care.

The tone is so open and heartfelt that one immediately forgives her for her first appearance, in which, after a string of bitterly sarcastic remarks, she crashes into the cocktail bar and is dragged away. In fact, it is difficult to see the actress, whose youthful poignance is so in tune with the mood of the music, capable of such behavior. All of them, as the cast album shows, really did convey the untested and naive charm that Prince heard in their voices. Frank Rich wrote that Sondheim had written "a half-dozen songs that are crushing and beautiful—that soar and linger and hurt."

One of the songs that would turn out to probe a painful memory, though for a different reason, was Sondheim's tribute, "Old Friends," to the many in

Old college friends: Howard Erskine, Sondheim, and Charles Hollerith

his life who had shared his triumphs, commiserated with his failures, and stuck together through the years. He was thinking particularly of his college friends—Dominick Dunne, Howard Erskine, Chuck Hollerith, and Ford Schumann—and he incorporated the latter's habitual toast into the song. Old friends, the lyrics state, provide the comfort of the familiar. They do not tell you when you are lying. Their attitude is, live and let live. Some people like to give free advice. Old friends just love you and forgive you. They accept you on your own terms.

> Most friends fade
> Or they don't make the grade,
> New ones are quickly made,
> Some of them worth something, too.
> But us, old friend—
> What's to discuss, old friend?
> Here's to us,
> Who's like us?
> Damn few.

Prince's original idea was that the set would be reminiscent of a high-school gymnasium and that makeup and costumes would be enough to make the necessary transformations. (Mary, in particular, has to look almost obscenely overweight when she first appears and dwindle, by degrees, to a normal weight by the end of the show, along with the other slight problem of growing twenty-five years younger.) But the costumes were not enough of a disguise; the cast just looked like youngsters dressed up. So that idea went. Then Prince had the idea of simplifying the set still further, using bleachers, with screen projections to set the mood and period. He dressed everyone in identical sweatshirts and pants. Then he had to add names emblazoned across the sweatshirts because the audience had difficulty telling the actors apart.

He said, "What do I regret? I regret that Steve wrote from the heart, he wrote openly, he felt all those things, and the score is beautiful. *We* let *him* down. I never knew how to direct it, because I work so much from 'What is it going to look like?' That becomes the motor of the show. I never could figure it out. I had *one* glimmering moment followed by a lot of cowardice. I called my office staff together and said, 'Look, it's a Broadway show. You know what the price of tickets is.' God knows it was less than it is now. 'But I'll tell you what I would do if I had the guts,' I said. 'I would have *no* scenery. I would have racks of clothes and these kids would come in looking like little kids, and they would pretend to be their parents as they see them. And let's see what happens. So we're talking *no* production costs, some lights, some kids; put on the story.' And everyone looked at me in the office and said, 'If that's what you think it should be, do it.' And guess what? I lacked the courage."

Prince had decided against taking the show to Boston or New Haven but held previews in New York in October 1981 at the Alvin Theatre. That was becoming standard procedure for Broadway shows, and it had worked to advantage with *Sweeney Todd*. But in this case it became clear that the musical was in much rougher shape than they thought. Sondheim said, "The irony was, the month of previews, during which we did so much work, was probably the most exhilarating time of our lives. Because we worked every single day and it felt like two kids putting on a show. Every day there were new changes and things to do," and when something was a success that had failed before, there was enormous euphoria. But by then the rumors had begun that *Merrily* was in trouble.

Prince said, "The trouble was that the newspapers snapped at our heels." He was referring to an article by Liz Smith in the New York *Daily News* that was published just ten days after the first preview with the damning headline, "Not So Merrily They Roll out of the Theatre." Smith wrote, "The walkouts from the new Hal Prince–Steve Sondheim musical are almost epidemic. There were about 140 people who left after the intermission at a recent performance. 'Terrible' and 'tacky' are the words most often being used . . ." Prince said the article was picked up everywhere "and you read everywhere the trouble we were in. Audiences began to storm out of the theatre . . ." It was particularly painful because he had brought in so many youngsters unprepared for this humiliating experience, especially his daughter, Daisy, who would come home and say, "They just kept walking out all night, Daddy." It was agonizing, and as he described it, tears came to his eyes. "I had cold sweats. I'd wake up in the middle of the night. You see, it went on and on and *on*. Night after night." The show continued to improve, but by then no one wanted to believe it. Lonny Price said, "I remember coming out of the stage door and someone asking me, 'Are they working on it?' and I said, 'Of course,' and the reply was, 'Well, the first act isn't working,' " and he went home in the cab feeling terrible. Prince concluded, "Was it one of our best shows? No. Does the show work still? No. Have I ever figured out how to make it work? No. Have they?" (A reference to several productions since.) "I don't think so, though there are critics who would disagree. So maybe it's just a bad idea." For his part, Sondheim thought it was "swell."

On opening night there were the usual cheerful telegrams for Sondheim, including one from "Mom," who had been reduced to this kind of communication since their rift. She sent love and kisses and best wishes. Arthur Laurents merely wrote, "Wishing," which summed it all up. At the cast party afterwards in the grand ballroom of the Plaza Hotel, there were drinks, food, and music and a mood of apprehension. "I remember exactly," Sondheim said. "We got the opening-night reviews at the party. I suddenly noticed that Hal and Judy had left, and then we all knew that the news was bad." The actors were equally in the dark. A great pal of Lonny Price's, Alex Bernstein, son of the conductor, had rented a limousine, so they piled into the car and went to some all-night newsstands on Broadway. "I remember sitting there with a bunch of my friends and crying. It was horrible." It was equally excruciating for Sondheim, who had, as he often did, brought a group of people back to the house. Among them was Lee Wright, and Sondheim recalled that he and Burt Shevelove were chattering away when he suddenly saw a look of profound sympathy on Wright's face and interjected, "Stop it, Lee!" He continued, "Pity is not what you want at a moment like that. Burt knew that. He knew that what you do is, you talk about anything else but that. The reviews are the reviews. That's it, we're here, let's have a good time." He did not want anyone feeling sorry for him. "It was out of the goodness of his heart, but I was really angry."

While admiring the score, Frank Rich, the *New York Times* critic, felt the book was "a shambles," because, although it showed how the three friends had parted, it never made the reason clear; "all we get is fatuous attitudinizing about how ambition, success and money always lead to rack and ruin." Edwin Wilson called the story commonplace. Only Clive Barnes, now critic of the New York *Post,* had kind words for the musical, which closed after sixteen performances. Even RCA Records, which was planning to record the cast album, wanted to renege on its commitment, and only a heartfelt appeal on the part of Sondheim's champion there, Tom Shepard, saved the day. A friend of Sondheim's said that after *Merrily* closed, everyone connected with it disappeared except Sondheim, who gave the cast moral support through the recording sessions. "He brought them to his house and buoyed them up. He felt so terribly for them. I was so impressed with his kindness."

Rich's review made a passing reference to a play by Harold Pinter that had recently opened, *Betrayal,* about the destruction of a marriage, which also told its story backwards, but in the manner of a mystery in which each step revealed a new clue to the puzzle. Arthur Laurents thought, as Rich did, that such a dramatic device could succeed if it were done well. After Laurents compared *Merrily* unfavorably with the Pinter play, Sondheim wrote reprovingly, "No matter what one thinks of a project, if one is a friend one doesn't undermine it at the beginning." It would take him some time to recover from that, and what was even sadder was that *Merrily* brought about a break with an even older friend, Ford Schumann.

After Williams, Schumann had gone on to become a painter. Whenever he would have a one-man show in Montclair, New Jersey, where he and his first wife lived, Sondheim would go to see his work. "It had nothing to do with whether it was a success or not, you know. That's his work. And they used to come in for every opening. They'd fly in from Aspen, then Scottsdale, he and his second wife, Susan." They were coming for *Merrily,* but since they could not be there for the opening night, Sondheim got tickets for the next night for them and another couple. The morning after the opening Schumann called to make his excuses. They could not come to the show after all. "And I knew he'd read the reviews and didn't want to take this couple to a flop. And I thought, that's not twenty years of friendship." No doubt he was also disappointed that his private tribute to his old friend, the toast set to music, had also been spurned. It was all too much to bear. Sondheim could not believe an old friend would betray him this way, as he saw it. (Schumann declined to comment.)

Merrily's disruptive influence on his life went further. Part of what was so devastating to Prince and Sondheim about the reviews was the way they felt they were being personally attacked. In a long article dissecting the failures of *Merrily*, Walter Kerr pointed to the theme of disenchantment which, he thought, was common to all the Sondheim-Prince musicals. "Compromise, the sellout, loss of integrity—these are not so much fighting words to Prince and Sondheim as they are creative words, words that help them choose their materials, words that drive them to work." There was nothing wrong with that, but their insistence on that theme was becoming monotonous. Prince said, "We were sitting pigeons. We had been overly celebrated as a team, and when the show didn't work as well as it should, the reaction was excessive. People say, 'Well, there must be hubris involved in this . . . No one else would make us see this flawed work but these two guys, who think they can get away with anything!' " He felt "black and blue." Before long Prince told Sondheim he thought their partnership had "run out of steam," Sondheim said. And that was that. Sondheim had lost the most important collaborator in his life.

HAL PRINCE HAS BEEN reluctant to describe in detail the reasons that led him to look for other artistic partnerships. It would appear that Sondheim, while obviously upset, never really comprehended why *Merrily* brought that association to an end. Perhaps the reasons are best understood in the context of another attempt to make the musical succeed, this one at the Arena Stage in Washington, D.C., in February 1990. That effort came after James Lapine's production of *Merrily* in La Jolla in 1985 showed that the musical was far from being as doomed as it had seemed to Prince. Douglas Wager, then a director at the repertory company, was convinced that *Merrily*'s problems were not insurmountable and had Sondheim and Furth's cooperation for the undertaking. The understanding was that if the revival was successful, it would go to New York for a Broadway production with himself as director.

Wager said, "The biggest change that happened with the La Jolla production was that it was cast with people who were the right ages rather than teenagers." There were new songs; the opening scene, which began with the group's graduation from high school, was changed to the grown-up party, the way Kaufman and Hart wrote it; and there were new sets and costumes and other refinements. Wager said, "There's a step in the Kaufman-Hart play that is critical, that is missed in the musical. It's a scene in the original play in which you find out why Frank has parted company with Charley over the issue of what they want out of life." In the musical, Charley describes his disapproval of Franklin in the song "Franklin Shepard, Inc.," but it is one in which Shepard takes no part. Wager thought an addition was essential because "in a classical tragedy there's a movement from ignorance to knowledge, and at the penultimate moment comes a moment of recognition and reversal, one in which the character recognizes his error and changes. But in a tragedy, that moment comes too late. If *Merrily* is a tragedy that goes backwards, then it begins with the moment of 'too late.' But the penultimate moment has to come very soon," and that was the pivot the script needed.

When the playwright was consulted, Wager said, "George felt that the problems did not lie with the book and any changes he would make would be cut-and-paste changes. He wasn't really willing to go back and open up that Pandora's box." Still, Wager thought they were making progress when disaster struck. There was a week of rehearsals in New York over the Christmas holidays in 1989. On New Year's Eve he and Furth had tickets to a matinee of the latest successful revival of *Gypsy*. Wager said, "We walked out onto the street and it was raining and I said, 'Let me go back in and get my umbrella.' I turned and stepped inside the hallway at Playwrights Horizons on a rubber mat that had water on it, and I hydroplaned and completely severed all four tendons of the whole muscle above one of my knees. I fell and passed out. When I came to, I couldn't move my leg because the muscle was detached. I've never felt anything like that pain."

Wager was hospitalized for ten days. The company moved to Washington without him; decisions were being made about slides and sets, and the choreographer went to work. He got back to rehearse the rest of the show in a wheelchair, aided by painkillers, with only two weeks of rehearsals left. "Numbers had been choreographed without my being there. They needed to be changed, but there was no time to fix them. It was worse than summer stock."

Wager said, "I think the chance to really fix the musical was ultimately taken away by my fall. That may be my own way of justifying it, because if I hadn't fallen there's no guarantee that it would have worked. But I live with it every day . . . Also, what was going on at that point in my life was eerily resonant with *Merrily*, which was that my marriage of ten years was breaking up, and the breakup really began the night that I fell." While rehearsals were taking place for *Merrily*, he was being evaluated for the position of artistic director of Arena Stage to replace its founder, Zelda Fichhandler. He was not at all sure whether he would get the job, and was hoping for a Broadway production in case he was not chosen. But the reviews were tepid; even Frank Rich, who had taken a particular interest in *Merrily*, was not encouraging. Nothing happened there, but at least he was named to succeed Fichhandler.

After that, Wager had "a fairly terminal falling out" with his good friend George Furth. "I'll never know why, except that I had such a bad taste in my mouth after this whole thing was over that I wasn't acting rationally."

CHAPTER 17

Finishing the Hat

HAL PRINCE'S REFUSAL to be cast down by defeat would be tested to its utmost during the next six years. Time after time he would begin a project only to have his hopes dashed and energies frustrated. Believing Comden and Green had a promising idea, Prince agreed to direct and co-produce a musical sequel to Ibsen's *A Doll's House*, called *A Doll's Life*. That closed after five performances. After directing several operas, along with revivals of *Candide* and *Sweeney Todd* on opera stages, he directed a new play by Joanna Glass, *Play Memory*. That also closed quickly. He went on to direct a play by Arthur Kopit, *End of the World*, which met a similar fate. He then decided to produce *Grind*, a new musical that, like *Follies*, used show business as a metaphor for "the dislocations of reality," Jack Kroll wrote. That was another flop. After *Merrily*, it seemed that the door to future success had been locked and bolted. Prince subsequently closed the production side of his office and took a year's leave of absence from the theatre. It was a traumatic period in his life, and if, he said later, he had not been willing to return once more despite the obstacles, despair would have overwhelmed him.

As for Sondheim, his mood after *Merrily*'s failure reflected that of Moss Hart after a similar experience. Hart wrote, "New York is not a city to return to in defeat. Its walls of granite and glass are not inclined to reassure the fearful or console the despairing." As a native New Yorker, he had always looked forward to going home, but now "the city seemed forbidding and impregnable. For the first time I felt as so many must feel who come from the little towns and hamlets to challenge the city—I felt swallowed up by it, erased; and I felt for the first time a hopelessness, a wretched awareness that the best thing I could do was to forget the theatre and take the first job offered . . ."

During an interview in February 1982, Sondheim was still defending the work he and Prince had done on *Merrily*. By June of the same year, he was seriously considering giving up the theatre; "the viciousness about this show," he said, "was so intense . . ." The slightest suggestion that the work was not good was likely to call up a mood of dangerous combativeness, with the questioner usually the loser. Such a defensive posture hid the truth: that the failure of *Merrily* had not only brought about a split with Prince but, because of a particular confluence of forces, left him stranded. After two boom years, when it was being said that more theatres were needed, during the 1982–83 season paid attendance had dropped 22 percent from that of the previous year, gross receipts had fallen 13 percent, and fifteen of Broadway's thirty-nine theatres were dark. Compared with two seasons before, business was off even more: 30 percent. Hal Prince's experience with *A Doll's House,* which had opened and closed within days, was typical. Only Andrew Lloyd Webber's *Evita* and *Joseph and the Amazing Technicolor Dreamcoat* and his new musical, *Cats,* were doing capacity business.

As Gerald Schoenfeld, chairman of the Shubert Organization, saw it, increases in costs and inflationary pressures were only a part of the story. The other had to do with the disappearance of an audience that had supported experimentation and made such works financial, as well as critical, successes. The decline of liberal-arts teaching in schools and colleges meant that the new audience was less cultured and intellectually oriented; wedded to television and movies, it wanted to be entertained rather than challenged. At the same time, because opportunities were dwindling, the pool of emerging talent was drying up. The riskier that musicals became as investments, the greater the pressures to produce for mass appeal. The huge and long-running musicals on Broadway had the same Barnum-and-Bailey combination of extravagant special effects, a minimal book, and the right kind of rock sound, Schoenfeld said. Meanwhile, accountants were assuming the roles once inhabited by such shrewd showmen as Kermit Bloomgarten and David Merrick. When Rodgers and Hammerstein launched *The King and I* for $360,000 in 1951, they raised the money themselves. The 1996 revival cost $5.5 million and was financed by a long list of corporations and production companies. The stable atmosphere and sense of community that had brought about what Arthur Laurents called a theatre of substance had disappeared, and what was left were cheap thrills: whirring helicopters and falling chandeliers.

Sondheim's old friend Roddy McDowall thought the reason any failure, whether on Broadway or in Hollywood, was so traumatic had to do with an awareness that success guaranteed nothing, and particularly not immunity from unfair criticism. Such words were taken at face value because, "ultimately, that is the currency of further employment," he said. "Criticism is a kind of shorthand or calling card. This amounts to the feeling that every time you, personally, launch a new role or idea you are going to the scaffold. Every actor I know with a brain in his head knows that the job he is doing is the last he will ever have. Montgomery Clift used to say, 'It's a great art form and a shitty profession.' " The only way to survive was to have a dogged faith in one's abilities that surmounted everything. He quoted Noël Coward, whose response to vilification and humiliation never varied: "It's perfectly simple. They're wrong." Then there was John Gielgud's calm comment that a bad review might interrupt one's breakfast but should never be allowed to disturb one's lunch. Sondheim said, "The thing that always annoys me about reviewers, or used to, anyway, was that they would all knock every show I ever did and stamp on it and sneer at it. Then, the next time around, they would refer to me as somebody who only had flops, which they had caused." He saw himself as a maverick, an artist in a completely commercial world. "I am serious, but I'm serious in an art that is hardly worth being called one. There's a case to be made for 'Am I wasting my time in the long run?' " When compared with *Pacific Overtures,* for instance, *Merrily We Roll Along,* with its Kaufman-Hart theme, its engaging cast, and nonexperimental score, could hardly be considered an avant-garde idea. But if *Merrily* could fail so spectacularly, what future could there be for a composer as quirkily independent as Sondheim? "Steve was in a very dark place in his head and his life," a friend said. "He was so despondent. It was bleak." The demise of *Merrily* seemed to have brought "the Sondheim age" of the musical to an end, Frank Rich wrote later. "He had run through the dance musical, the operatic musical and the musical play—only to end up, in *Merrily,* with an insular, self-martyring diatribe that blamed Broadway . . . for his own creative and commercial frustrations . . ."

TO BE PESSIMISTIC when things were going well was almost a reflex with Sondheim. In that respect he had something in common with Bernard Berenson. Living with a person as sunny-natured as his wife, Mary, Berenson said, terrified him, since the moment she made some optimistic statement he was convinced that the gods would take proper retribution. There are anecdotes attesting to Sondheim's similar response at moments when he might have been expected to luxuriate in his good fortune. Susan Stroman, who choreographed *A Little Night Music* when it was revived by the New York City Opera, recalled that the ovations were so prolonged on opening night that she, Sondheim, and the director, Scott Ellis, were ushered on the stage to take bows. Sondheim turned to them and said, "Don't forget this, because it's not always like this." His agent, Flora Roberts, said that whenever she called with some good news about sales or attendance figures, Sondheim's invariable response would be, "Yes, but for how long?"

The ability to find every silver cloud's black lining, which had so irritated Prince, had its compensatory aspect, one that showed whenever things were going badly, as during the months after *Merrily*. If Sondheim stayed in the theatre, it was because of a native resilience that seemed to be quite outside conscious control. And as Moss Hart observed, stamina in the theatre "is as necessary an adjunct to success . . . as talent itself." An interviewer who arrived for an appointment one morning found Sondheim exhausted. He had drunk too much wine the night before and had hardly slept. He warned the interviewer that he would probably fall asleep. But as the conversation progressed, he began to revive and was soon engaging in an eager exchange of ideas. When he left an hour later, bouncing down the street, he was walking so fast his companion could barely keep up with him. So although gloomily convinced that his career was over—he told Flora Roberts when he reached the age of fifty in 1980 that no work of any value by a Broadway composer had been created past that age—his ability to improvise in a crisis was about to get the best of him, as usual.

During the summer of 1982 he was in a reflective mood. He said during an interview, "I read this really nice phrase in a review of a book recently, that artists revise the world." It seemed his ability to create a world of his own imaginings had saved him when life was at its bleakest. If his themes were somber—the essential loneliness of the human condition and the death of illusion—in the end it was his ability to metamorphose his private anguish into something outside of himself that had saved him. As time went by, he began to see compensatory aspects emerging in his life, even a kind of richness. That interested him more and more.

The month of June 1982 was a pivotal one. He was approached by a producer, Lewis Allen, suggesting he collaborate with James Lapine, a young writer-director, on a musical version of a novella by Nathanael West, *A Cool Million*. As it happened, Sondheim already knew of Lapine's work, having seen his play *Twelve Dreams* at the New York Shakespeare Festival in 1981.

Sondheim was impressed by the play, which had to do with the Jungian dreams of a girl on the verge of adolescence, played against a spectacular three-level set. It occurred to Sondheim then that Lapine might be just the right person with whom to write a musical, but he did nothing about it. Then Allen made his phone call and Lapine entered his life.

Lapine was then in his thirties, twenty years Sondheim's junior, "a quiet man with a steady way of going about his business," an interviewer wrote. He began in photography, then took a job designing posters and programs at the Yale School of Drama, and soon began teaching graphic design. From there it was a short step to try his hand at directing and writing, making use of his pronounced visual gifts. His first attempt at directing, Gertrude Stein's *Photograph,* a poem in five acts, was considered a revelation, since it made her obscure and elliptical references suddenly meaningful, thanks to his use of vivid painterly and photographic images; the play was a huge success at the Open Space in SoHo in 1977. Lapine went on to write *Table Settings,* a play set around a table standing alone on a stage, and also directed a much-admired production of *March of the Falsettos,* William Finn's one-hour musical, at Playwrights Horizons. When they met in 1982, Lapine was staging a new production of *A Midsummer Night's Dream* for the New York Shakespeare Festival in Central Park, and turning the outdoor stage into part of the larger scene by using real grass, trees, flowers, and hillocks—even a small pond. Someone with such a pronounced visual imagination was bound to appeal to Sondheim.

Lapine said, "When I first met Steve he was very bummed out, in a very low state. He kept referring to himself as a dinosaur. He was complaining, very bitter, thinking about giving up the theatre, and I thought he was joking. I said, 'I am sure if you put your mind to it, you could do a big successful commercial show.' He looked at me and said, 'I would never do that.'

"We had this meeting at his house and lunch was brought in on a silver tray. It was bizarre and unbelievable," he said. "I was not that familiar with his work. I had only seen *Sweeney Todd,* so it was not like going to the glass house to have a conversation with Philip Johnson. I am glad, because otherwise I would have been too intimidated."

He found Sondheim very congenial. "He's so curious, he'll interact with everybody." The idea of writing a musical around *A Cool Million* was abandoned but they quickly decided to work together on something else. Rather than tell a conventional story, they liked the idea of writing a musical structured around a theme with variations. They tried to put together photographs of different people to see whether they were inspired to invent relationships between them. That did not work. They turned to painting, and Lapine immediately thought of *A Sunday Afternoon on the Island of La Grande Jatte,* the painting by Georges Seurat that he had used in *Photographs,* which had caught his imagination since the moment he first saw it. That famous nineteenth-century work depicts a group of people promenading along the banks of an island in the middle of the Seine, now a residential area of Paris, but then still bucolic. There are trees, children at play, a dog, a yacht, and people seated on the grass. For all of its activity, the scene has a transfixed quality, as if the inhabitants of the picture have, reversing Pygmalion's powers, been transformed from flesh and blood into statues.

Sondheim said, "All those people in that painting. You speculate on why none of them are looking at each other . . . Maybe someone was having an affair . . . or one was related to someone else. And then Jim said, 'Of course, the main character's missing—the artist.' When he said that I knew we had a real play."

As Sondheim began to read what little was known about Seurat's life, he became even more excited. "Here was this marvellous, mysterious genius who died of some strange disease, probably a rare form of meningitis. He led a double life—on the one hand, almost every night he had dinner at his mother's house. Only a few weeks before he died [he was only thirty-one] she discovered he'd kept a mistress and had a baby by her. The more I found out about him . . . the more I realized, 'My God, this is all about music.' "

What caused this particular awareness had to do with Seurat's theory of painting, which was based on the discovery that one could achieve a more striking result by placing, for instance, the primary colors of blue and yellow close together on a canvas, which the eye perceived as a brilliant green, than if the same colors were mixed beforehand on a palette. Seurat's contemporaries the impressionists were already using a variant of this technique, juxtaposing different shades and tones of one or more colors, with the aim of heightening the shimmering, flickering quality of their canvases. Seurat took the technique a step further, laying down speckled clusters of dots, blobs, and swirls that were calculated to leap into focus when seen from the right distance. Like the Impressionists, he, too, painted his areas of shadow with their complementary opposites, so that the vivid yellow-green of the grass would contain echoes of surrounding areas such as the sky, and its shadows would tend to be reddish purple. Similarly, the shadows in an orange-red dress would be painted as greenish blue. But while the Impressionists wanted their paintings to capture light and moving air, Seurat aimed for a quality of arrested movement that infused his scenes with the puzzling intensity of dreams.

In tackling a subject like Seurat, who rebelled against the prevailing style of Impressionism and whose career was scarcely made before it ended, and who had to endure similar criticism that his work was "all mind and no heart," Sondheim had found a subject whose parallels to his life were direct and unforced. Of *Sunday in the Park with George* (the title they chose), Sondheim said, "The show belongs to James. I'm not knocking it, the score is wonderful and I'm very proud of it, but that's James's show . . . I never thought of myself as Seurat, but I never think of myself as anybody in any of the shows. The only thing consciously autobiographical that I ever wrote was 'Opening Doors' in *Merrily.*" That did not, by any means, imply there was no connection. "What I'm doing when I'm writing is acting. That's why the best playwrights, with the exception of Chekhov and a couple of others, have been actors. And so I'm able to infuse myself. So when I'm writing the song 'Finishing the Hat' [from *Sunday*], half of it is writing about what I, Steve, feel, and the other is what Seurat feels. And I'm aware of both going on at the same time. I'm able to get into Seurat's head because there's a part of me that knows something about this, just as there's a part of me that knows something about Sweeney . . . I think all writers get attracted to stories that resonate in them," whether or not they know it consciously.

EARLY IN THEIR COLLABORATION Sondheim wrote the following note for *Sunday:* "The show is, in part, about how creation takes on a life of its own, how artists feed off art (we off Seurat); the artist's relationship to his material." That comment arose from weekly meetings that continued for a couple of months before the actual writing began in September 1982. Sondheim loved the idea of presenting a theme with variations. "Every time I listen to Rachmaninoff's variations on Paganini, I'm stunned, and I thought it would be a lot of fun to try theatrically. When we'd fastened on the idea of using Seurat's painting and showing how it was made for the first act, I was all excited because I thought the second act could be a series of variations or comments on the painting." It might take the form of a revue, with songs about various aspects of art, or the painting itself.

That idea was soon abandoned. "Jim's first response was, 'We must carry some kind of storyline from the first act or there'll be no focus of interest.' The danger always is to impose a form on material when you're just doing it because you like the form," he said. "That's probably the greatest pitfall of all writing, as far as I'm concerned, but I am constantly slipping towards that quicksand." The first act, in which Seurat is so obsessed with his work that he neglects Dot, his mistress, and she is obliged to leave him for a pastry baker and emigrate to America, came together fairly naturally. Their story was interspersed with vignettes about the others in the painting in which she figured prominently—a boatman, a nurse, a couple, a soldier—all of them with their own stories. As Lapine began to write and Sondheim to compose, they discovered that their working methods dovetailed in an interesting way. Lapine called himself "fast and sloppy." Sondheim worked with his usual exhaustive meticulousness. It was a relief to have someone like Lapine who "plunges in and worries later," Sondheim said. He began showing sketches to Lapine at earlier and earlier stages, despite his hard-and-fast rule, because Lapine had said, " 'Please, anything, just so it will help me write.' He wants to hear what I have in mind musically." Sondheim broke his own rule with no regrets. Lapine "was the first person I got to trust entirely with unfinished work," he said. For his part, Lapine worried that his responses were inadequate. "I consider myself not overly emotional. I don't enthuse the way Hal Prince does, and that is hard for him. Just when he needs me, I am suddenly catatonic. He plays a song and I'll say, 'That's nice.' "

Writing with Sondheim involved the usual requirement that the playwright contribute lengthy monologues that would never be used, but which would help the composer further define a character that had sprung to life in the mind of its originator. Sondheim said, "For 'Color and Light' . . . and even for the title song, James wrote interior monologues never to be spoken. They were sort of stream-of-consciousness pieces that I could take from." However, he became concerned that his colloquial use of language would be at odds with Lapine's style and "tear the extremely delicate fabric of Jim's prose." Lapine's sentences had been constructed with such care "that by merely changing one syllable—to make it work musically—I would kill the entire phrase." He eventually wrote lyrics using some of Lapine's passages as spoken interludes within the songs themselves.

The final version of act 2, which did not appear for months, takes the action forward to the present day. It describes George, a contemporary artist, working in light sculptures, who turns out to be the great-grandson of Seurat. But whereas Seurat was operating outside the conventional art world of his day, his modern counterpart has to solicit money, commissions, and patrons, if only to finance his expensive undertakings. He is experiencing, Frank Rich observed, a crisis that has some parallels with that of Sondheim after *Merrily.* In an attempt to revitalize his original vision George discovers his kinship with Seurat and returns to his roots, making a pilgrimage to Seurat's Parisian park. In so doing he also acts as a surrogate Seurat to reconcile at last with Dot, the rejected mistress, discovering Seurat's love and need for her. It is a crucial moment of recognition, the one that seemed to be missing from *Merrily* and only hinted at in *Sweeney Todd.* With the exception of *Forum,* it was a rare happy ending for a Sondheim musical and a highly significant event.

Rich wrote, " 'Connect, George, connect,' George tells himself—and that's what he and Sondheim finally do. *Sunday* allows Sondheim at last to channel his own passion into a musical that is not about marriage, class inequities or other things he doesn't seem sincerely to care about, but is instead about what does matter to him—art itself, and his own predicament as a driven artist whose austere vision, like Seurat's, is often incorrectly judged as heartless."

PLAYWRIGHTS HORIZONS, the Off Broadway group with which James Lapine was associated, had a sterling season in 1981–82, with five long-running hits, including Christopher Durang's black spoof about parochial school education, *Sister Mary Ignatius Explains It All for You*. Led by André Bishop, its thirty-four-year-old artistic director, the ambitious season was being produced in a tiny, 150-seat theatre, with very little width, no wing space on stage right, and no fly space. Despite these handicaps, its operating budget had jumped from $622,000 in fiscal 1980 to more than $2 million in 1982 and an estimated $3.5 million in 1983, the year *Sunday* was to receive its three-week series of workshop performances. Among the Off Broadway theatres (so defined according to the size of the theatre by Actors Equity rules), only the Public Theater, with a budget of almost $9 million, had more to spend. A good deal of the theatre's prosperity had to do with its ability to try out plays and musicals in its tiny home theatre and then act as its own producer to take a promising show into a larger house Off Broadway or even on Broadway. Using shrewd judgment, Playwrights Horizons had done so successfully on several occasions, and money that otherwise would have gone to Broadway producers had come back to it in the form of profits. There was every chance that if *Sunday* showed any promise at all, it would move to a larger theatre, although Sondheim was at pains not to give that impression. "This is not a way station to Broadway. It is a work in progress. We want to take a look at it and let it determine its own future course."

André Bishop said, "Because Steve was more eclectic in his tastes, or because he was working with someone young and new, he went into what was then the creative remnant of the American theatre, which is these non-profit theatres. None of the others, the remaining teams of what used to be known as Broadway writers, did so at the time. And the system was breaking down. It was simply too expensive, too difficult to mount musicals regularly any more, and Steve, either because of Lapine or because of something else in him, and a feeling that things had to change after the terrible disaster of *Merrily*, did something that was the inevitable right thing in the artistic life of anyone. He threw himself into a different world. He did something quite practical, whether he knew it or not. He found a consistent venue for mounting his shows. He clearly realized that it couldn't be just Broadway directly, like the old days. At a time when many writers I know have shut down or dwell in the past, or wish the old Broadway system they loved was still existing, he simply moved on. And he grew. His talent changed and refined itself."

At their first encounter, Bishop was very nervous. "We met at some restaurant and I had a million martinis just out of nerves and was trying to be impressive. I think Steve was then trying to decide whether he wanted to go ahead and do *Sunday* at Playwrights, and I probably said foolish things about French composers . . . Anyway, the meeting seemed to go well and we went ahead.

"I remember two things. He loved to argue, take the contrary view or challenge your view simply for the joy of discussion; and the other thing I remember, that is part of the makeup of very gifted writers, was that he listened. You could very easily, almost too easily, change his mind." Bishop "could not begin to imagine" how they managed to mount a full production of *Sunday* on their postage-stamp stage, "and I mean fully, not orchestrated, but fully cast, designed, costumed, with scenery and lights. It was a big deal for us." His only regret was that he was so busy trying to raise money that "I don't think I behaved as helpfully or strongly as a producer should. And when someone very eminent walks into a smaller venue and is the star of the event, you tend to ascribe to them powers that they may or may not have.

"He used to come in this old beige raincoat, this strange raincoat, and sit in the back, then leave. Then he and Lapine would meet and rework, and it was a heady, heady time. Parts of that show were never as good again, and some of that had to do with the space." At the end of the first act, Seurat has completed his great work and it springs to life in front of the audience, the actors precisely placed in their positions. Bishop said, "Because our theatre was small, with a real frame, the proportions of the stage painting to the auditorium were life size, and when that painting came together and all those actors started singing, people went wild, *wild,* from the joy of it, really. It was never quite as good on Broadway. The other thing I remember was that because we were doing workshops we would often make speeches before a performance. I used to appear every night, and occasionally Sondheim and Lapine would be coerced into making one. It was my turn to make the speech the night 'Finishing the Hat' went into the show. I said we were putting in a new song, I wouldn't say where it was going, but Mandy Patinkin [playing Seurat] would be reading the score because he hadn't got it memorized yet. His version of 'Finishing the Hat' was quite spontaneous and probably the

The poster for *Sunday in the Park with George*, 1984

Mandy Patinkin in the role of George Seurat

best performance it ever, ever was. Because no one had any time to fuss about it. And the audience quickly realized it was *the* song, and in my view it's the best one in the show, and one of his keynote songs ever, and the people went wild again, *wild*. It was a thrilling moment, and we never quite got it back."

Mandy Patinkin also remembered the first time he sang that song, which describes the inner battle between Seurat's longing for Dot, who is leaving him, and the act of creating, which is so revelatory and so transporting that it blots out every other need:

> Studying the hat,
> Entering the world of the hat,
> Reaching through the world of the hat
> Like a window,
> Back to this one from that.
>
> Studying a face,
> Stepping back to look at a face
> Leaves a little space in the way like a window,
> But to see—
> It's the only way to see.

One morning he, Paul Gemignani, and Sondheim went across the street to a coffee bar, where there was a piano in the basement that they could use. "Steve sat down and played this song, which I had been waiting for, for days—'Finishing the Hat,' which is also the story of his life. So by the time he was finished he was drenched in sweat, completely dripping. It wasn't at all hot in there. He was terrified, just terrified. I don't know whether he didn't think it was good—whether he needed our approval—but it's at moments like that when I love Steve forever. Because I'm terrified all the time myself. So we're sitting there after listening to this, and Gemignani is in tears and I'm like, 'I've got to do this! I've got to do it tonight!' So I taped the lyric sheet, just the words, on the back of the sketch pad I carried and worked on it all day. And I sang it. It was an evening when Mike Nichols was there and all of his friends. As the song ended the place went insane, an ovation I'd never heard before. And it crippled me for the rest of my life to try to sing that song, because I felt I could never do what I must have done then."

> And when the woman that you wanted goes,
> You can say to yourself, "Well, I give what I give."
> But the woman who won't wait for you knows

That, however you live,
There's a part of you always standing by,
Mapping out the sky,
Finishing a hat . . .
Starting on a hat . . .
Finishing a hat . . .
> [He is showing his sketch to the dog, Fifi]
Look, I made a hat . . .
Where there never was a hat . . .

Sondheim had been reluctant to consider Patinkin because he was a tenor, albeit with a wide, two-octave range, and he had conceived the part for a baritone. Patinkin, who with a beard would bear an uncanny resemblance to Seurat and would become one of Sondheim's principal interpreters, was reluctant to do the necessary audition, because he had played the leading role of Che Guevara in *Evita* on Broadway and thought he was past all that. But he finally did agree, learned "Color and Light," and sang it for Sondheim, Gemignani, and Lapine. Sondheim asked him to sing it in different keys and agreed he should play the part. Patinkin also remembers a funny episode involving the song Sondheim had written for Spot, a male dog, and Fifi, the female, who appear in the painting and are shown in cardboard outline on the stage. "Originally it was written for two offstage voices to sing the song," he said. Being an excellent mimic, Patinkin asked for the chance to invent voices. "It was remarkable—a tour de force," Sondheim said admiringly. "So these four grown men are in this room auditioning dog voices!" Patinkin said. "And Steve is literally saying things like, 'N-n-n-n-no. It's a little too Hermione [Gingold].' "

They had not seen much of Sondheim during the rehearsal period, since he was usually at home writing songs. Patinkin got to the moment in the plot when Marie, who is his grandmother, is trying to tell him about Dot. Patinkin kept waiting for the song to arrive, and Sondheim kept saying that the moment was already so perfectly expressed in the dialogue that a song was not needed. Then, one evening, after Patinkin expressed his frustration and Sondheim agreed to try to write one, they talked for hours about what the character was thinking and feeling. They talked at length about their mothers, Patinkin said. "I can't remember specifically what Steve said, but it was, essentially, the impossibility of getting through to his mother. I remember we talked about how much we wanted to love our mothers, connect with them and not hate them, and how hard the struggle was."

He also recalled a confrontation he had with Sondheim near the end of the rehearsal period. "When I started rehearsing, the only song written was 'Color and Light.' We went through four or five weeks of rehearsal and I was just sitting there drawing. I would walk to a mark, count to five, and then leave—that was supposed to be my song. It was quite torturing, and one day I lost my temper. And Steve just closed his book, got up, and left. I asked him years later, 'When you did that, Steve, it just seemed you were sitting on a volcano. How did you learn to do that?,' I said, because I needed to learn. He said he had learned long ago that he didn't dare confront someone, because he'd want to kill him."

Patinkin thought the character of Seurat was the hardest for Sondheim to write, because "George was Sondheim." He continued, "It's much easier to write about what George observed. The harder thing for Steve was to write what George was feeling." But that was the reason why he composed. "The words in his songs are his therapy, his lessons, his struggles. These are the things he is furious about, never wants to revisit again, from a confrontation with someone like me, or a mother figure, or anyone else, and the other side is everything he wishes he could embrace, everything he believes in, everything he feels . . . What spurs us on and tortures us all is this deep desire to connect."

Thanks to his collaboration with Lapine, Sondheim was also introduced to a new designer, Tony Straiges, and a talented young orchestrator, Michael Starobin, who would take on the role that had been dominated by Tunick, and acquit himself admirably. Starobin said that since Sondheim thought so well in pianistic terms, he tried to leave the piano part unchanged and just add instrumental color. "I represent his musical interests, but also the interests of the play, and I try to see how much I can get away with in adding my own creative impulses." After the first orchestral rehearsal, Sondheim said, " 'You don't need to make my songs work.' Meaning I was changing their textures too much, embellishing at moments when it wasn't called for."

Bernadette Peters made her memorable entrance into Sondheim's life at this time. A spirited actress, dancer, and cabaret singer, she had played leading roles on and Off Broadway and was cast as Dot by James Lapine. "The music is very complicated, something you really have to learn. I never thought I would find myself doing a Sondheim show." She enjoyed the challenge, which also involved playing the part of Marie. But when asked to appear in the Broadway production the following year she was hesitant.

"She said you sort of lose Dot after the first scene," Sondheim explained. "She makes appearances, but you don't know what she is going through . . . At first we thought, 'Well, she just wants a couple more songs,' or something like that. But the more we thought, the more it made sense, and we were wondering how to work her into the second park scene after 'Color and Light.' I don't know how it came up, but John Guare said, 'Why doesn't she learn to read while he's drawing?,' and it clicked . . . That kind of suggestion is invaluable." Peters was delighted. With her petite and shapely figure, her masses of golden brown ringlets, her porcelain skin and liquid, heavy-lidded eyes, Peters was the quintessential artist's model. Starobin recalled, "When they offered her the part, in the original script she is supposed to slip out of Marie's dress in the second act to show that it hides a young and beautiful girl and walk off—her last exit. But Bernadette said, 'I don't do nude,' so they took it out." (It should be noted that she did appear in déshabille a couple of times.) She was cast in the next Sondheim-Lapine show and joined the group of actors who would be invited back routinely for future undertakings. She was an asset to have on a stage, "because she brings such a joyous quality to anything she does," Sondheim said admiringly. In future cabaret performances Peters would become known for her skill at conveying the wrenching sweetness concealed beneath the tart exterior of some of Sondheim's best songs, including "Not a Day Goes By," "With So Little to Be Sure Of," "Being Alive," and many others. "The chemistry between the voice of the wise child and the lyrics of Broadway's ultimate sophisticate filled the hall with a profoundly bittersweet feeling of lessons learned on roads long traveled," Stephen Holden wrote. One of the photographs on her wall was autographed by Sondheim with the tongue-in-cheek words "You may not be talented, but you sure are beautiful. Yours forever, Steve."

LAPINE HAD TO STRUGGLE with a basic problem: how well could the sensibility of a nineteenth-century French painter be conveyed by twentieth-century Americans for whom his world would be inevitably remote as well as foreign? How did one convey that these puppetlike figures seemed to be part of a dreamlike drama taking place in the artist's mind? The fact that so little was known about Seurat's life was liberating in one sense, but on the other hand it meant that no clues existed to reveal whatever hidden meanings lay behind the statuesque images. Lapine's first idea was to draw the personages in the painting in depth, giving them scope and dimension. But not only did the first act become unwieldy—an hour and forty-four minutes in rehearsal—but the people themselves threatened to eclipse the figures of Seurat and his mistress. So their episodes had to be compressed into vignettes, and songs already written had to be dropped. The story had to focus on the ways in which such a work took over the artist's life, and its rewards, as well as the price to be paid, almost as if the central figure were an abstraction, a personification of obsession. How to extend that concept through another act proved extremely difficult to do. Act 2 had been performed only three times when the three weeks of workshops ended. The success of the project convinced everyone that *Sunday* had a great future, but it was only half-finished.

The Broadway producer Emanuel Azenberg, known for his productions of Neil Simon and Tom Stoppard plays, among others, was invited to see *Sunday* by Bernard Jacobs, president of the Shubert Organization, and his wife, Betty. He said, "Tom Stoppard has a quote, 'Public postures often take the configuration of private derangement.' It's from his play *The Real Thing.* So I went to *Sunday*, and it was a mystery to me. Why was this a musical? What is a musical that this one wasn't? Is it entertainment for the great dull bulk of the nation?

"The answer was that it was being done for private derangement. It's crazy if you think about it. There is no second act, and Bernie Jacobs is saying to me, 'Come on, let's do it.' " Azenberg agreed to co-produce the musical on Broadway. He spoke in particular of the songs "Finishing the Hat" and "Children and Art." "The work grows on you the more you hear it. It is not unlike a Stoppard experience. You have to invest something of yourself." He said, "I arrived at liking it somewhere in the middle. This one I did for private derangement, and it turned out to be humbling. I learned genuinely to like something I had no opinion about, by being confronted with it." He paused and said, "If there's a moment when I salute and respect Sondheim, it's to acknowledge that I heard the cry of the creator."

A budget of $2.1 million was set, and previews were announced for April 1984. The theatre chosen, the Booth, one of the smaller houses, lost a few more seats when a row was removed so as to uncover an old orchestra pit. The tedious process of refining act 1 and developing act 2 began. Lapine wrote every morning, rehearsed all afternoon, went to the evening performance, had a postmortem session after that, and snatched a few hours of sleep. Music director Paul Gemignani said that there was still no music for the second act. The only song that had been written was the opening number, "It's Hot Up Here." The cast would go as far as it could and then read the rest of the play. Patinkin said, "The first act was so brilliant and every night we knew the second act was a disaster and it was affecting our performances. I remember opening my dressing room door one evening and finding Lapine and Sondheim inside, and I'm saying to Steve, 'Write me anything. Even if it's a piece of shit! I don't care. Just write me anything!' And he is just sitting there saying, 'No, no, no, no. I know.' What he was saying was he couldn't write until he was ready."

Gemignani continued, "We got closer and closer to the previews and there was no music. I would call up Steve and he would say, 'I can't—I'm trying—' and you could hear him being nuts. Then one day he walked in with 'Children and Art' and 'Lesson #8.' Then after that he wrote the big, long middle song, 'Putting It Together.' All of that was three or four days before the first preview! He saved the show singlehandedly."

SEARCHING FOR the exact musical metaphor, Sondheim made use of repeated phrases, such as "bring order to the whole," "color and light," "connect," "get through to something new," and "move on," that would have a cumulative effect as the evening progressed; he did the same thing with musical themes. His principal motif, "an ornamental turn of three or four short notes followed by an upward-reaching interval, usually of a minor third or fourth," John Rockwell wrote, was introduced at the start and repeated as the refrain for "Color and Light" in the first act. "His use of these little building blocks hardly precludes soaring lyricism, however, especially with the warmly orchestrated sustaining lines to counterpoint the pointillism. At its best, this method recalls the lyrical climaxes in the operas of Leoš Janáček, which are similarly built up from interlocking motifs, repeated over and over in a climactic upward curve." Sondheim said later that he had been influenced by Benjamin Britten's operatic works, and called it "my Britten score."

The score builds towards Marie's aria, "Children and Art." Rockwell continued, "This song is vital conceptually as the clearest statement of the claims of life next to those of art . . . And it completes the upward-reaching opening phrase by inverting it into another ornamental turn followed by a downward reach of a minor third.

"Such parallelism isn't just clever; it knits the score together into a coherent whole that listeners sense even if they don't realize just what is going on. That is why it is so astonishing that 'Children and Art' was . . . only added in the final days . . . Perhaps just as Seurat groped for just the right combination of shape and color in his painting, Mr. Sondheim had to struggle intuitively to complete his musical painting . . . If so, then the last-minute composition of this crucial song becomes yet another proof that the artists' intuitions can speak more powerfully than their initial, conscious intentions."

Having arrived at a complete score, Lapine and Sondheim turned their attention to the finale. The idea of returning to the tableau, which ended the first act so effectively, was abandoned as being too repetitive. Another idea, which had the young George drawing his version of *La Grande Jatte*, was also discarded. Lapine said, "It would have spelled everything out and we wanted an ending that would be sort of ineffable." Sondheim said, "It's finding that line where everything isn't exactly explained, and yet doesn't rouse hostility in the audience because they're confused." Michael Bennett, Tom Stoppard, John Guare, and Hal Prince were all solicited for advice late in the previews. Then the final ending was decided upon, in which the young George accepts his human needs for connectedness and love and makes his way back to the demands of art.

WHILE *The Frogs,* his only other mature musical to have been initiated outside Broadway, had its full quotient of Sondheimian wit, it also contained a setting of Shakespearean verse from *Cymbeline,* "Fear No More," the kind of indulgence Broadway might not have allowed. His second attempt to write for another kind of stage had, similarly, allowed him to write with far more subtlety and stylistic freedom than would have been the case if his work had been burdened by the need to make huge profits. The pioneering experience had clearly energized him and allowed aspects of his talent to emerge with a new clarity and vitality. In contrast to his old friend Harold Prince, who battled the odds as he tried to remain on Broadway, finally ending up as the successful director of big, popular hits (*Phantom of the Opera, Kiss of the Spider Woman, Show Boat*), Sondheim had discovered how liberating it could be to experiment in a world that valued his art and nurtured his gifts.

"*Sunday,* not to mention its success with audiences, blurs old definitions," Frank Rich wrote, "those that separate Broadway from Off Broadway, show music and serious music, commercial entertainment and art, the theatre and musical theatre . . ." With this crowning achievement Sondheim, the logical heir to the American musical theatre tradition, had "changed the texture of the musical as radically as Hammerstein once did in *Show Boat* and *Oklahoma!*—but, even more than Hammerstein did, he has built a bridge between the musical and the more daring playwriting of his time. Should Sondheim keep moving on and moving others with him, he may yet become . . . one who leaves our theatre profoundly and permanently changed."

The enthusiasm of some critics was not shared by them all. For every critic who, like Jack Kroll, wrote, "To say that this show breaks new ground is not enough; it also breaks new sky, new water, new flesh and new spirit," there were others who thought the musical was boring, lacking distinction, thin and lifeless. The list of failings was a long one and caught its creators off guard. Lapine said, "I was in a state of shock. I thought, 'Okay, if they have mixed feelings about it, but pans?' " It was a kind of vindication of Prince's belief that Sondheim's work had become too rarefied for mainstream Broadway taste. Prince said, "It's a shocking thing to reach a certain age and say, 'I wouldn't go back for anything.' I wouldn't want to be twenty now and try to make the same career. I don't think anyone ever will again. Because you can't afford to fail any more. It's all about money. It wasn't. I didn't care about that. Why do you think one does *Pacific Overtures?* You go in and lose all the money, which wasn't a lot. And you could pick up and go on. Not anymore. So you don't do *Pacific Overtures,* or you take it Off Broadway. But it won't be the same."

That *Sunday in the Park with George* went on to have a successful run despite the negative reviews must have something to do with the first act, which culminates, as Bishop observed, in a magical moment, vis-à-vis the quieter and more demanding charms of the second. At the very least, *Sunday* was an arresting homage to the genius tutelae of a painting. It was also true that the *New York Times* played a central role in keeping the work before the public eye. Articles were being written about it throughout 1984, beginning in January and continuing through October. There was a particularly graceful tribute to Sondheim's career in the Sunday magazine section that spring, with a cover photograph of the composer himself, posed triumphantly in front of the musical's set. As Harold Evans, former editor of the London *Sunday Times,* who waged a successful campaign on behalf of the British victims of thalidomide, made clear, the trick of penetrating the public consciousness is the same message, endlessly repeated. If so, that message was being heard. *Sunday* ran for more than a year, closing in the autumn of 1985, having earned back three-quarters of its investment, which the judicious Bernard Jacobs thought was a good report card for a show the appeal of which would always be limited. Frank Rich admitted he was probably responsible for keeping interest in *Sunday* alive.

Its collaborators might be forgiven for thinking that even if the musical did not have a long run, it would be a winner in the annual Tony Awards. And even though it was competing against a much more commercial musical, *La Cage aux Folles,* the farcical French film that had been adapted by Harvey Fierstein and Jerry Herman and directed by Arthur Laurents, *Sunday* won the Critics' Circle Award on the first ballot by a margin of ten votes to four. It also received seven Drama Desk Awards, including that of outstanding musical. The number of Tony nominations—ten in all, including those for best musical, score, book, and direction—was flattering, and *Sunday* might have been expected to garner several of them. But, to everyone's surprise, the award for best librettist went to Fierstein, for best direction to Laurents, and for best composer to Herman, and *Sunday*'s consolation prizes were two awards, for best scene design (Tony Straiges) and best lighting (Richard Nelson). Herman said at the ceremony that his award proved "the simple, hummable show . . . was alive and well at the Palace!" Most people thought that was meant to be a criticism of Sondheim's work, including Sondheim, who was there.

But just as interest in *Sunday* was trailing off, it was revived by an announcement that could not have been predicted. It won the Pulitzer Prize for drama in the spring of 1985, only the sixth musical ever to be so honored. Sondheim learned the news in a conference call from Jacobs and his partner, Gerald Schoenfeld. That afternoon, following a matinee performance of *Sunday* at the Booth, Peters and Patinkin mobbed Sondheim and Lapine and everyone drank champagne. But the best news was at the box office, which was reporting ticket sales at the rate of $10,000 an hour, or twice the rate of the day before. Almost three years after the idea had first been discussed by Sondheim and Lapine, their work had reached its moment of triumph. *Time* magazine commented, "*Sunday in the Park* stands before its audience . . . a cool, unblinking object. Only a closer look reveals it as a shapely object of art."

André Bishop recalled that he would get a letter of thanks from Sondheim after every show. "And he would always say to me, or write, 'Dear André, Thanks for the use of the hall. Best, Steve.' And when I was younger I used to think, 'Well, we did more than just give him the theatre! Is that all he thinks we did? We raised money, we tried to help with the show . . .' But I realized, way back in Playwrights Horizons, that raising money for that first show, helping with the rewrites, being warm and supportive and caring, that's all fine. But actually, once again he nailed it. Because the best thing we did for him was to give him the use of the hall, at a time when he wasn't sure he wanted to go back into the hall at all."

CHAPTER 18

No More

S ONDHEIM'S DECISION to move into Off Broadway's liberating
atmosphere would be so pivotal, André Bishop maintained, that in
the next decade he would go from being the object of a cult to being the most
important figure in American musical theatre. Sondheim would, whenever
the subject arose, rebut that idea energetically, but it seemed clear, after the
success of *Sunday in the Park,* that the pioneering experiment brought with it
a new measure of respect. By the autumn of 1984, *Sunday* was doing a brisk
business at the Booth, a new production of *West Side Story* had opened at Her
Majesty's Theatre in London, *Pacific Overtures* was having its first revival, by
the York Theatre Company Off Broadway, and *Sweeney Todd* was being
revived on two opera stages, by the Houston Grand Opera and by the New
York City Opera at Lincoln Center. This showed that after two decades of
"wary regard as, variously, the savior of the American musical, a heartless
antimelodist or a closet opera composer," Alan Rich wrote, Sondheim had
finally come into his own. What once had looked like sheer perversity, a
determination not to give the audience what it wanted, was now seen as an
asset to be admired, for, as Ned Sherrin said, "It's also the reason why Stephen
is interesting. He will bold-headedly continue to not do what he's done
before. He's always knocking his head against another impossible subject."

After years of asserting his dislike of travel and his devotion to Manhattan, where, he said, cocooned in his second-story back room, he could hear nothing more distracting than bird song, he had bought a country house. His stepmother had died in 1980 at the age of seventy-six, leaving their house in Stamford, an old colonial built in 1776, in which his half-brother Herbert was also living. It needed various repairs and emergency work on the wide floorboards. Walter Sondheim said that by then Steve was looking for a country house and thinking of restoring it. So he hired a firm to sand down the floors. Somehow, Herbie was consulted about the way they should be refinished and wanted them just the way they had been, back to a dark stain. "Steve wouldn't talk to Herbie for a couple of months," Walt said.

Sondheim went looking elsewhere, in an unspoiled part of the state, and at length found another old colonial, white clapboard with black shutters, long and rectangular, half concealed behind huge rhododendrons. It was on about sixty acres, and across the road was a converted barn that was also on the property, with an apartment in it. Peter Wooster was invited to take possession of the apartment and oversee the design of the house and grounds. During the next few years he would transform a pleasant lawn into an exquisite formal garden and sitting area, where Sondheim frequently entertained. There was a swimming pool, there were guest quarters, and there would be plenty of room for Max, a raffish black poodle the size of a small horse with a romping, puppylike disposition. Although he had thought of it as a weekend house, Sondheim began to spend more and more time there. The formal rooms were decorated in his usual fawns and browns and had an unlived-in feeling, as if he spent his time on the large porch overlooking the garden, or in his study at the back of the house. That had a large picture window which overlooked the grounds, with a couch drawn up beside it; there was also a huge grand piano, buried under some kind of covering, with a portable keyboard on top. There was a spacious, friendly kitchen, and tucked into corners were memorabilia of all kinds, including a front-page photograph of himself, Peters, and Lapine outside the Booth the day *Sunday* won the Pulitzer Prize, and the painting his mother had made of Fox Hill Farm, whose resemblance to his own country house was "spooky," he said.

At home in New York he was being well cared for by Louis Vargas, who in addition to his culinary prowess had gradually taken over the complete running of the house. He supervised all the routine cleaning and house repairs, decided which clothes should be sent out for cleaning, even altered clothes and gave Sondheim his characteristic haircuts. He had mastered the art of dealing with Sondheim's hair, which changed from straight and lanky to crisp and curly as it went gray. Sondheim said, "He was the equivalent of a wife. In the traditional sense." Their harmonious relationship lasted until Louis's death of AIDS in 1993. When he knew he was ill and would not recover, he set about training his Brazilian replacement, Luiz Andrea Loureiro, who to avoid confusion was always known as Andrea. He learned to be almost as good a cook as Louis, and a houseman par excellence. Patricia Sinnott was in the office until 1987, taking charge of the myriad details of Sondheim's increasingly complicated professional life. She was the one who transcribed whatever late-night additions had been logged into the computer, and attended to his huge correspondence. "He would keep a regular régime even though it was his house. I never saw him late, or in slippers or a bathrobe. He would breakfast upstairs, where he had a separate little guest quarters with its own bathroom and small kitchen. He would sit there with the *New York Times* and coffee. By ten or ten-thirty he was already in the studio with the door closed, and he would truly work through until six." She added, "He would, at times, procrastinate and wait until the last-minute deadline, but he always came through, and then some."

She was the one who fielded the phone calls, sometimes from friends who wanted to know how he was but were hesitant to call his private number for fear of disturbing him. She was often approached by students with music they wanted to show the great man. There was a Japanese student who wanted to interview Sondheim for a thesis and who sent her flowers in a not very subtle effort to win preferential status. By then the word was out that Sondheim was generous of his time with students. "I just love teaching," he said later. "Teaching to me is a sacred profession, and I think art is a form of teaching anyway. My life was changed and saved by teachers," he continued, referring to Pollock, Barrow, Hammerstein, and Babbitt. "So any chance I get, I try to do it."

Sondheim had been involved with the Dramatists Guild for years, and its president for the last four, when, in 1977, he decided that what New York City needed was a festival for young playwrights on the model of the one which was held in London annually. He appointed a committee consisting of, among others, Mary Rodgers, Jules Feiffer, and himself and held a press conference. That was such a disappointment (only one theatre critic came) that the idea was dropped. But two years later, when he attended the festival in London at the Royal Court Theatre, it was such a moving and exhilarating experience that he returned to the project with renewed enthusiasm. Gerald Chapman, the man behind the British venture, was brought to New York to organize the first American Young Playwrights Festival for playwrights eighteen years old and younger, and it turned out to be as splendid an event as the one in London had been. The festival has been held annually since 1981, and many of its promising young writers have taken up theatrical careers. Sondheim also established a Dramatists Guild workshop for composers and lyricists and worked with ASCAP on a similar program. He said, "I always am astonished at the amount of sophisticated good work done by people who have had almost no public exposure." The situation had changed so much since the early days. When he was starting out, there was only Broadway, and if you could get your show on, you stood a chance of making some money. Now, with the appearance of Off Broadway and regional theatre, there was perhaps more opportunity but less money to be made, which meant that young writers had to have full-time employment elsewhere and had less time for writing. On Broadway an unknown had almost no chance of being heard. So many young writers wanted advice, which he did not give except to tell them to look for an agent. "You know, I don't tell about the bleakness of it all," he said. "But that's the whole thing. They should know that for themselves, if they can read newspapers."

Whether by accident or design he was becoming an effective mentor. Terri McKean recalled that as an undergraduate at Ohio State University, she decided to write about one of Sondheim's musicals for a history course. "The story was that he didn't answer letters," she said. But he replied to hers and even sent a tape giving detailed answers because, he told her, she had asked such intelligent questions. That led to an invitation to visit him in New York. "I didn't know what to expect when I went to his house, but we ended up talking for well over an hour," she said. "I don't think if I met Andrew Lloyd Webber . . ." Sondheim made her believe in herself. She has become a stage manager and hopes to work on a Broadway musical.

Freddie Gershon, chief executive officer of Music Theatre International, which licenses Sondheim's musicals, recalled one evening when he went to a brilliant reading at the Young Playwrights Festival. At the end, he left the theatre and was going down Forty-fourth Street when he saw Sondheim about fifteen feet ahead, moving fast. "Then I see him duck into Sardi's, and by the time I get there he has already ordered a drink. So I go up to him and he turns around and tears are streaming down his face. And I said, 'It's wonderful,' and he said, 'I know. I am just so moved when I see this whole new generation of talent that isn't trying to copy me or anyone else, but just trying to be themselves.' And so we're just there alone—it's like an odd hour, around nine o'clock at night—and he's later joined by Peter Wooster and some people who are wandering over from the theatre. I said to him, 'I know you answer every letter. How encouraging you are. Why?' And he said he thought a large part of it had to do with what Frank Loesser did for him when he was young and unknown."

SONDHEIM HAD REACHED that moment in his career when he seemed to be being considered for every kind of award. One of the most important was his election in 1983 to the American Academy and Institute of Arts and Letters, joining a select group of two hundred and fifty members, all of whom had made distinguished contributions to the arts. He was also being treated as a composer in his own right, rather than as one partner in a musical theatre collaboration. The concert in honor of his work in the spring of 1983 was one in a series about the works of composers organized by the Whitney Museum, and took the usual retrospective view, beginning with his earliest work and going through to the score of *Merrily.* A group of singer-actors was assembled, five of whom had already been seen in Sondheim musicals: George Hearn and Cris Groenendaal in productions of *Sweeney Todd,* Victoria Mallory in *Night Music,* and Liz Callaway and Steven Jacob in *Merrily;* only Bob Gunton and Judy Kaye had not performed Sondheim works before. Music director Paul Gemignani and producer and director Paul Lazarus decided to draw on Sondheim's extensive audition tapes and uncovered several songs that either came from the unperformed *Saturday Night* of 1954, were dropped from *Forum* at an early stage, or had been heard in New Haven in *The Frogs* but never in New York. The evening was to be recorded by Thomas Shepard of RCA Red Seal Records, the winner of ten Grammy awards, who had fought for Sondheim's cause in the past and done more to preserve Broadway music in general, it was said, than any record industry executive since the highly regarded Goddard Lieberson.

One of the high moments from the resultant record was "Someone in a Tree" from *Pacific Overtures,* in which four Japanese speculate about what might have gone on in the treaty house in which Commodore Perry's successful negotiations took place. It was a virtual Rashomon, Frank Rich wrote, as well as a metaphysical statement about "memory and history and existence." That the author of such a work of delicate feeling and complex musical structure could also be capable of the low humor of Marcus Lycus in *Forum,* as he lasciviously enumerates the attributes of his courtesans, was a tribute to the composer's wide range. One of the songs from *Forum* that did not get chosen for the record, "The Gaggle of Geese," is a brilliant rendering in song of the moment when three of its characters discover they all own the same ring, which sorts out what had up to that moment been a hopelessly tangled plot. The song was dropped from the score—presumably the authors decided to stage the moment rather than sing it—and has never been performed. Or they might have chosen "That Old Piano Roll," with its Gershwin-like, driving rhythm, or "Multitudes of Amys," or "I Remember," or so many others that came and went for a variety of reasons.

There was general agreement that the score of *Follies* had never received its due: the Capitol original-cast recording had been poorly engineered and radically edited to fit on one record. Just the same, the possibility of *Follies* ever having another Broadway production, given its immensely lavish staging demands, seemed remote. Then, in 1985, while he was attending a lunch of the Business Committee on the Arts, at which Sondheim was being given an award, Theodore Chapin, executive director of the Rodgers and Hammerstein organization, had an idea. Why not do *Follies* as a concert, in a recording studio? He raised the subject with Shepard, who took the idea a step further: why not do the concert on a stage? Shepard had produced about thirty albums for the New York Philharmonic, so he and Chapin approached the Philharmonic and an agreement was reached to do a joint benefit for the orchestra and the Young Playwrights Festival at Avery Fisher Hall. Shepard would direct and produce both the evening and the two-record album on RCA. Gemignani would conduct the orchestra. They started to talk about casting and "got some very strange vibes," Chapin said. "I thought Mary Martin singing 'Broadway Baby' would be a wonderful idea, but Tom Shepard didn't like it at all." Chapin got the idea of casting Arthur Rubin as Roscoe (as Shepard remembered it, this had been his idea), Betty Comden and Adolph Green to sing "Rain on the Roof," and Liliane Montevecchi singing "Ah, Paree!" Sondheim wanted Barbara Cook singing Sally's torch songs, and everybody, presumably, wanted Elaine Stritch, Carol Burnett, George Hearn, Mandy Patinkin, and Licia Albanese. Sondheim and Shepard had a heated disagreement over the casting of Phyllis Rogers Stone. Shepard very much wanted another actress for the part, which eventually went to Lee Remick. Then Ted Chapin, who was beginning to feel that the collaboration was not a comfortable one, dropped out. Meantime, Shepard was having a frustrating time at RCA. The recording was going to cost something like $300,000 to produce, Chapin said, but Shepard's superior—the famously disagreeable Jose Menendez, who a few years later would be murdered by his sons—overruled him, on the grounds that the record would never make back its costs. Shepard threatened to resign at RCA, and the project went ahead. Chapin thought that it was a member of the board of the Philharmonic who finally underwrote it and as it transpired, the album earned back its advance in three weeks.

Bill Young, who had co-produced the show *Marry Me a Little,* was hired as an assistant stage manager for *Follies in Concert,* as it came to be called, assisting choreographer Herbert Ross and also Paul Lazarus, who took over the direction when it was clear that Shepard was overburdened. *Follies in Concert* was to receive a single Lincoln Center performance on Friday, September 6, 1985, and, just to complicate matters, a BBC-TV film crew arrived to document the trials of putting on such a performance in a matter of days. Young said, "The documentary team came on a Tuesday, but we actually began rehearsing the principals on Monday because they had so much more to do, and we were working almost entirely in this one-windowed room right off the plaza at Lincoln Center. I spent virtually all day every day in the building for eighteen hours before the concert."

Carol Burnett claimed that when she agreed to the project, she had thought it was going to be a recording and had not realized it would be a performance as well. "It was like being shot out of a cannon," she said. So she insisted on having cue cards, and Young hired someone from David Letterman's television show to stand at stage left where she could see him but the audience could not. Elaine Stritch ("a whole theatre all by herself") was dancing around in shorts, a little white hat, and sneakers. Young remembers seeing her backstage at Avery Fisher Hall in her underwear, demonstrating how she gave herself insulin injections for diabetes. Lee Remick was "one of the most beautiful women" he had ever seen, "smart, funny, and nice." Having no confidence in her ability to sing, she had her own vocal coach; she was "very determined and worked very hard." Sondheim functioned almost in the role of second director. He was completely involved in the proceedings. Young said, "He doesn't pick away at a performance. He's very constructive. He's always terrific to work with professionally." Licia Albanese, the famous Metropolitan Opera soprano who had made her debut there in 1940 playing Madama Butterfly, sang "One More Kiss," written in the operetta tradition of Sigmund Romberg. Her voice was "in tatters," Young said, but something about her tremulous dignity was immensely moving. They all hated the BBC team, because they kept getting in the way, although they were grateful later that such a complete record of the event had been made. Friday was the only possible day for an orchestra rehearsal, because Shepard wanted to record some "clean" endings, i.e., songs uncontaminated by applause cutting into the final chords. But he agreed to have a small audience, and Young was delegated to assemble it. "All these incredible divas and the audience had strict instructions not to applaud! A friend of mine called it 'faggot torture.' At one point Stritch sang 'Broadway Baby,' and at the end there was the sound of a single clap. Everyone froze." Shepard was furious until he discovered that the ending had not been contaminated by this burst of irresponsible approval.

As for Mandy Patinkin, he was the innocent cause of a tense moment, which took place during the second performance, one eventually added to meet the demand for tickets. Young was standing at stage left wearing headphones when he noticed a red-haired young man with a beard talking to the hairdressers who gave a final touch to the coiffures before the actresses went on stage. At first he thought the man must be someone's boyfriend. "But then I got suspicious and asked politely who he was. He said he was Mandy Patinkin's brother. He looked to be in his late twenties, a little scruffy, but presentable," and Young was inclined to believe his story, but decided to check with the stage manager. "I said, 'Do we know anything about Mandy Patinkin's brother being backstage tonight?'" Patinkin was consulted and Young could hear him calling back, "I don't have a brother!" At that point Young got very nervous, because the actor was about to make a new entrance and he had visions of the stranger prancing on stage with him, or worse. "I was getting ready, in case I had to tackle him." But then two burly stagehands appeared and the "brother" meekly left. He had not been able to buy a ticket, so decided to see the show from the wings.

The demand for tickets had been enormous. There was a long queue after they went on sale, and over five thousand of them, varying in price from fifty to five thousand dollars, were sold in less than three hours. At a black-tie dinner that followed the first performance, guests were served raspberry soup at mock vanity tables decorated with old photographs and sheet music; the supper raised $216,000 for the two charities. As soon as the overture struck up and the stars began to make their stately entrances down a long ramp, the audience burst into applause, which only gathered momentum as the evening advanced. There seemed so much to celebrate: the reunion of stars like Burnett, Remick, and Cook, all on Broadway during its last fertile period and all, as the audience seemed to be saying, sorely missed; nostalgia for the Follies themselves; the rediscovery of a neglected treasure by an eminent composer. If, in 1971, critics had dismissed Sondheim's pastiches of vintage Broadway musical styles as pointlessly clever and his plot as too gloomy, with the virtue of hindsight it was evident that the musical carried considerable weight. "*Follies* wants nothing less than to bring us to tears, first sentimentally by awakening our deepest memories of youth and longing, and then bitterly by reminding us that our cherished fantasies of the past may only be illusions," Stephen Holden wrote in a review of the record. As "One More Kiss" demonstrates, Sondheim liked to set pretty themes "in ironic juxtaposition" to the messages being delivered: "Dreams are a sweet mistake, / All dreamers must awake / . . . All things beautiful must die." If Sondheim had demonstrated his ability to write in virtually any idiom, he had also cast those styles within the forceful framework of his own ironic sensibility. "Summing up a sixty-year musical tradition while rejecting its fundamentally optimistic philosophy, *Follies* closes the book on the past. Both the show and this stupendous new recording," Holden concluded, "add up to a valedictory stamped from beginning to end with greatness."

LIKE BERNSTEIN, Sondheim hated to let go of a project that held promise and would return to it with tenacious determination, as if in thrall to an incantation that, repeated often enough, could save any idea, however flawed. Perhaps that was why Burt Shevelove's sardonic comment about the folly of polishing worthless material had appealed to the ironist in Sondheim. If the problems of *Anyone Can Whistle* had been insoluble (and even that would return in concert form eventually), *Merrily* seemed to fit the category of shows that had never had a fair hearing. In Bernstein's case, the first successful revival of *Candide* was brought about by Prince, who restaged it to brilliant effect at the Brooklyn Academy of Music in 1973. But even he had been defeated by *Merrily*. Lapine, however, was eager to take up the chal-

Sondheim and Bernstein in 1985

lenge. He had seen an amateur production of the musical in New Jersey with Sondheim and Furth a few months before. So when he was invited to bring a production to the La Jolla Playhouse in the summer of 1985, he accepted with alacrity.

Lapine's decision to replace a young cast with seasoned professionals made immediate and practical sense. The three collaborators agreed that part of the problem also had to do with the fact that their main character, Franklin Shepard, remained a scoundrel, even though Furth and Sondheim had thought he became more likable as the musical carried him backwards into adolescent idealism. The clever and brittle wit that had given such shock value to *Company* seemed in this case to blast all hope for that sense of identification which, Oscar Hammerstein pointed out all those years ago when he reviewed *Climb High*, made all the difference. As a new version was hammered out and new songs written that took a more charitable view of Shepard as he traveled the road back from perdition, reviewers sensed a thaw. *Merrily* had become "less arty, more direct and at least fifty degrees warmer," David Richards wrote. Was it enough to rescue *Merrily*, despite the shortcomings of plot and character delineation, and the intractable problems that came from telling a story backwards? So far, *Merrily* has not returned to Broadway, although it went on to have a successful run in the York Theatre in 1994 Off Broadway.

IF THERE WAS one unfailing rule for a musical, it was, the British director Trevor Nunn said, that it was "an organism bent on self-destruction." As with that other perverse venture the play, the problems were never the same, as Moss Hart wrote in *Act One;* therefore, "the very mistakes that have been avoided in the previous play bear no relationship to mistakes that must be sidestepped in the present one." A playwright was, like Columbus, navigating the unknown, aware that even if he avoided a mutiny on the way, "those unfriendly Indian tribes—the critics and the public—will be lining the shores at the end of the voyage waiting to scalp him . . ." So Lapine and Sondheim faced a whole new set of problems as they turned to their next musical, *Into the Woods*. The page was a blank, but at least they could have confidence that Rocco Landesman, president of Jujamcyn Theatres, their new Broadway partners, was trying to forestall the problems that had doomed so many useful Broadway ventures. "We're trying to assume that we'll struggle to find an audience," Landesman said in 1987, three years after the group was formed. "So we've set up the machinery to do that without buying into the feast-or-famine notion so prevalent on Broadway. We're looking for that middle ground that used to be the lifeblood of Broadway. Shows that would run a while, never be a huge hit, but would make a little back for investors."

Jujamcyn was the name for five theatres that had been bought by James H. Binger and his wife (and named for their children, Judy, James, and Cynthia) and which offered attractive new terms. Jujamcyn would give a musical it wanted preferential treatment, i.e., require no rent until the show had reached a break-even point. On the equally difficult issue of attracting investors, the artistic team would agree to pool the weekly take from the start, rather than obliging investors to wait for returns that might never materialize. Jujamcyn's president was aware that its theatres were too small to attract the really profitable long-running shows. But Jujamcyn had already demonstrated with *Big River,* its opening hit of 1984, that a musical could begin in the provinces and then come to New York for a respectable run. For their part, Sondheim and Lapine were looking for an idea that was bright, lighthearted, and funny.

Their impulse was to write a new fairy tale from scratch. Developing that notion proved more difficult than Lapine had imagined. However, the idea of bringing together a group of familiar fairy-tale characters into a single story was more promising. Fairy tales had, of course, been used as the basis for operas, such as Rossini's *La Cenerentola* and Humperdinck's *Hansel and Gretel;* for films, such as Cocteau's magical *La Belle et la Bête;* and countless ballets. But what Sondheim and Lapine envisioned sounded closer to the freewheeling English pantomime, in which the story, whether of Cinderella, Aladdin, or Puss-in-Boots, acted as the barest pretext for a madcap romp full of local jokes, slapstick humor, a principal boy in tights (always a girl), and an obligatory widow (always played by a comedian in drag). Lapine had loved fairy tales as a child, when he was first introduced to the wonderful and sinister illustrations of Arthur Rackham. Of recent years, he had been influenced by Bruno Bettelheim's seminal work *The Uses of Enchantment.* Even though Sondheim had made perfunctory nods in their direction, such as the song "Two Fairy Tales," dropped from *A Little Night Music,* and had written the ironically titled "Happily Ever After" for *Company,* such stories had not peopled his youthful imagination. He had seen Disney films, like *Snow White* and *Pinocchio,* and of course he had seen *The Wizard of Oz,* but he once remarked jokingly that he had learned more from Barbara Stanwyck movies. Still, the idea had promise, if only to see what dimensions such stories would attain when filtered through Sondheim's "wicked but cherishing wit," as Jack Kroll wrote.

Lapine's book for the first act does not include the principal boy or the widow, but in other aspects it has something of a pantomime's zest and irreverence. There are Cinderella, Little Red Riding Hood, Jack and the Beanstalk, Rapunzel in her tower, the obligatory Witch (no Fairy Godmother, however), and also a new pair of characters, a childless baker and his wife. It turns out the Witch has made them barren but will grant them the baby they want if they assemble the required number of magical ingredients: a lock of Rapunzel's hair, Jack's cow, Cinderella's slipper, and Little Red Riding Hood's cloak. A furious romp begins in a suitably spooky wood as the baker and his resourceful wife try to assemble the necessary objects within the appointed hour, and other characters follow their own stories in a tangle of plots and counterplots reminiscent of the best moments of *Forum*. The characters, as envisioned by the authors, have real stature. Little Red Riding Hood has golden curls, a prematurely street-wise mentality, and enough budding curves to entice a real wolf, who, having swallowed her grandmother and found her on his road, sings, "Think of that scrumptious carnality / Twice in one day—! / There's no possible way / To describe what you feel / When you're talking to your meal." Cinderella runs away from her prince and his ball three nights in a row because she is delightfully and dizzily vague: "But then what if he knew / Who you were when you know / That you're not what he thinks / That he wants?" Meanwhile, the prince, wandering in the woods, has caught up with another frustrated prince, the one who is courting Rapunzel. They sing "Agony," in which they fatuously compete to see who is suffering more at that moment. The characters lament, tear their hair, miss each other, compete, agonize, exult, take pratfalls, and burst into songs laced with the best Sondheimian wit. They all live happily ever after at the end of Act One, or so it would seem.

As a first act it is a treasure, and even in an embryonic state its promise was apparent when a reading was held at Playwrights Horizons late in 1985. At that point Sondheim had written only an opening number. The following summer, in June 1986, two-thirds of the score for Act One had been written as well as Act Two. Bernard Jacobs of the Shubert Organization was invited to the two readings, and so was Landesman of Jujamcyn. Jacobs seemed lukewarm, but Landesman was eager to bring the musical to New York. An arrangement was worked out to give it a Broadway production after a tryout at the Old Globe Theatre in San Diego.

Into the Woods opened there on December 4, 1986, and ran for fifty performances. Reviews were mixed, and work continued on the book and score for another five or six months, while new actors were cast, the set was refined, and a choreographer brought in. Previews began at the Martin Beck Theatre in October 1987. In Act Two they would take their characters back into the forest to demonstrate that there are no happy endings in life, that one must be careful what one wishes for, and that each has a basic character flaw for which he or she must atone. This time, the forest is dark and sinister. An angry female giant is on the loose, and several characters meet squishy fates before the survivors assemble to sing the finale, "No One Is Alone." This decided shift in tone, not surprisingly, gave the authors some headaches. Landesman was delighted that he had been able to raise $4 million for the show—the advance sale was a satisfying $500,000—but not sure about the second act. "The device of the giant in the show was not something I embraced," he said later. "All of a sudden everybody was getting killed and it became very dark. Maybe that's what they wanted but I thought the show should have been more of a whole cloth."

Chip Zien, who took the role of the baker, confirmed that "people felt the second act was a problem. One night Steve was in the parking lot telling people to go back, because the show wasn't over yet." At one stage it was in "such a state of flux that I was nervous about it. I became obsessed with how it was changing. My preoccupation became, Will my character still be there when it opens?" By the time previews began, "Lapine and Sondheim were being buffeted around because the performances were not very successful and people like Jerry Robbins were giving conflicting advice."

Zien thought the darker tone of Act Two could have something to do with the characters of both creators. "They share a similar outlook. There is a certain melancholic view, a fear of flat-out enjoyment. I have it too, so I understand it. Is it the fear of getting what you wish for? It's more the feeling 'Be careful or you may be disappointed.' An underpinning of sadness. There is something not quite fulfilled that permeates the work."

IN DEPARTING FROM fairy-tale convention Lapine's book was at odds with the interpretation of such tales by Bettelheim. Happy endings, the latter wrote, are there to reassure children that a good life can be achieved despite adversity. In fairy tales, only the angry wishes of adults have bad consequences; those of the hero or heroine never do. The child can only wish for good things, since he or she is young and innocent. When Jack of beanstalk fame steals a bag filled with gold, a golden hen, and a golden harp, the young reader understands this is to illustrate the danger of relying on magic solutions, not to condone stealing. Killing the giant is another symbolic message, having to do with the necessity of a boy's outgrowing the father in himself.

Bettelheim's principal theme had to do with the lack of any kind of direct moral in a fairy story. If a child were being taught a lesson, it was in the most indirect possible way. "Fairy stories do not pretend to describe the world as it is, nor do they advise what one ought to do . . . The fairy tale is therapeutic because the patient finds his *own* solutions, through contemplating what the story seems to imply about him and his inner conflicts at this moment in his life." Could it be that Lapine and Sondheim were taking literally something that was always meant to be seen symbolically, and nudging their characters through too energetic a learning process? Just as Sondheim's new song for Franklin Shepard, "Growing Up," contained the lines "Every road has a turning, / That's the way you keep learning," so characters in *Into the Woods* declare at crucial intervals, "And I know things now, / Many valuable things, / That I hadn't known before" (Little Red Riding Hood). In making their themes explicit, something of value had been lost in Sondheim's work, Frank Rich thought: "The tension between his meaning and his expression of that meaning is what gives a Sondheim musical its theatricality . . . We care more about George reaching out to his "family tree" through the abstract art of painting in *Sunday* than about a baker literally finding his father among the trees in *Woods*." For Mimi Kramer the problem was not so much what Sondheim had contributed as Lapine's misguided approach to the material. "Give a child an old tale and he will make of it something wonderful and mysterious; give it to a grownup and he will reduce it to platitudes."

Sondheim dismissed criticisms of Act Two with the remark that "some people don't like to be surprised. Particularly in musicals. They want what they expect. Many of them want what they expected before they go into even the first act. Then, after Act One, they think they ought to get more of the same.

"To me, the theatre is about quite the reverse. It's about surprise. There are a lot of things in the second act that people—some people—don't want to think about, particularly in a musical, because a musical still means to many people something frivolous that's either pretty or spectacular. But whatever it is, it isn't nagging. It isn't something ambiguous. It's got to be one color. I don't think that way.

"If you want to really examine it, since I do like to deal in people's delusions, that is only an inch away from illusions. And illusions are only an inch away from fairy tales. The things we tell ourselves we want and don't want come under the headings of 'tiny little lies' or 'delusions' or 'self-deceptions.' The little fantasies that you experience today, the things that you told yourself that are not true, could all be put under the heading of 'fairy tales.' "

PERHAPS IT WAS INEVITABLE, given the subject matter, that reviewers would look for references to the parenting the collaborators had had. "If you hadn't already noticed, most of *Into the Woods* is about terrifying women," a critic noted, women with unpredictable moods, who lie and cheat and fly into murderous rages. "The men are either weaker or dumber—either way, better." Frank Rich noted that the theme of achieving adult independence in Sondheim musicals went back as far as *Gypsy* in 1959. Two of the actresses who played mothers in *Sunday*—Barbara Bryne, who was Seurat's mother, and Bernadette Peters, who was George's grandmother—were, curiously, cast as mothers again in *Into the Woods*. In both musicals the characters faded out of the picture as their children achieved self-assurance, as if the life of one could only be achieved at the expense of the other. It may just be a footnote, but Peters, who turned down the idea of being transformed from grandmother Marie into a nude model in *Sunday*, made a similar transformation (clothed, this time) in *Woods*. At a pivotal point she sheds her cloak, her cronelike features, and her rags to emerge as a young woman in all her satin-clad glory. That is also the moment when she loses her magical powers.

What reviewers seem to have missed is that, if there are not many fully drawn or likable women in Sondheim's musicals—one thinks with a shudder of Madame Rose, or the dissolute Mary in *Merrily*, or the termagant Joanne in *Company*—*Into the Woods* contains at least two of them. First there is the witch, convincing and enchanting as she mercurially dispenses pardons or damnation to her helpless victims in Act One, managing to be both sinister and engagingly frank. An even more attractive figure is the baker's wife, movingly played by Joanne Gleason. Here is a woman thrown into a milieu she barely understands, but grittily determined to come out alive, who is at the same time human enough to become temporarily diverted by Cinderella's faithless prince. *Woods* loses one of its most believable characters when, for impenetrable reasons, the authors decide to kill her off in Act Two. Meanwhile, stripped of her magical powers, the beautiful Peters has nothing to do.

There is a possibility that for Sondheim, *Woods* contains an emotional truth that has more to do with the relationship between fathers and sons, and it seems linked to the pivotal moment when a child has absorbed more rebuffs and disappointments than he can bear and resolves that wishing for anything at all is to believe in fairy tales. The moment that seemed to elicit the strongest reaction from him comes toward the end of Act Two, with the song "No More." The baker, having lost everything, including wife and home, abandons his last tie, his infant son, leaving the child with Cinderella. He will not even try to defeat the giant. He only wants to be left alone. Just at that moment he meets an old man who has figured on the periphery of the plot and learns that this is his own father, whom he thought was dead.

But the kind of recognition scene one might expect, the embraces and

With Bernadette Peters and author-director James Lapine on the set of *Into the Woods*

tears, never takes place. Emotionally, the baker is dead and only wants to be spared the pain of any more delusions. He sings:

> How do you ignore
> All the witches,
> All the curses,
> All the wolves, all the lies,
> The false hopes, the goodbyes, the reverses,
> All the wondering what even worse is
> Still in store?

Having nothing left to hope for, or give—it is an understandable state of mind for someone whose emotionally evasive father had left him alone "in the lion's den," and whose mother had wished he had never been born. He said during a television interview, "I remember the first time I heard Chip [Zien] sing that. I usually get a bit embarrassed when I hear my work sung, but I was really moved. It was funny, because he was five feet away . . . And it was really wrenching . . ." Nevertheless, in the story the baker does return to his child and does help slay the giant. We are all interconnected, Sondheim said. Or so he felt.

CHAPTER 19

Hit after Hit

THE PHILOSOPHY OF Jujamcyn Theatre management, that there was an audience to be found, had been supported with advertising specifically aimed at families; its success was reflected in strong box-office sales. *Into the Woods* was named best musical of 1988 by the Drama Desk and the New York Drama Critics Circle and nominated for ten Tony Awards. At the ceremony, otherwise dominated by *The Phantom of the Opera,* Sondheim won for best score, Lapine for best book, and Joanna Gleason was named best actress. In 1989 the musical received a Grammy Award for best original cast recording. A national company starring Cleo Laine went on the road, and *Into the Woods* became the first Sondheim show to have a road company begin touring before the original production closed. There would be an appearance on *American Playhouse,* the Public Television series, and the musical would go on to have an enduring appeal for amateur groups all over the country. When it closed on September 3, 1989, *Into the Woods* had run for 764 performances and 43 previews, making it the second-longest-running Sondheim show, for which he wrote music and lyrics, after *Forum.*

Sondheim was criticized for the sentiment "No One Is Alone," expressed in the closing moments of the musical, as inconsistent with his scrupulous regard for the truth. Halfhearted though the message might sound, it did end one of his musicals on a hopeful note. Either the composer was throwing his audiences a crumb of comfort or his habitual pessimism was loosening its hold. These days Sondheim had no serious competition in either New York or London, Leighton Kerner wrote. "From the latter oozes the sewer-spectacular school of rock operetta, embodied in that twin-blockbuster phenomenon that might be called *Les phantomes misérables.*" His newest musical, or any of the Sondheim works that had recently been revived, demolished the opposition.

By the time *Woods* closed, the man the London *Sunday Times* called "that rare thing in the musical theatre world: an intellectual heavyweight," was experiencing another surge in popularity. Part of that had to do with the revival of *Sweeney Todd* at the Circle in the Square; a new production of *Gypsy;* the show *Jerome Robbins's Broadway,* which contained scenes from *West Side Story, Gypsy,* and *Forum;* a revival of *Night Music* in London; a planned production of *Sunday* at the Royal National Theatre; a production of *Woods* in London, with Julia McKenzie playing the Witch; a new production of *Follies* in Long Beach, starring Dorothy Lamour, Juliet Prowse, and Yma Sumac; and three songs to be sung by Madonna for Warren Beatty's new film, *Dick Tracy.* Even Sondheim had to concede, late in 1989, that it had been a very good year. He was becoming wealthy (in 1987 he acknowledged that his income was over $1 million a year), but his tastes remained as unostentatious as ever. Some time after *Sunday* he went to an exhibition of Seurat drawings, which were selling in the neighborhood of $100,000 each, and remarked on how much he would love to own one, "but of course I couldn't afford it." And he had just been appointed Visiting Professor of Contemporary Theatre at St. Catherine's College, Oxford, for the Hilary Term, January–March 1990. The chair had been endowed by his good friend Cameron Mackintosh as a way of bringing instruction in drama and the performing arts to the university, which offered no degree in the field.

The title for his first public lecture was "Everything You Always Wanted to Know About the Theatre but Were Afraid to Ask." Sondheim dealt in the master classes with, for instance, the suitability of musical theatre as a topic for serious discussion—still a somewhat provocative idea in Britain—and whether everything in musicals should be set to music ("through-sung"), as it is in opera, or whether there was still room for the usual combinations of songs and spoken scenes. But the most important aspect of the course were the master classes for the thirteen students selected out of ninety-two who had applied. Sondheim took the appointment on fairly short notice because he thought the London production of *Sunday,* then going into rehearsal, could act as a prime example of the way a musical was assembled, because of its appropriateness for a course on creativity itself, and because it was an ideal opportunity to treat art and teaching as complementary activities.

The fact that none of the musicians and lyricists chosen for his classes on songwriting for the theatre was an Oxford undergraduate caused loud grumbling, and even the fortunate thirteen found themselves caught off balance. Stephen Keeling, a young composer whose musical *Maddie* would be performed in Britain a few years later, recalled, "On the very first occasion that I played anything to him, I remember him saying, 'May I hear that again?' Of course I was absolutely thrilled to be getting a second hearing. I grinned at the assembled crowd. Then I played again, and he said to me: 'That was great. Both times I lost interest in exactly the same place after about five seconds. I just wanted to be sure.'" Another student, Edward Hardy, recalled Sondheim's admonition that one must be prepared to defend every single word and note. "One of the classes allowed us each to play an example of an 'opening number' we had written . . . I had chosen a piece called 'Brand New Day,' from a musical I had written called *Living It Down*, which was a very graphic piece showing two working-class characters having sex. I played a recording of the song to the class and I was terribly proud of my work and at the same time very nervous . . . One of my classmates . . . asked me why I had chosen such a simplistic accompaniment. I had no idea how to reply, since the decision I had made to use this particular vamp had been made unconsciously . . . I fumbled in vain for an answer . . . Steve piped up and said I had obviously wanted to communicate the banality of the domestic environment . . . What a wonderful answer! Thus not only did he underline a very important point about writing, but he was generous enough to do my bullshitting for me."

Sondheim's emphasis on clarity and on being true to one's characters were points that Hardy would never forget. At the end of his stay Sondheim presented each of his students with his favorite rhyming dictionary, by Clement Wood. Although Hardy found it of limited use to an English lyricist (he pointed out that when pronounced by an Englishman, "dictionary" and "dairy" did not rhyme, for instance), he appreciated the kind thought. And then his teacher wrote, "Good luck—Steve Sondheim," which Hardy found odd, since the lesson had been pounded home that no one should count on luck. "He was always on about sweat and blood etc. Writing it in a rhyming dictionary was even odder. The whole point . . . is that you leave *nothing* to chance . . ." Hardy and a group of others formed the Mercury Workshop in London to produce new musicals, and Sondheim agreed to be patron. Hardy, who acted as its coordinator, said, "I owe so much of what I know about writing to Stephen Sondheim and my life is infinitely richer for it. At the same time I sometimes wish I had never met him. His influence, his judgment, his 'greatness' can sometimes hang around my neck like an albatross. Can any of us ever be as good as he is? . . ."

HAVING HAD a handsome success with *Into the Woods* gave Sondheim a new breathing space, artistically, in his continuing attempt to expand the limits of his chosen form. He knew he could try anything at Playwrights Horizons. He had come to value the freedom it offered, even depend upon it. Its subscription series meant that audiences had not been told by critics to dislike a production and therefore arrived in that state of perfect expectation which every playwright hopes for and so seldom gets. His next idea was perhaps his most radical to date. He decided to make a musical about assassinations, a subject that, even in a time of vanishing limitations, would seem a preposterous choice for a musical. That was, of course, one of the reasons why he wanted to do it.

The idea had begun to germinate, as had so many others, some years before he did anything about it. About a decade earlier he had acted as a judge for entries by young playwrights to the Musical Theatre Lab founded by Stuart Ostrow, and one of the scripts he read was by Charles Gilbert. Its title was *Assassins*.

He said, "I looked at the title and thought, 'What a great idea for a musical.' " Gilbert had based his play on a book about assassins and the intense feelings of desperation and alienation they had expressed during court proceedings. His own work evolved into a story about a Vietnam veteran who is goaded into assassinating a President. Sondheim was struck by a poem that Gilbert had quoted by Charles Guiteau (President James Garfield's assassin), written on the day of his execution. It began, 'I am going to the Lordy.' "That poem, and the letters and diaries, were what was most interesting about it. The narrative seemed to weigh the piece down, so we never did it. But I thought, 'I wish I had had that idea.' " Nothing more happened. Charles Gilbert went on to work on other projects and eventually to teach in the theatre department of a college in Delaware. Then, in 1988, John Weidman, with whom Sondheim had collaborated on *Pacific Overtures*, approached him with an idea for a musical about Woodrow Wilson and the Paris Peace Conference. Sondheim thought the subject more cinematic than theatrical. But that reminded him of *Assassins*. Weidman was immediately intrigued. Sondheim wrote asking Gilbert whether he could use the idea. Gilbert said, "I was pretty cheeky—I offered to work on it with *him*—it was like writing a letter to God. He phoned, very cordial, and said he had someone else in mind." Lawyers were called in, Gilbert gave his consent, and the idea went ahead.

"John and I sat down and tried to find a form for this thing. The one thing we knew from reading Charlie's play was that a storyline didn't work." Sondheim thought it might be possible to frame the subject matter in a revue form, analogous to the structure they had decided on for *Pacific Overtures* and that had worked so well in *Company.* "But it took us many weeks to decide *how* to do that, because the problem with a revue, particularly a musical, is that each scene, each number, has to be better than the one before it, because there's nothing to pull the audience through, no narrative tension." That led to an investigation of the possibilities suggested by a revue form loosely linked with a narrative. "The idea that people from different eras would have scenes together was exciting," Sondheim said. "I loved the notion that John Wilkes Booth could talk to somebody who lived fifty years after he died. Once the barriers are down, you can allow yourself to cross eras and find parallels and contrasts."

At first Weidman and Sondheim took the long view, going back to the assassins of Julius Caesar and incorporating Charlotte Corday. "It was going to be an epic piece: what does it mean to kill a political figure?" The field proved to be so well populated that the authors had to keep eliminating categories and finally narrowed the cast of characters to Presidential assassins: Booth, who killed Lincoln; Guiteau; Leon Czolgosz, who murdered William McKinley; Giuseppe Zangara, who tried to kill President-elect Franklin Roosevelt; Lee Harvey Oswald, Kennedy's assassin; Samuel Byck, who tried to kill Richard M. Nixon; Lynette (Squeaky) Fromme and Sara Jane Moore, who both shot at Gerald Ford on different occasions; and John Hinckley, who wounded Ronald Reagan.

Weidman said, "Presidents have never been attacked for purely political or economic reasons," as they were in Europe, and no assassin has been black. That was because "by the time black kids grow up they have a realistic sense of their own limitations." Men and women who had attempted to kill Presidents believed that everyone had a right to happiness, not just to its pursuit. When their dreams, however delusory, were not fulfilled, they looked for someone to blame. "These are stalkers with a grievance." Each had his own story to tell, but taken together they were alienated and disaffected, acting out their rage and turning it on the most tempting of targets. "There is a lot to be learned from looking at them," Weidman said.

Sondheim shared Weidman's political perspective—he characterized himself as a "fierce liberal"—but was not attracted to the subject for this reason alone. "One of my objections to Brecht is that it's always politics to the forefront and the characters to the rear, and what I hope we have done with *Assassins* is to put the characters to the forefront and the political and social statements all around."

In writing "an anti-musical about anti-heroes," as Frank Rich wrote, Sondheim evoked the sound of American music, drawing from John Philip Sousa, Stephen Foster, Scott Joplin, the ballads of the seventies, and back again, using these themes in ironic counterpoint to the violent events in the foreground. Thus the attempted assassination of President-elect Roosevelt is played out against the Sousa march "El Capitan," a song about guns gets a barbershop quartet, and Charles Guiteau's final moments, as he mounts the scaffold, are set to a cakewalk. The opening number, "Everybody's Got the Right to Their Dreams," set at a shooting gallery in a fairground, is a jaunty little tune with an ominous message:

> No job? Cupboard bare?
> One room, no one there?
> Hey pal, don't despair—
> You wanna shoot a President?"

The actor Booth, who committed suicide in a barn, believing that history would finally recognize him as a martyr; Zangara, who turned on Roosevelt in a rage because nothing had assuaged his persistent stomach cramps; Czolgosz, who struck a blow for social justice; Fromme, who thought a mass murderer was the son of God; Hinckley, trying to prove himself worthy of a movie star's love; Guiteau doing the cakewalk; Byck in a Santa Claus suit; Oswald, portrayed here as the lone gunman and a potential suicide—the characters are unforgettable. "All you have to do is squeeze your little finger," they sing in the "Gun Song." "Squeeze your little finger . . . You can change the world." And the cast, led by Victor Garber as Booth, Terrence Mann as Czolgosz, and Jonathan Hadary as Guiteau, was impeccable.

This had to be Sondheim's most important score, the *Gramophone* reviewer later wrote of the cast recording. "He has taken on the 'American Dream,' challenged its validity, exposed its falsehood; he has taken on the assassination of Presidents, the rule of the gun, the laws that make it possible; he has taken on the promises, the lies and the deceit of politicians, the social injustices, the anger of the losers and the deprived . . . In nine short songs he has taken on issues that some in the U.S. would rather forget . . . Every single word is an indictment; the musical means could hardly be pithier, or wittier, or sadder." And there was no doubt that hopes were high as the previews began in December 1990 at the 139-seat main theatre at Playwrights Horizons. (It officially opened at the end of January.) All the seats soon sold out. A columnist at the *Daily News* called it the "toughest ticket" in town to get and reported that people queued for cancellations for hours. A parade of Sondheim's prominent friends did get tickets, including Hal Prince, Arthur Laurents, Jerome Robbins, Mike Nichols, John Guare, Lauren Bacall, and even Katharine Hepburn. The reaction was positive. That did not prevent Sondheim's usual eleventh-hour jitters. Mandy Patinkin recalled going to the first workshop performance and sitting in the front row. He sat there with a pad and pencil making occasional notes about songs he wanted to remember, unaware that taking notes in front of actors was considered the height of bad manners by Sondheim. A few days later a furious letter was dispatched asking him how he dared do that to Garber, playing Booth. Patinkin was sure Sondheim would never speak to him again.

If Sondheim were particularly apprehensive about critical response to *Assassins,* he had good cause. Its opening coincided with Operation Desert Storm and the war in the Persian Gulf against Iraq. Paul Ford, who began as a rehearsal pianist and became an indispensable member of the Sondheim team, said, "There was a television set downstairs in the dressing room and the actors were all watching developments and groaning, because they knew the implications." André Bishop said, "We had queues in the dead of winter blizzards. We could have run it there for months. But we couldn't afford to, and the actors couldn't have stayed at that salary level. It was a very odd time. I will never forget the day President Bush came to town to go to the United Nations or something. They would come through one of the tunnels and up West Forty-second Street. The motorcade went past *Assassins* with these giant posters and this long line of woebegone people, and there was the Presidential limousine with all the flags flying, and I thought, Well, this sums it all up."

John Simon thought the show in extremely bad taste. "When the terrible events in the Gulf began, Sondheim & Co.—all affluent folks in no great need of turning a buck—could have done the gallant thing and shut down, or shot down, their not very viable brainchild." Jack Kroll wrote, "You can swallow the savage comedy, but not the show's moral fuzziness . . . 'Everybody's Got the Right to Their Dreams' is a pretty pathetic rationale for the complex questions that Sondheim does raise." "The tone of these scenes is windily self-important, the intellectual content embarrassingly slight," William A. Henry III wrote. One would have thought from the tone of the reviews, Benedict Nightingale observed, that Sondheim "might almost be recommending that George Bush be shot." David Richards in the influential

Times was one of the few who thought that Sondheim and Weidman had written a major work.

"Nothing . . . quite prepares you for the disturbing brilliance of *Assassins,* unless it is the irony that has always been the constant in Mr. Sondheim's work. And even that has been raised to teeth-chattering levels," he wrote. The authors had made everyone look at "a shadow America, a poisoned, have-not America," and insisted that the prosperous majority pay attention to something it would rather sweep under the rug. "Mr. Sondheim has real guts. He isn't ashamed to identify with his assassins to the extreme point where he will wave a gun in a crowded theatre, artistically speaking, if that's what is needed to hit the target of American complacency."

Unlike assassinations in Japan, where the weapon was a knife, or in the Middle East, a hand grenade, in the United States the ordinary man or woman with a grievance always uses a pistol or a rifle, "the common pathway of social pathology," observed Robert Jay Lifton, director of the Center on Violence and Human Survival. Americans tended to want to think of assassinations as an anomaly, a product of a deranged mind, he wrote. That was to minimize the effect of social breakdown and to ignore the national insistence on easy access to weapons of murder. Lifton wrote, "The laws that permit our society to be saturated with guns can be seen as a national refusal of political and moral growth—a constitutional literalism ('the right to bear arms') so anachronistic as to qualify as a form of political fundamentalism."

If Weidman and Sondheim agreed with this analysis, as seems logical, they concealed their own views so successfully that it was difficult to tell, one critic wrote, whether the musical was intended as savage political satire or veiled approval. Even those critics who admired the work, like Julius Novick in the New York *Observer,* thought the musical's tone seemed "jarringly trivial" to those who did not understand that broad jokes could express anguish, and hoped its creators would do more to clarify the focus. For his part Jerry Zaks, the director, admired for the dash and polish he brought to the work, fretted about the scene changes, too slow to suit him, the limitations of the tiny twenty-five-foot stage and skeletal orchestra. It was too large a concept for such a setting and should have been moved to a Broadway theatre right away, he said. He poured scorn on the idea that anyone could have thought they were trying to "glorify" political assassinations. And some of the scenes that did not quite work should have been cut. But the worst problem had been the unfortunate timing. "The ground wasn't fertile, if it ever could be." André Bishop, who went on to become artistic director of the Lincoln Center Theatre, said, "The show was greatly underrated by the critics. Audiences were divided. In the Kennedy scene, which was the only fully realized stage set, when you saw this guy in the Texas Book Depository listening to country music, you knew. And some people simply couldn't deal with it and would look away, or cover their faces." He added, "I would love to revive it some day at Lincoln Center." He had thought of doing so in 1992, but Bill Clinton had just been elected President and it did not seem appropriate. Given such an explosive subject, and the very real danger with which every modern President is faced, one might well wonder whether there ever will be a right moment.

THE LONDON REVIEWERS had taken the unusual step of reviewing the New York production, an indication of the status Sondheim had achieved there. Unlike the New York reviewers, for whom the macabre subject matter cut too close to home, in London *Assassins* was just the most lethally brilliant of a series of such experiments that they had come to expect from Sondheim. As a political satire it was a devastating assessment of the American Dream turned nightmare. Such events could, of course, always happen in Britain, but history had shown them to be exceedingly rare, thanks in part to stricter gun control. The show demonstrated, John Peter wrote in the *Sunday Times,* that America was "a breeding ground of simple, ordinary megalomaniacs busy in the pursuit of happiness brandishing a gun."

The Donmar Warehouse production of the musical in Covent Garden followed two years later and sold out its twelve-week run. The setting was equally small, but the designers decided to turn this to advantage by transforming the theatre itself into a fairground, and setting the assassins up in nine shooting booths on stage. Placed prominently above an invitation to shoot a President and win a prize was Uncle Sam himself, aiming a gun at the audience. Behind the contrived vulgarity, the deadly counterpoints, and the mocking jauntiness was a sense of rage and frustration that was almost palpable. "One mystery of this work's off-Broadway failure . . . was the complaint that it had no viewpoint," Irving Wardle wrote in the *Independent.* "From the transatlantic perspective its viewpoint is as clear as a Presbyterian sermon." For Nicholas de Jongh of the *Evening Standard* the ending, as all the assassins gathered around Lee Harvey Oswald, urging him to immortalize his name by murdering Kennedy, was the most surreal of all. "The scene encapsulates *Assassin's* eerie, enthralling appeal—dangerous Americans possessed and ruined by dreams," he wrote. "Yes, you may make a musical about assassins and live to triumph—if you happen to be Stephen Sondheim."

Sondheim said a few years later that he was comfortable in London in a way that he was not in New York—a real compliment from someone who had spent all his life as a New Yorker. "I have been tempted to originate shows here and even to live here. If I were a younger man I probably would. But it's too late now." He admired the versatility of the English actor's training, which allowed him or her experience in everything from contemporary drama to Restoration comedy. It was a luxury to be able to attend so many musicals and plays. Every free afternoon and evening in London was spent at the theatre, and *Time Out* was the first magazine he bought when he got off the plane. He would soon have further cause to appreciate London when the Royal National Theatre mounted a revival of *Sweeney Todd* with Declan Donnellan as director and Julia McKenzie as "the definitive" Mrs. Lovett. That brought forth another round of critical praise, none so fervent as from Sondheim himself. The musical was now exactly as he had imagined it, he told Donnellan, and called him the best director in London. Donnellan well remembered the reception that followed opening night and seeing Sondheim in the middle of a group of fans. Suddenly Sondheim began calling, "Declan, get me out of here!" and Donnellan realized that the group of young men bearing down on him purposefully were all wearing Stephen Sondheim bow ties. "He was caught like a fly in amber by forty spiders," but there was nothing Donnellan could do, as he, too, was being carried off by the crowd.

Sondheim was in demand. "One month, he's a high-profile part of the repertoire of the . . . National Theatre, occupying an auditorium more frequently given over to Chekhov and Shakespeare; the next, he's generating sellout business [with *The Frogs*] in the unlikeliest of sites—a West London public swimming pool," Matt Wolf reported. While Sondheim's musicals covered the theatre pages, no less than five Andrew Lloyd Webber hits were bringing in huge crowds in the West End. There was a general belief that Lloyd Webber, as the younger man (curiously, both were born on the same day, March 22), would do anything to have achieved Sondheim's *renommée*, while Sondheim would do anything to have had as big and popular a success. Comparisons were almost inevitable, given that Lloyd Webber's opulent lifestyle included a country estate in Berkshire where the visitor, having run the gauntlet of security staff, butler, and maids, was likely to be taken on a formal tour of his dazzling collection of Victorian art that did not encourage questions or conversation. On the other hand, on a visit to Sondheim's country house the host, alone in the house, would be mixing drinks in the kitchen and ready for a relaxed conversation in the garden.

A Sondheim retrospective was almost inevitable, and one was duly held at the Drury Lane Theatre bringing together such luminaries as Elaine Stritch, Ned Sherrin, and Petula Clark. Keith Warner, who had directed *Pacific Overtures* at the English National Opera and was in charge of the show, an AIDS benefit, recalled that during the interval Sondheim expressed a wish to meet the royal visitor, who happened to be Princess Alexandra. They chatted amicably for a while. After Sondheim left the princess wanted to know whether Mr. Sondheim was married. Warner explained that he was a homosexual. There was a silence. Then the princess said kindly, "Oh yes, he does look rather a sad man."

One person Sondheim could no longer count on for social introductions in London was Burt Shevelove, who had died in 1982. Nancy Ryan had telephoned to say he had died at the age of sixty-seven; she herself would die not long afterwards. Sondheim recalled that when they were writing *Forum,* he and Larry Gelbart made up obituaries and the one they liked best was "Here lies Burt Shevelove, finished before his apartment." He said, "Burt was a presence in everybody's lives, and I doubt whether a week goes by when I don't miss him. He was the world's best person."

Of recent years he has lost many people who had been close to him. There was Michael Bennett, who died of AIDS in 1987. There was also Lee Remick. After she married Kip Gowans and moved to London, he visited them regularly in St. John's Wood and sent presents. One was a wooden heart made in the shape of a puzzle, with an arrow inscribed with their initials, L and K. She looked happy and in the peak of health when she presented Sondheim and Lapine with their Tony Awards for *Into the Woods* in 1988, but learned the following year that she had kidney cancer. The first treatments seemed to be successful, but then malignancies were found in her lungs which eventually traveled to her brain. "She was immensely brave," Gowans said. "She had to have an injection every night for a year that was very painful but she bore it like a trouper." She died in 1991, and although Sondheim did not attend her memorial service on the West Coast he was deeply affected. Patinkin had not understood why Remick was cast in the *Follies* concert in 1985, because she was a terrible singer, he said. But then, when Sondheim came on stage to take a bow and the person he hugged was Lee Remick, Patinkin said, "I stood there and thought, 'He loved her.' "

In 1993 Sondheim would lose not only Louis Vargas but his half-brother Herbie, the one who had been so ill as a child. Walter Sondheim said, "He was a wonderful child who became very self-destructive, with a fatalistic sense about a disease that would kill him." Stephen Sondheim said that Herbie gambled and smoked and was always in debt. Walt said, "He was warned that

With Lee Remick at a post-performance party for *Follies in Concert,* 1985

if he did not change his lifestyle his kidneys would fail, and two and a half years later, that is what they did, after a lot of suffering." (Herbert Sondheim, Jr. died in May 1993 at the age of forty-nine.) "Herbie went on living at the same hellish pace. I didn't know my brother's kidneys were only working at ten percent of normal capacity." One Christmas Eve Herbie was rushed to hospital. Walt was living in New Mexico and very hesitant to ask Steve to go to Stamford, but Herbie seemed seriously ill, so he finally called and asked him. "The minute Herbie was out of that immediate crisis, Steve was out of there," Walt said. That fitted his pattern, Walt thought, of being unable to deal with illness. One might have thought him uncaring, but not his old

With his half-brother, Herbert Sondheim, Jr.

friend Milton Babbitt. The latter recalled that Sondheim had attended a benefit in his honor, had said a few kind words, and then dissolved into tears because his brother had died the day before.

His friends were aware of the tides of feeling that could overwhelm him without warning. When Dorothy Hammerstein died in 1987 at the age of eighty-eight, Jamie Hammerstein said, "We had the memorial service for my mother and there was a reception in a room at the back of the church, with a staircase leading from it to a back exit. We were drinking champagne when Steve was suddenly overcome with tears and ran down the stairs. Half an hour later he tried to come back, but he only got halfway up and then disappeared again, he was so overcome." As has been noted, that was in stark contrast to his reaction when his own mother died five years later, in the spring of 1992. His new secretary, Steven Clar, and Foxy's retirement home took care of the arrangements for her funeral. Sondheim did not even know where she had been buried.

IN DECEMBER AND JANUARY OF 1990–91, while *Assassins* was still at Playwrights Horizons, Sondheim hoped that despite the mixed reviews, the musical would transfer to Broadway, as had every other musical he had written. At the same time he was working on an idea for a film musical, *Singing Out Loud* with William Goldman. In his years as a Hollywood screenwriter, Goldman had achieved fame for his Academy Award winning scripts: *Butch Cassidy and the Sundance Kid* and *All the President's Men,* and Sondheim asked him whether he thought *Company* would make a movie. Goldman said, "*Company* is one of those shows, along with *Gypsy* and *Pal Joey,* that I think of as the greatest, quintessential, most beloved musicals. I remember seeing *Company* five times and I loved it, and I had a huge, fucking problem, which was that the main character's gay but they don't talk about it. Hal, George, and Steve all think it's about a guy with a commitment problem. Anyway, I loved the show. And I figured out a way—I've forgotten it now—to change it, keep the score but give it some narrative, which is the real problem for a movie. And Steve was pleased. We were going to do it, and then the choreographer Herb Ross came to town. He had dinner with Ross and called me the next day. Ross had told him that no matter how good the movie was, it wouldn't be as good as the play. So Steve didn't want to do it. And I remember thinking, Gee, how vulnerable that guy is!"

Most people did not realize, he continued, that anyone in the middle of creative work was going to be volatile and easily discouraged. "You see, here's the deal. We don't know what we're doing. Young people think we do but we don't. If Steve knew what he was doing, half his songs would be as popular as 'Send In the Clowns.' And as well received. Because don't think for a minute Steve would not like to have written—Steve would not have wanted to write *Phantom of the Opera,* but he would have loved the grosses. He hates it when people say, 'Well, the shows don't pay off.' . . . He's not above any of that; it's just basically his sensitivity, his sensibility, is such that he can't do it."

The idea of *Company* was dropped, and nothing more happened until the director-producer Rob Reiner of Castle Rock Productions called Goldman one day and said he had an idea for a musical. It would be about a movie musical that was in trouble. Goldman called Sondheim and, to his great surprise, Sondheim jumped at the idea. Sondheim said, "Film musicals, as opposed to stage musicals, are a territory that fascinates me, because film is a reportorial medium and theatre is a poetic medium. I've rarely seen musicals work on film, musicals that tell stories and explore character, and I'd like to have a go at solving that problem."

Goldman said, "We worked for something like three drafts and Steve wrote a fabulous score of six or eight songs. I'll give you a story about Steve. He's very brave as to what he'll try creatively. We were sitting around one day talking, Rob and his partner and Steve and myself. There's a section for a scene in the recording studio, where the heroine sings a song, but she's lacking in confidence and can't sing . . . It's just a huge scene; it takes place over eight to ten minutes. And Steve says, 'I can try that.' I remember thinking, Wow, that's a lot of work to do. And he did it. It's a great, great scene. Most guys would say, 'I can write the song and you guys make the book work.' But Steve was willing to get in and do the whole thing."

Nothing came of the film, which was titled *Singing Out Loud*. Goldman thought that was because the director changed his mind after another movie musical was a huge flop, and the cost was projected as $50 million, considered high. Castle Rock still owns the score, and both Goldman and Sondheim want to work on the idea again. Rob Reiner said, "These things never completely die, and it may be resurrected. For a film that wasn't made it was one of the greatest creative experiences I ever had."

EARLY IN 1991, Sondheim was deeply involved in negotiations for a Broadway production of *Assassins*. By February 4, while the musical was still playing to sold-out houses at Playwrights Horizons, *Variety* was reporting uncertainty about its future because of its subject matter, the political situation, and mixed reviews. The owner of the Promenade Theatre, a larger house Off Broadway, had made an offer, but no decision was forthcoming, and so he had booked another show instead. The transfer would have cost more than $1 million, and despite interest from the Shubert Organization and Geffen Music, which was Sondheim's publisher at that time, less than half that sum was raised. *Variety* reported that there was friction between the Shubert and Geffen camps. The rumor was that David Geffen had withdrawn his offer after the Shuberts would not meet his exacting terms. Goldman said, "My memory of what happened is everybody kept going back on the deal. I mean, the Shuberts would say, 'No, it's got to be money from Geffen's bank account. Not money from the cap profits, it's got to be real money.' And finally it was clear that Steve, who was trying to get the two parties together, was caught in a personal vendetta." Just at that moment, Peter Jones entered his life.

Peter Jones, later referred to as P.J. to distinguish him from Peter Wooster, was one more in a series of young men who in recent years had knocked on Sondheim's door, hoping to become his pupil. He had been born in a large Catholic family and grew up in Wyoming and had spent most of his life in Denver, eking out a living as a composer and lyricist for children's theatre and working in the school system teaching creative dramatics. He had several relationships with both sexes and had been living for the past three years with an electronics engineer in Denver, with whom he had exchanged wed-

Peter Jones, 1997

ding rings. But he was ambitious to try his luck in New York. Finally his partner urged him to write to Sondheim to see whether there was an apprentice-
ship program of some kind in which he could enroll. Jones wrote and
received a prompt reply during the Christmas holidays of 1990. Sondheim
said that if he were ever in New York he would be happy to see him. Jones
immediately bought a cheap train ticket and arrived in New York on February 15, the closing night for *Assassins,* a date that would seem highly significant to him in retrospect. He moved in with a friend from college days who
lived in Queens, and got in touch with Sondheim. He said, "I was running
out of money. By then I only had a few hundred dollars and a meeting was
being delayed by Steven Clar," Sondheim's secretary. One day he went out to
mail three résumés and when he returned there was a message from Sondheim on the phone machine inviting him to come by that day at six o'clock.
Jones went by public transportation.

Jones is slight, of medium height, with glasses, a mass of curly brown hair,
a square chin, regular features, and the look of a young poet. He has the
relaxed manners of a westerner, is a vegetarian, does not drink alcohol, and is

interested in New Age theories about time and space—in particular, the way random events can seem to conspire to bring about a certain result, or what Jung called synchronicity. He arrived at the house and was let in by Sondheim himself, something he would discover the composer rarely did. He was sure Sondheim was inwardly dreading this encounter with yet another fan, an impression that was reinforced when Sondheim disappeared upstairs to make a phone call. The composer at length returned and sat some distance away on the couch. A conversation began, and, Jones said, "to my surprise the time just flew. I thought, Here am I, an uneducated man, talking to this sophisticate." Sondheim took him on a tour of the house, and that was when they discovered their mutual attraction. After some hesitation Jones decided to accept Sondheim's invitation for a weekend in the country and they left next morning.

By then it was February 24, and negotiations for *Assassins* were on the point of collapse, and did, in fact, break down four days later. Sondheim said, "We arrived and there was a slight sprinkling of snow on the ground." He was showing his guest the grounds and wearing moccasins, the wrong kind of shoes. He slipped a couple of times. Jones urged him to change his shoes, but Sondheim dismissed the idea and they continued their walk. "The third time I slipped, I heard a sound I will never forget," Sondheim said. "It was a crack like a rifle in the woods. And I thought, That can't be what I think it is!" Jones and Wooster helped him back into the house and the doctor advised him to see an orthopedist the next day. By then his ankle was really starting to hurt. "It was very, very painful even to climb on the examining table," he said. While the X-rays were being developed, "I was lying on the table feeling sorry for myself, and I heard the student nurse come in to take a look, and then she said 'Oh boy!' and I knew I had some classic fracture that she'd been taught in school." The senior nurse showed him the film of the break, "and it was as if someone had drawn a pencil line right across the bone. Thank God it wasn't in fragments." His leg had to be encased in a cast for the next two months and he hobbled around on crutches. He felt helpless.

As Peter Jones later realized, he had arrived at a serendipitous moment. The acute disappointment of *Assassins'* closing—in Sondheim's eyes, since it had not transferred to Broadway and therefore was a great disappointment—coupled with breaking his ankle, acted as a salutary jolt of fate. Almost without his awareness, those paralyzing insecurities that had kept him safe in his self-imposed and loveless isolation had relinquished their hold on him. He was suddenly aware of the powerful extent of his vulnerability, but also of his need. "Want something," Bobby is told in "Being Alive," the words that always used to affect Sondheim most deeply. He asked Jones to stay and help, and the latter agreed, parting amicably from his friend in Denver. The informal living arrangement soon became a permanent one. A few weeks or months later, Sondheim was telling his friends that he was in love, really in love, for the first time in his life.

CHAPTER 20

And That I Learned from You

P *assion,* the third musical by Sondheim and Lapine, has a curious history. It derived from a nineteenth-century novel by Iginio Ugo Tarchetti, who wrote it as a serial for a Milanese periodical. (It was then titled *Fosca.*) Tarchetti's epistolary novel languished in complete obscurity until 1971, when Italo Calvino chose it for a paperback series of classic novels that he was editing, and its author suddenly joined the company of such distinguished authors as Dostoevsky, Henry James, and de Maupassant. Thus rediscovered, his novel attracted the attention of the Italian filmmaker Ettore Scola, who made it into a film titled *Passione d'amore.* Sondheim saw it in 1981 and immediately wanted to adapt it as a musical. Then *Sunday in the Park* intervened and the idea was dropped for the time being.

Fosca, or *Passione d'amore,* or *Passion,* tells the story of Giorgio, a young soldier who is having a passionate affair with Clara, a married woman with a child. He is posted to another town and thrown into contact with Fosca, the cousin of his commanding officer. She, like himself, is only in her twenties, but the disfigurations of epilepsy have turned her into a grotesque figure. She fastens on Giorgio and pursues him shamelessly. He is repelled but something about her also fascinates him. At the end of the book his affair with Clara is over and he and Fosca have become lovers. But he is forced to fight a duel, she dies shortly afterwards, and he is left a mental and physical wreck. It was a variant on Mme. de Beaumont's *La Belle et La Bête,* with the roles reversed and a twist at the ending.

The novel was considered extremely daring for its time. Not only did it paint an unblinking portrait of illicit relationships, but it also presented an early challenge to the social convention that what women had for sale on the marriage market were looks alone, and that their reasons for being depended upon the roles they played in the lives of their men. A love like Clara's ought to be justifiable, even celebrated, Tarchetti wrote in *Fosca,* arguing that it was society's attitudes toward women that were corrupt, not the behavior of women. But he also drew on the fashionable nineteenth-century idea that there was something particularly erotic about illness; that Fosca's emaciation somehow conferred a heightened and more spiritual sensibility, as well as endowing its victim with more passionate responses. In Tarchetti's novel Clara represented the conventional bourgeois ideal; Fosca, all that was rebellious, decadent, and transfiguring. Seen as a study in relationships, *Fosca* presents an interesting conundrum. Is this the story of a man redeemed or destroyed? Did Tarchetti intend to portray the triumph of a woman who, even as she faces death, has the courage to defy convention, or someone in the grip of an obsession?

Tarchetti's novel is drawn with enough fine attention to nuances that there is a case to be made for both interpretations, although the one to be made for the destructiveness of the affair is stronger. The author makes it clear that Giorgio's decision to become Fosca's lover has more to do with his own state of mind than with Fosca. He has just received a letter from Clara breaking off the affair and is devastated. He turns to Fosca, convincing himself that hers is the "real" love, since she alone has renounced everything for his sake; she alone is therefore truly deserving of it. Yet he cannot get past his revulsion at the thought of making love to her, or thoughts of Clara, as the moment looms: "Oh! Clara, Clara, why have you killed my heart?"

Fosca is similarly torn by ambivalent feelings. Her emotion seems naked, almost infantile in the primitiveness of its need. In fact, it seems inspired chiefly by the need to prove she is sexually desirable, and there is something even more disquieting, an interlinking of love and hate. Love, it would seem, is not possible without suffering, sacrifice, and being abused ("Someone to hold you too close, / Someone to hurt you too deep . . ."). In her unsuccessful marriage to an abusive count, briefly described, Fosca was at someone else's mercy. Now, for what would seem the most loving of reasons, she has assumed the predatory role and is manipulating and controlling in her turn. Scenes from the novel in which she uses every kind of emotional blackmail, and in which she gains the power over Giorgio that she is determined to have, were retained in Scola's film. His ending, which portrays his hero as a pathetic and ravaged figure, makes his conclusion unambiguous.

In deciphering the riddles posed by *Fosca,* the issue is complicated by the fact that Tarchetti's novel was never finished. He died just before he was to have written the culminating scene in which Giorgio becomes Fosca's lover. That chapter was written by another young Italian novelist, Salvatore Farina, who was a close friend. So although no one knows exactly what dénouement was planned, it is a reasonable assumption that Farina's ending reflects the one the author intended, and it seems completely consistent with the previous scenes that Tarchetti did write.

The story is particularly poignant because it presents yet another case of art imitating life. Tarchetti also served as an officer in the Italian army. While staying with a friend in Milan, he met a neighbor named Clara in much the same way that Giorgio meets her namesake. Their love affair, as described in the novel, closely resembled its real-life counterpart, and Tarchetti was transferred to another post where he, too, met his commanding officer's cousin, named Angiolina, who was ravaged by epilepsy. Like Fosca, she, too, pursued him until he capitulated, and, like Giorgio's, his feelings remained extremely ambivalent. In a letter to a friend Tarchetti wrote, "I have a terrible superstition: I feel as if this woman were dragging me to the grave . . ." He, too, was discharged from the army because of poor health. He died of tuberculosis in 1869, at the age of twenty-nine. Ironically, Angiolina survived him by some years. Every November 1, All Saints' Day, she would place a wreath on his grave.

ACCORDING TO Peter Jones's chronology, at the time *Assassins* closed Sondheim was finishing *Singing Out Loud* with Bill Goldman and then involved with *Putting It Together,* a revue starring Diana Rigg, which had opened in Oxford the month before and which would be brought to the Manhattan Theatre Club with Julie Andrews in the spring of 1993. In the minds of Sondheim and Lapine, the *Passione* project seemed too short for full-length treatment. It ought to be on a double bill, and when the composer was working on *Assassins* with Weidman they considered the idea of twinning the work with *Passione,* but the two works seemed too disparate.

Then Lapine came up with an idea that did seem related to *Passione,* a book named *Muscle* by Sam Fussell. Sondheim said, "*Muscle* is a memoir about the son of two American academics who goes to Oxford and then comes back to New York. He was tall and thinly built and . . . nervous about violence in the city. One day he was crossing the street to avoid an altercation and he ducked into the only kind of refuge he knew, a bookstore . . . As he was idly flipping through books he came across the biography of Arnold Schwarzenegger and a sea change happened. He became a bodybuilder, and it started to take over his life . . . Suddenly he was bullying people at the office, so he quit his job and trained eighteen hours a day. He went to California to compete in a tournament and . . . came in second. The obsession was shattered and he became normal again, so to speak . . .

"On page two of *Fosca,* Giorgio says (I'm paraphrasing), 'I want to tell you the story of two loves, one the kind of love that all of us know and encounter, the other a disease.' The first sentence of *Muscle* begins (and again I paraphrase), 'Body building, or the disease as we call it . . .'

"What a coincidence, I thought. Both books are about outward appearances. In *Passione* Fosca is concerned with her homeliness, her ugliness, and Fussell's great insight is that he was building . . . a fortress around himself because he was afraid of the world, so that his appearance would keep people away, just as Fosca's appearance keeps people away . . ."

Sondheim and Lapine held a first reading at Lincoln Center, with Michael Hayden in the role of the bodybuilder. That convinced Sondheim that "I had to go back to the drawing board . . ." Meantime he and Lapine began to work on *Passione,* which showed real promise. As the work grew (it eventually became a one-act opera that played for an hour and fifty minutes without interruption), the idea of *Muscle* was shelved.

Even when a subject fascinated him—and the only other musical that had been his idea was *Sweeney Todd*—Sondheim tended not to examine the reasons. But when *Passion* was produced, he was pressed to explain, and recalled that when he first saw the film he could hardly believe what the plot seemed to portend, that a handsome soldier in love with a beautiful woman was about to be taken over by a grand affair with the ugly Fosca. "This woman is appalling looking, I mean, science-fiction horrifying, but she fixes her eye on this guy and in an instant I knew he was going to end up falling for her. And in that instant I knew I wanted to musicalize it." To him the story was romantic and ennobling and had a universal message. "We're all Fosca. I think we're all also Giorgio . . ."

Giorgio, Sondheim also said, realized there were layers of love, and that unconditional love was the kind he had never had and never given, but it was the only kind worth having. In an interview at about that time, Sondheim made a reference to what John Mortimer called "the blurred connections between art and life." "There was some personal connection clearly," he said. "I think it's about a desire to open up, a desire to be like Giorgio." He added that, coincidentally, while he was writing *Passion* his life changed.

If Giorgio had gained from the relationship, in Sondheim's view, then so had Fosca. She learned she was someone worthy of love, and the awareness made her gentler, less bitter, and less bizarre. His friends remarked upon the benevolent change in Sondheim after Peter Jones entered his life. He was obviously happy, Lucy Beldock said, "and I couldn't hope for more than that for a loving friend." Hal Prince agreed he was more mellow and that that was partly the result of feeling himself loved. Peter Stone, another friend, said, "He's always been wise about certain things, but now I think he's a little wiser." Arthur Laurents said, "Peter Jones I think has been wonderful for Steve. He's a different man."

All those years of analysis had prepared him "not to be ashamed, either of the way I felt, or [of] my sexual feelings or anything else, and be vulnerable and take a risk," Sondheim said. And despite the disparity in their ages and backgrounds, his friends liked Peter. Ned Rorem said, "Sometimes when famous people have friends, the friends try to be as important as everyone else, and P.J. didn't do that. He listened to my music; spoke when spoken to." Laurents liked the fact that he had his own interests and original opinions: "If you asked him a question, you'd get a real answer." Other friends had some general concerns, since they knew how much of a risk Sondheim was taking.

As *Passion* was being written during the early summer of 1992, Jones left New York to take a job as musical director in summer stock in Minnesota, and work on a children's musical and other compositions. He was anxious to get back to composing, something he had not been able to do for months. Then he started a new relationship and wrote to say he was not coming back. Being in the position of teacher to his lover was one Sondheim found attractive, but a friend of Jones's thought it was difficult for the pupil, who would be bound to wonder whether he could measure up to the standard being set. Then there was the fact of what years alone had instilled in Sondheim: the ability to shut a door and remain oblivious for hours and days.

Jones said it took time to realize that Sondheim was the quintessential absentminded professor, capable of being so immersed in his work that he was oblivious of the world around him. The relationship had taken them both by surprise. Jones was used to being physically, but not emotionally, attracted to men. On the other hand, Sondheim was being very reserved about whatever it was he felt. Jones believed he was just a good friend, and had no inkling of the special place he had assumed in Sondheim's life. By then Peter Jones knew he was in love and had said so. There were times when Sondheim seemed especially warm, and he would respond, and then, Jones felt, Sondheim would withdraw to a safe distance. During that first year he was never given Sondheim's private number, meaning that he would always have to go through his secretary during business hours. Jones did not want to make any demands for fear of being thought unreasonable. It was much easier for him just to leave, but then Sondheim discovered just how large a place Jones had assumed in his life. "And I got catatonic! I lost a lot of weight in about three days. It's a great way to lose weight! Because you're so depressed you can't eat . . . Three days later I looked at myself in the bathroom mirror after a shower and thought, Gee, what am I losing weight for? I want to die!"

Later that summer, the two resumed contact. Jones thought Sondheim might have written the opening scene for *Passion*. "I was working in summer stock, and every afternoon for about a week I would call him up from a phone booth. It was about ninety degrees, and I would be in there crying and talking. We learned more about each other in that one week than we had in an entire year. One day he calmly told me he loved me." Sondheim was in Connecticut, and as this was happening his neighbor Mia Farrow, who lived about ten minutes away, was defending herself against a custody suit brought by Woody Allen. She recalled, "I was going through my unpleasantness just as this was happening with Peter, and Steve and I would stumble through the woods to find each other, with tears streaming down our faces." Sondheim even tried to accept the fact of someone else in P.J.'s life and insisted on meeting him, but, as P.J. feared, the encounter was "very difficult and emotional." Some months later Jones decided to return and the two cemented their relationship by exchanging wedding rings on January 15, 1994. Sometime afterwards, one of Sondheim's anniversary gifts to P.J. was the title page of *Passion*, reprinted and framed, with a dedication to him. Life, it seemed, was now imitating art.

JAMES LAPINE READILY AGREED that there were two radically opposed ways of looking at Giorgio, as presented by Tarchetti, as a man either redeemed by love or destroyed by it. Deciding on the former was "not a conscious decision," he said. "We just didn't want him to be defeated by the experience, because that made Fosca a destructive character, and that isn't what appealed to me about it." Despite this, he and Sondheim followed the outlines of the Tarchetti plot closely, including scenes in which Fosca's unlikable aspects are faithfully rendered. At one point, Giorgio, who has become really ill, is sent on sick leave for forty days. He gets on a train and finds Fosca already waiting for him. Horrified, he makes her get off at the next station. While they wait for another train back to the barracks, there is a waiting-room scene in which he reproaches her for what contemporary viewers would consider her relentless pursuit. Sondheim and Lapine also allowed Clara to end the affair as she does in the novel. But in terms of the story's emotional dynamics, that made their most important departure from the novel the least convincing aspect of their script. Instead of taking Fosca to bed with as much loathing as longing, unable to forget Clara, Lapine and Sondheim have Giorgio renouncing his past love affair and experiencing a change of heart. He has fallen genuinely in love with Fosca. Although the abruptness of his volte-face is never really convincing, the moment when Giorgio tells Fosca he loves her is genuinely affecting, the high point of the musical. Sondheim said later, "Every time this happens I go to pieces."

In Fosca, Sondheim has created one of his truly grand and larger-than-life characters, as mesmeric in her obsession as Madame Rose, if for different reasons. He and Lapine knew that the musical's success or failure would depend on finding the right leading lady, and that would be a tall order. It had to be someone who did not mind being seen as revoltingly ugly (in the Scola film, the actress Valeria d'Obici was just that), someone who could sing, act, and dance if necessary. They were prepared for a long search, and then Donna Murphy appeared. Sondheim said, "Hers was one of the most astonishing auditions I have seen." She was given Fosca's entrance song to learn in two days, and her performance was so well realized that it appeared virtually unchanged on stage. "I have never known an actress to understand a character that thoroughly . . . It was absolutely extraordinary." He was also "proud to have written the song—that's how good the audition was." Unfortunately, in one respect, Murphy was quite unsuitable. She was much too pretty for the part, and much tinkering with false noses and hairlines never achieved the right result; at worst, she simply looked plain.

Marin Mazzie, a tall, vibrantly lovely actress with a clear, strong singing voice, was cast as Clara, and Peter Gallagher, a darkly handsome figure with mobile, almost boyish good looks, played Giorgio. They rehearsed for close to four weeks and gave three performances for invited audiences at Lincoln Center in the fall of 1993, in a small studio theatre with minimal scenery and costumes. André Bishop, by then artistic director at Lincoln Center, offered them the Mitzi E. Newhouse stage for the following season. But Gerald Schoenfeld and the late Bernard Jacobs were offering one of the Shubert theatres on Broadway for that same season. Bishop said, "Artists don't want to wait if they're hot. We felt very sad to lose the show but felt they were probably right to go to Broadway because they could go on working without interruption. Steve was afraid of a repeat of *Assassins,* that he'd have a modest run in a subscription theatre and it wouldn't be movable. I completely understood this . . ."

Donna Murphy had some difficulties with the characterization of Fosca as shown in Scola's film and reflected in Sondheim's music. "I was so turned off by it. I found it very over the top, so exaggerated. It became a kind of horror show with a black comic edge." Shortly after rehearsals for the workshop began, Sondheim arrived to give some musical coaching. "We got to Fosca's entrance, and even though I thought a lot of what he was saying was brilliant and justifiable, it didn't jibe with my instincts. For instance, he wanted a lot of movement in and out of different tempos and dynamics," to make the character more melodramatic, she thought. "I remember someone saying, 'It's becoming a little Norma Desmond' [of *Sunset Boulevard*], and Steve said, 'What's wrong with that?' I went home that night and listened to the tape sitting on my couch in the living room, and I was crying my eyes out. Because if I did what Steve wanted, I wouldn't feel connected. It didn't feel honest to me." She was sure she was the wrong actress for the part and just knew she was going to be fired. But both men reassured her on that score, and "Fosca continued to evolve. There was no debate about making her plausible. We all wanted her to be someone who acted from the heart, sometimes without thinking about the way she hurt others."

As the musical moved towards a Broadway opening, set for the spring of 1994, changes were made in the casting. Peter Gallagher, who had looked and acted the part ("He's so sexy," a member of the company said, "you'd have no difficulty understanding Fosca's reaction"), had other commitments, so a long search began for his replacement. He had not been a strong singer, and Otts Munderloh, who became the sound designer, said, "Unfortunately, on Broadway shows, when people change their minds the pendulum tends to swing too far in the other direction." Jere Shea, his handsome replacement, was a fine singer, but his performance had less definition, and he lacked the kind of features that had made the other actor seem so open and guileless. His deep-set eyes were almost always in shadow, and there seemed to be something skull-like about his face. Still, it was felt that the casting was strong, and morale was high. "A lot of actors accepted secondary roles because they would be working with Sondheim and Lapine," said Beverly Randolph, the production stage manager. "Everybody was very happy to be doing this." She thought that Sondheim had considerable influence on the development of the concept, although he and Lapine presented such a united front that it was impossible to tell to what extent.

Several in the company expressed chagrin that Sondheim was so seldom at rehearsals. Munderloh said, "When he did come, his notes for actors were so exactly right that you wished he were there more often." In the difficult role of writer-director, Lapine was under double pressure. Randolph said,

"When you are developing the pieces, the atmosphere gets very heated. You're under the gun twice. And when Jim is on the defensive, sometimes he will withdraw. He'll get short with actors, or accidentally send mixed signals. He will ask for help with a problem and then not like the solution. And he likes to have his company around, which irritates performers as it means a lot of waiting." When Sondheim worked with Prince, the last word had belonged to Prince. "In this particular case Sondheim had the power, and James was someone who can direct in an age when there are not many directors left," Munderloh said. The problem was, Randolph added, "no matter how good James makes it, Sondheim gets the credit."

SONDHEIM'S SCORE WAS as original and unanticipated as this latest choice of a subject, which, he noted, lacked the wit of *Into the Woods* and *Company,* the intellectual detachment of *Sunday,* and the stylish irony of *Night Music.* It was "a straightforward, nonironic love story," he said later. The exception was some comic relief provided at intervals by the soldiers in Giorgio's garrison. But that made it a show "with no protection." His decisions about the score were risk-taking ones on a level none of his other works had quite approached, even the daring *Sweeney Todd.* The book was almost entirely musicalized, and the resulting structure was so fluid that titles of individual songs would not even be listed in the program. Michiko Kakutani wrote, "While the harmonic language of *Passion* is reminiscent of such soaring ballads as 'Johanna' and 'The Barber and His Wife' in *Sweeney Todd,* its highly patterned use of motifs recalls *Sunday in the Park with George.* Each of the three main characters in this show possesses distinct musical motifs. Clara's songs, which are essentially written in major keys, have a bright waltzy feel to them that gradually mutates into something sadder, when she begins to miss Giorgio in the latter part of the show. Fosca's songs, by contrast, possess a melancholy minor-key quality that gradually becomes more buoyant . . . as she comes closer to realizing her love."

As was his usual practice, Sondheim began at the beginning with *Passion* and worked his way methodically through the book, using the text Lapine had written as a kind of blueprint for those moments that would emerge as fully fledged ballads. In, for instance, the letter Fosca has forced Giorgio to write, Lapine has her dictating the words: "Having finally thought carefully about you, I've come to realize the love you have shown me to be stronger and purer than any I have known or could ask to know. I have come to see you in a new light, and what I see is beautiful, and virtuous, and sound . . . Your love will always live on in me . . ."

Working for about a week, eight to twelve hours a day, Sondheim hammered out his ballad, looking for a shape: "This is stream of consciousness and free association. I note principal points I want to make, and then check the ones I definitely mean to keep," he told Annette Grant of the *New York Times*. These included the opening phrases, "I wish I could forget you" and "I know I've upset you." Almost all the ideas that appeared in the final version evolved from these early sketches: "Getting the outline is half the battle, and that goes for musical outlines, too," he said. As the rhyme scheme began to take shape, so did the melody. He wanted this score to feel rhapsodic and lyrical, for, as he said on another occasion, "I always describe it as one long rhapsody . . . it's all about yearnings between two people." He decided on a minor key for this particular ballad, experimenting with an arpeggio accompaniment based on an earlier Fosca theme. "The result, which uses rapidly changing harmonies and rippling chords to suggest emotions welling up, helps Sondheim delineate a character who is agitated, feverish and impassioned." Finally, there are the lyrics themselves:

> For now I'm seeing love
> Like none I've ever known,
> A love as pure as breath,
> As permanent as death,
> Implacable as stone.
> A love that, like a knife,
> Has cut into a life
> I wanted left alone.

Sondheim and Lapine had received much admiring comment during the Lincoln Center performances, and the major unresolved issue then seemed to be whether or not there should be a flashback describing Fosca's unhappy marriage. When consulted, the film director Louis Malle said "Absolutely," while John Guare, who had contributed such a wonderful suggestion for *Sunday*, said at the same moment, "Take it out!" That showed how radically brilliant minds could differ, Sondheim said. Still, the comment was illustrative of the kind of reaction they had received. As the show wound its way toward its first preview at the Plymouth Theatre in the spring of 1994 and further adjustments were made, the company was confidently expecting *Passion* to be a tremendous hit. There was just one catch: its weeks of previews had to be played on Broadway. The era of the out-of-town tryout had gone forever, mostly because musicals had become so technologically complicated that they had to be confined to the particular theatre in which they would be performed. Sondheim said, "God knows there used to be people who would follow the trail of blood up to Boston and to New Haven. I know—I was one of them. Maybe there was a bitchy intent, but I wanted to be the first on my block to see *My Fair Lady* so I could come back and tell everybody I had seen [it]. But there weren't a lot like me back then." There was the further danger that one might leave a nurturing workshop situation thinking that scenery was all that was needed to bring the idea to its perfect realization.

Despite the cautionary lessons of past experience, neither Sondheim nor Lapine was prepared for the reception *Passion* received when previews began. In this particular case, the audiences were not just those armchair critics who went in order to dislike the work, or assistants to rival producers and press agents whose job it was to put out a bad word, but the large and amorphous musical-theatre audience itself, many of them tourists, who are the biggest audience for musicals nowadays. Those people could not believe what they were seeing. As Sondheim had realized after Billy Wilder's warning about *Sunset Boulevard* all those years ago, they were laughing in disbelief, and not just in the moments of comic relief already provided. Otts Munderloh said, "Every day Donna would go into the train scene and get laughs. She'd come off the stage crying." People were yelling from the balcony, "Die, Fosca! Die!" It was said that a prominent Broadway director began howling with laughter ten minutes after the curtain went up and had to be hushed up by Sondheim's fans. Theatre-group organizers were apologizing to their clients. The authors later identified twenty places in the musical where the wrong kind of laughter was being heard.

The explanation advanced was that philistines in the audience simply could not accept the idea that an ugly woman could win a handsome man, although they would flock to the same story told in reverse when Disney's *Beauty and the Beast* opened on Broadway a month later. But more than this was involved. It was as if, Benedict Nightingale wrote, Michael Douglas had lifted Glenn Close from the bathtub in which she meets her doom in *Fatal Attraction*, removed the knife, and given her "a big, doting kiss." If the Fosca-Giorgio story had seemed a manifesto for a love that defied convention in the nineteenth century, it was a concept that modern audiences were likely to find difficult, Lloyd Rose wrote. "In the late twentieth century, the all-for-love Fosca seems more like a clinical case than a heroine. The story might make sense as an examination of the perversity and self-destruction of love if we understood what egotism or weakness in Giorgio responded to Fosca, if it were clear that when he talks about feeling a 'duty' to her he is fooling himself . . . But . . . Giorgio . . . has no dark side. He's a decent young fellow whose basic innocence leads him into the web of Fosca's obsession . . ." If this was supposed to be a paradigm for true love, audiences seemed to be saying, they knew better.

Early in the previews, Munderloh recalled, Lapine had no solution for Donna Murphy's problem except to tell her to be prepared for laughs. The producer Gerald Schoenfeld said that the laughter was not addressed immediately "on the grounds that the artistic integrity of the work was being impugned." He was an advocate of immediate change. The question seemed to be "How much more could this woman do to make herself repugnant?" he said. "So as each escalation took place, the audience responded with disbelieving laughter." Fosca "had to be someone you could believe was ultimately lovable." Donna Murphy agreed that Lapine and Sondheim had been slow to respond. "In the bedroom scene when Fosca was very, very sick she was wearing some long braids. She was very vain and, in the book, said when she died she would leave him one of her braids. At the end of the piece when he got a box of her things, and took out the braid, the audience thought it was hilarious. That went very fast, but in the main, Jim and Steve were reluctant to compromise. If you have chosen to write a piece you know will make people uncomfortable, who do you listen to?"

The parallels in *Passion,* if indeed they were there, put Sondheim at great emotional risk. Certainly, he found the laughter "excruciating," Arthur Laurents said. "We take each other to dinner on our birthdays, and the year *Passion* was on, I had seen the workshop and had not liked it, and I told him and he got very angry. And it got to the point that I said to him, 'Don't invite me to a preview or any of this, because when I criticize you turn on me. Our friendship is more important.' And he brought up the fact that I hadn't liked *Sunday.* I said, 'Yes, I told you I didn't like the second act, and it still isn't fixed!' So, getting to the point, I had gone to a preview of *Passion,* and at our dinner he said, 'Now, we have to get the spikiness out of the way right away,' and he's drinking up a storm. He said, 'Did you think you could go to a preview without anybody knowing you were there?' And I said, 'Well, yes.' Actually I had sat next to his half-brother Walt, and this is how he found out. And he said, 'Why didn't you ask me?' And I said, 'Because I didn't think you'd care.' And he burst into tears."

THE CONTRAST BETWEEN Plymouth Theatre audiences and those at Lincoln Center was striking. That supported the popular wisdom that different venues attracted audiences with differing expectations, as well as the idea that *Passion* showed Sondheim at his most operatic. "*Passion* is not an opera because there is so much dialogue," he said, "but it is an opera in its attitude towards people." He added, rightly, "If it were all sung and done at the Metropolitan Opera House nobody would laugh because this is the way Salome behaves and . . . Electra behaves, and you accept it . . ." *Passion* can be seen as a testament to the ways in which the lines between opera, opéra comique, and musical theatre have become increasingly blurred in recent years. David Patrick Stearns wrote, "It shouldn't be surprising that Sondheim is bridging the gap between the popular theatre and opera. Virtually all of his predecessors—Charles Ives, Aaron Copland and especially George Gershwin and Leonard Bernstein—have never comfortably fitted into pop and classical categories." If early works like *Forum* had conformed to conventional formulae, recent scores had not merely been a collection of songs but scenes in which the marriage of music and dialogue had been brought to a level of sophistication once reserved for "serious" works. In fact, in discussing Sondheim's works versus opera as such, said Keith Warner, who directed *Pacific Overtures* for the English National Opera, the dividing line became so blurred as to be meaningless. One could say of so many of his works what Sondheim said of *Carousel,* that they inhabited a "twilight zone" between opera and the musical. That could also be said about *Passion.*

Sondheim often said that he did not like opera, although the list of those he did like was substantial: all of Puccini, Gershwin's *Porgy and Bess,* works by Britten, Debussy's *Pelléas et Mélisande,* Alban Berg's *Wozzeck.* To him opera was about orchestra, staging, and the production of the human voice, with the emphasis on who was singing, whereas, with a few exceptions, musical theatre had the reverse emphasis. "For me, *Sweeney Todd* is not an opera; it's a black operetta in feeling and form. The only thing is it deals with extremely melodramatic material. Operettas tended to deal with lighthearted subjects. But if you look at the form *Sweeney Todd* is, let's say, eighty percent sung, and it's almost all songs and arioso singing. Not much recitative. And that is true of operetta.

"*Passion* is closer to a chamber opera, like [Britten's] *Rape of Lucretia,* in which, although there is dialogue, there is a sense of through composition." That did not alter the fact that he thought categories were irrelevant. "This is glib to say, but I really believe it: when *The Medium* and *The Telephone* [by Gian Carlo Menotti] were done on Broadway, they were Broadway musicals; when they were done in opera houses, they were operas," because the different expectations of the audiences had such an effect on the performances of the works.

Although *Pacific Overtures, Sweeney Todd,* and *A Little Night Music* have all been revived by opera companies, Sondheim has always resisted writing a work specifically for an opera house, at least partly for practical reasons. Some new operas might be performed only a few times in a single season, whereas on Broadway, the writing team would have weeks of previews in which a work could be cut, lengthened, rewritten, and polished before being subjected to a critical appraisal that would otherwise have been premature. Frank Rich commented, "He's right about that. But on Broadway everything is in a great rush, and maybe you can write 'Send In the Clowns' in ten minutes and maybe you can't. The trouble is, even for the best writers, the meter is always running."

What intrigued Sondheim when *Sweeney Todd* was performed by the New York City Opera was not the style of delivery, which was not that different from its Broadway performance, since it was mostly cast with performers who straddled the opera and musical-theatre worlds, but that the audience was so surprised by the plot. He said, "Even though the New York State Theatre is only fourteen blocks away from the theatre district, it was apparent that nobody had ever ventured down there, because they were all shocked at the revelations at the end of *Sweeney Todd* . . ." Given the gulf separating the two worlds, it had to be an advantage to have his work introduced in a completely new setting. Stearns said, "It seems hard to believe that he is more than a breath away from writing a genuine opera, particularly since he doesn't seem a bit intimidated by operatic form . . . [And] he says opera is much less restrictive than creating characters within the . . . Broadway musical." Sondheim was not at all sure *Passion* should be done on an operatic stage, because he thought operatic singers had not been trained to perform in the dramatic parlando, or speaking style (perfected by such actors as Rex Harrison and Richard Burton), and when dealing with the naturalistic settings of his own songs they would merely sound stilted. All that being so, Frank Rich observed, "His loyalty to Broadway is the real issue, much bigger than who he worked with or didn't work with. You've got to admire him for being the last major artist in the American theatre who believes in Broadway." But there was a price to be paid in trying to squeeze his material into a popular mold. In *Passion*, "they're trying hard not to commercialize it too much, and end up with something that doesn't fit comfortably into either mold. I am saying that Sondheim's working environment is basically hostile to the kind of work he is trying to do."

Passion was being performed without an interval, in order that the mood Lapine and Sondheim had created would be sustained unbroken. This being the case, the problem of the unwanted laughter eventually had to be dealt with. Sondheim said, "There are moments when . . . [Fosca] does behave in such a way that it's okay . . . for the audience to laugh because her behavior's outrageous . . . She's an operatic character in a musical comedy." Two or three laughs were acceptable; a dozen or more were not. "So we immediately took out, or ameliorated, the lines or moments that would trigger the laughter, either by removing the line or . . . just changing the tone." One night Giorgio visits Fosca's sick room and she invites him to sit on the bed beside her and then urges him to "put his feet up." The audience thought that was hilarious, and it sounded much too contemporary an invitation, so the line was changed to "Rest your feet on the bed." That still prompted a ripple of amusement occasionally. As Lapine said, getting rid of unwanted laughter was "a little like putting out a wildfire: you put it out here and it bursts out somewhere else."

Scenes were also rewritten. The one in which Clara broke off the affair was removed and replaced with a scene in which Giorgio demanded that she leave her husband and go off with him. When she begged him not to insist, knowing that she would lose her child, he turned on her. "Is this what you call love?" he sang. "Love isn't so convenient / Love isn't something scheduled in advance, / Not something guaranteed . . . / What's love unless it's unconditional?" The song was designed to make Giorgio's emerging love for Fosca more convincing, but it also made his behavior towards Clara seem brutally insensitive. But the pivotal change had to do with the all-important train scene, in which the portrait of Fosca as a flawed personality was replaced by that of a woman whose love is selfless. "Loving you / Is not a choice, / It's who I am." She would die for him, she said, and that was the truest kind of love there was.

OPENING NIGHT WAS delayed for two weeks before *Passion* was judged ready to meet its fate on May 9, 1994. Then the telegrams rolled in. "It is both painful and moving to see our story up there on stage," Mike Nichols wrote, tongue-in-cheek. Laurents recalled the theatrical incantation designed to ward off disaster: "Break a leg." Then he added (referring to Peter Jones), "Look what an ankle did!" The infinite pains taken were rewarded by predominantly favorable reviews. As always, the comments of the *New York Times* were all-important. Vincent Canby wrote, "It's now apparent that though *Passion* is technically a period piece, it's the boldest, most modern musical work to arrive on Broadway in years." Robert Brustein, often a Sondheim critic, found himself "sobbing uncontrollably," and compared the work to Puccini's *La Bohème*. *Variety* called it a great work, "the most emotionally engaging new musical Broadway has had in years." So did Stearns in *USA*

Donna Murphy in the role
of Fosca in *Passion*

Jere Shea as Giorgio and
Marin Mazzie as Clara in
Passion

Sondheim and James Lapine, center, confer during recording sessions for *Passion* as Steve Murphy, president of Angel Records, at rear, Tony MacAnany, and Phil Ramone await the verdict.

Today, Peter Travers of *Rolling Stone* called it "a thrilling meditation on the power of awakened feelings." Howard Kissel was full of compliments in the *Daily News*, and Clive Barnes, in the New York *Post*, was equally admiring: "Once in an extraordinary while, you sit in a theatre and your body shivers with the sense and thrill of something so new, so unexpected that it seems, for those fugitive moments, more like life than art." Sondheim, his orchestrator, Jonathan Tunick, and Lapine had finally created "the first serious Broadway opera."

There were some dissenting voices. William A. Henry III called it "the darkest, most depressing show of [Sondheim's] career." Then there were the more cautious assessments, led by David Richards of the *New York Times*, who felt the work's ambitions exceeded its achievements. It was, nevertheless, a bold and highly admirable one. Lloyd Rose of the Washington *Post*, while praising *Passion* for being "disturbing, musically brilliant and astonishingly adult," found it ultimately unsatisfying. Edwin Wilson of the *Wall Street Journal* had great trouble believing the story meant what Lapine and Sondheim clearly thought it meant. "The musical, like the film, emerges as more a pathological study than the illuminating probe of the heart it might have been," he wrote. "*Passion* has so many compelling moments and holds out such promise that the sense of loss when the story falls apart becomes an ache of the heart—not the kind Fosca or Giorgio feels, but the kind one feels when the possibilities of art are made so apparent and yet are not achieved."

Even those critics who had not liked *Passion* were united in their admiration for Donna Murphy. Hers was a stunning performance, John Lahr wrote, of a character out of Gothic romance: "the shadowy figure descending the long, gloomy staircase; the black-shrouded silhouette; the doomed, spectral presence." John Simon thought she was "almost too spookily perfect" as Fosca. Somehow, in the quietest possible way (a novelty for Broadway musicals), Murphy managed to impose herself as both "suffering martyr and relentless fury."

Not surprisingly, Murphy was the favorite to receive the Tony Award for best actress in a musical that year. The all-important awards, which meant so much in terms of box-office sales, had been on everyone's mind, and the only real competition that season was Disney's *Beauty and the Beast,* an extravagant production based on the animated film. Although doing capacity business, *Beauty* was "resented among insiders for having the subtlety of an Ice Capades," Laurie Winer, theatre critic for the Los Angeles *Times,* wrote. The irony, of course, was that in past years the awards community resented Sondheim "for not having the subtlety of an Ice Capades." The 1993–94 season was, by general agreement, stronger on revivals, both musicals and plays, than on original works. So perhaps it was not too surprising that *Passion* triumphed with four awards: for best musical, best original score, best book, and best actress. When his musical was named, Sondheim "gave the room a nice thumbs-up sign and shouted, 'Let's sell some tickets!' " That *Passion* continued to do. By the end of August, *Variety* reported that the musical had returned $675,000 to its investors, or about 15 percent of its capitalization. By October, it was still selling well ahead of the minimum of $200,000 a week needed to keep the doors open. It was filmed for television and recorded before it closed on January 7, 1995, a typically slow month on Broadway. It had stayed afloat for eight months, and that was a respectable run, Lapine said. He added, "The night the show closed, the audience began to applaud as soon as the lights were lowered, and I found myself in tears. At the end they brought Steve and me on stage for a bow, and we had a little party afterwards."

The mood, as so often happens, was closer to exhaustion than exhilaration. As the arguments died away, all that seemed clear was that another experiment had been fought through to an honorable conclusion. As an artistic statement *Passion* was always likely to provoke mixed verdicts. But in human terms, there was no doubt about its landmark status in Sondheim's life. That continuing conflict between head and heart (behind which one might glimpse a suppressed romanticism), one that was once so admired; that defusing wit, the one that kept painful feelings at bay: all the usual defenses had been abandoned. It would have been so much more characteristic for Sondheim to have treated *Fosca* as a black comedy, deftly skewing its affectations and illusions with another bleakly ironic portrait. But that was before the composer had begun to discover a compensatory richness in his life, as he had described it a decade earlier; and the more he looked, the more he saw.

> Love without reason, love without mercy,
> Love without pride or shame.
> Love unconcerned
> With being returned
> —No wisdom, no judgment,
> No caution, no blame.

CHAPTER 21

_____

I'm Still Here

THE FILMED PERFORMANCE of *Passion* (which was shown
on Public Broadcasting stations in the autumn of 1996) was being
given editing sessions in the spring of 1995 in a West Side office building that
was a rabbit warren of sound studios. Two technicians were at work on the
soundtrack, and two more were working on the film, with Paul Gemignani
presiding. Huge platters of meat and cheese were in evidence, accompanied
by mounds of salads and dips and plenty of rolls. James Lapine stopped in
briefly, as did Donna Murphy. Sondheim arrived after they left—he was
always a few minutes late, Gemignani said—and when asked how he was,
said, "All right." He collapsed on the sofa, wearing his usual baggy brown
pants and well-worn sweater, and locked his hands over his eyes. But his eyes
were soon fixed on the screen, his hand sought a sandwich, and he devoured a
pickle in a single bite. He leapt up and swung his arms with vigor while mut-
tering a barrage of comments on the dialogue, all of it unflattering. When
Fosca declared, "Now I want to live!" he said it reminded him of a film starring Susan Hayward. The advertising campaign for that, he quipped, had
been "Filmed on location inside a woman's soul." He always mocked his own
lyrics, Gemignani said, especially when they became "serious." Sondheim
took out a handkerchief at the end of the film. For him, *Passion* caused the
same response no matter how many times he saw it. He could perfectly

understand why some people thought it was "the slowest show in the world," but this never happened to him, he said, blowing his nose.

He had some sharp comments for the singers, saying "Oy vey!" in disapproval when Donna Murphy scooped a note. He wanted more bass notes during one of Clara's songs and left the room briefly while the technicians tried to accommodate him. "Where's the restroom, as they say in this country? Where's the loo?" He was waving his arms above his head in comic despair as he went. "I worked for days on that note!" He made another suggestion for an obvious improvement when a singer came in a fraction too late on a note. After it was corrected, he said, "Perfect!" There was a pause. "Now make it better." Everyone laughed.

Gemignani was equally irreverent, with a gift for keeping the mood lighthearted. As they were waiting for Sondheim to appear, he joked they should run the ending of the film so that he would see the final credits rolling as he walked in. The banter between the two men was constant. Sondheim was always in a good humor at such moments, Gemignani said. One could not go wrong appealing to his sense of the ridiculous. Bonnie Weiss, who performed annual birthday cabaret tributes to Sondheim, discovered to her pleasure that the composer actually liked having his songs parodied even when the wit was quite pointed. "Another hundred people just got off of the train" from *Company* became "Another hundred lyrics just flew out of my brain." The spoof, written by Lauren Mayer, was one long singer's lament about the impossibility of singing Sondheim:

> We try to follow the internal rhymes
> And infernal counts
> With the tricky meter and the picky words
> In absurd amounts.
> And we lose our places where the phrases change
> With a rhythmic flounce.

Christopher Durang, another skillful Sondheim parodist, recalled that *Sweeney Todd* and *Evita,* Andrew Lloyd Webber's musical about Eva Perón, were both playing when he and Sigourney Weaver were performing one of their famous cabaret evenings. He said, "Sondheim came to it and I didn't know he was there, which was lucky. We were told he laughed and laughed, especially when we got to our song about the 'Demon Lady of Buenos Aires.' He doubled up, apparently, after we started to count, which was a reference to how rhythmically complicated his songs were." Over the years, Durang's parodies continued to appeal to Sondheim's sense of humor, so perhaps it was no surprise when a new revue, *Putting It Together,* was announced for New York during the summer of 1992 and Durang was offered a role.

Putting It Together began, as *Side by Side by Sondheim* had done years before, in England. Julia McKenzie had just staged a successful version of *Merrily We Roll Along* in London, Cameron Mackintosh had just produced his own, gentler version of *Follies,* and the idea was launched for a revue that would make use of songs from the later musicals, including *Sweeney Todd, Merrily, Sunday,* and *Into the Woods.* (The title was taken from the song in *Sunday* about the way a work of art is created.) The revue was given the loose structure of a dinner party at which the hosts and their guests discuss the vagaries of love and marriage, play games, drink too much, and arrive at some predictably wry conclusions about their lives. Diana Rigg starred as the hostess in an early version of the revue at Oxford early in 1992. Julie Andrews, who would recreate the role for the New York production, had not been seen on Broadway since *Camelot* some thirty years before. Mackintosh said that the offer was "an irresistible five hundred dollars a week to work a five-show weekend sharing a dressing room in a basement with no star billing!" A meeting took place in Sondheim's study to demonstrate the idea for Andrews, who sat there in immaculate jeans "and a wonderful white shirt, looking about twenty-two years old," McKenzie said. The latter was trying to display the possibilities of the songs chosen without giving Andrews the impression that "the song belonged to me." She was getting drowned out by Sondheim at the piano, who was throwing himself into the mood of the moment rather too energetically. Mackintosh was sure Andrews did not like the idea, but to everyone's surprise, she did.

The only change involved one of her songs, "The Ladies Who Lunch" from *Company.* Diana Rigg had handled the demands of the song with aplomb, and although she was willing to try it, Durang said, Andrews was finally defeated by the necessity of having a New York accent and the impossibility of dispensing with her own clipped British one. So that song went, to be replaced by "Could I Leave You?" The revue had a limited run at the Manhattan Theatre Club in the spring of 1993 and received favorable notices, with the exception of Frank Rich's, who thought the choice of material confirmed the critical view of Sondheim as a brittle intellectual gamesman who specialized in "knee-jerk romantic disillusionment."

During the course of the second act the guests played a party game. In England the one chosen was Truth or Dare, which was not thought to be well known in the United States, so Durang was consulted to suggest a replacement. He offered several, but Sondheim eventually invented his own, "Whom in This Room [Would You Marry]," as a pretext for other songs.

Inventing a new game was an increasingly rare pleasure for Sondheim, since although his love of game parties had not diminished over the years, the opportunities had. None of his friends were interested in them nowadays, he said somewhat wistfully. But he would leap at the offer if consulted, as he was in May of 1994. James Lapine was organizing a benefit for the Millay Colony for the Arts and asked Sondheim to create a treasure hunt that would act as a fund raiser. A private club had been offered for the event; Lapine and Sondheim examined the facilities, and Sondheim invented an elaborate set of clues based on Edna St. Vincent Millay's poetry and particularly her birthdate of 1892. The treasure hunt would culminate in the basement, and the numbers in the birthdate would unlock a particular locker. To do this, however, the lock's combination had to be changed. When he learned at the eleventh hour that this could not be done, Sondheim had to come up with a completely new set of clues. It was a huge amount of work, but on the other hand, it did raise $20,000 for the charity.

Sondheim occasionally found himself in quandaries of this kind. He offered to write a song as a prize for a PBS-TV benefit. He said, "It's the only song I've ever written that nobody's ever heard except the guy I wrote it for. I never even met him, but he wanted a song about his mother and we talked on the phone. I said, 'Send me her characteristics,' and one of these was, she was no good at telling jokes. The entire family just covered their faces in embarrassment every time she told a joke, so I wrote a song about telling jokes. I worked it so the family would sing a song, and they would cue her, she would tell a joke, and their terrible reaction would be in the song." It was a great success, but "I'll never do it again, because it took a month out of my life."

SONDHEIM HAD ENTERED his sixties in fine physical and mental fettle. "Sondheim: A Celebration at Carnegie Hall" in June 1992 paid tribute, as John Simon wrote, to his "cleverness and breadth" if not his asperity and depth. In 1994 there was a tenth-anniversary concert version of *Sunday in the Park* that reunited the original cast. *Anyone Can Whistle* received its concert version, an AIDS benefit, somewhat less successfully the following year, although it raised almost $1 million for the cause. His career was celebrated at length by the Kennedy Center in Washington in 1993 when he received an award for his lifetime achievements. The National Endowment for the Arts, embroiled, in the summer of 1992, in a bitter controversy over an attempt to cancel its more controversial grants, wanted to award Sondheim the National Medal of Arts. That was during the Bush administration, and he, along with author Wallace Stegner, declined the honor. Early in 1997, Sondheim accepted the same award from President and Mrs. Clinton and went to the White House dinner afterward, taking Arthur Laurents as his guest. It was gratifying to have one's achievements widely acknowledged, even though he sometimes did not want to be reminded about how much time had passed. "Stop!" he told an interviewer jokingly. "I'm really twenty-two years old. Don't you know I'm just very precocious?"

Dear friends celebrated his birthdays. Hal and Judy Prince threw a lavish party for his sixtieth at their home in Florida which continued all weekend, with boat trips, lunches, and a grand dinner at a mansion built by the Van-derbilts. Soon after *Passion,* Prince invited him to join forces in a musical retelling of the Leo Frank story. Frank was a factory manager who was falsely accused of murdering an Atlanta child in 1913 and lynched. The musical was to be called *Parade,* and Sondheim said, "I instinctively thought it was a good idea." But after mulling it over he decided it was "extremely intense" and wanted to do something in a lighter vein. Still, there was no doubt about the warmth of his feelings for his old collaborator. One of the two photographs in his study was of himself and Prince, seated on a piano bench, the summer they were working on *Merrily.* The greeting said, "Hey, Old Friend! Love, Hal." There was the elaborate party given by Hank and Mary Rodgers Guet-tel for his sixty-fifth birthday, which featured a string trio and a birthday cake in the shape of a Steinway with an anagram on top for him to decipher. But birthdays were always special occasions. Faced with Sondheim's fifty-ninth, Mary Ann Madden had composed a poem that began:

> Once upon a night divinish
> Came a thought so bleak and swinish
> As of someone not refinish
> Knocking at my chamber door.
> While I nodded, quite bovinish
> Clouds became all silver-linish
> Jesus Christ, Steve's fifty-ninish.
> And I'm only thirty-four . . .

It was titled "What to Do for Steve's Birthday—Again."

"PUTTING IT TOGETHER" is a theme that occurs repeatedly in *Sunday in the Park with George.* The artist deplores the emphasis upon novelty at any price, the necessity of finding backers, the competitiveness of art itself, and the gulf separating a work's inception and its execution: "a vision's just a vision if it's only in your head . . ." The other theme expressed in the song of the same title would have had particular relevance for him personally. Seurat's grandson George sings, "If no one gets to see it, it's as good as dead." For a musical dramatist, what counted even more than the agony of creativity and the vagaries of critical acceptance was the necessity of being performed. Without a performance his works did not exist, and although his work was frequently being revived (besides a London production of *Passion,* there were new productions of *Company, Forum,* and *Night Music* being planned in London and New York), these were works he had long since polished to a high gloss and which therefore no longer held his rapt attention. He wanted the exquisite agony of putting together a new project, something he could bring to life, and had returned to the idea of a musical he had considered thirty years before, after reading Alva Johnston's book *The Legendary Mizners.* Now John Weidman had agreed to the new venture. Sondheim said his original interest had been in Wilson, the writer, and that he had seen Addison, the architect, as a minor figure. "But as I talked to John the relationship between the two became central. What was funny was that when I reread *The Legendary Mizners* I realized I'd forgotten the first four or five chapters were about Addison. John wanted to explore the relationship between them and he's absolutely right, and that's what the show will be about."

Sondheim and Weidman went to Florida for a week early in February of 1995 and spent it visiting some of the palatial homes Addison Mizner had built, and looking at his grand designs for the new town of Boca Raton, which included a canal rivaling those in Venice and a vast highway linking the new resort with the rest of the world. Although, as Johnston noted, its twenty lanes made it the widest highway in the world, it was also the shortest, being only half a mile long. "In boom maps and blueprints El Camino Real rolled its twenty traffic lanes past a series of colossal nonexistent cities," he wrote. "In real life, it died away in brambles and swamps."

The new musical was being commissioned by the Kennedy Center in Washington, D.C., but when they went to Florida that year they were still looking for a producing partner for Roger Berlind, who had agreed to co-produce the musical, which would acquire the tentative title of *Wise Guys.*

Howard Erskine said he had met an enormously rich couple, with "his and her Gulf Stream jets" and a lovely old house in England that they were restoring, and who owned one of the great houses in Palm Beach. Erskine knew the wife had been a singer and was interested in Sondheim's work. Somehow she learned that Sondheim was due to arrive in Palm Beach and rang Erskine to say she wanted to give him a dinner party. Sondheim was not terribly keen on that idea, but since the new musical was likely to be expensive—Erskine thought $5 million–$6 million—he agreed to go for cocktails. "He really didn't want to do it but he did it because it was me. When we got there we had a marvelous time because this house was just unbelievable, one of the great houses, with a courtyard, tennis courts . . . As we drove in, Steve said, 'I'm sure these people are anti-Semitic,' and I said, 'No, they just hate Jews! Don't worry about it.' Steve was grumbling and John was telling him to shut up." The couple were dressed in their best, the bejeweled hostess was charming, inquired about the new project and plied them all with drinks. Soon Sondheim sat down and began to play at one of the two pianos. Erskine thought the hostess was just about to start singing and so did Sondheim, because he stopped. They stayed for an hour, enjoying the luxurious ambiance, the servants, the fine wines, the vintage champagne, and the mounds of caviar. Erskine was sure the couple were about to make an investment. But in the end, Scott Rudin, the multimillionaire filmmaker who had, with Berlind, co-produced *Passion*, decided to join Berlind on *Wise Guys*.

The musical was to have received its premiere during the Kennedy Center's twenty-fifth anniversary season, 1995–96, but the date kept getting postponed. That was partly because Weidman had a prior commitment to another musical, *Big*, the opening of which kept getting delayed. It was also because Sondheim, too, was having difficulty writing. "I think my trouble is partly loss of confidence, loss of brain cells and some kind of creative energy that leaves you." Meantime there were all the reasons why he should lend his name to charities, go to dinners and give speeches, even when it was the last thing he wanted to do. The suspicion that there were too many demands had grown over the years, after he became president of the Dramatists Guild. "And boy, you hate to turn anybody down, because they need you." As he said in another context, there was an obligation to help. If he really put his mind to it, he could probably analyze every show he had written, beginning with *Anyone Can Whistle*. "It's about nonconformity. Surprise, surprise! And it's one of the bases for my friendship with Arthur, that we were nonconformists." Sondheim used to have a sign posted on the bulletin board of his office, the gist of which was, "If you do what everybody expects, you're not doing your job." He believed this although "I'm scared to death of being a nonconformist . . . I worry so much about what other people will think of me."

IN 1995 SONDHEIM HAD JOINED forces with an old collaborator, George Furth, and written his first play. It was a murder mystery set in the dowdily elegant offices of a West Side psychiatrist, in a turn-of-the-century building replete with gargoyles that was about to be demolished. Here some

patients gathered every Saturday afternoon for group therapy. But this particular afternoon the doctor did not appear. He had been murdered, evidently
by one of them. In a plot reminiscent of Agatha Christie's famous novel *And
Then There Were None,* each participant was murdered and the murderer
escaped seconds before the building went up in smoke. The play received its
premiere in the summer of 1995 at the Old Globe Playhouse in La Jolla, California, and the reviews were encouraging.

The plot was developed with meticulous attention to timing and considerable wit and style. But the authors created an almost insuperable problem
for themselves by revealing the murderer's identity at the end of the first act
and were never able to invent an even more audacious climax for the end of
the second, although they tried mightily. Some members of the audience
objected to having the murderer get off scot-free, and this was also rewritten
at the eleventh hour. The fact that the play's title kept changing before its
authors finally settled on *Getting Away with Murder* seemed symbolic of the
problems they were having in giving the right focus to their "comedy
thriller," as it was called. One morning, although groggy from lack of sleep,
Sondheim was still laughing about what had happened at the preview in New
York the night before. The murderer's gun refused to fire and the actor was
reduced to strangling his victims one by one while the others politely awaited
their turn. Sondheim, lying on his couch, was flailing his legs and arms at the
irresistible silliness of it all. "What do you do?" he said. "Isn't that wild?" His
ability to laugh at his own dilemmas, and those of others, was as pronounced
as ever. When Howard Erskine returned from a visit to the island of North
Haven, Maine, where he lunched with the late Tommy Watson, heir to the
IBM fortune, he was full of stories about his host, then an octogenarian, who
was still flying his own plane. "Just think," Erskine said, "he told us about the
time he went skywriting." Quick as a flash, Sondheim replied, "He's beginning to misspell, I hear."

Getting Away with Murder opened at the Broadhurst on March 17, 1996,
to a barrage of negative reviews. One headline advised, "Stick with the day
job, Stephen," and few others were any more encouraging. It was clear that
the end was near. Before and during previews Roger Berlind had used a gargoyle holding a smoking gun to advertise the play. But once the closing date
was set, he had the advertisement redrawn to show the gun pointing at the
gargoyle's head, along with the message "Goodbye, cruel world . . ." It
showed a gallant spirit on the part of a man who, people thought, must have
lost millions of dollars. On his way to Heathrow Airport, after attending
rehearsals of *Passion* in London a few days before *Murder* closed, Sondheim
said, "I had such a good time writing it, the audiences enjoyed it, but it gave

Terrence Mann, as Gregory Reed, and John Rubinstein, playing Martin Chisholm, in *Getting Away with Murder,* 1996

the critics a chance to shoot me through the heart, the chance they'd been waiting for, for years. I was surprised how vicious they were."

Being mortally wounded sounded hyperbolic for the disappointment felt, but there might have been another reason for the anguished feelings. He and P.J. had attended the opening, slipping into the theatre with impeccable timing just as the curtain rose. The moment it came down for intermission Sondheim, with practiced ease, again escaped, leaving P.J. to his own devices. Jones, in a well-tailored raincoat and turtleneck, seemed ill at ease and distracted. He did not know where Sondheim had gone and was disinclined to discuss his own project, a musical version of *Peyton Place,* one he had been working on for some time. The very thought of it seemed to embarrass him.

The two men moved between New York and Connecticut and seemed to have established an easy and comfortable relationship, but cracks were beginning to show. Jones said that problems were to be expected when someone young and untested is drawn into the orbit of a famous person. He joked that he felt exactly like the second Mrs. de Winter in *Rebecca,* but instead of a dead wife, his rival for the affections of Sondheim was the past and all that it implied. He was being relegated to a corner into which, since he was young and malleable, he could be made to fit. The "Manderley" in this case, the house in Connecticut, inspired feelings of domesticity in him, but there was nothing to be done because the whole estate had been arranged around the tastes and habits of one person. Similarly, in New York, he did not have a room to call his own, a depressing state of affairs which was further eroding a sense of self-worth that he readily conceded was fragile. He said that Judy Prince once asked him whether he always nodded agreement to whatever Sondheim said. He replied that he did not always agree, but "I don't get a chance to get a word in edgewise. It's hard for me to talk freely when I'm in his presence with other people, because he naturally holds court." Since self-assertion was so difficult for him, Jones took the easy way out. He began a relationship with someone else, in this case a college teacher. Sondheim tried to accept the fact that P.J.'s affections were divided, but "it didn't work," Sondheim said. "I got too upset." Jones said he was given an ultimatum. Sondheim offered to help him pack. In a fury, Jones walked out of the house in the rain but returned in five minutes to gather his belongings and call a taxi. He arrived in New Haven that night and stayed with his friend until he could find an apartment and a job.

Sondheim put the most diplomatic construct on the break, saying P.J. needed to have his own space. But to have been rejected must have been painful, and it would be small comfort when P.J.'s new relationship also foundered. "The damage had been done," Sondheim said. He was helped through the crisis by his psychiatrist, Arthur Laurents, and Judy Prince. Then Jones became enrolled in a program of Freudian analysis four mornings a week. Sondheim said the change in him was remarkable. Meanwhile, they cautiously tried to begin again. It was agreed that Jones would keep his New Haven apartment and spend three days of every week in New York. That arrangement was made in the spring of 1997 and they would see how things worked out. They were no longer wearing wedding rings. Sondheim reflected that he had been experiencing in the last few years the "Sturm und Drang" most people went through in their twenties and thirties, because "I had opened myself up."

Meantime, he had other concerns. At the end of February 1995, shortly after work began on the Mizner project, Sondheim had agreed to write some new songs for a film, *The Birdcage*, being directed by Mike Nichols, a new version of the French film and Broadway musical *La Cage aux Folles*. So Sondheim, Nichols, P.J., and Clar went off to a restaurant in Greenwich Village famous for its drag shows. Jones recalled they left shortly after eight o'clock. Andrea, the houseman, already suffering from the effects of AIDS that would kill him the following year, was asleep upstairs in his apartment; Max, the poodle, was with him.

Moments later, at 8:12 p.m., a fire started in the office on the second-floor front. Sondheim said the desk lamp was kept burning night and day. After ten years he and Steve Clar had long since forgotten the cord was there and had piled cartons full of photographs directly on top of it. That, they subsequently learned, is one of the commonest causes of fire, since an electrical wire without adequate ventilation will eventually overheat. "From the pattern of charring on the wall and what was left of the lamp it was clear that the fire had started there." The fire brigade arrived almost immediately, but by the time the blaze was discovered the second floor, housing all of the manuscripts, archives, scrapbooks, and reference books, was in flames. Andrea had to be rescued with a ladder. Max, the dog, died of smoke inhalation. All this took place while Sondheim and party were still at dinner.

When they returned, "We didn't see anything wrong right away," Jones said. "As we got out of the car and walked up to the door, I noticed some broken glass on the steps and thought, Oh, we've been vandalized." The door was open, but he assumed that merely meant Andrea was cleaning things up. Then Andrea himself appeared in tears, and they suddenly realized that every window in the front of the house was broken. Even floors not badly damaged by smoke and ash, which rose up and coated everything with an oily black layer, were permeated by an unpleasant chemical smell, which had even penetrated the clothes in drawers. Thanks to a heavy wooden door, some items in the office closet, including music manuscripts and scrapbooks, had been saved. But the collection of photographs was destroyed, and so were some antique playing cards and games, and many other objects of real or sentimental value. Fortunately, firemen had covered his grand piano with a tarpaulin to protect it from water damage, and it survived relatively unscathed. But a week or so after the fire, an upstairs toilet erupted and flooded the ground floor with two inches of water. The whole house had to be completely gutted, and it would be almost two years before he could live there again. He and P.J. took a furnished apartment forty-five floors up on Fifty-seventh Street (Sondheim joked of the height that P.J. could not look up and he could not look down) and enlisted the help of Peter Wooster to redesign and restore the house. Eventually, it would be handsomer than ever. Steve Clar discovered a flame-licked copy of one of the songs from *Follies* and had it framed, where it occupied a place of honor. It was "I'm Still Here."

IF *Sunday in the Park with George* was the breakthrough, the personal renaissance that both confirmed and reinvigorated Sondheim's role as the major musical dramatist of his time, it also had an important role to play in his per-

June 1961

sonal life. For his emotions operated on two levels, levels that allowed him to know things without knowing them. (How many times had he begun work on something just because it attracted him, and found out much later how close the subject matter was to home?) *Sunday in the Park* was the quintessential vehicle for feelings that had been mangled in childhood. And that musical, which on the surface displayed such a clinical dissociation from feeling, perhaps paradoxically revealed the most. Loneliness, the sense of being an outsider, a feeling of continually groping toward something just beyond one's reach—these were themes he knew and had already expressed, always superimposed upon by irony and disillusion, those reliable defenses against painful emotions. *Sunday's* arrival in his life had taken him a long step closer to reconciliation, not just with life and others but with his essential being.

As Carl Jung explained in a superb essay, *The Spirit in Man, Art, and Literature,* every creator tried to maintain an uneasy equilibrium between opposing qualities: "On the one side he is a human being with a personal life, while on the other he is an impersonal creative process. As a human being he may be sound or morbid, and his personal psychology can and should be explained in personal terms. But he can be understood as an artist only in terms of his creative achievement." Art, Jung thought, was "a kind of innate drive that seizes a human being and makes him its instrument," and that being the case, such a person was driven to work and create almost despite himself. He was, equally, "mastered by an impulse for constant growth and development—he knows not whither."

If, as some of his more perceptive friends believed, Sondheim might never know that inner contentment which is perhaps the most elusive of all human states—Yeats's description of that was "a heavenly mansion, raging in the dark"—Jung believed it was not one that the artist could achieve, even if he most desired it. "A person must pay dearly for the divine gift of creative fire. It is as though each of us was born with a limited store of energy. In the artist, the strongest force in his make-up, that is, his creativeness, will seize and all but monopolize this energy . . ." The price for such a gift was bound to be "a deficit on some other side of life."

To some degree, Jung continued, the work of an artist met the psychic needs of the society in which he lived, whether he was aware of it or not. Since he was only the instrument, one had no right to expect him to be an interpreter as well. "A great work of art is like a dream; for all its apparent obviousness it does not explain itself and is always ambiguous." That, perhaps, is a particularly satisfying explanation for *Sunday in the Park,* for those hypnotic, arrested images from Seurat are both blankly noncommunicative and yet, somehow, insistent on the importance of their secret metaphor. After much anxious inner questioning, Lapine and Sondheim found the exact ending, one that would give them the sense of haunted incompleteness they sought but one that could just as easily be seen from a different perspective. For George sings at the end,

> I want to move on.
> I want to explore the light.
> I want to know how to get through,
> Through to something new,
> Something of my own—

And as he examines his work, populated by so many ghosts, they begin to leave the stage quietly, one by one. All that remains, finally, is a blank canvas, an empty space. It is that most tantalizing of colors: white.

Acknowledgments

I FIRST MET Stephen Sondheim when I was at work on a biography of Leonard Bernstein and went to interview him about the part he played in the creation of *West Side Story.* His front door opened directly off the street and the silence of that long living room, spotlit at intervals, was in marked contrast to the din behind the door. Once we got past the standard questions it was clear that here was a trenchant and quicksilver mind. I was struggling just then to understand the moment when Bernstein's exuberant creativity began to fade, to be replaced by works as labored and pedantic as *A Quiet Place,* and Sondheim said something that provided a clue to the puzzle. He remarked that Bernstein had a bad case of "important-itis." I retained an image of Sondheim stretched out on a beige sofa—he had just broken his ankle—and talking, as it seemed, into the air but in ways that addressed my concerns. Some time later I approached him with the idea of writing his biography. He declined at first, but I persisted, and once he had agreed, submitted to many hours of interviews, and helped in every conceivable way. That this most reticent of men was willing to undertake such a self-revelatory task was remarkable. Not surprisingly, I came to admire him greatly. Keeping a certain distance from one's subject has always seemed desirable to me, and I can only hope that my partiality did not lead me too far astray.

Many of Sondheim's friends were willing to assist this project, some of them at length. The help and advice of Arthur Laurents and Mary Rodgers

ACKNOWLEDGMENTS

Guettel have been invaluable at every stage, and for Sondheim's recent years I am indebted to the reminiscences of Peter Jones. Sondheim's friends from childhood, Henry ("Skippy") Steiner and his sister, Felicia Lemonick, could not have been kinder or more helpful. Walter Sondheim, half-brother, has also helped unselfishly at every stage, with materials that included precious family photographs and many personal reminiscences. On his father's side, Arthur Persky, the late Barbara (Bobbie) Rosenberg, her sister, Janet (Johnnie) Eisler, Myra Berzoff, Doris Gorman, Patti Gorman, and, in particular, Joan Barnet were invaluable guides in reconstructing the Fox family history and the early life of Janet ("Foxy") Sondheim. I cannot thank them enough.

For his days at George School, I was particularly indebted to Hugh Cronister and Rosamond Earle Matthews, who befriended him and remembered him well. For his relationship with the Hammerstein family I drew heavily on the reminiscences of William and Jamie Hammerstein, sons of Oscar Hammerstein II, and would like to make a special mention of the insights of Susan Blanchard, Oscar's stepdaughter. For his days at Williams College, Sondheim's lifelong friends Charles Hollerith, Howard Erskine, and Dominick Dunne could not have been kinder or more helpful. I was also very much helped by John Anderson, Stephen Birmingham, Charles W. Halleck, Andrew D. Heineman, H. Baekeland Roll, Professor Irwin Shainman, Dr. Sidney Werkman, and Ford Wright. Professor Milton Babbitt and his wife, Sylvia, were other witnesses to the talents of the young Sondheim, as was D. D. Ryan, whose reminiscences were particularly vivid and perceptive.

Hal Prince gave me the benefit of his reminiscences and his unique perspective on Sondheim's career, as did his children, Daisy and Charles Prince; they have my great gratitude. The playwright John Guare added his insightful comments, as did William Goldman, André Bishop, and James Lapine; all of their remarks have influenced me one way or another. Sondheim's immensely competent and hospitable chargé d'affaires, Steven Clar, has endured my many demands on his time with patience and good humor. When Paul Salsini, editor and founder of the Sondheim Review, learned that a great many of Sondheim's files had been consumed by fire, he insisted that I pay him and his wife a visit, and put his own extensive archive at my disposal. I am so grateful for his help, which came at a crucial moment.

For all those who also offered advice, encouragement, words of wisdom, and concrete help, I want to extend further thanks: Michael Adams, Bob Allen, David Aukin, Bob Avian, Alan Ayckbourn, Emanuel Azenberg, Ben Bagley, Scott Baldinger, Professor Stephen Banfield, Keith Baxter, Lucy Beldock, Nancy Berg, Roger Berlind, Anne Bernays, Arnold Bernstein, Professor Norwood and Martha Beveridge, Patricia Birch, Robert W. Bloch, Patricia Bosworth, Dwight Blocker Bowers, Adrian Bryan-Brown, John Breglio, Robert Brustein, Lucy Perry Buchanan, Len Cariou, Theodore S.

Chapin, Martin Charnin, Stephen Clark, Stephanie Coen, Barbara Cook, Alice Crouthers, William D. Curtis, Nancy Davis, June Wells Dill, Rick Donahue, Declan Donnellan, Barry Drogin, Christopher Durang, Scott Ellis, Beverly Emmons, Roger Englander, Milton B. Eulau, Harvey Evans, Dr. Lee Evans, Mia Farrow, Bernard Felch, Bert Fink, William Finn, Paul Ford, Hugh Fordin, Robert Fryer, Bruce-Michael Gelbert, Paul Gemignani, Freddie Gershon, Bob Gillespy, Joanna Gleason, Ricky Ian Gordon, Martin Gottfried, Lois Gould, Kip Gowans, Jesse Green, Edward Hardy, the Earl of Harewood, Judge David Harfeld, Ron Harris, Rosalie Harris, John N. Hart, Stanley Herman, Toby Himmel, Stanley L. Hirsch of Camp Androscoggin, Jeffrey Hogrefe, Ann Hoops, Mark Horowitz of the Library of Congress, Dr. Carol Ilson, Dr. Richard A. Isay, the Reverend Bruce Janiga, Bix Janni, Diane Johnson, Dr. David I. Joseph, Howard Kissel, Florence Klotz, Albert F. Koenig Jr., Jack Kroll, John Lahr, James Lapine, Sondra Lee, David Levine, Jeffrey Lonoff, Craig Lucas, Patti LuPone, Sir Cameron Mackintosh, Roddy McDowall, Terri McKean, Julia McKenzie, Paul McKibbins, Barbara Barondess MacLean, Joseph McLellan, John McMartin, Richard Maltby, Laurence Maslon, Edward Matthews, Sam Mendes, Joanna Merlin, Barbara Michaels, Larry Miller, Charlotte Moore, James Morris, Otts Munderloh, Donna Murphy, Marty Jacobs, Lawrence Newman, Mildred Newman, Phyllis Newman, Mike Nichols, Jack O'Brien, Cynthia O'Neal, Mrs. Frank W. Packard, Tim Page, Mike Palter, Professor Frank Rizzo, Mandy Patinkin, D. A. Pennebaker, Mr. and Mrs. Robert Persky, Robert S. Persky, Bernadette Peters, Dan Pinck, Lonny Price, Beverley Randolph, Rob Reiner, Bruce W. Remick, Frank Rich, David Richards, Martin Richards, Phil Rinaldi, Flora Roberts, Jill Robinson, Barbara Rollin, Ned Rorem, Jay David Saks, Rita Salzman, Sanford J. Schlesinger, Gerald Schoenfeld, Susan H. Schulman, Peter Shaffer, Thomas Z. Shepard, Ned Sherrin, David Shire, Mark E. Swartz, Jean Simmons, John Simon, Patricia Sinnott, Professor Irving Sirkin, Michael Starobin, David Patrick Stearns, Peter Stone, Elaine Stritch, Nancy Swift, Anthony Tommasini, Jonathan Tunick, Michael Turkic, Jack Viertel, Doug Wager, Jim Walton, Tony Walton, Keith Warner, Sir Andrew Lloyd Webber, John Weidman, Charles Winecoff, Susan Woelzl, William Baldwin Young, Craig Zadan, Jerry Zaks, Chip Zien, the late Sharman Douglas, the late Janet Hayes, the late Tommy Valando, and the late Benay Venuta.

Some biographies get written despite every obstacle that fate, or circumstance, can contrive. This one has led a charmed life, and not just because, as I am again reminded, strangers can be so amazingly forbearing. That so many people have been willing to help is a testament to their devotion to my subject. My former agent, Murray Pollinger, saw the project off in high style before breaking the sad news that he was retiring. But I was passed along to Bruce Hunter of David Higham, whose diligence and genuine interest have helped fill the gap he left. As always, I am indebted to the perceptiveness of my editor, Victoria Wilson, who has perfected the art of administering criticism and encouragement in judicious amounts. Our happy association is in its tenth year. Finally, I must thank my husband, Thomas Beveridge, who has endured a steady diet of Sondheim for breakfast, lunch, and dinner these past four years with hardly a murmur of protest.

Notes

ABBREVIATIONS

BA *Broadway,* Brooks Atkinson, 1970.

BAN *Sondheim's Broadway Musicals,* Stephen Banfield, 1996.

BSS *Broadway Song and Story,* Dramatists Guild Inc., 1985.

COH Columbia Oral History.

F *Getting to Know Him: A Biography of Oscar Hammerstein II,* Hugh Fordin, 1995.

GOL *The Season,* William Goldman, 1984.

HUB *A Stephen Sondheim Lecture,* edited by Eugene R. Huber, typescript, 1986.

IL *Harold Prince,* Carol Ilson, 1992.

JAN Interview with Stephen Sondheim by the Reverend Bruce Janiga on CompuServe, 1994.

MUS *Musical Comedy in America,* Cecil Smith and Glenn Litton, 1991.

NOL *Notes on Lyrics,* Oscar Hammerstein, 1949.

RNT *Platform Papers,* Royal National Theatre, 1993.

RR *Musical Stages,* Richard Rodgers, 1995.

SI Typescript of interviews with Stephen Sondheim by author.

THE "The Musical Theatre," a talk by Stephen Sondheim, *Dramatists Guild Quarterly,* Autumn 1978.

Z *Sondheim & Co.,* Craig Zadan, 1989.

An Institutionalized Child

3 The day it first opened: *New York Times,* September 21, 1930.

4 Marriage to Bertha Guttenstein: on June 19, 1894.

5 Gave him a job: from a press release by Eleanor Lambert, undated.

9 "young women traveling together": from an interview with author.

"...she was a dress designer": SI, pp. 194–5.

"...a doozie": interview with author.

11 "...she must have been very hurt": interview with author.

"That was dangerous": interview with author.

"it was a bargain": SI, p. 3.

12 Central Park's Hooverville: *Central Park: The Birth, Decline and Renewal of a National Treasure,* Eugene Kinkead, 1990, p. 101.

The finest apartments in the city: *Mansions in the Clouds: The Skyscraper Palazzi of Emery Roth,* Steven Ruttenbaum, 1986, pp. 139–40.

13 "I was strolled naked!": SI, p. 3.

14 "...those were my Saturdays": SI, p. 6.

16 "I thought it was swell!": SI, p. 15.

"...a very ordinary kid.": SI, p. 15.

17 This parlor trick: COH, 1–12.

"...a wonderful invention...": SI, p. 8.

18 "The Sondheim Straw Hat Chorus": from a series of advertisements published in the summer of 1946.

"The Rodgers and Hart...": obituary in *Women's Wear Daily,* August 2, 1965.

19 She and Kern won an Academy Award: F, pp. 144–5.

Sondheim had no idea: SI, p. 96.

20 "...on his little finger": SI, p. 9.

"...really a lump": SI, p. 9.

"...humming things": COH, 2–67.

"very strongly attracted": COH, 2–69.

But remembers nothing: SI, p. 24.

21 "...and badly abused": interview with author.

"I didn't cry...": SI, pp. 10–11.

22 "...a lonely voice": "The Brass Goddess," Stephen Sondheim, *The Purple Cow,* Williams College, March 1947, p. 5.

"...that's how I found out": SI, p. 12.

Children Will Listen

23 Chapter title is taken from the song of the same name by Stephen Sondheim in *Into the Woods.*

24 "...something of a vogue..."; "...she left her husband...": SI, p. 12.

"She wasn't pretty . . .": interview with author.

"I thought it was terrific": SI, p. 12.

25 ". . . our Sunday uniforms": SI, p. 57.

". . . I sort of knew . . .": SI, p. 56.

". . . pulling every green button . . .": COH, 1–15.

28 "immoral purposes": *Frank Lloyd Wright*, Meryle Secrest, 1992, p. 243.

A legal separation: on October 22, 1941.

29 ". . . a very vindictive woman": SI, p. 14.

Married in a registry office: on March 6, 1943.

30 Finally obtained his divorce: on May 29, 1946.

". . . a little fortress . . .": SI, p. 15.

Believed his father had abandoned him: SI, p. 98.

Foxy blamed her son: from an interview with Howard Erskine.

". . . really upsetting . . .": SI, p. 11.

". . . all moderately naive": SI, p. 11.

31 ". . . treat me like dirt . . .": SI, p. 12.

"lacks appropriate sexual controls . . .": *Healing the Incest Wound*, Christine A. Courtois, 1996, p. 70.

Similar histories: In *Mother-Child Incest, Characteristics of the Offender* (1986) L. M. McCarty found that "the typical offender had a troubled childhood (92%) during which she was sexually abused (78%), usually by a brother" (pp. 456–7).

"the incesting mother forces . . .": *Between Mothers and Sons*, Evelyn S. Bassoff, 1994, p. 84.

"The unremembered plight . . ." *Thou Shalt Not Be Aware*, Alice Miller, 1986, pp. 160–1 (Miller's italics).

32 "Foxy's chutzpa . . .": interview with author.

33 "infiltrating the house": COH, 1–22.

". . . very much in love . . .": interview with author.

A year younger: he was born on March 21, 1931.

34 ". . . she was not reliable": interview with author.

34-5 ". . . reminded me of Albee's play . . .": interview with author.

35 ". . . it was difficult . . .": SI, p. 39.

". . . making me alienated . . .": SI, p. 13.

36 Did not think she really minded: SI, March 13, 1997, p. 3.

". . . bought rabbits": SI, p. 35.

"some pretty bitchy fights": interview with author.

About to begin work: F, p. 182.

"a romantic, florid . . .": RR, p. 207.

37 ". . . wounds have been inflicted . . .": SI, p. 39.

"His idea of fun . . .": interview with author.

37 "would reduce everyone . . .": SI, p. 38.

39 ". . . your heart beating": SI, pp. 34–5.

40 "I trudged down there": interview with author.

"The women didn't notice . . .": SI, p. 167.

43 "the remnant": F, p. xi.

"I am there still": from "Someone in a Tree," by Stephen Sondheim.

"nothing made sense . . .": SI, p. 67.

". . . the black terrors . . .": *Sleuth,* Anthony Shaffer, 1977, p. 76.

Became the leitmotif: SI, pp. 66–7.

". . . he grabbed my arm": from an interview with author.

The Brass Goddess

44 Operation to improve her nose: SI, p. 68; letter, March 29, 1996.

45 ". . . that maddening smirk": "The Brass Goddess," Stephen Sondheim, *The Purple Cow,* Williams College, March 1947, p. 5; ". . . polished, lonely house": ibid., p. 7; ". . . making yourself unpleasant . . .": ibid., p. 7; "I hate her!": ibid., p. 20.

A not very kind caricature: SI, p. 58.

"Don't brag.": SI, p. 211.

tended to stammer: SI p. 132.

Had severe acne: SI, p. 58.

46 Nose was "forever running": *Necessary Objects,* Lois Gould, 1988, p. 77.

Suffered from hay fever: SI, pp. 57–8.

Destroys the score: *Necessary Objects,* Lois Gould, 1988, p. 182.

End of a concert-career: SI, p. 23; COH, 1–15.

"so hopelessly bad . . .": *Period Piece,* Gwen Raverat, 1981, p. 273.

Shoes lacking any polish: Hugh Cronister, interview with author.

47 "I was precocious . . .": SI, p. 65.

Make a point of doing the reverse: SI, p. 76.

". . . so that nobody would think . . .": SI p. 65.

". . . and bright as could be": interview with author.

Excited him about language: SI, p. 23.

48 "I had no family . . .": SI, p. 207.

50 ". . . my idea of real sophistication . . .": SI, p. 124.

"unable to think . . .": NOL, p. 8.

". . . the direct and honest approach . . .": NOL, pp. 8–9.

51 ". . . waiting to be used": NOL, p. 10.

Just like Oscar: SI, p. 36.

". . . worlds of creative possibilities": SI, p. 58.

The biggest success: George School *News,* May 31, 1946.

52 Truly bad lyrics: "There is a desire to create the illusion of a magic touch and infalli-
   bility, and I think this does a great deal of harm": NOL, p. 36.

   "There are limits . . .": NOL, p. 39.

   ". . . fancy rhymes and foolish jokes . . .": NOL, pp. 34–5.

   ". . . I said it was terrible": Z, p. 4.

   Was absolutely right: SI, p. 114.

   Did not quite please: NOL, pp. 24–5.

53 ". . . a single expression": NOL, p. 15.

   His advice was asked: SI, p. 59.

   ". . . it moved me so much": SI, p. 124.

54 "It wasn't about money . . .": SI, p. 60.

55 Bad behavior: SI, p. 60.

56 Commanded them to be quiet: F, p. 255.

   ". . . I am trying to recreate . . .": SI, p. 172.

   ". . . my entire view of the world": Sondheim Guardian Lecture, reprinted in *Biased*,
   Spring–Summer 1980, p. 40.

   ". . . through her eyes": "The Brass Goddess," Stephen Sondheim, *The Purple Cow*,
   Williams College, March 1947, p. 21.

57 ". . . how rare it was . . .": SI, p. 116.

58 ". . . soft, watery material . . ." *Bequest*, Stephen Sondheim, p. 46.

59 "a sick, empty, lonely feeling . . .": "The Brass Goddess," Stephen Sondheim, *The
   Purple Cow*, Williams College, March 1947, p. 25.

60 "of course" he believed her: SI, p. 76.

   ". . . totally unstable . . .": interview with author.

No Sad Songs

61 Moved in with his father: SI, p. 99.

   ". . . not sure that she wanted me . . .": SI, p. 25.

62 ". . . He was old enough . . .": interview with author.

   His father felt uncomfortable: SI, p. 21.

   "I had a stepson": Sondheim, interview with Charlie Rose, June 3, 1994.

   ". . . 'How's your mother?' . . .": SI, p. 98.

   ". . . in the lion's den . . .": SI, p. 98.

   Find himself becoming tense: SI, p. 11.

63 ". . . she didn't get it . . .": SI, p. 22.

   ". . . wouldn't have wanted to recognize . . .": SI, p. 25.

64 "I was appalled . . .": SI, p. 40.

   ". . . a nagging, demanding mother . . .": SI, p. 99.

65 ". . . telling the truth": SI, p. 99.

   "I might have been institutionalized": interview with Charlie Rose, June 3, 1994.

65 Enrolled as an English major: SI, p. 49.

66 "there was a smell of money . . .": interview with author.

"It was very explicit": interview with author.

67 Late-night movies: Shainman interview with Paul Salsini, p. 2.

". . . the only anti-Semitism . . .": SI, p. 63.

". . . someone was always playing . . .": interview with author.

68 ". . . It was so sadistic . . .": SI, p. 64.

The Russian romantics: Sondheim Guardian Lecture, reprinted in *Biased,* Spring–Summer 1980, p. 56.

"The muse came . . ." interview with Martin Gottfried, October 29, 1993.

". . . dogmatic and difficult . . .": Shainman interview with Paul Salsini, p. 3.

". . . invention comes with craft": SI, p. 49.

69 ". . . I don't think he ever went . . .": Shainman interview with Paul Salsini, pp. 1–3.

". . . required to make music . . .": interview with author.

". . . quite extraordinary . . .": SI pp. 45–6.

69–70 Daringly modern works: SI, p. 46; "all the way up . . .": ibid.

70 Given four performances: April 30, May 1, May 7, and May 8, 1948.

". . . make some money . . .": Stephen Sondheim in *The Arts,* August 1960, p. 52.

". . . hopefully satirical . . .": John S. Wilson in *The Arts,* August 1960, p. 53.

". . . they won't believe it": SI, p. 63.

71 ". . . a much better prop . . .": interview with author.

72 ". . . the highlight of the show": letter to author, May 17, 1995.

Gave him a record: BAN, p. 12.

Ravel was the one responsible: Sondheim Guardian Lecture, reprinted in *Biased,* Spring–Summer 1980, p. 56.

". . . the pervasive influence . . .": BAN, pp. 400–1.

". . . the three dramatic categories . . .": interview with author.

"First take a play . . .": SI, pp. 44–5.

". . . think of *something!*": *Broadway Anecdotes,* Peter Hay, 1989, p. 238.

73 ". . . any good second-act curtains?" Ibid., pp. 238–9.

A remarkable work: BA, p. 234

"honest garrets": Williams *Record,* March 23, 1949.

". . . the romantic Artist . . .": "*Waiting for Lefty*" *and Other Plays,* Clifford Odets, Introduction by Harold Clurman, 1979, p. xi.

74 They all went up one Sunday: interview by Paul Salsini, November 14, 1991.

"Steve would play . . .": Ibid.

"I extend endings . . .": SI, p. 113.

"pewter ashtray making": SI, p. 115.

76 ". . . tried to make passes . . .": SI, March 13, 1997, p. 3.

77 "But she never died . . .": SI, p. 70.

"We used to worship . . .": interview with author.

"He had professors . . .": interview with author.

". . . he was very shy": interview with author.

"It was a parody . . .": interview with author.

79 ". . . I was flattered . . .": SI, p. 46.

Early in 1947: the date was January 18.

80 Thought it was funny: SI, p. 27.

". . . it's as though you have to kill . . .": *Three Plays by Thornton Wilder,* 1970, p. 132.

Sondheim played Garth: May 15 and 16, 1947.

The role of the blind seer: January 23, 1948.

He played Cassius: on February 18, 1949.

He got to "kill" Sondheim: letter to author, May 17, 1995.

82 "I became a confirmed . . .": SI, pp. 65, 26.

"Nobody would dare to watch . . .": *Night Must Fall,* Emlyn Williams, 1988, p. 93.

"the orgasm was over": SI, p. 27.

"to the high talents . . .": Williams *Record,* June 2, 1948.

For a student revue: June 18, 1950.

83 "Sing no sad songs": from "Song" by Christina Rossetti.

Climbing High

84 " 'What the hell . . . ?' ": COH, 1–7.

". . . the best on Broadway": Salsini interview, p. 3.

85 "It could have been six months . . .": interview with author.

". . . I was a fool . . .": COH 1–43b.

He very much cared: *New York Times,* October 6, 1996.

86 ". . . a perfect combination": ibid.

A musical about Helen of Troy: it was never performed.

". . . the best corned beef sandwich . . .": Salsini interview, p. 4.

87 ". . . more than a song": COH, 2–75.

"I am his maverick . . .": *New York Times,* October 6, 1996.

88 ". . . a charmer and a ladies' man . . .": SI, p. 46.

89 Already a marked trait: BAN, p. 26.

Hammerstein was concerned: in a letter dated August 6, 1953.

90 ". . . foretastes of phrases . . .": BAN, p. 25.

". . . I feel quite certain . . .": F, pp. 306–7.

91 ". . . had to get somebody else": SI, p. 62.

92 A stellar cast: *Capote,* Gerald Clarke, 1988, p. 237.

93 Largely a matter of waiting: Sondheim, letter dated March 4, 1953; "We have a great time . . .": ibid.

94 "He knew how starstruck . . .": SI, p. 108.

". . . wide-bosomed suits": letter is undated.

97 Exactly sharpened pencil points: letter dated July 31, 1953; "cute and fun . . .": ibid.

" 'Who was that man?' ": interview with author.

98 The script, which she returned: ibid.

". . . It isn't bad . . .": letter dated July 31, 1953.

". . . By following your moves . . .": SI, p. 86.

99 ". . . Why don't they love me . . . ?": letter dated July 31, 1953.

". . . an inch from her nose . . .": SI, interview on March 13, 1997.

"A Star Is Born" was dated March 29, 1954.

100 ". . . I lost interest": SI, p. 71.

Did not interest him at all: SI, pp. 70–1.

". . . 'Can I build you . . . ?' ": SI, p. 122.

". . . I could squeeze past . . .": SI, p. 122.

"the typical Capote woman . . .": *Capote,* Gerald Clarke, 1988, p. 291.

102 He was always invited: SI, March 13, 1997.

"the cheapest they had . . .": SI, p. 123.

103 ". . . a recording of the work . . .": SI, p. 125.

Called the play "ramshackle": BA, p. 375.

It was a flop: SI, p. 125.

"I got paid for it": SI, p. 125.

". . . he would feel the aura . . .": SI, p. 125.

Told in the form of a monologue: SI, p. 94.

104 "It never sold": SI, p. 93.

". . . say to Walter, 'Butt me' . . .": SI, p. 95.

105 ". . . there was great reluctance . . .": interview with author.

". . . we never did anything . . .": SI, p. 126.

". . . induced to go straight": *Broadway Anecdotes,* Peter Hay, 1989, p. 63.

". . . floating down a sewer . . .": *A Girl Like I,* Anita Loos, 1966, p. 21.

106 A wonderful idea: letter dated August 6, 1953.

In the summer of 1954: on June 7.

". . . an Afghan hound . . .": COH, 3–107, 108.

". . . great social ambitions": COH, 3–109.

107 ". . . a very sweet show . . .": COH, 3–110.

108 He almost dropped: COH, 3–111.

110 ". . . heartfelt show": interview with author.

A date was set: *New York Times,* September 17, 1954.

"... a complete blood transfusion ...": SI, p. 48.

A closely guarded secret: COH, 3–108.

"... adjusting to the transfusion ...": SI, p. 48.

Then one day Ayers died: on August 14, 1955.

One Good Break

111 Chapter title is taken from "When I Get Famous" in *Climb High* by Stephen Sondheim.

Gabel had interested Laurents: the account of Arthur Laurents differs in some important particulars from that given by Leonard Bernstein, recounted in his diaries and published by Humphrey Burton, one of his biographers, in 1992.

"... thought was brilliant ...": *Leonard Bernstein*, Meryle Secrest, 1994, p. 213.

112 "on the wrong side of forty": Letter to author from Laurents, October 6, 1997.

"... smote his forehead ...": Z, p. 11

"A true luck story": London *Times,* January 13, 1972.

"... this show wasn't for them": *Leonard Bernstein*, Meryle Secrest, 1994, p. 213.

113 "... an organized calamity": BA, p. 418.

There were still eighty-seven productions: BA, p. 418.

"... you could invest ...": SI, p. 105.

It was *The Pajama Game,* SI, p. 105.

114 "... no one can tell ...": GOL, p. 9.

A friend of his: in her biography, *Montgomery Clift,* 1978, p. 136, Patricia Bosworth states that it was Clift.

"... a very brief outline ...": BSS, p. 40.

Romeo would be Jewish and Juliet Catholic: Bernstein's diary gives the reverse but Laurents says this is incorrect. Letter to author, October 6, 1997.

Origins of the musical: BSS, p. 40.

Abie's Irish Rose set to music: letter to author, October 6, 1997.

Was committed to writing a screenplay: Ibid.

A convenient excuse: *Leonard Bernstein*, Meryle Secrest, 1994, p. 212.

115 Writing the score: from February to May, 1954.

The moment had come: Z, p. 15.

Still waiting to be explored: *Leonard Bernstein,* Humphrey Burton, 1994, p. 248.

"... Lenny's idea of poetry": SI, p. 100.

"... That was Lenny": Washington *Post,* May 3, 1972.

116 "... extremely self-conscious": SI, p. 100.

117 "Nobody knew ...": HUB: pp. 5–7.

"... he never beat me": *Leonard Bernstein,* Meryle Secrest, 1994, p. 215.

Having a wonderful time: SI, p. 114.

"... that's the form ...": HUB, p. 7.

119 "... all that work ...": JAN, pp. 2–3.

" '... make it a song' ": BSS, p. 43.

"... the two-four part ...": RNT, p. 38.

Could also illustrate tragic themes: MUS, p. 235.

"Not many laughs ...": SI, p. 22.

120 "... like an operetta": SI, p. 106.

He does not remember: SI, p. 123.

Sounded like Stravinsky: SI, p. 102.

121 "... that was the end of that": SI, p. 102.

"... the windows were open ...": *Leonard Bernstein,* Meryle Secrest, 1994, p. 215.

"... 'Send it to us' ": SI, p. 102.

122 "... He's a master artist": SI, p. 103.

123 "it just froze me ...": JAN, p. 6.

"... Try that again ...": SI, p. 118–9.

Had to "plot and plan": THE, pp. 18–9.

124 "That's what we all say": interview with James Lapine.

Wishing him luck: on August 19, 1957.

"... which warm our hearts ...": Undated letter.

Saw fit to mention: on August 20, 1957.

"... that single remark ...": SI, p. 129.

Opening night: on September 26, 1957.

125–6 "The evening hurtles ...": New York *Herald Tribune,* September 27, 1957.

126 "I didn't want to see ...": SI, pp. 17–8, 109–10.

People had a chance: THE, p. 8.

"It got excellent ...": BSS, p. 228.

127 "... I can't blame him ...": SI, pp. 210–1.

Coming Up Roses

128 "... dancing merrily ...": *New Yorker,* October 5, 1957.

129 "sound lumpen and old-fashioned.": from a memoir written by Keith Baxter, pp. 1–4.

"It is Shakespeare pillaged ...": London *Sunday Times,* December 14, 1958.

130 There were bound to be errors: letter, October 23, 1957.

"... I'll be hostile ...": letter, September 26, 1957.

131 "... it might change ...": New York *Herald Tribune,* September 22, 1957.

It was a unique experiment: SI, p. 116.

Forced to sue: COH, 3-117–9.

"a humiliating, awful ...": COH, 2-78–80.

132 "Didn't I tell ...": SI, p. 112.

". . . No one ever remembers . . .": interview with author.

133 ". . . I was too grand . . .": *Advocate*, May 16, 1995.

Took an immediate dislike: interview with the late Benay Venuta.

His musical versatility: *New York Times*, September 21, 1994.

134 ". . . it filters into . . .": SI, p. 113.

Much as he disliked: COH, 1–43A.

So long as her name: BSS, p. 56.

135 "If you don't cry . . .": New York *Herald Tribune*, May 22, 1959.

"We'd discuss it . . .": BSS, p. 74.

"It just . . . feels right . . .": BSS, p. 246.

". . . he is the greatest . . .": interview with author.

136 "I was really proud . . .": BSS, pp. 66–7.

"We howl about it . . .": interview with author.

" 'That's what it says here . . .' ": interview with author.

". . . didn't see it coming": SI, pp. 113–4.

He criticized the show: *David Merrick: The Abominable Showman*, Howard Kissel, 1993, p. 168.

Far fewer opportunities: Z, p. 45.

138 ". . . he was furious . . .": SI, p. 101.

". . . I started to ad lib . . .": RNT, p. 38.

139 ". . . burst into tears": S, p. 46.

That was the climax: Z, p. 49.

". . . put a big ending . . .": BSS, pp. 69–70.

140 ". . . there is a way . . .": Ibid.

"That's what Steve understands.": interview with author.

". . . four dollars and ninety cents": SI, p. 129.

141 ". . . black-and-white pumps . . .": *Advocate*, May 16, 1995.

"dead silence": SI, p. 22.

142 Just over a year later: on August 1, 1966.

" 'but Lloyd Weill made a million . . .' ": SI, p. 22.

"No metaphor there": SI, p. 127.

COMEDY TONIGHT

144 Chapter title is taken from the song of the same name by Stephen Sondheim in *A Funny Thing Happened on the Way to the Forum*.

"It isn't like Rubinstein . . .": SI, p. 131.

They shook hands: SI, p. 20; to somebody else, ibid.

Advised him to buy: SI, p. 131.

145 ". . . thought . . . I would go to jail . . .": SI, pp. 20–1.

146 ". . . mostly Victorian games . . .": Washington *Post*, November 30, 1975.

". . . a slow reader . . .": SI, p. 68.

"She would bring him fruits . . .": SI, p. 175.

147 ". . . he's had it stuck . . .": interview with author.

"There's nothing more horrifying . . .": SI, p. 132.

"his hair hanging lankly . . .": *Playbill*, 1970.

". . . I got a high commendation . . .": NRT, p. 29.

"one of the eight wonders . . .": SI, p. 84.

148 "He had a way . . .": SI, p. 84.

". . . into a cabbage": interview with author.

". . . so he was responsible . . .": SI, p. 84.

"Well, I'm polishing . . .": COH, 2–47.

149 "The problem was . . .": SI, p. 118.

150 ". . . a very reserved man . . .": SI, p. 118.

151 ". . . never getting it right . . .": *A Funny Thing Happened on the Way to the Forum*, Introduction by Larry Gelbart, 1991, pp. 4–5.

"He needed the work . . .": SI, p. 119.

"giving the audience a needed break . . .": *New York Times*, July 21, 1996.

"a salon score . . ." BSS, pp. 232–3.

". . . the golden rule of collaboration . . .": ibid., p. 232.

152 ". . . you cannot *not* laugh" ibid., p. 232.

"So we put it all back . . .": Z, p. 70.

"refused to close the show . . .": SI, March 13, 1997.

" '. . . You had better call in George Abbott' ": SI, p. 119.

Looked at him in horror: BSS, p. 45.

154 Identified as a Communist: *Zero Mostel*, Jared Brown, 1989, p. 177.

"I did write that . . .": SI, p. 120.

Mechanical stage effects: New York *Journal-American*, May 9, 1962.

" 'I could do this so much better . . .' ": SI, p. 120.

155 "But you don't do it there . . .": SI, p. 121.

". . . they just get bored": SI, p. 121.

"genial and felicitous": Anthony Tommasini, *New York Times*, July 21, 1996.

156 "virtue implausible . . .": New Haven *Register*, April 3, 1962.

". . . lowdown comedy": May 21, 1962.

". . . so beautifully contrived . . .": *Evening Standard*, October 4, 1963.

". . . Falstaff-like . . .": *New York Times*, May 9, 1962.

". . . a whole road company . . .": New York *Herald Tribune*, May 9, 1962.

157 "impish and mocking": *Evening Star*, April 11, 1962.

A success on the whole: New York *Herald Tribune*, May 9, 1962.

Not even nominated: *Sondheim Review,* Summer 1996, p. 11.

"I should have mentioned . . .": SI, p. 121.

"Steve was so unhappy . . .": interview with author.

"I wanted you to know . . .": letter dated May 31, 1962.

158 ". . . won't really be a member . . .": *Broadway Anecdotes,* Peter Hay, 1989, p. 250.

ANYONE CAN WHISTLE

159 Chapter title is taken from the song of the same name by Stephen Sondheim in *Anyone Can Whistle.*

". . . hacks and gag men . . .": NOL, p. 41.

". . . I could do something . . .": COH, 3–119.

160 ". . . contemporary, satirical . . .": New York *Herald Tribune,* May 21, 1962.

161 Then considered daring: *Delphian,* April 26, 1972.

162 ". . . it's so moving . . .": interview with author.

It helped him write: BSS, p. 235.

"using pastiche . . .": SI, p. 134.

". . . rather gentle but gingery . . .": *Delphian,* April 26, 1972.

A comprehensive musical structure: BAN, p. 123.

". . . highly romantic": HUB, p. 12.

"They weren't about . . .": Z, p. 95.

163 ". . . an atonal show . . .": SI, p. 135.

". . . not in my nature . . .": Z, p. 90.

"wiping up the stage . . .": SI, p. 195.

Lansbury found out: Z, p. 90; "I remember screaming . . .": ibid.

164 Guardino . . . became depressed: Z, p. 87.

165 "We were just killing . . .": Z, p. 85.

". . . there was no time . . .": BSS, p. 389.

She had to stop them: Z, p. 92.

". . . did not come to blows": interview with author.

166 ". . . it got dark at night": *Clinging to the Wreckage,* John Mortimer, 1995, p. 131.

"We were trying . . .": HUB, p. 12.

"It is exciting . . .": April 6, 1964.

". . . 'good and rotten' . . .": *How I Got to Be Perfect,* Jean Kerr, 1978, p. 215.

"the total embodiment . . .": April 6, 1964.

168 "a quality of truth . . .": June 7, 1960.

". . . I can't be something . . .": *New York Times,* July 3, 1991.

169 ". . . not . . . feminine": interview with author; ". . . looked like Miss America": ibid.

170 ". . . part of the fun . . .": SI, p. 196.

"Doesn't she realize . . .": interview with author.

171 "I was terribly jealous": interview with author.

"She was delightful": interview with author, March 13, 1997.

172 ". . . he almost could not function . . .": interview with author.

Had Harry Nilsson record: SI, p. 159.

173 ". . . more serious about me . . .": interview with author, March 13, 1997.

174 An unofficial engagement: interview with author.

". . . immensely dramatic . . .": *New York Times,* October 16, 1952.

". . . 'I will try' ": SI, p. 143.

175 ". . . something small and rather dirty . . .": New York *World Telegram and Sun,* March 13, 1965.

"a monster": *New York Times,* November 6, 1964.

"it would make Daddy so happy": SI, p. 145; "the sacrificial goat": ibid.

". . . rightfully angry . . .": interview with author.

". . . burned to death": interview with author, March 13, 1997.

176 "We get together . . .": *New York Times,* November 6, 1964.

". . . a sad little comedy . . .": RR, p. 318.

"I . . . stomped out . . .": Z, p. 102.

"That was especially needed . . .": RR, p. 318.

Made her less likable: RR, p. 319.

"I wrote lyrics . . .": interview with author, March 13, 1997.

178 Shevelove had been asked: ibid.

To prevent people from entering: interview with author.

". . . some kind of affair": SI, p. 144; "the imagined slight": ibid.

". . . It was a dead show . . .": SI, p. 146.

179 ". . . this whole happy experience . . .": letter, November 15, 1973.

He blamed his co-creators: RR, p. 319.

"a cold man . . .": interview with Baxter.

Rodgers was the reverse: Z, p. 102; *Newsweek,* April 23, 1973.

179–80 ". . . he was sensitive . . .": interview with author; "I'd hit a bottom": ibid.

180 "I was just . . . unhappy . . .": SI, p. 96.

181 "There's not a man . . .": interview with author.

"He was . . . the first . . .": SI, p. 196.

Held in the Shubert Theatre: on March 11, 1973.

182 "I always thought . . .": interview with author.

BEING ALIVE

183 Chapter title is taken from the song of the same name by Stephen Sondheim in *Company.*

184 Singing as she went: MUS, p. 92.

"Rubble in the daylight": *After Dark,* June 1971; "A 'who'll-do-it' . . .": ibid.

185 ". . . someone fires a gun . . .": Z, p. 135.

"Steve was very encouraging . . .": interview with author.

186 "Gee, I had nothing . . .": SI, p. 169.

". . . I didn't know how . . .": Z, p. 119.

Either ignored or lost: Z, p. 119.

A new director . . . had been engaged: Z, p. 116.

187 ". . . The light flashed on . . .": *Sondheim Review,* Summer 1994, p. 21.

"didn't pay that well . . .": SI, p. 149.

188 ". . . we still had illusions . . .": Z, p. 116.

"Jerry can be . . .": interview with author.

189 Pass his pages under the door: ibid; ". . . a feeling of horror . . .": ibid. Sondheim's version is less dramatic. He says he and Robbins re-signed at a lunch at the Harvard Club with Guare and Bernstein.

"I was ashamed . . .": Z, p. 116.

190 Comic-book boxes: IL, p. 129.

"I showed them to Hal . . .": SI, p. 151.

191 Sondheim went to work: Z, p. 120.

". . . the view from the peephole . . .": London *Sunday Times,* May 3, 1970.

"*Company* says very clearly . . .": *Time,* March 5, 1971.

192 "It kept me awake . . .": *New York Times,* April 24, 1970.

The only solution: SI, p. 183.

193 ". . . the hardest song to find . . .": SI, pp. 152–3.

195 ". . . trapped and exposed . . .": *The Theatre Art of Boris Aronson,* Frank Rich and Lisa Aronson, 1987, pp. 220–1; two elevators: ibid., p. 222.

"The director is free to change . . .": IL, p. 171.

"like a shock wave": Z, p. 126; "a landmark": ibid.

"human perplexity . . .": Z, p. 130.

197 "sweetly laconic cynicism": *New York Times,* April 25, 1970; "It's the kind of . . .": ibid.

"On re-hearing . . .": Z, p. 130.

198 "This is terrific . . .": interview with author.

"missed his cue . . .": ibid.

"Jonathan will sometimes add . . .": BSS, p. 242.

199 "I unhesitatingly recommended . . .": *New York Times,* January 29, 1984.

"this exceptionally energetic . . .": program for the Donmar Warehouse production of *Company* in London's West End, March 7, 1996.

200 A successful revue: *Side by Side by Sondheim,* 1976.

"He looked *terrible* . . .": Z, p. 126.

202 Seemed to frighten audiences: IL, p. 172.

"I get chills . . .": SI, p. 160.

203 Chapter title is taken from the song of the same name by Stephen Sondheim in *Follies.*

"I hadn't liked the show!": interview with author.

204 ". . . all the desired rewards . . .": *New York Times,* October 31, 1971.

206 "the first Proustian musical": April 12, 1971.

"the death of vaudeville . . .": *The Theatre Art of Boris Aronson,* Frank Rich and Lisa Aronson, 1987, p. 231.

207 "If you see a statue . . .": ibid., p. 232.

". . . there's a minute or two . . .": *Newsweek,* July 26, 1971.

". . . I told him the truth . . .": ibid.

209 "I put myself . . .": Z, p. 183.

". . . a unique talent": interview with author.

"expecting egos . . .": IL, p. 318; ". . . someone so bright . . .": ibid.

"a screamer and . . ." *The New Yorker,* June 2, 1997.

210 "we never talked . . .": interview with author.

"Directors tend . . .": BSS, p. 325.

". . . listening to records . . .": London *Times,* January 13, 1972.

211 "It's not about being smart . . .": unidentified television interview.

"marvellously foolish": *New York Times,* April 11, 1971.

"a strangely poetic quality . . .": Tom Prideaux, *Life,* April 12, 1971.

"It saved a great . . .": IL, p. 188.

212 ". . . an object lesson . . .": *New York Times,* April 11, 1971.

". . . I wasted some time . . .": *New York,* November 11, 1974.

Sondheim took the trouble: Theodore S. Chapin's reminiscences about his role as director's assistant during *Follies* from an interview with author.

"No one would undertake . . .": BA, p. 444.

213 "I couldn't make . . .": *Newsweek,* July 26, 1971.

214 "Something Charles Ives . . .": interview with author.

215 ". . . something is wrong . . .": *Newsweek,* July 26, 1971.

216 "But they want to believe it . . .": GOL, p. 273 (italics Goldman's).

"I wish we'd thought of that . . .": SI, p. 89.

A bone of contention: interview with author.

They never worked together: Michael Bennett died at the age of forty-five on July 2, 1987.

217 No one knew: interview, March 13, 1997.

"I heard no whisper . . .": from a memoir by Keith Baxter, p. 10.

"get out of the graveyard . . .": *New York Times,* April 5, 1971.

218 "Send him back . . .": letter, *New York Times,* May 2, 1971.

"with its complex . . .": *New York Times,* May 2, 1971.

"platforms bearing jazz bands . . .": *New York Times,* April 11, 1971.

". . . a pastiche show . . .": Z, p. 146.

"a brilliant show . . .": *Newsweek,* April 12, 1971.

A daring act: *Time,* April 12, 1971.

"It's not merely . . .": *New York Times,* September 7, 1985; a bootlegged tape: ibid.

219 " 'Can I sit with you?' . . .": interview with author.

". . . scream with laughter . . .": COH, 1–43.

220 She actually wanted to live with him: SI, p. 41.

"A truly compulsive liar . . .": SI, pp. 2, 4.

"gay and animated . . .": interview with author.

222 ". . . this elaborate charade . . .": SI, pp. 16–17, 40.

"I made up a story . . .": interview with author.

224 Account of Foxy Leshin's suicide attempt from interviews with Stephen Sondheim, Harold Prince, and the late Benay Venuta.

The Boy in the Bubble

225 "Something happened . . .": interview with author.

226 ". . . one of the best writers . . .": *New York Times,* January 16, 1997.

"I've always been very smart": SI, p. 110.

"adore and worship": interview with author.

"He was aloof . . .": interview with author.

Found him so inhibiting: interview with author.

Confessed to being frightened: interview with author.

"He's scary . . .": *Sondheim Review,* Fall 1995, p. 10.

". . . He's so bright . . .": interview with author.

227 An amusing encounter: interview with author.

He was simply shy: interview with author.

His quick wit: interview with author.

Something comically endearing: interview with author.

228 Difficult person to describe: interview with author, March 13, 1997.

Took a kind of pride: interview with author.

229 "He's not cynical . . .": interview with author.

He was more vulnerable: interview with author.

"a highly, nervously charged energy . . .": interview with author.

A sweet-sour aspect: interview with author.

Public humiliation: interview with author.

"The entire room turned around . . .": SI, p. 35.

229 ". . . you always know . . .": interview with author.

230 "he had a little list": interview with author.

He was always tense: BSS, p. 368.

En route to Canada: interview with author.

Characters in musicals as puppets: SI, p. 181.

Returned to analysis: SI, p. 197.

". . . became the lingua franca . . .": ibid.

"There was . . . something striking . . .": *Lytton Strachey,* vol. 1, Michael Holroyd, p. 187.

231 View of himself is prosaic: SI, p. 115.

Consider himself a fox: The comment was made during a television interview at Southern Methodist University in 1994.

" '. . . It ain't going to happen' ": *David Merrick,* Howard Kissel, 1993, p. 164.

". . . the smallest flaw . . .": SI, p. 154.

"I've always been a low . . .": SI, pp 96–7.

232 "When you get it right . . .": *Sondheim Review,* Fall 1995, p. 10.

". . . that kind of investment . . .": interview with author.

"It is difficult . . .": *Touched with Fire,* Kay Redfield Jamison, 1993, p. 19; "Write me immediately . . .": ibid.; "I am like water . . .": ibid., p. 311; "we have the best possible . . .": ibid., p. 54.

233 "The small cast . . . had now swelled . . .": *Making Scenes: A Personal History of the Turbulent Years at Yale, 1966–1974,* Robert Brustein, 1981, p. 179.

234 ". . . descent into Hades": interview with author.

235 An unfortunate oversight: interview with author.

". . . would have exploded . . .": interview with author.

236 An ambitious treasure hunt: London *Sunday Times,* March 9, 1969.

". . . a yacht in France . . .": SI, p. 183.

"Not having to write lyrics . . .": COH, 2–97.

237 ". . . an actor's point of view . . .": Sondheim Guardian Lecture, *Biased,* Spring-Summer 1980, p. 41; ". . . a really good gimmick . . .": ibid., p. 42.

Crime and Variations: JAN, p. 2.

His own version of *The Thin Man:* COH, 2–98.

239 The one intelligent question: COH, 2–102.

". . . a wonderful time": COH, 2–97.

240 "Tony and I . . .": London *Sunday Times,* March 9, 1969.

"If Steve couldn't boil . . .": interview with author.

Quite wearing: London *Sunday Times,* March 9, 1969.

Prince always won: *Newsweek,* July 26, 1971.

241 For his fiftieth birthday: in 1968.

"So the players are . . .": SI, p. 136.

"As a game . . .": London *Sunday Times,* March 9, 1969.

242 A games-playing man: *Sleuth,* Anthony Shaffer, 1977, p. 76.

243 ". . . all about order . . .": *New York Times,* March 10, 1996.

Applause for the Clowns

244 Chapter title is taken from the song "Send In the Clowns" by Stephen Sondheim in *A Little Night Music.*

". . . Love and foolishness . . .": *Wall Street Journal,* February 27, 1972.

245 Only about fifty opened: *Wall Street Journal,* February 27, 1972; "My little investors . . .": ibid.

A composer could easily make: GOL, p. 166.

246 ". . . Hal has a sense . . .": Z, p. 182.

Warmth and compassion: *New York Times,* March 27, 1973.

". . . and multiples thereof": Z, p. 182–3; ". . . plaintively memorable waltzes . . .": ibid., p. 190.

247 ". . . It was maddening . . .": Z, p. 185.

". . . the ruffled feathers . . .": *New York Times,* March 4, 1973.

"wanted the humor . . .": *Wall Street Journal,* February 27, 1972.

". . . 'I'll sing it again . . .' ": Z, p. 185; ". . . too much for me . . .": ibid., p. 185.

"I walked out . . .": interview with author.

249 "When *Company* opened . . .": interview with author.

250 ". . . jauntily battered . . .": *New York Times,* February 26, 1973.

251 "The sound they made . . .": *The Theatre Art of Boris Aronson,* Frank Rich and Lisa Aronson, 1987, p. 254.

". . . rattle, rattle . . .": *Wall Street Journal,* February 27, 1972.

Broke all the china: ibid.

"I've dined out . . .": interview with author.

". . . one of his biggest successes": interview with author.

253 She was Garn Stephens: Z, p. 189; Stephens was fired: ibid.

"It hurt morale": interview with author.

The banquet table left: *Wall Street Journal,* February 27, 1972.

254 ". . . style and imagination": February 26, 1973.

". . . an adult musical!": *New York Times,* February 26, 1973.

He sent a telegram: SI, p. 126.

". . . in devastating comic form . . .": September 28, 1995.

255 "The score is so delicate . . .": *A Little Night Music,* music and lyrics by Stephen Sondheim, book by Hugh Wheeler, introduction by Jonathan Tunick, 1991, p. 6.

256 ". . . the complete absence of rests . . .": ibid., p. 4.

257 "brilliantly funny . . .": Tom Sutcliffe and Paul Sheren, *Theatre '74,* edited by Sheridan Morley, p. 204.

258–9 "... poems for the theatre": ibid.

259 "desperate to make it": Sondheim Guardian Lecture, *Biased,* Spring-Summer 1980, p. 48; "... style over substance ...": ibid., p. 35.

"... about savoring moments": SI, p. 184.

Suicidally wrong-headed: *New York Times,* March 8, 1978.

260 "... you've done your bit": Washington *Post,* March 13, 1973; "... like organizing a peace march": ibid.

Dozens of socialites: ibid.

262 "... your music is not much": ibid.

Someone in a Tree

263 Chapter title is taken from the song of the same name by Stephen Sondheim in *Pacific Overtures.*

"it had as little to do ...": *Another Part of the Wood,* Kenneth Clark, 1974, p. 145; "Absurd as it sounds ...": ibid., p. 211.

264 "... intelligently crafted ...": *Newsweek,* April 23, 1973.

"... a stronger debut ...": interview with author.

"I have no life-style ...": *Time,* March 19, 1973; "All I ever ... wanted ...": ibid.

265 "... the end of the world ...": interview with author.

His eyes were smudged: *Time,* March 19, 1973.

"Unfortunately I had ...": SI, p. 198.

"... not enjoying it ...": SI, p. 132.

"It's very good ...": SI, pp. 198–9.

266 "... I have a small circle ...": *Newsweek,* April 23, 1973.

267 "... a really good eye ...": interview with author.

"My Christmas shopping ...": interview with author.

268 "The old game ...": New York *Daily News,* August 7, 1980.

A mask out of music paper: interview with author, March 13, 1979.

They bought a sheepdog: ibid.

"He became a great friend ...": interview with author.

269 "... he made a pass ...": interview with author.

270 Her son had been plagiarized: interview with author.

She wrote him a letter: *New York Times,* March 20, 1994; SI, pp. 40–1.

271 Until she died: On April 13, 1992.

Tried to make amends: interview with Benay Venuta.

"... an impossible person": SI, p. 42.

"... she never asked any questions ...": interview with author.

"Lou was very kind ...": interview with author.

272 "Thanks for the plate ...": letter, April 26, 1985.

" 'Oh, I forgot . . .' ": interview with author.

". . . deeply unhappy . . .": interview with author.

". . . ease up . . .": interview with author.

Interviewed Sondheim: in 1977.

274 ". . . should sound natural . . .": JAN, p. 4.

". . . Don't censor anything": SI, p. 131.

275 ". . . a terrible sound . . .": *New York,* November 11, 1974.

". . . the joke has lost . . .": Previn interview.

276 "to help make the line terse . . .": HUB, p. 21.

"That's not exceptionally . . .": *New York,* November 11, 1974.

"one of the quick . . .": COH, 2–91; it was easy: ibid.

276-7 "The Song Is Ended": *New York Times Magazine,* June 2, 1996; "showed people . . . that they could keep . . .": ibid.; "What was the point . . .": ibid.

277 "At best, one discrete . . .": ibid.; "the songs are so . . .": ibid.

Releasing his music on records: *The Companion to 20th Century Music,* Norman Lebrecht, 1992, p. 202.

Company . . . has sold: interview with Paul McKibbins.

Sondheim named his company the Burthen Music Company, after the term Jerome Kern had used for the refrain or chorus of a song, a term that has become archaic.

279 ". . . My kind of work . . .": "Stephen Sondheim," Joseph Kastner, essay in the record album *American Musicals,* Time-Life Records, 1982.

"the most bizarre . . .": *New York Times,* January 4, 1976.

280 "We were all dragged . . .": interview with author.

"the fragility and delicacy . . .": *Horizon,* October 1981.

281 It held together: COH, 2–75.

Finding the right lyric style: THE, p. 10.

282 "Are we seeing . . .": *Wall Street Journal,* January 13, 1976.

"more humanity": Z, p. 214.

". . . entirely about ideas": THE, p. 9.

"spectacle and bombast": *New York Times,* October 26, 1984.

After it opened: January 11, 1976.

". . . a Japanese show": Z, p. 219.

Lost its entire investment: Z, p. 221.

284 ". . . kaleidoscopic patterns . . .": *Maclean's,* December 24, 1985.

Made him seem condescending: COH, p. 44.

Appeared to admire: *New York Times,* January 4, 1976.

Badly misquoted: COH, p. 44.

". . . meant to damage . . .": Z, p. 219.

". . . taciturn, withdrawn . . .": New York *Observer,* April 10, 1995.

DIES IRAE

285 A mock dialogue: *Leonard Bernstein,* Meryle Secrest, 1994, p. 198.

286 "Nor did she know . . .": interview with author.

287 "I had done . . .": interview with author.

288 ". . . dream of a show": *New York Times,* April 19, 1977.

289 "the greatest lyric poet . . .": *Punch,* May 12, 1976.

Established Sondheim's preeminence: December 13, 1995.

". . . the wit and wisdom . . .": *Sweeney Todd,* music and lyrics by Stephen Sondheim, book by Hugh Wheeler, introduction by Christopher Bond, 1991, pp. 3–4.

290 ". . . it would be perfect": RNT, p. 32.

"This new version . . .": THE, p. 16.

"I was moving house . . .": *Sweeney Todd,* music and lyrics by Stephen Sondheim, book by Hugh Wheeler, introduction by Christopher Bond, 1991, p. 5.

291 They were "dead drunk . . .": SI, p. 189

"semi-permanent state": *Sweeney Todd,* music and lyrics by Stephen Sondheim, book by Hugh Wheeler, introduction by Christopher Bond, 1991, p. 5.

". . . a satisfying laugh . . .": RNT, p. 33.

"a private murderer . . .": SI, p. 189.

292 "the hardest thing . . .": Z, p. 246.

"All I wanted . . .": THE, p. 16.

"all . . . the groundwork . . .": BSS, p. 365; "as scary as . . .": ibid.

293 "I'll never forget . . .": Z, p. 249.

294 "I always found . . .": Z, p. 248.

No orchestra call: BSS, p. 358.

295 "It's an open secret . . .": NRT, p. 34.

"I never start . . .": NRT, p. 39.

". . . 'it's Grand Guignol' ": SI, p. 208.

"They're missing the point . . .": SI, p. 209.

296 "I found the nature . . .": interview with author.

Dwarfed and degraded: IL, p. 292.

"There was a peaked . . .": IL, p. 391.

A black comedy: BSS, p. 385.

"I realized . . .": interview with author.

"I meant it to be done . . .": NRT, p. 8.

297 "I took it out . . .": interview with author.

"There's a scene . . .": SI, p. 166.

". . . obscure and sometimes slyly obscene . . .": London *Daily Telegraph,* December 13, 1995.

"repellently cheap.": *New York Times,* December 13, 1984.

298 "... Sondheim's darkest statement...": *Journal of American Drama & Theatre,* Spring 1991, p. 35.

"*Sweeney Todd* is brilliant...": *Newsweek,* March 12, 1979.

"an overwhelming obsession...": *New York Times,* September 15, 1989.

"howls piteously...": September 25, 1989.

299 "... He was so afraid...": interview with author.

"didn't raise a cent": Stephen Sondheim, *Dramatists Guild Quarterly,* Summer 1991, p. 15.

"The show got lost...": interview with author.

300 "... filled with tears": from a memoir by Keith Baxter, pp. 17–18.

301 "It was awful...": Z, p. 255.

"There is more...": March 2, 1979.

"... A modern American opera": interview with author.

302 "transfixing": London *Observer,* June 6, 1993.

Doomed to fail: IL, p. 296.

Repaid more than half: The actual figure was 59 percent.

"I think the most...": Z, p. 390.

OLD FRIENDS

303 Chapter title taken from the song of the same name by Stephen Sondheim in *Merrily We Roll Along.*

A terrible pain: COH, p. 169.

"... I could have died...": SI, pp. 201–2.

"... a sense of impending...": COH, p. 168.

"I felt not bad...": SI, p. 202

304 "... when the door opened...": interview with author.

305 "I just want to prepare you...": SI, p. 204.

"... So I never can believe...": SI, p. 203.

306 "he is far fitter...": interview with author.

"I didn't see him...": interview with author.

"I had seen *Company*...": interview with author.

308 "We made the mistake...": interview with author.

"... the exalted impulses...": *New York Times,* October 1, 1934.

309 "... It is best remembered...": BA, p. 235.

"It was the first time...": Z, p. 269.

"what this country...": BAN, p. 314.

When an artist loses sight: SI, p. 60.

310 "It's much easier...": BAN, p. 311; "popular music's first...": ibid., p. 315.

"They were introduced...": February 21, 1990.

310 "... this happy, upbeat ...": interview with author.

311 "I wanted to show ...": IL, p. 301; "But it certainly ...": ibid., p. 302.

An aspect of himself: comment to author, March 24, 1997.

She was cast as Meg: interview with author.

312 "I was charmed ...": *New York Times,* November 15, 1981.

He hardly felt adequate: interview with author.

313 "... a very successful song ...": *New York Times,* November 15, 1981.

"real, thirty-two-bar songs": HUB, p. 29; "... like modular furniture ...": ibid., pp. 28–9.

The same themes: Z, p. 270.

315 "to place an individual signature ...": New York *Post,* November 17, 1981.

"a half-dozen songs ...": *New York Times,* November 17, 1981.

317 Names across sweatshirts: interview with Robert Fryer.

"What do I regret? ...": interview with author.

Article by Liz Smith: October 18, 1981.

318 "and you read everywhere ...": IL, p. 309.

"They just kept ...": interview with author.

They piled into a car: interview with author.

"Stop it, Lee!": interview, March 13, 1997.

319 "a shambles,": *New York Times,* November 17, 1981.

"No matter what one thinks ...": letter, December 4, 1981.

"It had nothing to do ...": SI, p. 77.

320 "Compromise, the sellout ...": *New York Times,* December 13, 1981.

"We were sitting ...": interview with author.

"run out of steam": SI, p. 204.

"The biggest change ...": interview with author.

FINISHING THE HAT

322 Title taken from the song of the same name by Stephen Sondheim in *Sunday in the Park with George.*

Show business as a metaphor: IL, p. 328.

Despair would have overwhelmed: IL, p. 388.

"New York is not ...": *Act One,* Moss Hart, 1959, p. 89.

323 Still defending the work: COH, 1–43.

A mood of combativeness: Ricky Ian Gordon.

Doing capacity business: *New York Times,* January 3, 1983.

Disappearance of the audience: interview with author.

324 "... that is the currency ...": interview with author.

"The thing that ... annoys me ...": SI, p. 180.

He was a maverick: SI, pp. 172–3.

"He had run through . . .": New York *Times,* October 21, 1984.

325 "Don't forget this . . .": interview with author.

"is as necessary . . .": *Act One,* 1959, p. 152.

"I read this really . . .": COH, p. 155; a kind of richness: ibid., p. 156.

326 He did nothing: Z, p. 295.

"a quiet man . . .": *New York Times,* April 29, 1984.

"When I first met . . .": interview with author.

". . . a dinosaur.": *Show Music,* Fall 1994, p. 16.

327 "All those people . . .": HUB, p. 29; "Here was this . . .": ibid., p. 30.

328 "The show is all about . . .": SI, pp. 208–9.

"The show is, in part . . .": *New York Times,* June 10, 1984; weekly meetings: ibid.; "Every time I listen . . .": ibid.

"Jim's first response . . .": *New York Times,* June 10, 1984.

329 He began showing sketches: SI, p. 154.

His responses were inadequate: interview with author.

". . . James wrote interior . . .": *Dramatists Guild Quarterly,* Spring 1991, p. 14.

". . . I would kill . . .": *New York Times,* June 10, 1984.

330 ". . . his own predicament . . .": *New York Times,* October 21, 1984.

". . . a work in progress . . .": *New York Times,* June 17, 1983.

". . . the creative remnant . . .": interview with author.

333 "Steve sat down . . .": interview with author.

334 ". . . a tour de force": *New York Times,* May 22, 1984.

335 "I represent his musical . . .": interview with author.

"The music is very complicated . . .": interview with author.

"She said you sort of lose . . .": *Dramatists Guild Quarterly,* Fall 1994, p. 10.

336 ". . . a joyous quality . . .": *New York Times,* November 1, 1987.

". . . the wise child . . .": *New York Times,* December 11, 1996.

337 "Tom Stoppard has a quote . . .": interview with author.

Snatched a few hours: *New York Times,* April 29, 1984.

"The first act was . . .": interview with author.

338 "We got closer . . .": interview with author.

"my Britten score": in a television interview.

"This song is vital . . .": *New York Times,* July 29, 1984.

"an ornamental turn . . .": ibid.

"It would have spelled . . .": *New York Times,* June 10, 1984.

339 ". . . blurs old definitions . . .": *New York Times,* October 21, 1984.

"To say that this show . . .": *Newsweek,* May 14, 1984.

". . . a state of shock . . .": Z, p. 314.

340 ". . . you can't afford . . .": interview with author.

Graceful tribute: By Samuel G. Freedman, April 1, 1984.

The same message: *Good Times, Bad Times,* Harold Evans, 1983.

He was probably responsible: *Rocky Mountain News,* January 27, 1985.

341 ". . . alive and well . . .": Z, p. 315.

Everyone cried: New York *Post,* April 25, 1985.

Reporting ticket sales: *Newsday,* April 26, 1985.

". . . a cool, unblinking object . . .": May 14, 1984.

"And he would always say . . .": interview with author.

No More

342 Title taken from the song of the same name by Stephen Sondheim in *Into the Woods.*

West Side Story had opened: on May 16, 1984.

Its first revival: October 11, 1984.

By the Houston Grand Opera: June 14, 1984; at Lincoln Center: October 11, 1984.

Had come into his own: *Newsweek,* October 29, 1984.

". . . He's always knocking his head . . .": *Time Out.*

343 "Steve wouldn't talk . . .": interview with author.

344 ". . . the equivalent of a wife . . .": SI, p. 175.

"He would, at times . . .": interview with author.

". . . My life was changed . . .": Chicago *Tribune,* November 10, 1995.

345 "I always am astonished . . .": interview with Charlie Rose, June 3, 1994; an unknown had no chance: ibid.

". . . the bleakness of it all": COH, 1–41.

". . . he didn't answer . . .": interview with author; letter, June 22, 1995.

". . . I am just so moved . . .": interview with author.

346 Done more to preserve: Frank Rich, *New York Times,* July 24, 1983.

347 Not a comfortable collaboration: interview with author.

Shepard was overburdened: interview with author.

349–50 ". . . in ironic juxtaposition . . .": *New York Times,* November 17, 1985; ". . . a valedictory . . .": ibid.

351 ". . . fifty degrees warmer": Washington *Post,* February 9, 1990.

Has not returned to Broadway: as of winter 1997.

"an organism bent . . .": *New York Times,* October 20, 1996.

"those unfriendly Indian tribes . . .": *Act One,* Moss Hart, 1959, pp. 167–8.

". . . feast-or-famine . . .": *New York,* September 28, 1987.

352 Barbara Stanwyck movies: Chip Zien to author.

"wicked but cherishing wit": *Newsweek,* November 16, 1987.

353 A reading: held on November 14.

354 A basic character flaw: Z, p. 338.

"The device of the giant . . .": Z, p. 348.

"people felt . . .": interview with author.

355 "Fairy stories do not . . .": *The Uses of Enchantment,* Bruno Bettelheim, 1986, p. 25.

"The tension between . . .": *New York Times,* November 29, 1987.

"Give a child . . .": *New Yorker,* November 16, 1987.

"some people don't . . .": *Insight,* August 28, 1989.

". . . it was really wrenching . . .": from a television interview.

We are all interconnected: *New York Times,* November 1, 1987.

Hit After Hit

358 A road company began: Z, p. 352.

359 "From the latter . . .": *Village Voice,* April 19, 1988.

Three songs for Madonna: *USA Today,* February 12, 1990.

". . . couldn't afford it": London *Sunday Times,* January 14, 1990.

The usual combinations: *TheaterWeek,* July 9–15, 1990.

360 Performed in Britain: at the Salisbury Playhouse, September 1996.

"On the very first occasion . . .": London *Daily Telegraph,* September 4, 1996.

"One of the classes . . .": letter to author, October 12, 1995.

361 State of perfect expectation: *TheaterWeek,* July 9–15, 1990.

"I looked at the title . . .": Philadelphia *Daily News,* January 14, 1990.

362 "John and I sat down . . .": *New York Times,* January 27, 1991.

"Presidents have never . . .": interview with author.

"One of my objections . . .": *Dramatists Guild Quarterly,* Spring 1991, pp. 10–11.

363 "an anti-musical . . .": *New York Times,* January 28, 1991.

His most important score: April 1992.

364 The end of January: January 27, 1991.

A parade of friends: New York *Daily News,* January 29, 1991.

A furious letter: interview with author.

The motorcade went past: interview with author.

Extremely bad taste: *New York,* February 4, 1991.

"you can swallow . . .": *Newsweek,* February 4, 1991.

"The tone of these scenes . . .": *Time,* February 4, 1991.

". . . Bush be shot": London *Times,* January 28, 1991.

365 "Nothing . . . quite prepares you . . .": *New York Times,* February 3, 1991.

"the common pathway . . .": *New York Times,* September 9, 1990.

366 "A breeding ground . . .": November 1, 1992.

"One mystery of this work's . . .": November 1, 1992.

". . . eerie, enthralling . . .": October 30, 1992.

367 "I have been tempted . . .": London *Evening Standard,* March 26, 1996.

Sweeney Todd revival: June 2, 1993.

". . . caught like a fly . . .": interview with author.

"in the unlikeliest . . .": *New York Times* News Service, October 1, 1990.

Would do anything: interview with David Richards.

368 ". . . rather a sad man": interview with Keith Warner.

Died in 1982: On April 8.

". . . the world's best person": SI, pp. 84–5.

Inscribed with their initials: interview with Kip Gowans; ". . . immensely brave": ibid.

He was deeply affected: interview with Roddy McDowall.

". . . 'He loved her' ": interview with author.

". . . a wonderful child . . .": interview with author.

370 "We had the memorial service . . .": interview with author.

Where she was buried: Janet Fox Leshin's ashes were buried on the family plot at Mount Lebanon Cemetery, Glendale, New York.

371 ". . . the main character's gay . . .": interview with author.

". . . a repertorial medium . . .": *Dramatists Guild Quarterly,* Summer 1991, p. 17.

". . . a fabulous score . . .": interview with author.

372 ". . . never completely die . . .": interview with author.

No decision was forthcoming: *Variety,* February 4, 1991.

". . . a personal vendetta": interview with author.

373 "I was running out of . . .": interview with author.

374 Did, in fact, break down: on February 28, 1991.

". . . I heard a sound . . .": SI, p. 207.

AND THAT I LEARNED FROM YOU

376 Chapter title is taken from the song by Stephen Sondheim in *Passion.*

378 ". . . a terrible superstition . . .": *Passion,* I. U. Tarchetti, 1994, p. vii.

"*Muscle* is a memoir . . .": *Dramatists Guild Quarterly,* Autumn 1994, p. 3.

379 ". . . I started crying": London *Evening Standard,* March 26, 1996.

"We're all Fosca . . .": interview with Charlie Rose, June 3, 1994.

"the blurred connections . . .": *Murderers and Other Friends,* John Mortimer, 1994, p. 112.

His life changed: *New York Times,* March 20, 1994.

380 Less bitter and less bizarre: interview with Charlie Rose, June 3, 1994.

He was obviously happy: interview with author.

He was more mellow: interview with author.

"He's always been wise . . .": interview with author.

"Peter Jones . . . has been wonderful . . .": interview with author.

"not to be ashamed . . .": SI, p. 197.

". . . when famous people . . .": interview with author.

Jones left New York: in May 1992.

381 ". . . I want to die!": SI, p. 203.

"We just didn't want . . .": interview with author.

382 "Every time this happens . . .": said at the audio mix for *Passion,* spring 1995.

"proud to have written . . .": *Dramatists Guild Quarterly,* Autumn 1994, p. 6.

"Artists don't want . . .": interview with author.

383 "I was so turned . . .": interview with author.

"Unfortunately, on Broadway . . .": interview with author.

384 ". . . Sondheim gets the credit": interview with author.

". . . no protection": interview with Charlie Rose, June 3, 1994.

"While the harmonic language . . .": essay on *Passion* written for the album.

385 Description of Sondheim's working methods: *New York Times Magazine,* March 20, 1994.

". . . one long rhapsody . . .": Chicago *Tribune,* November 10, 1995; ". . . feverish and impassioned": ibid.

Brilliant minds could differ: *Dramatists Guild Quarterly,* Autumn 1994, p. 5.

Its first preview: On March 24.

386 "God knows there used . . .": *Dramatists Guild Quarterly,* Autumn 1994, p. 10; the further danger: ibid.

Had to be hushed up: New York *Daily News,* April 5, 1994.

Opened a month later: Previews were in mid-April 1994.

"a big, doting . . .": London *Times,* March 28, 1996.

". . . more like a clinical case . . .": Washington *Post,* May 19, 1994.

387 Advocate of immediate change: interview with author.

"In the bedroom scene . . .": interview with author.

The parallels in *Passion:* interview with author.

"*Passion* is not an opera . . .": *Dramatists Guild Quarterly,* Autumn 1994, p. 9.

388 "It shouldn't be surprising . . .": *Gramophone,* August 1988.

A "twilight zone": *Dramatists Guild Quarterly,* Summer 1991, p. 16.

"For me, *Sweeney Todd* . . .": RNT, p. 36; SI, pp. 167–8.

389 ". . . The trouble is . . .": interview with author.

"Even though the New York . . .": RNT, p. 36; "It seems hard . . .": ibid.

". . . I am saying . . .": interview with author.

"There are moments . . .": interview with Charlie Rose, June 3, 1994.

390 ". . . it's the boldest . . .": *New York Times,* June 19, 1994.

"sobbing uncontrollably": *New Republic,* August 1, 1994.

390 "the most emotionally engaging . . .": May 16–22, 1994.

392 *USA Today:* on May 10, 1994.

"a thrilling meditation . . .": May 10, 1994.

Full of compliments: May 10, 1994.

". . . your body shivers . . .": May 10, 1994; "the first serious . . .": ibid.

"the darkest, most depressing . . .": *Time,* May 23, 1994.

Bold and highly admirable: May 10, 1994.

". . . musically brilliant . . .": May 19, 1994.

". . . a pathological study . . .": May 20, 1994.

393 A stunning performance: *New Yorker,* May 23, 1994.

". . . spookily perfect": *New York,* May 23, 1994.

"suffering martyr . . .": Toronto *Globe and Mail,* June 4, 1994.

She was the favorite: *New York Times,* May 26, 1994.

"resented among insiders . . .": June 14, 1994; ". . . an Ice Capades": ibid.

". . . a thumbs-up sign . . .": *TheaterWeek,* July 4–10, 1994.

Selling well ahead: *Variety,* October 24–30, 1994.

". . . I found myself in tears . . .": interview with author.

I'm Still Here

395 Chapter title taken from the song of the same name by Stephen Sondheim in *Follies.*

396 Sondheim parody from *TheaterWeek,* July 11–17, 1994.

"Sondheim came to it . . .": interview with author.

397 "an irresistible . . .": interview with author.

". . . romantic disillusionment": *New York Times,* April 2, 1993.

398 A new set of clues: SI, p. 89.

"It's the only song . . .": SI, p. 191.

"cleverness and breadth": *New York,* May 22, 1992.

A tenth-anniversary concert: on May 15, 1994.

Raised $1 million: April 8, 1995.

His career was celebrated: December 5, 1993.

399 Accepted the award: on January 9, 1997.

". . . very precocious?": *New York Times,* November 27, 1989.

"I instinctively thought . . .": interview with author.

The summer they were working on *Merrily:* It was dated August 28, 1981. The other photograph in the study was a portrait of Margaret Sullavan in a silver frame.

"Once upon a night . . .": The poem was sent as a present for Sondheim on his fifty-ninth birthday, March 22, 1989.

400 "But as I talked . . .": SI, p. 28.

"In real life . . .": *The Legendary Mizners,* Alva Johnston, 1953, p. 238.

An enormously rich couple: interview with author.

401 "It's about nonconformity . . .": SI, p. 211.

402 "Isn't that wild?": SI, p. 190.

"He's beginning to misspell . . .": interview with author.

"Stick with the . . .": New York *Post*, March 18, 1996.

Closing date was set: for April 1, 1996.

403 ". . . I was surprised . . .": London *Evening Standard*, March 26, 1996.

His rival was the past: interview with author, May 31, 1997.

404 "Sturm und Drang": interview, March 13, 1997.

405 "From the pattern . . .": SI, p. 107.

406 "On the one side . . .": *The Spirit in Man, Art and Literature*, C. G. Jung, 1972, pp. 100–5.

Index

Page numbers in *italics* refer to illustrations.

ILLUSTRATION CREDITS

Joan Barnet, 10, 221

Jonathan Becker, 369

Leonard Bernstein Archive, Music
    Division, the Library of Congress, 95

Robert W. Bloch, 21

Eileen Derby, 150

Howard Erskine, 316

Charles Hollerith Jr., 70

David Inman, 373

The Kobal Collection, 161

James Lapine, 350

Judy Levin, 234

Museum of the City of New York, 193,
    194, 332

Hans Namuth, 406

New York Public Library, 101, 102, 118,
    125, 137, 153, 160, 167, 196, 199, 205,
    208, 248, 249, 294, 314

Photofest, 92, 96, 164, 238, 239, 273, 283,
    332, 357

The Rodgers and Hammerstein
    Organization, 34, 35, 38, 177

Barbara Rosenberg, 10, 370

D. D. Ryan, 107

John Barry Ryan, 93

Jay David Saks, 283

Stephen Sondheim, 180, 196, 238, 255,
    261, 314

Walter Sondheim, 6, 13, 15, 19, 26, 27, 29,
    40, 41, 49, 141

Henry "Skippy" Steiner, 17

Benay Venuta, 223

Tony Walton, 269

Williams College Archives, 81

A NOTE ON THE TYPE

This book was set in Adobe Garamond. Designed for
the Adobe Corporation by Robert Slimbach, the fonts are
based on types first cut by Claude Garamond (c. 1480–1561).
Garamond was a pupil of Geoffroy Tory and is believed to have
followed the Venetian models, although he introduced a number
of important differences, and it is to him that we owe the letter we
now know as "old style." He gave to his letters a certain elegance
and feeling of movement that won their creator an immediate
reputation and the patronage of Francis I of France.

Composed by North Market Street Graphics,
Lancaster, Pennsylvania

Printed and bound by Quebecor Printing,
Martinsburg, West Virginia

Designed by Cassandra J. Pappas

MERYLE SECREST was born and educated in Bath, England. She has written biographies of Romaine Brooks, Bernard Berenson, Kenneth Clark, Salvador Dali, Frank Lloyd Wright, and Leonard Bernstein.